W9-BCF-247

Sentimental Twain

Sentimental Twain

Samuel Clemens in the Maze of Moral Philosophy

by Gregg Camfield

University of Pennsylvania Press

Philadelphia

Library of Congress Cataloging-in-Publication Data
Camfield, Gregg.
    Sentimental Twain : Samuel Clemens in the maze of moral philosophy
/ by Gregg Camfield.
        p.   cm.
    Includes bibliographical references and index.
    ISBN 0-8122-3285-2
    1. Twain, Mark, 1835–1910 — Philosophy.   2. Twain, Mark, 1835–1910 —
Ethics.   3. Sentimentalism in literature.   4. Philosophy in literature.
5. Emotions in literature.   6. Ethics in literature.
I. Title.
PS1342.P5C36   1994
818'.409 — dc20   94-5007
                                                              CIP

To the memory of my grandparents, ROLAND and HELEN CAMFIELD, for their early encouragement of my curiosity; to my parents ROLAND and JUANITA CAMFIELD, for their boundless pride in me; and to my wife, EILEEN KOGL CAMFIELD, whose love and humor inspire me daily.

Contents

Preface

Mark Twain, variously called a skeptic, a cynic, and a curmudgeon, and Harriet Beecher Stowe, the exemplar of American sentimental writers, seem about as far apart on the literary scale as can be imagined of two people who shared a neighborhood. Or so it seems from a late twentieth-century perspective. But consider the comments of George Parsons Lathrop, who, writing about Hartford's Nook Farm "literary group" in *Harper's Magazine*'s October 1885 number, described a connection between Stowe and Mark Twain that he expected his readers to see with minimal difficulty:

> A few steps only from Mrs. Stowe's brings you to Mr. Clemens's house, and still fewer, if you take the short-cut through the lawn and shrubbery, by which brief transit you pass from old New England to modern America — from the plain quarters of ethical fiction to the luxurious abode of the most western of humorists. It is not difficult to trace, however, the essential kinship between Sam Lawson of *Old-Town Folks* and the equally quaint and shrewd but more expansive drollery of Mark Twain; and, on the other hand, those who see much of this author in private discover in him a fund of serious reflection and of keen observation upon many subjects that gives him another element in common with his neighbor. (731)

Lathrop sees not only the apparent distance between the two, he sees, in the figurative sense of his short-cut through obscuring ornamental bushes, an essential similarity. Not only does Stowe's sentimental world-view embrace humor, but Clemens's putative modernity is qualified by a deep moral concern, says Lathrop, that is fundamentally like Stowe's ethics of emotional concern. Is Lathrop merely inventing connections, or did Clemens really belong in Nook Farm? Was he, too, a pillar of genteel culture in spite of his front of comic buffoonery?

The answer is a qualified yes. Often in spite of himself, Samuel Clemens was a sentimentalist, and his writing was almost always inspired by the intellectual tension between his sentimental leanings and his energetic efforts to believe in anti-sentimental versions of realism, especially the naturalistic determinism that became so prominent in American letters toward the end of the nineteenth century. In other words, the battle over the moral value of sentimentalism was not the battle between genteel cultural insiders and vigorous outsiders who advocated a more modern understanding of ethics and psychology, it was an inside battle all along, and in no one person's career is the nature of that battle better represented than in the career of Samuel Langhorne Clemens as he worked himself into the center of the world of American letters. What he read, whom he knew, how he thought: all show that he was not a gifted outsider who helped tear down the genteel tradition in both philosophy and literature. On the contrary, he belonged, and his efforts to purify literary culture were the efforts of a committed insider who followed the fracture lines of his culture's ideas and pursued them to their extremes out of the depth of his commitment.

To support these contentions, I have followed Clemens's journey through the convolutions of nineteenth-century moral philosophy, especially as related to the epistemological and ethical conflict between sentimental and naturalistic world views. It should be clear immediately that I construe sentimentalism in a much larger sense than most critics now do. Even though feminist critics of the last two decades have done admirable work reclaiming the political dimensions of sentimentalism, little work has yet been done to show how widely sentimental philosophy ranged from its base in a psychology and ethics of sensation. Thus, my work is substantially a reconstructive history, one that traces ideas over a long historical curve in order to describe as fully as possible their content and impact. What surprised me early in the study was how, in spite of the twentieth-century bias against sentimentality in the narrow sense of the word, much of the larger sentimental world-view is alive and well as we look toward the twenty-first century.

The introductory chapter investigates some of this sentimental residue as a way of examining the continuing relevance of these issues to our current understanding of the works of Mark Twain. This chapter, setting the stage for the entire study by concentrating on reactions to the problem of race in *Adventures of Huckleberry Finn*, reveals that sentimental ethics persist, though buried, in American culture and that Americans' ambivalent responses to sentimentalism explain in part some of the continuing controversy surrounding Mark Twain's work. Specifically, insofar as the liberal agenda remains substantially sentimental — especially when dealing with issues of race — today's readers of Twain participate in the same dialectic between sentimental compassion and "realistic" cynicism that Clemens himself confronted. The remainder of the book explores this dialectic through the full range of ideas contained in the nineteenth-century discipline of moral philosophy as Clemens came to know it.

But before I could come to understand Clemens's intellectual quest, I had to know the culture's starting point, what exactly sentimentalism meant to Americans more broadly. I explore this background in chapter two, which traces the tangled and often conflicting strains of sentimental moral philosophy from their Enlightenment roots to their high water mark in American letters in the works of Harriet Beecher Stowe. I had no idea what I was getting into when I began the study; what I found was a vast, virtually untapped, intellectual gold mine, one that, while it had been discovered, had not been developed because it was difficult to extract the ore. In *Roughing It*, Mark Twain prefaced a chapter on the technical aspects of silver mining with an invitation to his casual readers to skip if they found it too dry. I do not have the same luxury with my chapter. The ideas here are foundational to the rest of the study, which, I hope, will more than repay the difficulties of following both my excavations into over a century and a half of philosophy and my narrative of its transmission into American culture.

What comes out of this second chapter, finally, is an understanding of the source of Clemens's obsessive ambivalence over sentimentalism in the internal contradictions of sentimental moral philosophy itself. The remaining chapters trace Clemens's changing uses of these contradictions. In chapter three, I follow his *ad hoc* exploitation of sentimental ethics as fodder for Mark Twain's newspaper comedy. In chapter four I uncover how his commitment to a life in Hartford as a member of the literary community forced him to take intellectual stands, and the first ones he took were rather conservatively in support of most of the agenda of people like his neighbors Harriet Beecher Stowe and Charles Dudley Warner. But as Clemens committed himself to a career as a serious literary moralist, he found that the philosophical contradictions that once provided him with comic contrasts caused him moral unease. Consequently, as I show in the remaining chapters, he vacillated between idealistic sentimental and naturalistic interpretations of morality, ultimately ending his career with a tentative reformulation of philosophical pluralism — much like William James's Pragmatism — that was founded on sentimental voluntarism as a counter to materialistic determinism. Ultimately, I find in Twain's career a strange transmission to the twentieth century of sentimental ideas packaged in an anti-sentimental rhetoric.

This study concerns itself primarily with Clemens's conscious reactions to ideas as he was exposed to them, either as they were simply part of a broadly dispersed set of cultural constructs or as Clemens, after his move to Hartford, studied them in their more academic and systematic forms. Of course, the intellectual history and Clemens's deliberate reaction to it that I sketch in this study explains only some aspects of the Twain canon. Indeed, of our major writers, Clemens was perhaps less in control of his writing than any. But I think it is important to look at his efforts to control his gift because he was only able to articulate ideas, however playfully protean, however unconsciously motivated, through the intellectual patterns available to him. To cite a telling example: after Samuel and Olivia Clemens's daughter Susy died, the Clemens family "celebrated" the anniversary of her death as if ritualized mourning were both a duty and a joy. It is easy to psychoanalyze the motives for such a display, but lying behind the individual psychopathology of the action on the part of each member of the Clemens family lay a cultural vocabulary of grief that encouraged such displays, as Ann Douglas admirably documents in *The Feminization of American Culture*. Indeed, well before Susy's death, Clemens wrote "The Californian's Tale," in which an entire community indulges in a ritual anniversary of the death of a woman. While Clemens often denigrated such sentimental displays, he was neither averse to using them in fiction when he needed to turn a little cash, nor to articulating his own emotions through similar patterns when his grief needed an outlet. I say nothing unusual, then, when I say that one must uncover cultural commonplaces to understand how an author articulated his or her particular reactions to the world.

But to say this does not explain my insistence on following intellectual history as if Clemens were a professional philosopher rather than a writer of *belles lettres*. As I will discuss below, Clemens came to consciousness in a culture that was suspicious of *belles lettres* and justified them only as an adjunct to moral philosophy. Granting that as a humorist he occupied the lowest position in the literary world, he still aspired to serious consideration as a moralist, and as such he undertook an extended study of moral philosophy. His study was patchy, to be sure, but he exposed himself, either directly or through popularizations, with the thought of all of the philosophers I discuss in the following pages.

Even if literary culture and tradition had not pushed Clemens toward an intellectual approach to fiction, his own psyche would have. He was raised in a family that was suspicious of play and positive emotion. Not surprisingly, Clemens expressed his attraction to powerful feeling in negative terms, though undoubtedly his satirical attacks on sentimentalism express a veiled desire for it. As a satirist, his approach to any set of emotions would be mediated by an intellectual detachment, however fatuous or self-deceptive such detachment may ultimately have been. Thus, the process by which Clemens came to reconcile himself to his own creative gifts would be a singularly intellectual one, and thus a study of intellectual history will pay dividends in increased understanding of the shape of Twain's career.

This book is, then, an intellectual history, an attempt to create thick historical contexts, to explore the power of those contexts over our culture's development. But I do not surrender my final interest in a particular author. I emphasize those epistemological and moral questions that Samuel Clemens attended in order not merely to show how context creates meaning—that is a rather flat given—but rather to see how a mind negotiates the fissures in that given in order to create agency, to find the possibility of creativity within social and psychic constraint. I find Clemens to be a fascinating subject for such a study because he confronted the philosophical questions of freedom and constraint so energetically and courageously, if rarely wisely. His effort speaks to me, and by taking his effort seriously, I hope to help it speak to others.

This book could not have been possible without the explorations of all the Twainians, Americanists, and other scholars whose work has influenced mine. While the citations and the bibliography annotate the most obvious borrowings, the debts I owe to an entire community of scholars are beyond mere documentation. I want to discharge some of those debts here. I have been fortunate at various times over the years this project has been in the works to have been able to draw on the insights, criticism, and support of Eric Sundquist, Fred Crews, Mitch Breitwieser, Carolyn Porter, Julia Bader, John Traugott, Alex Zwerdling, Tom Leonard, Cindy Weinstein, Larry Howe, Conrad Olson, Susan Scheckel, Bob Rennicks, Lisa New, Bob Regan, David DeLaura, Thomas Wortham and, for last minute comments and more help with the manuscript than I could ever have expected from anybody not related to me, Vic Doyno. And I want to thank Sears Jayne who remains always in my mind as the ideal teacher/scholar.

As with any work on Mark Twain, mine has benefited from the help of the entire staff of the Mark Twain Papers, not only for their impressive scholarship, but for their friendliness and helpfulness to me when I was working in the Papers. I want to thank in particular Bob Hirst, Robert Browning, Vic Fisher, and Sunny Gottberg, all of whom showed remarkable tolerance of my most inane questions and helped me to navigate the papers themselves. I also appreciate the permission to publish previously unpublished Mark Twain material.

I thank my students for demanding that I bring my theories down to earth. I am not sure how successfully I have met their challenge, but I am certain my work is better for the effort. More particularly, I want to thank Max Grant, Penn graduate student and fellow Mark Twain fanatic, for calling to my attention the quotation with which I began this preface and for much needed help in proofreading.

For the material support that also went into this book I thank the University of California for a Graduate Research grant that enabled me to go east to study in Hartford, New Haven, and New York City. In the Mark Twain Memorial, in the Beinecke Library, and in the American Academy of Arts and Letters I met with none but helpful staff members. For the money to return to Berkeley in order to study Mark Twain's autobiographical dictations, I thank the University of Pennsylvania Research Foundation.

I am grateful to the University of California Press for permission to reprint here those portions of Chapters One and Two that appeared in *Nineteenth-Century Literature* under the titles "Sentimental Liberalism and the Problem of Race in *Huckleberry Finn*" (46: 96–113) and "The Moral Aesthetics of Sentimentality: A Missing Key to *Uncle Tom's Cabin*" (43: 319–45).

I also want to say how much I appreciate the staff of the University of Pennsylvania Press. In particular, Jerry Singerman, the editor who invited me to submit my manuscript in the first place, and Alison Anderson have been uniformly friendly and efficient, no matter how often I disrupt their daily routines by dropping in unannounced.

Finally, I want to thank my parents, my in-laws, my brother and sister, my friend Peter Meyer, and my wife, all of whom have endured my obsessive work on this book with real grace and love.

Abbreviations

I have followed the Mark Twain Project's standard abbreviations as used in the Iowa-California edition of the Works of Mark Twain and in the California edition of the Mark Twain Papers for citing collections of Mark Twain's works and significant works about him. For volumes of collected materials that do not have standard abbreviations, I have used my own. For a full list of works by Mark Twain cited in my discussion, see the list of Works Cited and Works Consulted under "Clemens."

ET&S   *Early Tales and Sketches.* Ed. Edgar Marquess Branch and Robert H. Hirst. Berkeley: University of California Press, 1979.

FM   *Mark Twain's Fables of Man.* Ed. John S. Tuckey. Berkeley: University of California Press, 1972.

HH&T   *Mark Twain's Hannibal, Huck & Tom.* Ed. Walter Blair. Berkeley: University of California Press, 1969.

LLMT   *The Love Letters of Mark Twain.* Ed. Dixon Wecter. New York: Harper & Brothers, 1949.

LOM   *Life on the Mississippi.* 1883. New York: P. F. Collier & Son Company, n.d.

MTB   *Mark Twain: A Biography.* 4 vols. By Albert Bigelow Paine. New York: Harper & Brothers, 1912.

MTE   *Mark Twain in Eruption.* Ed. Bernard De Voto. New York: Harper & Brothers, 1940.

MTHL   *Mark Twain-Howells Letters.* Ed. Henry Nash Smith and William M. Gibson. Cambridge, MA: Belknap Press, Harvard University Press, 1960.

MTLH   *Mark Twain's Letters from Hawaii.* Ed. A. Grove Day. Honolulu: University Press of Hawaii, 1975.

MTMF   *Mark Twain to Mrs. Fairbanks.* San Marino, CA: Huntington Library, 1949.

MTMS   *Mark Twain's Mysterious Stranger Manuscripts.* Ed. William M Gibson. Berkeley: University of California Press, 1969

MTTB   *Mark Twain's Travels with Mr. Brown.* Ed. Franklin Walker and G. Ezra Dane. New York: Alfred A. Knopf, 1940.

MTS   *Mark Twain's Speeches.* New York: Harper & Brothers, 1910.

N&J1   *Mark Twain's Notebooks and Journals, Volume 1 (1855–1873).* Ed. Frederick Anderson et al. Berkeley: University of California Press, 1975.

N&J2   *Mark Twain's Notebooks and Journals, Volume 2 (1877–1883).* Ed. Frederick Anderson et al. Berkeley: University of California Press, 1975.

N&J3   *Mark Twain's Notebooks and Journals, Volume 3 (1883–1891).* Ed. Frederick Anderson et al. Berkeley: University of California Press, 1979.

SN&O   *Sketches New and Old.* Hartford, CT: American Publishing Co., 1875.

TIA   *Traveling with the Innocents Abroad.* Ed. D. M. McKeithan. Norman: University of Oklahoma Press, 1958.

WIM   *What Is Man? And Other Philosophical Writings.* Ed. Paul Baender. Berkeley: University of California Press, 1973.

WWD   *Mark Twain's Which Was the Dream? and Other Symbolic Writings of the Later Years.* Ed. John S. Tuckey. Berkeley: University of California Press, 1968.

1. Two Views of Twain

I

Both academics and the larger public love Mark Twain, but it should surprise no one that the academy and the public admire him for different reasons. In fact, the images the two groups have created of Twain differ so greatly that they seem to describe two different men, or, rather, two different cultural icons.[1] These two images are about as different as the two Providences that Huck Finn learns about from Miss Watson and the Widow Douglas:

> Sometimes the widow would take me one side and talk about Providence in a way to make a body's mouth water; but maybe next day Miss Watson would take hold and knock it down again. I judged I could see that there was two Providences, and a poor chap would stand considerable show with the widow's Providence, but if Miss Watson's got him there warn't no hope for him any more. (14)

Outside the academy, America has many Widow Douglas-like interpretations of Mark Twain. America's "Phunny Phellow," the author whose *Innocents Abroad* sold so well as to put it nearly in the league of the sentimental *Uncle Tom's Cabin*, has always had interpreters who see nothing but the sweet vision of American innocence that Twain's works undoubtedly play with.[2]

And one could expect such treatments of what is arguably Twain's most widely popular book in America, *The Adventures of Tom Sawyer*. Consider, for instance, the nostalgic vision of Middle America that Disney created in Disneyland's Tom Sawyer's Island. Like the entire park, the island offers a self-contained haven of adventure, where fantasies of piracy and treasure hunting, of endless summertime and endless youth, are colored with enough that is frightful to make them interesting, but are perfectly safe, endlessly repeatable, always charming, and quite saccharine.

What is surprising is the enduring popularity of *A Connecticut Yankee in King Arthur's Court*. The book that ends with a holocaust and that has its narrator say that it would be better to hang the entire human race and end the farce, has been turned into a happy stage musical and into several films. One of these films, a thirty minute animated Bugs Bunny version, at least maintains the anarchic violence and the vicious satire of feudal ways, but the others completely omit or subvert any of Twain's political meanings and gloss over his pessimistic fulminations in a sweet vision of American innocence and ingenuity. The best known of these, the Bing Crosby musical version, reduces the entire political content of the book to two short speeches and to one song and dance, the refrain of which is, appropriately, "We're busy doin' nothin'."

Even those popular treatments that acknowledge Twain's pessimism manage to transmute it into a sentimental optimism. The most telling of these, and an enduring favorite of American popular culture, is the Frank Capra film, *It's a Wonderful Life*. The film alludes in much of its structure to Twain's late publications, "Extracts from Captain Stormfield's Visit to Heaven" and, more importantly, *The Mysterious Stranger*.[3] When the film's protagonist, George Bailey, after facing bankruptcy and perhaps even a jail term, contemplates suicide, he is interrupted by an angel named Clarence, who convinces George that his life has made a difference. The sentimental denouement brings tears to the eyes of even many a hard-hearted moviegoer, and that it has remained a perennial favorite, even while so many old films now seem hokey, attests to the power of the vision.

One of the crucial pieces in this sentimental ending is Clarence's gift to George of his copy of *The Adventures of Tom Sawyer*, which obviously serves as something of a Bible for this awkward guardian angel. When called upon by off-screen, heavenly voices to rescue George, Clarence asks whether successful completion of his "mission" to save Bailey will earn him his wings.[4] The divine voice, in an apparent *non sequitur* replies, "What's that book you've got there." Clarence responds, "Oh, ho, *The Adventures of Tom Sawyer*," to which the voice replies, "Clarence, you do a good job with George Bailey, and you'll get your wings." But what appears a *non sequitur* at first is apparently an extension of an earlier remark, when the voices are discussing the value of Clarence as a guardian angel and the one says the Clarence has the "I.Q. of a rabbit" to which the other replies, "but the faith of a child." This heavenly voice puts his faith not only in the children per se, but in Twain's "hymn" to boyhood. By movie's end, the viewer who catches the Twain references gathers that the film argues against Twain's late pessimism in favor of the sentimental good humor of his earlier work.

The popular treatment of Twain, then, often seems either ignorant or dismissive of the dark side of his vision. But in academic discourse we find the Miss Watson interpretations of Twain. Although much academic criticism of Twain up to the 1960s also tried to rescue Twain's humor from his pessimism, the line of criticism that now seems dominant began at least as early as with George Santayana and H. L. Mencken and was part of a powerful anti-genteel school of criticism. One of the things such critics liked about Twain was his pessimism.

For instance, in a review of A. B. Paine's *Mark Twain: A Biography*, Edna Kenton published in the radical, pacifist *New York Evening Mail* that she looked forward to the "new note" found in Twain's unpublished, unedited literature, such as "Three Thousand Years Among The Microbes," a brief extract of which Paine published in the biography. She praised the excerpt for the promise that its message "will not be the flaccid optimism that passes for vision in the current cant." She further attacked Paine, whose *Biography* sedulously tries to create a genteel vision of Twain, for employing hypocritical editorial policies. She noted that Paine enjoyed "Three Thousand Years Among the Microbes" but called it "unprintable." "Paine derogates it and its 'printability' so hastily, after such a huge and reminiscent laugh as to make the apperceptive feel that his sense of censorship is working after the usual Anglo-Saxon manner, not for himself, but for others."[5] Kenton's, Mencken's, and Santayana's were among the early voices in a tradition of criticism that not only "discovered" but praised the "dark" side of Twain's oeuvre. The degree to which the critical perception of Twain's output focuses on the anti-sentimental and violent even in Twain's middle works can be summed up in the title of James Cox's recent essay on *Huck Finn*, "A Hard Book to Take."[6]

Yet it would be absurd to dismiss the popular interpretations of Twain as wrong; much good evidence exists to support the contention that Twain was a sentimentalist. Indeed, although Twain did often attack sentimentalism on utilitarian grounds, he often endorsed sentimental conventions by using them straight, especially when his generally liberal politics required him to garner sympathy for his pet causes. In some of his later works, such as "A Horse's Tale" and "A Dog's Tale," the overt sentimentality has been an embarrassment to critics who have considered Twain a "masculine," which in their terms is to say an anti-sentimental, writer. They pass over such pieces in uncomfortable silence, dismiss them as occasional accidents, or use them to damn Twain altogether for capitulating to a "feminized" culture. Such criticism could be defended as a matter of personal taste, with critics who dislike sentimentalism noting that Twain was a transitional figure who wrote seriously on both sides of the fence that he erected. But the problem with such a defense, besides the elitism that dismisses a literary mode that still attracts such a wide popular following, is that it ignores the fact that sentimentality remains at the critical center of all of Twain's important works. Moreover, critics have long refused to acknowledge their own continued reactions to the sentimentalism through which these works treat some of their most important issues. Nowhere is this more clear than in the reactions of critics to the issue of race in *Adventures of Huckleberry Finn*.

II

Adventures of Huckleberry Finn has always sparked controversy. From the earliest reviews attacking it for promoting vulgar morality, *Huck* has found readers who impugn and who defend its moral vision. The first battle it provoked was waged in explicitly sentimental terms. Clearly, many of the genteel moralists of Twain's day were up in arms about his world-view; equally clearly, his promotion of what Henry Nash Smith has called a "vernacular" perspective led to Twain's "canonization."[7] But while Twain's very use of vernacular has been considered a liberating, democratizing artistic innovation, at least one aspect of that vernacular, the way it describes Jim, has fueled the most important and long-lived debate about the book, namely whether or not it is racist.

The public battle over the racial attitudes the book conveys began in 1957 when the NAACP condemned the book for its diction, for the gross affront to the dignity of a whole race of human beings implicit in the use of the vernacular term "nigger." Since then, a whole literature has sprung up trying to deal with the characterization of Jim and the conclusions we can draw about the book's racial attitudes contingent on that characterization. Naturally, African-American readers have been no more immune to controversy over the book than have been members of any other group. While the NAACP and many black critics have vigorously condemned the book's depiction of blacks — Chicago educator Dr. John Wallace, for instance, calls the book "the most grotesque example of racist trash ever written" — some of the most spirited and interesting defenses of the book's characterization of Jim have come from black authors.[8]

In particular, many of these critics suggest that Huck is often manipulated by Jim precisely because Jim can always hide behind the mask of stereotype created by whites for their own psychological protection.[9] Such responses seek to demonstrate the richness and complexity of Jim's character throughout the book in order to suggest that Jim is not a weak role model who will necessarily undermine black readers' perceptions of themselves or reinforce white stereotypes about blacks. The trade-off, here, is that Huck's character is diminished in contrast. Clearly Huck, with no sense of humor or of irony whatsoever, is susceptible to Jim's manipulation, as we can see in Huck's treatment of one of Jim's superstitions: "Jim said bees wouldn't sting idiots; but I didn't believe that, because I had tried them lots of times myself, and they wouldn't sting me" (55). Such a boy is often duped and even controlled by Jim.

Thus, in trying to make Jim a dignified character capable of controlling circumstances as well as he possibly can, such critics implicitly argue for an uneasy equality between Huck and Jim, what Robinson calls "an equality in suspicion and fear" that creates a "tenuous bond of mutual protection."[10] Still, such readings, while allowing for racial equality and a vital community of interest between Huck and Jim, diverge from the traditional liberal view of Huck and Jim as embodying inter-racial harmony. Many readers wish to see the community of Huck and Jim in these larger symbolic terms, and, consequently, many of them complain that the so-called evasion chapters betray the book's humane potential.

Although few supporters of the book like to admit it, such a vision of racial harmony stems ultimately from a sentimental view of the world, a view that Twain, though he also disliked to admit it, to a large degree shared. The sentimentality of this vision should come as no surprise if one considers that anti-racist thought originated in the antislavery movement of the eighteenth century. As David Brion Davis points out, the very movement to abolish slavery coincided with and was significantly shaped by the rise of sentimental moral philosophy.[11] In fact, antislavery was part of a dramatic paradigm shift in Western thought: "The emergence of an international antislavery opinion represented a momentous turning point in the evolution of man's moral perception, and thus in man's image of himself." Davis notes that Locke, whose psychology of the sensations undergird the development of sentimental moral philosophy by the likes of Shaftesbury & Hutcheson, "was the last major philosopher to seek a justification for absolute and perpetual slavery."[12] The generation he taught "to take an irreverent view of past authority" and to see the "importance of personal liberty" began the attack on race slavery by appealing sentimentally to universal human longings for freedom, self-determination, and familial affection. The same movement that began the attack on slavery provided, as Gary Wills has shown, the liberal strain of thought that sanctioned the American Revolution.[13] Canonized in many of the texts of the Revolution, these ideas have had a formative role in almost every democratizing and egalitarian movement in the history of the United States.

Furthermore, it could be argued that most events that have moved the nation toward a democratic ideal have been catalyzed by the problem of race as articulated in sentimental terms. The Civil War stands as an obvious example, with the sentimental rhetoric of the antislavery movement significantly influencing the advent of the war that ultimately led to the Constitutional embodiment of equal protection under the law. Less obviously, the Civil Rights movement of the 1950s and early 1960s also drew on this sentimental tradition. Exploiting the news media's hunger for sensation, Civil Rights leaders publicized and often even provoked confrontations that generated scenes of grotesque violence. But the movement succeeded not merely by finding the sensational — the so-called drug wars of today do that constantly without generating any sympathy for the American underclass; it succeeded by interpreting striking images through the sentimental rhetoric of universal brotherhood.

Sentimentalism, then, which is latent in American political and social ideology and which has been present since the inception of the nation, comes strikingly to life around questions of race. It therefore stands to reason that readers' reactions to the question of racism in *Huck Finn* are complicated by, in fact may even be governed by, conflicting responses to the sentimentality in that novel. The book's advocacy of racial equality, though buried in irony, is almost completely sentimental, and that fact may well account for both the spirited attacks on and equally spirited defenses of Twain's attitudes toward race as manifested in his depiction of Jim.

That Clemens's advocacy of racial equality is sentimental is not self-evident, especially given his own ambivalent attitudes toward sentimentalism. In the late 1870s and early 1880s, as I will show later, he preferred utilitarian ethics; his marginalia in his copies of W. E. H. Lecky's *History of European Morals* and of Darwin's *The Descent of Man* show quite clearly that he consciously rejected many of the fundamental ideas — epistemological, aesthetic, and psychological — of sentimental moral philosophy.

As Clemens knew from his reading and from his discussions with his neighbors and fellow writers — including Harriet Beecher Stowe, Horace Bushnell, and Charles Dudley Warner — sentimental literature was professedly realistic even as it was didactically reformist. According to sentimental aesthetic and moral theory, which I will treat in the next chapter, for sentimental literature to promote moral change, it must recreate in the reader's mind a sense of psychic reality. Such responses depend on shared associations and sympathy. Still, such sentimental reactions are easily upset by conflicting associations and by anything that might impede sympathy. Thus, by these standards, a writer must purify representations of external reality in order to evoke pure, ideal, morally uplifting responses.

At about the time he began writing *Huck Finn*, Clemens had come to believe that such artistic idealization sacrifices truth. In part, the physical distortions of idealized art annoyed Twain, as any reader of "Fenimore Cooper's Literary Offenses" knows. In larger part, he felt that an aesthetic that called itself a synthesis of realism and idealism enabled sentimentalists to lie to themselves about their own motivations, particularly those based on sympathy. He usually rejected the idea that human beings ever act altruistically, and he deliberately crafted many episodes in *Huck Finn* to try to demonstrate the absurdity of a moral system predicated purely on the power of sympathy. Persons who act out of sentimental motives, he suggests, act for the pleasure they will get from experiencing vicariously someone else's emotions. Further, since they are more interested in apparent intention than in consequences, they often cause more ultimate harm than good.

To take an episode from Chapter Five for example, the new judge causes this kind of harm when he tries to reform pap. He shows more concern for a sentimental model of family as the ideal institution than for the real good of either pap or Huck. In other words, perceiving reality through the medium of ideal stereotypes, he ignores particulars to the detriment of all concerned. Pinning the blame for the breakdown of pap's family on alcohol alone, the new judge sets up a theater of reform. Pap signs the pledge, bringing him in the two strokes of the pen needed to make his mark from the depths of degradation to the apex of social respectability. Add new clothes and the sentimental scenario is complete. Here are ideal emotions, purified of their mundane complications, enabling everyone to weep with joy.

With minimal investment of time and with no conception of the real difficulty of changing a person's life, the new judge and his wife wallow pleasurably in pap's tearful confession. But Clemens forces a practical reality back into the scene. Pap stays reformed for all of an evening before returning to his habits; no reformation can really change the future without hard, grinding, daily work. In seeking another man's change of heart, the new judge finds momentary sentimental bliss for himself, but when faced by the ruins of his spare room the next day he concludes that "a body could reform the old man with a shot-gun, maybe, but he didn't know no other way" (28). His anger, of course, stems not only from his sense of failure, but also from his awareness that he had been pap's gull in a small but humiliating con game. Later in the book, Clemens ups the ante with the various sentimental con games the king and duke perpetrate, most notably their effort to defraud the Wilks girls out of a sizable fortune. They almost succeed because they are so good at manipulating others with their sentimental "tears and flapdoodle" and "soul-butter and hogwash" (213). Clemens clearly feared that sentimentality could be the key not to truth and virtue but to deceit and vice.

This was how Clemens had, at this point in his career, consciously developed his reaction to sentimentalism. But what about his treatment of Jim? One of the central episodes that ironizes Huck's educated bigotry by showing Jim's humanity comes when Jim gets homesick. Huck often overhears Jim lamenting the loss of his family, but he is most struck by, and relates to us in minute detail, the story of Jim's treatment of his daughter:

> "What make me feel so bad dis time, 'us bekase I hear sumpn over yonder on de bank like a whack, er a slam, while ago, en it mine me er de time I treat my little 'Lizabeth so ornery. She warn't on'y 'bout fo' year ole, en she tuck de sk'yarlet fever, en had a powful rough spell; but she got well, en one day she was a-stannin' aroun', en I says to her, I says:
> "'Shet de do'.'
> "She never done it; jis' stood dah, kiner smilin' up at me. It make me mad; en I says agin, mighty loud, I says:
> "'Doan you hear me? — Shet de do'!'
> "She jis' stood de same way, kiner smilin' up. I was a-bilin'! I says:
> "'I lay I make you mine!'
> "En wid dat I fetch' her a slap side de head dat sont her a-sprawlin'. Den I went into de yuther room, en 'us gone 'bout ten minutes; en when I come back, dah was dat do' a-stannin' open yit, en dat chile stannin' mos' right in it, a-lookin' down en mournin', en de tears runnin' down. My, but I wuz mad. I was agwyne for de chile, but jis' Den — it was a do' dat open' innerds — jis' Den, 'long come de wind en slam it to, behine de chile, ker-blam! — en my lan', de chile never move'. My breff mos' hop outer me; en I feel so — so — I Doan know how I feel. I crope out, all a-tremblin', en crope aroun' en open de do' easy en slow, en poke my head in behine de chile, sof' en still, en all uv a sudden I says pow! jis' as loud as I could yell. She never budge! O, Huck, I bust out a-cryin', en grab her up in my arms en say, 'O de po' little thing! de Lord God Amightly fogive po' ole Jim, kaze he never gwyne to fogive hisseff as long's he live!' O, She was plumb deef en dumb, Huck, plumb deef en dumb — en I'd ben a treat'n her so!" (201–2)

I quote here at length in order to call attention to many conventionally sentimental aspects of this scene. Notice that the tale is a recollection sparked by association between a sound and a remembered sound. According to sentimental aesthetics, as I will explain in the next chapter, the emotional power and moral value of sentiment come from this associational characteristic. Particular experiences, according to this aesthetic, become the motives for our emotional and moral lives even though we must, by the constitution of our minds, categorize those experiences to make them universal. In the book's continuation of Huck's moral reformation at the hands of Jim, Huck's particular experience of Jim's altruism finally convinces Huck to "go to hell" in an effort to free his companion. And in the reader's experience of Jim, this particularity becomes a profound source of the sentimental conception of Jim's reality as a human being.

Note also that the agent of moral reformation is an innocent girl. Jim demonstrates his "full humanity" in sentimental terms by the tenderness of his heart when confronted by the sufferings of a girl who has been ill. Although this may be the only case in sentimental literature of a sick girl not dying (usually of tuberculosis), she nonetheless succeeds in performing her sentimental task. As a girl she is, by cultural commonplace, supposed to be closer to the ideal in two ways. By the tenets of sentimental dualism, while all life is compounded of both matter and spirit, some people have naturally more spiritual tastes than do others. Furthermore, innate tastes notwithstanding, some people experience life so as to encourage spiritual tastes while others develop their more earthly sensations. The ideology of the sexual spheres arose in part from these sentimental distinctions, assigning to women the attributes of spiritual affinity. Thus Jim's daughter, by virtue of her gender, is supposed to be spiritual by nature. Also, the culture exalted children as closer to spirit because they had not yet had time for worldly pursuits to color their moral sensibilities. Thus by virtue of her age Jim's daughter again is supposed to figure spiritual purity. Here, then, is sentimental idealization at work in the manipulation of stock cultural symbols.

Finally, note the tears, this time presented not derisively but rather to guide our responses. And as Jim's tears guide us, so does the way he tells the story; he purifies his tale of any accidental characteristics — we have no idea of his circumstances or of his history with his daughter, so we cannot know if his ill use of her stemmed from a more complex reality than he gives us. So his abuse of her, especially as he reveals it to us, evokes a simple, clean emotional response of pity. Since Jim berates himself for his behavior, the reader has no need to do it, too; Jim's mea culpa in fact yields, by a sort of transitive property of emotion that is central to sentimental liberalism as a whole, a reader's pity for Jim and a sense of his nobility in his capacity to, as Harriet Beecher Stowe put it in *Uncle Tom's Cabin*, "feel right."

The very next episode after Jim's recollection provides an interesting counterpoint to this sentimentality. When the king and the duke masquerade as dead Peter Wilks's English brothers, the duke must play the part of someone "deef and dumb" (208) in a kind of perverse mutation of Jim's daughter. And in fact the "goo-gooing for sympathy" (248) of these imposters is precisely the "soul-butter and hogwash" that so disgusts Huck. On first glance it seems as though what Twain giveth in one chapter, he taketh away in the next, but the episode is not exclusively anti-sentimental, and again the tensions revolve around issues of race and gender.

The king and the duke, while able to impose on the townspeople by crying, are successful partly because the people as a whole cannot distinguish the truth, and especially because the Wilks girls, as innocent as they are supposed to be, put their faith in the frauds. The townspeople, when challenged by the skeptical Dr. Robinson, follow the lead of innocence.[14] But when the "rapscallions" sell off the Wilks's slaves to a slave-trader, they lose some of the reputation their tears had gained them. Huck "thought them poor girls and them niggers would break their hearts with grief; they cried around each other, and took on so it most made me down sick to see it." And as Huck was made sick, so were the townspeople: "The thing made a big stir in the town, too, and a good many come out flatfooted and said it was scandalous to separate the mother and the children that way. It injured the frauds some" (234).

The frauds are injured in Twain's reprise, apparently without irony, of the classic anti-slavery argument made in exclusively sentimental terms. Even slave-holders, it seems in this version of Twain's Southern town, are able to form attachments to the slaves as people and to recognize the slaves' familial attachments to one another, and the abrupt sacrifice of those attachments paves the way for the people to reject the sentimental claims of the king and the duke. When the new pretenders to the fortune arrive, the people are quickly willing to turn their allegiance from the king and the duke, suggesting that in scandalizing the town's sensibilities about the role of black families, they loosen their hold on the town's sympathies.

In the narrative economy of the story, it is easy to forget that the townspeople abandon their faith in the king and duke before they hear from Mary Jane Wilks that Huck has exposed them as frauds. On the contrary, the reader's reaction to Huck's doing the right thing gives a narrative sense of ethical resolution, so that the sudden shift in the town's faith in the frauds comes as no surprise. Huck's decision to help Mary Jane and her sisters is a further sign of Twain's ambivalence about sentimentalism. Even though Mary Jane's innocence exposes her to the designs of the king and the duke in the first place, it operates successfully on Huck's sympathy for that innocence. Huck decides to risk his own well-being for the well-being of the Wilks girls precisely because he cannot bear to see innocence imposed upon. The implication of a dawning sexuality as part of Huck's motive is clearly present, but again according to sentimental convention — and Twain was almost always sentimental when writing about sex — sexual feelings themselves are among the strongest spurs to the moral behavior of good men. Huck surrenders his self-interest under the double goad of sympathy and sentimental sexuality.

This treatment of sexuality is related to the episode of Jim talking about his daughter. Jim teaches Huck about the value of family in emotional terms that Huck's own life has been unable to give him. Many commentators, noting Jim's self-sacrificing behavior and his terms of endearment, have described his relationship to Huck as maternal. Many forget, however, that by sentimental convention, men, too, were supposed to act with great gentleness toward their children and wives and to sacrifice their personal interests to the interests of their families. Again, it is the black man who serves as the catalyst for these ideas in *Huck Finn*. Not only does Twain use sentimentalism to elevate the character of Jim, he reciprocally uses Jim to elevate the value of sentimentalism in the face of his own skepticism about the worth of sentiment.

So even though much of the book militates against sentimentalism as a morally legitimate ideology, its sentimental portrait of Jim and the narrative consequences of that portrait give us a different sense of Twain's attitudes. In particular, we see Twain using sentimentality to tell the reader to sympathize with the black man's humanity. We can see here, even at the high point of Clemens's attack on sentimentalism, how difficult it was for him to reject the humanity of sentimental morality in favor of the pessimistic conclusions of his consciously chosen utilitarian materialism. By the end of his career, he would, much as did William James at about the same time, self-consciously reject his earlier monism in favor of a pluralistic vision founded on sentimental epistemology. This intellectual journey will unfold throughout the following chapters; what interests me here is that, in spite of the ironic context in which it is embedded, the plea for sympathy works for so many readers yet creates such controversy.

The academic argument over Jim often hinges on accusations of naïveté made from a standpoint of professional sophistication. On the one hand, those who defend the book accuse its detractors of naively failing to see the book's irony, that Twain realistically depicts a bigoted world in order to satirize that bigotry by comparison to the emotional bond between Huck and Jim. On the other hand, those who condemn the book as racist accuse its defenders of naively defending the depiction of Jim as realistic. They say that Jim is merely a version of the stereotypical "Uncle Tom," and that any investment in Jim's reality is a projection of the reader's expectations and desires onto the reality of race relations in the United States.[15]

The central term in the debate, then, is that slippery term "realism," and it might help us to understand our reactions to keep in mind how sentimentalists wished to define it. At best, they sought a psychological mimesis; they tried to represent not the simple physical reality of the world, but the psychological reality of how we perceive it. That reality begins, they said, with natural senses providing the mind with complex categories of perception, and these categories in turn provide categories of understanding based on the associations we accumulate through life. The epistemological difficulties of sorting objectivity and subjectivity according to this model were not lost on Clemens. His early rejection of sentimentalism was contingent on his belief that physical experience alone can tell us the truth, but his later recurrent interest in sentimentalism as a philosophy that better explains human consciousness fueled many of his late literary extravaganzas. Neither were the epistemological difficulties of sentimentalism lost on those who developed it; the radical intuitionists like Hume and Smith — who had the greatest impact on sentimental literature — described the conception of reality that arose from their model of mind as one that cannot be rationally explained.[16] It can be no more than felt through the power of sympathetic imagination, a human power superior to logos, superior to the terms by which we try to articulate it.

Still, sentimentalists did try to articulate it, and insofar as sentimental literature strives for psychological mimesis, it walks a thin line between describing particular experiences and reducing those experiences to general categories, between describing reality or an idealized preconception of reality. When such literature describes people, that representational dilemma becomes a moral dilemma. Sentimental characterizations balance precariously between oppressively stereotyping the "other" and recognizing his or her particular humanity.

As a result, sentimentalism blurs the distinction between stereotypical and particular representations. For the sake of securing the connection between the particular and the universal, sentimentalists hoped to do precisely that: to confuse the particular and the categorical, the real and the ideal. That confusion has, in part, led to much of the recent criticism of what Huck Finn does in depicting Jim. As readers, we do not know how we are supposed to respond to Jim. Are we to see him as a realistic portrait of a black man? If so, we can't help noting all the things wrong with this depiction. Are we to see him as the image of a black man that a kind-hearted but bigoted boy might have as he struggles to realize an ideal of love? If so, we shift our gaze from Jim as he is, to Jim as Huck feels about him.

The text itself, then, accounts for our conflicting responses to the book in two ways. For one, it entails the representational ambiguities of sentimental realism itself; for another, it reflects Clemens's own ambivalent attitudes toward sentimentalism. Later chapters will elaborate on the intellectual journey that moved him from utilitarianism back to sentimentalism, but, as I am trying to explain our reactions to an instance of his ambivalence, I must briefly note the emotional impulse behind his change. Clemens found the reduction of all human behavior to the basest motives to be emotionally intolerable even though it took him a long time to change his belief that logic proved his cynicism even though his logic contradicted his emotional experience. Extrapolating from my own experiences as a reader and from my reading of many critics who have written about whether or not *Adventures of Huckleberry Finn* is a racist book, it seems possible that modern readers share the same tension between cynicism and sentimentalism and respond to the characterization of Jim at least in part depending on which they embrace.

Speaking of my own experience as a reader, I find that my fear of sentimentalism stems from my ambivalent reactions to commercial culture. The fact that, through sentiment, the manufacturers of kitsch have turned Twain's works and life story into a crude commodity, and in the process have reduced the complex satirist to a toothless funny fellow, stimulates my anxiety. It is easy to feel manipulated by the purveyors of sentiment, and I fear, especially, the political implications of that manipulation. I often turn to my professional training to protect myself from this fear, and I do not think I am alone in doing this: certainly the modernists who installed Twain in the canon for his services in attacking sentimentality shared this fear, and I do not think recent critical theories have allayed it.

Trained in post-structuralist analysis, many contemporary critics want, when reading nineteenth-century literature, to describe the psychological mimesis of sentimentalism as a power strategy, to see the emotional coercion as oppressive, and to deny the capacity of writers and readers to see the full humanity of the "other" as long as they tend to see that "other" only through universalizing categories. In this vision of sentimentality, we see a need to purge ourselves of our own emotional responses in order to free ourselves from and to expose the oppressive language that has ordered those responses.[17]

Still, we have no choice but to describe people through the necessarily limited categories our language gives us; the question is whether such categories are necessarily oppressive or whether the intention behind language has some impact on what it does. The controversy surrounding Twain's book suggests some interesting answers. Those readers who do not see Twain's depiction of Jim as oppressively stereotypical may at some level reject the idea that language is necessarily oppressive. In insisting that the book attacks racism, many still insist that Jim is a noble character with whom it is easy to sympathize as a "real" person even as they acknowledge the limits and political dangers of that realism.

In other words, all other biases notwithstanding, some of us react according to a continued emotional affinity with sentimentalism. Perhaps this affinity lies in the hope that human beings do have shared interests that are prior to the language we use to try to describe them, that with good intentions we can communicate meaningfully in terms other than those of domination and submission, that, as Ralph Ellison says in his 1982 introduction to *Invisible Man*:

> If the ideal of achieving a true political equality eludes us in reality—as it continues to do—there is still available that fictional vision of an ideal democracy in which the actual combines with the ideal and gives us representations of a state of things in which the highly placed and the lowly, the black and the white, the Northerner and the Southerner, the native-born and the immigrant are combined to tell us of transcendent truths and possibilities such as those discovered when Mark Twain set Huck and Jim afloat on the raft.[18]

In this I think Ellison may have discovered much about the power of sentimentalism in addressing the American problem of race, that in blurring the distinctions between reality and ideality, it engages our sympathy and allows us to imagine human connections that we cannot fully articulate.

As this history suggests, Clemens's stance to sentimentalism is complicated. The meanings of this complexity have been almost entirely obscured by the modernist response to sentimentality, a response that dismissed the entire intellectual tradition behind American sentimental literature so effectively that only in the last ten or fifteen years have scholars seriously begun to unearth the nineteenth-century intellectual context in which sentimentalism flourished. Derived from a model of mind and morality first postulated by Locke, developed by, among others, Shaftesbury, Hutcheson, Hume, and Adam Smith, and popularized in America by the Scots Hugh Blair and Archibald Alison and by Americans such as Catherine Beecher, American literary sentimentalism was sophisticated and powerful.[19] But the New Critical mythology of a desiccated genteel tradition has so thoroughly cut us off from that power that we cannot see its full impact on the works of Mark Twain in their own right, nor on our perceptions of those works. We have shelves of books discussing Twain's doubleness, but without a sense of the continuing importance of ideas that, while no longer called sentimental, persist in our cultural dialogue, we cannot use Twain to help us see our own doubleness.

III

In saying that critics often do not take into account their own doubleness in reading Twain, I do not mean to say that most critics pretend that he was a consistent writer. On the contrary, they have always noticed the doubleness in Twain, the fact that Twain's works come to life through fundamental conflicts.[20] Traditionally, critics have explained those conflicts in psychological terms or in terms of a historical vision of progress. In both cases, they have tended to view Mark Twain the humorist as the progressive, democratic voice of dissent in opposition to Samuel Clemens the repressed, conservative voice of Victorian authority and order.

Neither of these points of view should come as a surprise, given their historical origins in the Van Wyck Brooks/Bernard De Voto controversy. These critics, both of whom were important advocates of literary modernism, defined the terms of Twain criticism at least through the 1960s. According to Brooks, Mark Twain killed his creativity when he capitulated to commercial, Victorian, and feminine conventionality. In response, Bernard De Voto accepted that Eastern culture was oppressively sterile and that Mark Twain's worst writing came under its aegis, but argued that his Western background gave him a protean, dynamic, masculine set of ideas and values from which he could forge his own art in triumphant opposition to Eastern gentility.

The two differed in most of their conclusions and in their respective emphases on personal psychology and cultural influences, and both ways of looking at Mark Twain's radical inconsistencies have the power that comes from elegantly simple statement of substantial truth. But more important than their disagreements, perhaps, is their fundamental agreement on a questionable assumption. Brooks and De Voto both assumed that Eastern culture had an internal consistency that could tolerate little, if any, opposition. They assumed, therefore, that any challenge to Eastern gentility had to come from outside the culture, either in the artistic impulses of an individual genius or in the countervailing codes of a cultural frontier.

By acknowledging the existence of other traditions than those of the literate East, De Voto at least accepted that Twain found his original voice in a rich social context rather than in the romantic imagination of a great genius, and from this emphasis arose the plethora of excellent source studies of Mark Twain's art. However, even while source studies show alternative conventions that Twain drew on, no emphasis on sources alone has yet thoroughly overcome the critical acceptance of anti-conventionality as the hallmark of his genius. A brief analysis of Henry Nash Smith's excellent and influential *Mark Twain: The Development of a Writer*, the best example of this interpretive school and, incidentally, probably the closest thing we have to a book-length study of Clemens's moral thought, will show that an emphasis on Mark Twain as an opponent of conventionality finally raises more questions than it answers about his uses of sentimentality.

Smith accepts Santayana's thesis that "America . . . 'is a country with two mentalities, one a survival of the beliefs and standards of the fathers, the other an expression of the instincts, practices, and discoveries of the younger generations'" (2). Smith sees in Mark Twain the first clear expression of the alternative philosophy, the "vernacular perspective" (viii) that came to dominate American letters.

Mark Twain's genius, according to Smith, was to show through his style exactly how hollow and morally inappropriate to real life America's conventional philosophy was. For instance, discussing Huck Finn's moral dilemmas, he says:

> The conflict in Huck between generous impulse and false belief is depicted by means of a contrast between colloquial and exalted styles. In moments of crisis his conscience addresses him in the language of the dominant culture, a tawdry and faded effort at a high style. . . . It is . . . the issue . . . of fidelity to the uncoerced self versus the blurring of attitudes caused by social conformity, by the effort to achieve status or power through exhibiting the approved limits of sensibility. (122–23)

Here Smith aligns personal moral and artistic integrity on the one hand against conventional sensibilities on the other. Not accidentally, the term "sensibility" conjures up the entire opposition to Mark Twain's art as defined by most critics. According to Smith, sentimental morality and art are all part of the gentility that Mark Twain struggled to reject. The correlative oppositions drop in parallel positions underneath the moral and artistic: democracy versus elitism, freedom versus constraint, pragmatic realism versus sentimental idealism.

These polar oppositions, though, begin to collapse if put under pressure. Take, for instance, the putative source of Mark Twain's moral vision, his "intuitions that always reached farther than his means of expression" (69), his capacity in vernacular English, to express "the intuitive good sense of the common man, which was assumed to be valid because it had not been perverted by upper-class affectations and stereotypes" (182). Yet the sentimental morality that Smith assumes to have been no more than a mark of upper-class affectation actually arose out of an anti-authoritarian belief in the innate goodness of each human being and a belief in each person's access to that goodness through intuitive knowledge of good and evil. Thus, the intuitive morality Smith describes Mark Twain as advocating was, in reality, a restatement of conventional sentimental morality.

Humor itself, which Smith deems the central source of Twain's vernacular intuitions of honesty, was also highly conventional, as Smith himself admits. He wants us to accept, however, the implicit premise that as a low-brow tradition, humor represented a more dynamic American reality than could any high-brow aesthetic, presumably ossified by gentility and suffering osteoporosis from lack of "real" food. But as Kenneth Lynn points out in *Mark Twain and Southwestern Humor*, Southwestern vernacular comedy arose from English courtly models. Vernacular comedy conventionally mocks low-style characters for their crude stupidities, and even when these characters reveal truths humorously, readers recognize the superiority of the message to the messenger, and their own superiority to both. Especially as satire, comedy tends to be a conservative medium. It may be no coincidence that, in Britain, the age of sentiment was also the age of satire, and the latter was more frequently the tool of Tories than of Whigs. Twain's satire, then, may indeed be anti-sentimental, but how does it represent a democratic and anti-conventional tradition?

Consider, too, the distinction between Twain's humor and his satire. The very term "humor" as an artistic category was born under a sentimental rubric, as Stuart Tave points out in *The Amiable Humorist*. Twain's contem-

poraries understood the sense of humor to be one of literary sentimentalism's many sensibilities, and much American humor was primarily sentimental. Often, indeed, writers used sentimental humor to domesticate and
elevate "low-life" characters, as did, for example, Bret Harte in "The Luck
of Roaring Camp," and "The Outcasts of Poker Flat," or as did Harriet
Beecher Stowe in developing many of her humorous vernacular characters. Certainly Smith recognizes this in his discussion of "stalwart" Scotty
Briggs:

> The word ["stalwart"] calls up a cluster of sentimental attitudes that formed a
> part of the popular culture. It is a shorthand designation for the formula by
> which crude, impulsive strength could be transformed from a threat to estab-
> lished values into a means of defending them. The unrefined character is
> shown to be a loyal defender of basic principles of justice even though he
> outrages the niceties of etiquette. (66–67)

If one refuses to accept the legerdemain in distinguishing between "popular" and "vernacular," one sees that Smith acknowledges in fact that sentimental gentility, rather than being alien to vernacular culture, was part of it,
and served substantially to give the common person the same moral legitimacy in intuitive, impulsive goodness that Smith credits Twain with having given to Huck Finn and for having in his own moral and artistic vision.
So even if it is pragmatic and realistic, the vernacular character's individual
integrity begins to look remarkably romantic, idealistic, and sentimental,
to use three terms that Smith uses synonymously to describe an elitist
philosophy.

So, insofar as Smith is correct that Mark Twain's writings succeed
when they show faith in the common man, this does not necessarily imply
that in doing so Twain had to oppose vernacular voices to genteel ones.
Correlatively, insofar as Samuel Clemens was torn between his own elitism
and his leveling impulses, his attacks on gentility could just as well, as I will
show later, come out of his own elitism as out of his desire to establish a
vernacular alternative to the culture's sentimental snobbery.[21]

The problem with Smith's thesis, then, is that he, like his predecessors, views historical dialectic teleologically, with clearly opposed, virtually
monolithic ideologies passing in succession, with the morally superior
one — in this case a democratic, American, vernacular one — succeeding the
archaic one. I do not disagree that Twain's works are driven by fundamental
opposition; I wish to relocate the site of that opposition from between

conflicting world-views, to within the rather multiform and paradoxical ideology of American liberalism.

In locating the culture's dialectic within the dominant ideology I am participating in a recent trend of criticism that often shows sentimentalism in a broader perspective. In particular, Jane Tompkins and Philip Fisher have begun to examine sentimentality in terms not of literary convention but in terms of its functions in the culture at large, what they call its "cultural work." Their analyses have arisen out of a growing interdisciplinary focus on the interplay between social ideology and literary movements that has been fueled substantially by feminist criticism of literary canonization and of the cultural roles of women as workers, wives, and writers. Having uncovered the social value of sentimentalism in nineteenth-century America, these critics have revealed the possibility that Mark Twain's uses of sentiment may have had a social content larger than just the desire to clear room for realism in literature or even, as Henry Nash Smith more generously puts it, to advocate American pragmatism over European traditionalism.

I wish to add to this recent criticism by recovering our knowledge of the intellectual richness of this cultural ideology. As I hope to show in the next chapter, sentimentalism, rather than being merely a set of literary conventions, was part of a plastic and vital cosmology. A case can be made for the intellectual content of American sentimentalism only if we surrender the idea that there was a monolithic "genteel" philosophy that writers could either defeat or succumb to. While some scholars in other fields give credit to the vitality and variability of the nineteenth-century moral philosophies that included sentimentalism, literary historians have not yet explored these significant cracks in the intellectual facade of genteel culture.

For example, Terence Martin, whose *The Instructed Vision* still stands as the definitive study of the literary influence of the Scottish Philosophers who popularized sentimentalism in America, insists that the intellectual underpinnings of literary gentility were both consistent and conservative:

> Common Sense thought consistently helped to articulate a need for social order in America. An 'academic' philosophy from the time of its entrance into the Colonies, it suggested stability. . . . Not that all the Scots held precisely the same philosophical positions; they were eminently capable of disagreeing among themselves. But the disagreements were intramural, as it were, and it is possible to speak of a Common Sense school of thought which gained a widely favorable reception in America. (5)

Martin makes this assertion in the face of his own notice, in Chapter One, that the Common Sense philosophers were important preceptors to such cultural progressives as Thomas Jefferson and William Cullen Bryant. A philosophical tradition that served both Federalists and Democrats does not appear consistently conservative.

Martin may be right that various moral philosophers wished to encourage stability in the Western world. After all, their foremost task was to synthesize a bridge between faith in God and a belief in practical science. The first British moral philosophers in particular wished to provide an alternative to fundamentalist Calvinism without endorsing pure materialism, and most American moral philosophers shared this agenda. But the task precluded the possibility of a stable agreement. By trying to combine virtually all academic disciplines — including what we now call theology (then divided into natural and revealed theology), sociology, psychology, epistemology, ethics, natural science, political science, and aesthetics — into consistent philosophical systems, nineteenth-century moral philosophers threatened the stability they sought. They found themselves disagreeing over the relative importance of various bits of knowledge that they all accepted as true, and their consensus opinions were susceptible to pressures from new knowledge gained in any of their fields of interest. Consequently, the "genteel" culture resting on these philosophies could be no more than a loose, shifting alliance of ideas, attitudes, ideologies, and conventions, many of which were at many points in conflict with others though able to collaborate in the battles against atheism and Calvinism.

Samuel Clemens aspired to the literate culture that rested on these shaky and shifting intellectual foundations. His divided mind, I will argue, came not so much out of his conflict with "genteel" culture as out of his participation in it. As long as he participated in literate America's moral battles, he had to choose sides, and like the professional moral philosophers around him, he shifted alliances depending on his target.

His vitality as an artist, and finally as a thinker, depended on his ready ability to shift sides in spite of his desire to find absolutely unshakeable moral truths. He was not immune from the cultural habit of trying to fashion consistent philosophical systems, and, again like the professional moral philosophers around him, when he felt sure of his "truths," he grew quite numbingly didactic, as any reader of *What Is Man?* can testify.

Fortunately, Clemens's method of testing truths kept him from ever complacently accepting any one system. His technique — developed under the umbrella of sentimental justifications and definitions of humor — of juxtaposing conventional voices, produced an ironic vision that always consumed any truth he wanted to believe. His irony enabled him to explore the validity and practical value of the entire range of moral options his culture made available to him. When none of these options proved satisfactory and his much heralded despair set in, he finally experimented with trusting his ability to hold opposites in tension without trying to resolve inconsistency. Only then did he hesitatingly and partially pick up the pieces of moral systems he had earlier discarded in order to synthesize a new, less rigid moral vision.

To understand how sentimentalism fits into the larger picture of Twain's work, we must suspend the idea that he was on the side of a victorious "realist" viewpoint that destroyed literary sentimentalism. Instead, we must see, as the internal contradictions of this century's criticism show, that the moral and literary tensions that drove Twain's works have persisted — not because the ideas are those of fundamentally opposed world-views, but because they are part of the fundamental paradoxes of the modern world, or at least of Western culture's liberal formulation of modernity. Never were these paradoxes more acutely and consciously debated than among intellectuals of the late nineteenth century. Insofar as Clemens participated in this dialogue, he was always struggling toward conscious understanding, and insofar as his career as Mark Twain represents the trajectory of that dialogue, we can see that his doubleness is not, then, primarily between the superego and the id, the past and the future, the real and the ideal, the West and the East, or Europe and America; it embraces all of these oppositions because they lie within the very structure of liberal thought at the center of American moral ideology.

This book, then, is the story of Samuel Clemens's attempt to come to terms with these contradictions, and while his particular effort marks a major shift in the way literate culture perceived its mission — in particular in the way the vocabularies of science and morality would be articulated in modern literature — his effort also shows how in their ostensible death, the ideas and forms of sentimental literature were reinscribed in the modernist project that Twain's later writings so interestingly forecast.

2. The Real and the Ideal in the Sentimental Tradition

I

> If Cooper had any real knowledge of Nature's ways of doing things, he had a most delicate art of concealing the fact. For instance: one of his acute Indian experts, Chingachgook (pronounced Chicago, I think), has lost the trail of a person he is tracking through the forest. Apparently that trail is hopelessly lost. Neither you nor I could ever have guessed out the way to find it. It was different with Chicago. Chicago was not stumped for long. He turned a running stream out of its course, and there, in the slush in its old bed, were that person's moccasin tracks. The current did not wash them away, as it would have done in all other like cases — no, even the eternal laws of Nature have to vacate when Cooper wants to put up a delicate job of woodcraft on the reader.
>
> — Mark Twain, "Fenimore Cooper's Literary Offenses" (172–73)

> Damnation! I said to myself, are we real creatures in a real world, all of a sudden, and have we been feeding on dreams in an imaginary one since nobody knows when — or how is it?
>
> — Mark Twain, "The Great Dark" (130)

According to Sydney J. Krause in his study of Mark Twain as a literary critic, "when a writer is at once a realist and a satiric humorist, he is ipso facto committed to judging things, and where there is judgment, there must of necessity lurk some system, some standards, some decided way of looking at the world" (3). If it is true that Mark Twain is the father of American realism, the author of the one great book from which, as Hemingway put it and countless others have quoted, "All modern American literature comes," then his literature must have been completely at odds with genteel standards of literature. And in fact, ever since Santayana, this is how critics have interpreted Twain's relationship to the genteel tradition. They have usually scorned his contemporaries for writing unrealistic, overly formal, narrow-minded fiction that was out of touch with actual American values.

Such judgments, relying on twentieth-century definitions of realism, fail to take into account that the sentimental novel itself, the main target in attacks on literary gentility, was considered in its time to be realistic. How, then, do we discriminate between the realism that sentimentalists purported to write and the realism that Clemens supposedly began? Or to phrase the question differently, if Clemens held himself to be a realist who was committed to judging by realistic standards, how did he define realism, and how, if at all, did his definition contradict the genteel one? We need to have a historically accurate understanding of nineteenth-century definitions of realism before we can answer such questions.

We can best build such an understanding by tracing America's peculiar development of the British philosophies that undergird genteel culture. Many scholars have studied the wide-ranging and deep impact of Scottish Common Sense Philosophy on the ante-bellum American mind.[1] Parrington, Miller, May, Pearce, Curti, and Howard among others have explored the Scottish influence in the eighteenth and early nineteenth centuries generally, while other scholars have shown the impact more specifically on such things as American literature (Martin), Unitarianism (Howe), abolitionism (Davis), and theology (Ahlstrom). Miller seems justified in calling the Scottish philosophies America's "official metaphysic" for over half of the nineteenth century (ix). Given their overwhelming centrality in American culture by 1850, the Scottish philosophies could not have entirely disappeared after the Civil War, yet twentieth-century scholars often insist that they did. As Perry Miller describes the intellectual climate during the bulk of Clemens's career as a writer,

> it is a curious fact that one of the most radical revolutions in the history of the American mind took place in the two or three decades after the Civil War without exciting appreciable comment: the philosophy and the philosophers of Scottish Realism vanished from the American colleges, leaving not even a rack behind, and were swiftly replaced by expounders of some form of Idealism. (ix)

That Common Sense realism would give way to idealism in American universities seems all the more surprising given the vogue of mechanistic materialism and social Darwinism in large parts of American culture as the century drew to a close.

The "curious fact" cannot be explained without looking at what Daniel Walker Howe calls Common Sense dualism. He notes that the popularity of Common Sense philosophies in American culture depended substantially on their advocacy of the equal reality and importance of both heaven and earth, of both matter and spirit. Either could teach us much, said the

Scots, about the other, but neither could be given primacy in explaining the world or determining morality. Furthermore, the Common Sense realists did not predicate their dualism on any form of relativism or doubt; they insisted on the absolute, demonstrable reality of both heaven and earth. Consequently, their dualistic balancing act required not metaphysical hair-splitting but rope-splicing between the essentially idealistic, a priori and deductive Christian religion and the essentially materialistic, a posteriori and inductive system of science.

So, far from leaving "not even a rack behind," Common Sense Philosophy provided the foundations on which both the various forms of idealism and materialism were built. To understand how this philosophy could continue to exist in such opposed forms toward century's end, one needs to look at the pressures peculiar to America in the development of this country's version of Common Sense philosophy and then to the pressures, intellectual and social, that split the dualism into its component parts. This understanding in turn will make it possible to understand Clemens's particular treatment of the intellectual schisms between sentimentalism and realism, idealism and materialism.

II

> [Isabella Beecher Hooker] and her sister, Harriet Beecher Stowe, were near neighbors of ours in Hartford during eighteen years. I knew all the Beecher brotherhood and sisterhood, I believe. . . . There was not an ungifted Beecher among all those brothers and sisters, and not one that did not make a considerable name.
> —Mark Twain, Autobiographical Dictation, March 1, 1907†

> Once, when Mr. Clemens, at the solicitation of his wife, called on Mrs. Stowe, he was so absent minded as to put on neither collar nor necktie. On Mrs. Clemens remonstrating on his return, he said he would make it all right, and accordingly sent a collar and tie of his over to Mrs. Stowe in a box.
> —*Mark Twain Laughing*, Anecdote #111

A study of Harriet Beecher Stowe's career provides a perfect window into the cultural controversies that ultimately informed Clemens's writing. Her career spanned the era in which Common Sense versions of sentimentalism rose to prominence as a "realistic" alternative to Calvinism and then came under attack as idealistic utopianism. She self-consciously involved herself in the effort to spread Common Sense philosophy through the country, first in her teaching and then in her writings, both fiction and non-fiction. The enormous popularity of her works gives a loose sense of how widespread her version of moral philosophy was from Clemens's teens through his early years as a writer.

Not only was she one of the most influential writers of the literary generation that preceded Clemens's, she also belonged, through family ties and intellectual affinity, to the Hartford community — Nook Farm — that Clemens chose as his home. Like him and many other members of the Nook Farm community, she saw herself as a moralist whose writings served to promote reform. In some ways, she served as Nook Farm's tutelary spirit, the primary example of what the community stood for. Insofar as Clemens would react against a "hereditary philosophy" or accept it as his own, that philosophy would be well represented in Stowe's works.

Given the usual criticism of her writings, however, it is not easy to see how Common Sense philosophies influenced Stowe. A recent and rather peculiar trend in criticism places Stowe firmly in the Calvinist intellectual tradition of her father, brothers, and husband at the same time that she allegedly articulated, in fiction, a feminist alternative to the androcentricity of Calvinist religion.[2] Ignoring for the moment that her father in particular objected to almost all fiction on the traditional Puritan grounds that such "lies" are immoral because both worldly and false, Stowe wrote her greatest work not as a Calvinist allegory such as *Pilgrim's Progress*, but as a sentimental novel.[3] Perhaps feminist critics, in order to reform Stowe's reputation as an artist, would rather attach her to an intellectual tradition American literary critics take seriously than to one they have disparaged so effectively that even now one may speak of the cultural work of sentimentalism, as do Philip Fisher and Jane Tompkins, but not of its intellectual content.[4]

In fact, with the exception of Jay Fliegelman, whose *Prodigals and Pilgrims* treats the impact of sentimental moral philosophy on the literature of the Revolutionary era, no one yet has precisely addressed Herbert Ross Brown's influential complaints about all American sentimental fiction. Brown begins his discussion of American sentimental novels with *The Power of Sympathy* (1789), and he finds very little philosophical content in America's earliest, most clearly derivative novels. He finds the formal influence of Richardson, Sterne and to a lesser extent Goethe, but little substantive influence. Thus, he dismisses the early American sentimentalists' philosophical justifications as so much propaganda:

> The sentimental formula was a simple equation resting upon a belief in the
> spontaneous goodness and benevolence of man's original instincts. It could
> point to what passed for philosophical justification in the admired writings of
> Shaftesbury, Hutcheson and Adam Smith. (176)

In suggesting that philosophies of the sentiments merely passed as justification for American novels, Brown implies that sentimental novels actually
contained no philosophy at all.[5] Leaving aside the fact that he does not take
Shaftesbury, Hutcheson, or Smith seriously in the first place, Brown er-
roneously believes that British philosophers influenced American writers
only indirectly through popular British fiction. Assuming that no American
sentimental fiction could have been directly based in the British philosophical tradition that gave birth to the best of British sentimental fiction, Brown
concludes that American sentimental fiction merely and mindlessly repeated various stock plots and characters.

Stowe did, of course, draw on the sentimental literary tradition disparaged by Brown, but she creatively used stock plots, characters, vocabulary, and tears as vehicles to carry her theological and philosophical beliefs.
Consider, for instance, Stowe's treatment of the conventional sentimental
courtship. The earliest American novels often followed Richardson in depicting true love thwarted by the mercenary greed of cruel parents. Herbert
Brown notes that many a novel wrings many a tear out of some sweet child's
need to choose between her favorite suitor and filial loyalty, which impels
her to marry the rich beast her parents insist upon (34–35). In *Uncle Tom's
Cabin* Stowe uses the convention, but with a remarkable twist. When she
sketches out a conventional romance in which cruel parents estrange their
daughter from her true love, Augustine St. Clare, she uses the tale not to
garner pity for the young woman but to explain how, with his dreams
broken, Augustine St. Clare has hardened his naturally soft heart. If Stowe
were merely following what Brown describes as the sentimental formula,
she would not have to explain a hardened heart because such a thing could
not be. On the contrary, Stowe seems to be engaged in a serious defense of
the sentimental ideal; she is trying to explain how naturally good human
beings can lose their sensitivities to goodness. In other words, she is trying
to explain the existence of evil in the best of all possible worlds.

The "problem of evil" was less of a problem to Stowe's basically
orthodox Calvinist father, husband, and older brothers. In fact, the very
question of how God could have allowed evil in the best of all possible
worlds would have struck them as heretical. Human beings, according to
their theology, brought evil upon themselves in Adam's fall; his transgres-

sion imputed sin to all. To believe in the natural goodness of the human heart was to indulge in sinful pride, further alienating the soul from God. On this point at the very least, Lyman Beecher and Calvin Stowe were absolutely orthodox Calvinists, believers in a fundamentally deductive system based on an absolute, a priori faith in the literal truth of the Bible.

Harriet Beecher Stowe, in an 1863 attempt to whitewash her father's Calvinism, said that "though he firmly believed in total depravity, yet practically he never seemed to realize that people were unbelievers for any other reason than for want of light, and that clear and able arguments would not at once put an end to skepticism" ("Early Remembrances" 394). While Lyman's practice may have brought about his trial for heresy and may have ultimately given his children room for their own Arminianism by the 1850s, his firm "belie[f] in total depravity" was intimidating enough to drive one of his sons to suicide over his despair at not feeling grace, to drive his eldest daughter, Catherine Beecher, to open apostasy, and finally to hound Harriet, whose conversion wasn't convulsive enough to satisfy the orthodox, into fits of extreme doubt not only about her own soul but about the existence of God altogether. In this context, and substantially under the guidance of her sister, Harriet turned to a metaphysical tradition founded on John Locke's formidable epistemological challenge to Calvinism so that she could support her own faith.

III

> Miss Watson she took me in the closet and prayed, but nothing come of it. She told me to pray every day, and whatever I asked for I would get it. But it warn't so. I tried it. Once I got a fish line, but no hooks. It warn't any good to me without hooks.
> —Mark Twain, *Adventures of Huckleberry Finn* (13)

John Locke, formulating his philosophy of the mind substantially in reaction to the Puritan revolution in seventeeth-century England, attacked Calvinism at its deductive roots. He suggested that human beings, born with no innate ideas, learn their world almost exclusively through the agency of their external senses. Sense impressions leave their marks in the mind in the form of simple ideas, with a perfect correspondence to the reality of the sensory impressions. By combining these simple ideas into complex ones, human beings come to know the world but also find the ability to misconstrue reality. The memory and the imagination, working together, can create ideas of things that not only never have been, but never could be. To Locke, deductive systems are intrinsically subject to error because based on fanciful association of ideas, on the mind's natural empiricism gone awry. To find truth, one must resist the temptation to imagine by strictly applying the mind's natural empirical method, by using reason alone to mediate between perception and understanding in all but the very few, simplest intuitive cases.[6] To do so, Locke suggests that we should eschew figurative language in order to remain true to sensory impressions. Only from clear perception and by the light of reason can we generalize experience into a discovery of natural laws.

The corollaries to Locke's theory of mind dispense with the fundamental tenets of Calvinism. For one, Locke implied that the mind, while responsive to its environment, is essentially free to make choices; that is to say, human destiny is not predetermined. He implied further that the soul and matter fundamentally agree. Then too, if the mind is a tabula rasa at birth, it is not innately depraved. Its salvation and damnation alike depend on education, not conversion. And, most importantly, the pursuit of an ethical life, not devotion to God, is the highest human purpose. "Morality," says Locke, "is the proper science and business of mankind in general . . . who are both concerned and fitted to search out their summum bonum" (4: 11–12). Essentially, then, Locke's psychology supports an Arminian over a Calvinist religion, and this emphasis explains its popularity among Christians in spite of its deist leanings.

Regardless of his attack on deductive systems based on unproven or fanciful assumptions,[7] Locke postulated the existence of God and of natural law in order to support the idea that the senses in fact do objectively perceive extra-mental realities. The epistemological problems attendant on these assumptions inflamed the metaphysical debates Locke had hoped to quell with his philosophy. On the one hand, a strictly materialistic empiricism calls into question the very existence of God, as Hobbes had already shown. On the other hand, the problems of mediation between reality and sensation and between sensation and understanding call into question the possibilities of really knowing the external world empirically. Locke in fact seems to have been aware of these problems; he dismissed them in the only reasonable way by stressing understanding as the end product of determining probabilities. But to the absolutist metaphysicians who surrounded him, probabilites were not enough. Berkeley deduced from the epistemological weaknesses of Locke's psychology that in fact there is no reality but a transcendent or ideal one. Berkeley salvages God only by abandoning the reality of the world. Hume, in his skepticism, questioned whether we could, through ideas contingent on sensation, know anything at all, since our belief in natural law relied on our sensory perceptions and our belief in the reliability of our sensory impressions in turn circularly relied on natural law. In Hume's hands, Locke's psychology threatened faith in God and creation both.

With faith in God at risk through the epistemological problems of Locke's philosophy, morality, too, was called into question. Specifically, by postulating that the human mind knows the external world only through its senses, Locke created a threefold problem for moralists. For one, such a psychology cast doubt on the medieval conception of the human being as compounded of both heavenly spirit and earthly clay. Philosophically and theologically, Locke's model of the mind suggests that human beings are simply the most intelligent of the animals and have no intrinsic kinship with the spiritual or ideal world. Like animals, they only respond to external stimuli in searching for pleasure and avoiding pain. While the deistic implications of the concept of natural law kept Locke from emphasizing the materialistic and hedonistic implications of his philosophy, Hobbes's works showed how such a materialistic philosophy could warrant gross sensualism.

While postulating that true self-interest corresponds to conventional morality so that sensual hedonism can never be a problem, Locke's system nonetheless implies that human beings as animals can only discover morality — that is, self-interested behavior in accord with natural law — empirically. Experimentation, as long as human beings could perceive the universe exclusively through the five external senses and through the internal faculties of memory and reason, would lead to a self-interested, utilitarian morality and, worse, to a utilitarian faith. It did not take a David Hume to alert the clergy and various philosophers to the relativistic potential of such a doctrine.

At least two influential English moralists, both widely read in America and both studied by Harriet Beecher Stowe and by Samuel Clemens, tried to adapt Locke's utilitarianism to support conventional Christian faith. William Paley used Locke's insistence on natural law to articulate a religion based on hard science. He evoked devotional feeling out of "natural philosophy" by showing the sublimity of God's perfect, immutable design. His argument had great emotional power, and was central to the faith of many Americans who rejected Calvinism.[8] But because Paley's religion was based on God's power and on the rigidity of his law, its emotional impact was similar to that of Calvinism.

Joseph Butler, too, tried to build an empirical religion, but he did so by first stressing the importance of probability as the fundamental source of knowledge. Citing Locke's authority in rejecting systematic thinking, Butler proposed that we calculate probabilities by analogy, that is by comparing one observed situation to another that we know well by previous, repeated observation. By analogy, he decides that there is an after-life and that in it we must be able to feel both pleasure and pain. He then defines human prudence as the wisdom to avoid pain. Since pain probably will exist in the afterlife, says Butler, a prudent person, acknowledging that hell is a possibility by analogy to the pain in this world and that one might earn one's place in hell by immoral behavior, would prudently follow a moral path in this world even though it might not maximize earthly pleasure. Butler accepts Locke's utilitarianism but counters hedonism with hell-fire in order to support conventional morality.

Such a utilitarian morality, however, seemed almost as hard as the Calvinism it tried to replace. In a slightly different approach to finding a middle ground between Puritanism and skepticism, various latitudinarian divines began to interpret 1 Corinthians 13 in light of Locke's psychology of sensation, thereby stressing the pleasures of Christian charity (Crane 208, 221, 230). Working from this growing latitudinarian tradition in England, the third Earl of Shaftesbury formulated his idea of the moral sense, an additional human faculty that could innately perceive right and wrong by allowing one person to experience another's pains and pleasures through the power of sympathy. While such a sense could not, perhaps, distinguish as certainly between right and wrong as the tongue could between sweet and sour, it allowed Shaftesbury and his protégé Hutcheson to put absolute morality back into Locke's world. Endowed with this sense and in accordance with the empiricism of the pleasure principle, human beings could, suggested Shaftesbury, behave philanthropically without the added stimulus of the pain of punishment.

Shaftesbury's own deism notwithstanding, his ideas gave British liberal theologians a system they could adapt to their purposes. By suggesting that God inspired the moral sense in order to encourage human beings to renounce the purely physical pleasures of this world, they managed to retain the moral and theological benefits of Locke's philosophy—namely free will, the possibility to earn grace through works, and the manifest presence of God's love throughout a creation designed to secure human happiness—without having to accept totally any of its shortcomings. The only thing that remained was to address the epistemological problems.

IV

> There is a Moral Sense, and there is an Immoral Sense. History shows us that the Moral Sense enables us to perceive morality and how to avoid it, and that the Immoral Sense enables us to perceive immorality and how to enjoy it.
> —Mark Twain, *Pudd'nhead Wilson*, epigraph, Chapter 16

> Grief can take care of itself; but to get the full value of a joy you must have somebody to divide it with.
> —Mark Twain, *Following the Equator*, epigraph, Chapter 47

Inheritors of the sentimental ethical tradition, the philosophers of the Scottish Renaissance were extremely influential in America, as well as in much of the Western world. Often called the Scottish Realists for their opposition to Berkeley's idealism, their usual name, the Common Sense philosophers, hints at their solution to the epistemological problems raised by Locke's philosophy. In the expression "common sense" itself, these philosophers expressed their disdain for deductive systems that sophistically denied the reality of a world outside of the mind. Their name also alludes to their model of psychology with the word "sense" specifically referring to the innate faculties of perception by which we know the world. We could, they believed, understand the reach and limits of these senses through introspective analysis, giving us not only the capacity to perceive the world at large but also the capacity to perceive our own abilities to perceive. They did not claim that our senses could give us all possible knowledge of the world, but their faith in God and in God's benevolence toward us gave them faith—rather circularly—that our senses provided all the information we needed to secure understanding of God's intentions toward us and to secure our own happiness. In these beliefs, they merely followed Locke.

They countered the objections of idealists, relativists, and skeptics that introspection could yield only subjective knowledge of one person's inner states in two ways. First, they elevated sensory impressions to the level of intuitive truth. Locke had postulated that we know of our own existence intuitively, and he further suggested that certain moral precepts are as self-evident as many mathematical propositions. The Scots elevated sensory impression to the same status, thereby circumventing the possibility of pure subjectivism in sensation. Secondly, they allowed for corroboration of knowledge by emphasizing that the senses on which they relied were common to all normal human beings. Thus they began to add empirical techniques to the art of understanding human psychology.[9] Of course, few of the Scottish philosophers accepted the relativistic potential of their own technique; that is, when they found societies whose moral codes, for example, cast doubt on their idea of the moral sense, they dismissed those societies as abnormal or perverted. Thus their standards of normalcy once again became a rather question-begging ground for their studies.

In spite of such methodological shortcomings, however, in adopting the language of physical science the Common Sense philosophers adopted much of its spirit, taking several radical, though probably unintentional, steps toward positivism. At the very least, they began to dismiss many metaphysical questions on the grounds that such speculations made no practical difference either to human understanding or to human behavior.[10]

These common characteristics notwithstanding, the entire intellectual tradition embraced weaknesses and inconsistencies enough to encourage fundamental disagreements among the various members of the school. In the very origins of the system, Shaftesbury conflated the differences that threatened to split this school of thought into radically opposed camps. By adding the moral sense to Locke's list of the human being's mental faculties, Shaftesbury implied that people have innate, intuitive access to certain kinds of complex understanding. No longer a tabula rasa, the mind in Shaftesbury's system was more like a color-by-numbers picture. A moral question is not tangible as was the stone Dr. Johnson reputedly kicked in order to confound philosophical skepticism. No wonder that, when Shaftesbury talked about how the moral sense could allow one to build a moral algebra, he used as his metaphor an abstract, logical system that enables one to solve equations for a missing variable.[11]

Shaftesbury's choice of metaphor, then, shows the problem he bequeathed to "mental and moral science," namely, determining the respective roles of reason and emotion in mediating between perception and understanding. If the moral sense directly perceives right and wrong, then no moral algebra should be required; emotional reaction should be a sufficient intuitive guide to truth. If, however, the moral sense must be used to create complex ideas from the simple ideas of perception, as Locke suggests all human understanding must, then the best way to determine the truth in ethical matters, as in all other matters, would be to reason it out. In both cases, the motive for doing good comes from the pleasure it will entail and thus is "utilitarian" in the strictest sense of the word. But the emphasis on direct emotional response gave rise ultimately to sentimental morality, whereas the emphasis on reason as a guide to morality gave rise to the strictly utilitarian branch of moral philosophy. As these ideas moved into the Scottish Renaissance, the various philosophers filtered themselves out into something of a continuum with Adam Smith, best known in his lifetime for his *The Theory of the Moral Sentiments*, on the sentimentalist extreme and Thomas Reid on the utilitarian extreme.

Shaftesbury's "discovery" of the moral sense encouraged other thinkers to discover yet other "senses." Francis Hutcheson, for instance, enumerated not only the five standard senses, but many "finer powers of perception" including the senses of honor and shame, decency and dignity, the sense of the ridiculous, more commonly known as the sense of humor, and, of course, the moral sense. All of these "finer" senses Hutcheson felt provided greater pleasures than did any of the "gross" senses, and all of them had the ability to color simple perceptions, adding, for instance, a moral valence to kinds and amounts of food (87). The moral sense Hutcheson held to be the most important; "from its very nature [it] appears to be designed for regulating and controlling all our powers" by forcing a person to sacrifice "lower" desires to higher (61). This power in turn lends coherence and purpose to human existence:

> Without a distinct consideration of this moral faculty, a species endued with such a variety of senses, and of desires frequently interfering, must appear a complex confused fabrick, without any order or regular consistent design. By means of it, all is capable of harmony, and all its powers may conspire in one direction, and be consistent with each other. (74)

The harmony Hutcheson felt the moral sense pursued ultimately was the harmony of human beings acting in concert for the good of other human beings, as the moral sense requires the exercise of the "benevolent affections" (62–64).

According either to Hobbesian naturalism or to the Calvinist doctrine of innate depravity, benevolent affections do not exist naturally. Yet to Hutcheson, they were the center of human nature because human nature, in his system, is primarily gregarious. Since no social animal can pursue merely selfish interests, Hutcheson assumed an agency of sociability in a primary sensibility, namely, the sense of sympathy. By sympathy, Hutcheson meant an ability to feel along with others both in "compassion" for their troubles and in "congratulation" for their happinesses. Following Hutcheson, the "sense of sympathy" as a sign of human sociability became a commonplace of the Scottish Renaissance. The social impulse, whether named gregariousness, benevolence, or sympathy, served an important purpose to all of the Common Sense philosophers insofar as it ratified the idea that human beings were able to determine truth by comparing their ideas and experiences. Furthermore, to Adam Smith and the sentimentalists, this sense served an even greater purpose, too. To them, the sympathetic social impulse was the fundamental precondition of society and in turn of moral behavior. As they conceived of sensation, it allowed human beings not only to perceive, it inspired also an emotional reaction that impelled a person to appropriate action. Thus sensation ceases to be passive reception, as in Locke's world, and becomes instead instinct. From sense to emotion, from emotion to impulsion, this line of inquiry pushed its adherents ever closer to a belief in innate ideas. From there, it was but an easy step to idealism.

Not that Reid and his more utilitarian followers rejected the idea that emotion moved people to action; they simply remained closer to Locke in distrusting sympathy and imagination as acceptable determinants of truth and therefore of moral action. After all, sympathy, requiring the activity of the imagination to conceive of rather than merely perceive the mental states of other human beings, required human beings to react to something other than tangible, extra-mental reality. Consequently, Reid and his followers helped promote the utilitarian idea that one determines the moral value of an action by judging its consequences; the sentimentalists on the other hand judged the moral value of behavior by the intention behind an action.

Given these disagreements, that the Common Sense philosophers remained a school depended at least as much on having common opponents as on sharing common methodologies. Beginning from a dualistic belief in the reality of both heaven and earth, they all had to defend themselves against the idealisms of Calvinists, of Berkeley, and of Kant on the one hand and against materialism on the other. Reid, not surprisingly, concerned himself mainly with Berkeley (Martin 85), while the sentimentalists shadow-boxed mostly with the ghost of Hobbes. In both cases they wanted to argue for a benevolent God who created an actual world according to natural laws. These laws gave human beings the greatest possible good by allowing free will, the power to earn happiness in this life, and the power to earn eternal happiness in the next. But the materialistic implications of natural law threatened a deterministic universe almost as morally offensive as the Calvinists' and also threatened to turn self-interested behavior into the death of altruism. The sentimental alternative, on the other hand, approached dangerously close to idealism in a way that threatened the reality of this world. The extremes of the school, in defending against one philosophical enemy, always threatened the possibilty of veering into the next. Perhaps the greatest talent of most Common Sense philosophers was to reconcile the extremes by ignoring the conflicts between them.

V

> Until near midnight I wallowed and reeked with Jonathan [Edwards] in his insane debauch [On Feedom of the Will]; rose immediately refreshed and fine at 10 this morning, but with a strange and haunting sense of having been on a three days' tear with a drunken lunatic. . . . He seems to concede the indisputable and unshakable dominion of Motive and Necessity (call them what he may, these are exterior forces and not under the man's authority, guidance or even suggestion) — then he suddenly flies the logic track and (to all seeming) makes the man and not these exterior forces responsible to God for the man's thoughts, words and acts. It is frank insanity.
>
> — Mark Twain, letter to Joseph Twichell, Feb. 1902

These conflicts lived a vigorous life in nineteenth-century America, as Harriet Beecher Stowe's works show. Typically for a nineteenth-century American, Harriet Beecher Stowe arrived in the Common Sense camp by way of her opposition to Calvinist doctrines that she could not reconcile to her own ideas of Christian love and justice. Looking back at her adolescence from the perspective of 1866, she rather disingenuously complained that her father's doctrines were made of "hair-splitting distinctions and dialectic subtleties" that "were as unintelligible to me as . . . Choctaw" (Fields, *Stowe* 50). In the late 1820s when she expressed her doubts about Calvinist doctrines to her brothers and father, they tried to badger her back into orthodoxy. She resisted on the grounds that God's compassion could not allow Him both to circumscribe human behavior and then to hold human beings accountable for it:

> I have been reading carefully the book of Job, and I do not think that it contains the views of God which you presented to me. God seems to have stripped a dependent creature of all that renders life desirable, and then to have

answered his complaints from the whirlwind; and instead of showing mercy and pity, to have overwhelmed him by a display of his power and justice. . . . With the view I received from you, I should have expected that a being who sympathizes with his guilty, afflicted creatures would not have spoken thus. Yet, . . . in the New Testament I find in the character of Jesus Christ a revelation of God as merciful and compassionate; in fact, just such a God as I need. . . . Mr. Hawes always says in prayer, "We have nothing to offer in extenuation of any of our sins," and I always think when he says it, that we have everything to offer in extenuation. The case seems exactly as if I had been brought into the world with such a thirst for ardent spirits that there was just a possibility, though no hope, that I should resist, and then my eternal happiness made dependent on my being temperate. Sometimes when I try to confess my sins, I feel that after all I am more to be pitied than blamed. (Fields, *Stowe* 67–68)[12]

British moral philosophy provided a fitting alternative for someone who objected to the image of God and to the very limited possibilities for human freedom proffered by Calvinism.

While her biographers do not know whether Stowe read the most important of the British philosophers—namely, Hutcheson, Reid, and Smith—she certainly was exposed to their ideas. In an autobiographical sketch of 1863, she mentions her first contact with these philosophies:

Much of the training and inspiration of my early days consisted, not in the things which I was supposed to be studying, but in hearing, while seated unnoticed at my desk, the conversation of Mr. Brace with the older classes. There from hour to hour I listened with eager ears to historical criticisms and discussions, or to recitations in such works as Paley's "Moral Philsophy," Blair's "Rhetoric," Alison "On Taste," all full of most awakening suggestions to my thought. ("Early Remembrances" 398)

She began her studies under Brace in the summer of 1819 at the age of eight and continued to the autumn of 1824 (Wilson 36–95).

Stowe's continued observations in "Early Remembrances" suggest that this contact with the Scots impressed her deeply:

I remember I could have been but nine years old, and my handwriting hardly formed, when the enthusiasm he [Brace] inspired led me, greatly to his amusement, I believe, to volunteer to write every week. The first week the subject of composition chosen by the class was "The difference between the Natural and the Moral Sublime." One may smile at this for a child of nine years of age; but it is the best account I can give of his manner of teaching to say that the discussion which he held in the class not only made me understand the subject as thoroughly as I do now, but so excited me that I felt sure I had something to say upon it. (398)

This composition could well have come in response to Blair's Common Sense rhetoric, but more likely arose in response to Alison's Common Sense treatise on aesthetics.[13] In any event, the subject itself was not likely to come out of Calvinist doctrine. Thus, while her father spoke the doctrinal equivalent of "Choctaw," Stowe at the age of nine found Common Sense philosophies both understandable and exciting.

If Stowe's studies had ended here, it would make little sense to argue that a precocious child's brief contact with moral and aesthetic philosophy could dominate her entire career. However, she continued her studies in order to teach, which she did intermittently until the publication of *Uncle Tom's Cabin*. In the early part of the century, children learned from books not graded to their supposed abilities; they learned from college texts or they learned not at all. It seems likely, then, that she would have mastered much of this and similar material simply because it constituted much of the American school curriculum.[14] She certainly studied Butler's *Analogy* well enough by 1833 to write a parody of Butler's "outrageous style of parentheses and foggification" (Fields, *Stowe* 83).[15]

More particularly, Stowe came to understand moral philosophy under the guidance of her sister Catherine. In 1824, Lyman Beecher pulled Harriet out of Miss Pierce's Litchfield school, where she had studied under Brace, in order to send her to Hartford as a student in her sister Catherine's new school. Harriet paid her way by preparing to teach as soon as possible, and one of the first subjects she taught was moral philosophy, conning Butler's *Analogy* just ahead of the class she taught. At the same time, her sister was undertaking a thorough study of Scottish moral philosophy.

The attraction of moral philosophy to Catherine, as to Harriet, was its power as an alternative to such doctrines as innate depravity, limited atonement, election, and justification by faith alone. As early as 1831, while running her Hartford Female Seminary, Catherine wrote one of America's first volumes of moral philosophy on the Scottish model, *The Elements of Mental and Moral Philosophy, Founded upon Experience, Reason, and the Bible*. She printed it at her own expense but suppressed publication in reaction to orthodox clerical opprobrium.

When in 1857 she revised the book and published it with Harper & Brothers under the title *Common Sense Applied to Religion, or the Bible and the People*, she claimed a consistent purpose over the course of her entire career, of "opposing theological theories, that seemed at war with both the common sense and the moral sense of mankind." She personally found her father's doctrines repugnant because predestined election "was so nearly like a matter of mere chance, and there seemed so little adaptation of means to ends, that, to one so hopeful, and, at the same time, so practical, there was very little motive of any kind to lead to a religious life" (xviii). Worse, after her fiancé died without having experienced a saving "change of heart," she reacted violently against the injustice of Calvinism, declaring, "I remember once rising, as I was about to offer my usual, now hopeless prayer, with a feeling very like this: that such a God did not deserve to be loved" (xxii). She felt that her reactions were commonplace and could explain why "there is apparent a manifest and strong tendency, especially among the young and most highly-educated of both sexes, to infidelity" on account of "dogmas . . . which are revolting both to the intellect and to the moral nature of man" (x). Thus, while she began her studies of moral philosophy in order to find her own religion, she continued in order to fight "infidelity" throughout the nation.

One of her first converts was her younger sister. According to Stowe's son, "No mind more directly and powerfully influenced Harriet's than that of her sister" (Fields, *Stowe* 54), and the influence became most significant when Harriet first confronted her religious doubts as a teenager. Catherine kept track of Harriet's feelings, writing to their father in 1827 when Harriet was living in Boston with Lyman while Catherine remained in Hartford: "I have received some letters from Harriet to-day which make me feel uneasy. She says, 'I don't know as I am fit for anything, and I have thought that I could wish to die young, and let the remembrance of me and my faults perish in the grave'" (Fields, *Stowe* 63). Catherine responded by arguing that Harriet should return to Hartford to study and teach with Catherine rather than stay in Boston with their father:

> If she could come here . . . it might be the best thing for her, for she can talk freely to me. I can get her books, and Catherine Cogswell, Georgiana May, and her friends here could do more for her than any one in Boston. . . . I can do better in preparing her to teach drawing than any one else, for I best know what is needed [letter to Edward Beecher, winter 1827] (Fields, *Stowe* 64).

What Catherine thought best, apparently, was not only society and drawing, but also her own influence.

The influence turned out to be life-long and ultimately reciprocal. When the entire Beecher clan left New England for Cincinnati, both Catherine and Harriet once again established a school; they also collaborated in writing textbooks. Catherine's failure as a school principal led to a temporary falling out during the early years of Harriet's marriage when Catherine was considered by most of the Beechers to be something of a pariah. But after Harriet read Catherine's *The Duty of American Women to their Country* (1845), Harriet once again fell under her sister's influence, then becoming Catherine's champion to the rest of the family (Sklar 233–34). Catherine returned the favor, helping manage Harriet's household in Brunswick, Maine, when Harriet was writing *Uncle Tom's Cabin*. Significantly, the ideas Catherine expressed in *Duty* that so impressed Harriet arose out of Catherine's understanding of moral philosophy (Sklar 78).

Beecher's writings fairly well reflect the Common Sense school except that she has a bias toward Butler's use of analogy as a weaker standard of "proof" for her arguments than would have been used by most of the Scots.[16] Under this weaker standard, her works easily embrace the most extreme differences in the Common Sense school. For instance, she asserts as one of the intuitive truths of the human constitution that human beings have free will, yet her wholehearted endorsement of the concepts of natural law and the idea that the human being is a "well-regulated machine" suggest that the will can be governed by mechanical habits and tricks of mind. Similarly, she simultaneously believes that a world governed by rigid natural law uniformly and implacably punishes immoral behavior and rewards moral behavior, yet the morality of any action lies in the intention behind it rather than in any "involuntary results." That these could be in conflict she acknowledges tacitly by willfully refusing to consider the justice of rigid natural law:

> The question of the justice or injustice of such natural penalties involves the great question of the right and wrong of the system of the universe. Is it just and right for the Creator to make a system in which all free agents shall be thus led to obedience? . . . This question will not be discussed here. (144)

Her way of dismissing such questions also follows the Scottish pattern of dismissing as useless such metaphysical speculations.

She also expresses a rather typical ambivalence toward the role of reason in human affairs. On the one hand she feels that reasoning on the basis of intuitive truths will yield universal agreement on all questions of morality and that such agreement will yield a millennium of perfectly moral behavior (27); on the other, she also believes that emotions cause human behavior even to the point of providing subconscious motivations — predicated on habit, association, and desire — that disguise themselves as conscious ones (32 et seq.). Typically, her ambivalence on these and other points arises out of her dualism, out of her efforts to promote belief in heaven by way of earthly means.[17]

Besides her extraordinary ability to straddle intellectual fences, Beecher's moral philosophy is noteworthy in two ways. For one, she exaggerated Hutcheson's hierarchy of pleasures in order to argue that self-sacrifice is the highest possible good. She begins by analyzing the mind's

> desires and propensities for various kinds of enjoyment. These are gratifications secured by the senses, the pleasures of taste, the happiness of giving and receiving affection, the various intellectual pleasures, and the still higher enjoyment resulting from our moral nature. All these are common to the race, though in varied degrees and combinations. The mind is also constituted with susceptibilities to pain and suffering from all the sources from which enjoyment may spring. (32)

Key here is the idea that "our moral nature" gives us higher pleasures than the merely physical nature of our being. Since, as Beecher would have it, our pursuit of these pleasures and our avoidance of these pains is the "Grand motive power to the mind" (33), and since these sources of pleasure are often in conflict, the organism naturally pursues the higher pleasures over the lower. From this point she derives her absolute "laws" of morality: "always . . . sacrifice the lesser for the greater good, having reference to the future as much as to the present," and "The lesser good of the individual is always to be sacrificed to the greater good of the many, having reference always to the future as much as to the present" (36).

To a point, this sounds like Bentham, but the conclusion that Beecher finally draws supports self-sacrificial martyrdom over any really utilitarian pleasure:

> Thus life commences with desires that are to be controlled and denied, first by parental power and influence, and next by the intellect and will. . . . And as self-denial always involves more or less pain, it becomes a fact that happiness is to be gained only by more or less suffering. (36–37)

By concentrating on the sacrifice of one pleasure to the next, Beecher virtually forgets the next pleasure per se and finds joy only in renunciation. She paradoxically exorcises the specter of selfishness by finding the self's greatest expression in total selflessness and at the same time reconciles her ethical system with Christian values.[18]

Catherine Beecher's systematic justification of suffering was certainly central to Stowe's version of Christian piety. Commentators often see the traditional aspects of Christianity in Stowe's use of martyrdom. Uncle Tom, after all, can only tolerate his martyrdom by fixing his spirit on heaven so that the earth ceases to be real for him. But it is important to recognize that he required his earthly attachment to Eva to teach him how to submit to suffering, and she taught him by demonstrating her own sympathy with people of this world.

> That's what troubles me papa. You want me to live so happy, and never to have any pain, — never suffer anything, — not even hear a sad story, when other poor creatures have nothing but pain and sorrow, all their lives; — it seems selfish. I ought to know such things, I ought to feel about them! (*Uncle Tom's Cabin* 403)

Here Eva uses her own feelings of pleasure and pain as a standard by which she judges moral behavior and thereby learns to renounce lower pleasures for higher. Her renunciation is only possible through her sense of sympathy, through her attachment to human community, through her love of the world.[19]

Stowe also uses this standard to explain how human beings should respond morally to pleasure, as when the Quaker Ruth wants to tell Eliza that her husband will soon join her rather than wait to surprise Eliza with a fait accompli:

> "Hush thee, dear!" said Rachel, gently; "hush Ruth! Tell us, shall we tell her now?"
> "Now! to be sure, — this very minute. Why, now, suppose 't was my John, how should I feel? Do tell her, right off."
> "Thee uses thyself only to learn how to love thy neighbor, Ruth," said Simeon.
> "To be sure. Isn't that what we are made for? If I didn't love John and the baby, I should not know how to feel for her." (220)

Stowe describes here a sentimental education that uses the sense of self and its attachments merely as a step in expanding one's moral sphere beyond the self and the home. In Stowe's moral system, selfhood serves to teach how to transcend the self, and while the last step requires the suffering of mortality, she sees the pleasures of this world as leading one to that beatifying final self-renunciation.

Perhaps even more significant culturally, and to Stowe's ethic in particular, was Beecher's development of Common Sense principles to justify the "sexual spheres."[20] She implicitly postulated a correspondence between the masculine "sphere" and common sense realism on the one hand and between the feminine "sphere" and common sense idealism on the other. As she put it in *Common Sense Applied to Religion*, "in regard to domestic relations. . . [t]he one who has most physical strength goes forth to provide supplies; the delicate one remains behind, by domestic ministries to render home the centre of all attractions" (207). Here Beecher equates woman's work with moral evangelism in the word "ministries," by which she implies that women do nothing practical but provide "attractions," or motives to moral behavior. On the other hand, a man's sphere sends him in pursuit of the lower, that is bodily, comforts such as food, clothing, and shelter. Beecher found this arrangement quite sensible in its efficient "division of labor" (*Treatise* 4–5), but quite dangerous to the morality of men in their public sphere. "A Man that has been drawn from the social ties of home, and has spent his life in the collisions of the world seldom escapes without the most confirmed habits of cold, and revolting selfishness" (*Elements*, quoted in Sklar 87).

This division of labor places women in a position to redeem men from the potential evils of worldly life, especially since as mothers, women "are perfect illustration[s] of self-sacrificing love" (*Common Sense* 207). With so much practice renouncing self, women in domestic circles maintain a moral purity that men in their worldly sphere cannot. But in order to maintain that purity, women must, according to Beecher, renounce practical and political equality with men. Thus, Beecher converts the relative moral position of women to one of superiority to men, but only so long as women renounce practical authority in this world to masculine control. Much as Beecher finds pleasure in renouncing pleasure, she finds power in renouncing power.

Stowe became more doctrinaire on these points than did Beecher, insofar as Stowe argued that woman's proper role was defined by her natural mental as well as physical differences from men. She felt that women are more emotional, sensitive, and idealistic than hard, practical men, as we can see clearly in her description of a significant exception to her rule, Augustine St. Clare:

> In childhood, he was remarkable for an extreme and marked sensitiveness of character, more akin to the softness of woman than the ordinary hardness of his own sex. Time, however, overgrew this softness with the rough bark of manhood, and but few knew how living and fresh it still lay at the core. His talents were of the very first order, although his mind showed a preference always for the ideal and the aesthetic, and there was about him that repugnance

to the actual business of life which is the common result of this balance of the faculties. (*Uncle Tom's Cabin* 239–40)

In Stowe's vision of the sexual spheres, this is what is largely wrong with Augustine, that although more sensitive than most men, he cannot act according to his sensitivities. The proper balance, according to Stowe, is between a woman who regulates a household according to her superior moral proclivities and a man who acts with masculine efficiency, as in the case of Mary and Senator John Bird. In the Bird household, Mary rules "more by entreaty and persuasion than by command or argument" (143), and her abilities to play on her husband's emotions through her own superior moral insights enable her to convince John to help Eliza to freedom in spite of his political convictions to the contrary.

Less ambiguously, Eliza Harris subdues her husband's anger and promotes his work ethic just by her very being:

"Yes Eliza," said George, "I know all you say is true. You are a good child, — a great deal better than I am; and I will try to do as you say. I'll try to act worthy of a free man . . . so long as we have each other and our boy. O! Eliza, if these people only knew what a blessing it is for a man to feel that his wife and child belong to him! . . . Why, I feel rich and strong, though we have nothing but our bare hands." (285)

Prompted by the domestic "attractions" of such virtual, and ironic, ownership, George's strengths and abilities slide into socially productive and orderly channels rather than into revolution.

Scholars of Common Sense philosophy stress that this conservative social function in part made the philosophy popular in America. In stressing ethics over piety, moral philosophy shifted the locus of moral accountability from an omnipotent God to the individual moral sense. Although this frees the individual from the central control of the Puritan clergy, it reestablishes order in the domestic circle and in civic responsibility. Thus Common Sense thought justifies democracy while hedging against anarchy.

Common Sense philosophy had other benefits as well, especially in promoting the arts in an unreceptive culture. Certainly Catherine Beecher, who in 1825 was still suspicious enough of such "luxuries" that she enjoined Harriet from writing poetry so that she could study Butler and "discipline [her] mind" (Fields, *Stowe* 49), eventually used Common Sense philosophy to justify fiction as useful for recreation, as long as it does not "throw the allurements of taste and genius around vice and crime" (*Treatise* 256).

Not surprisingly, as a disciple of Reid, Beecher endorsed fiction reticently. But Stowe, with her belief that the "preference for the ideal and aesthetic" was a natural trait of women, had other sources for her aesthetic in the works of Blair and Alison, the two Common Sense philosophers who so excited her when she studied under John Brace in Litchfield and who, along with Lord Kames, gave America its most cogent and popular expositions of aesthetics.

Blair, although relatively conservative in his belief in absolute standards of taste, strenuously advocated the value of novels as teachers of youth. He felt that even though true taste requires a balance between intellect and emotion, children and young people respond much more readily to emotion than to rationality, to imagination than to reality. Thus, fiction in general and novels in particular serve as excellent preceptors of true taste. Like Alison and Kames, Blair felt "that the exercise of taste is, in its native tendency, moral and purifying" (Hugh Blair 1: 15). Accordingly, the use of fiction to develop taste in the young could help promote morality. What a relief that must have been to Stowe who, struggling against her father's condemnation of fiction, complained to her brother Edward in 1829: "You speak of your predilections for literature having been a snare to you. I have found it so myself. I can scarcely think, without tears and indignation, that all that is beautiful and lovely and poetical has been laid on other altars" (Fields, *Stowe* 66). Of course, while Blair may have convinced Stowe that novels were not profane, he certainly wrote nothing to convince her that adults should read them. Perhaps under this influence Stowe originally ended her novel with a farewell to the children rather than to the Senator Birds whose Fugitive Slave Law did so much to inspire her to write in the first place.

Alison, more theoretical than Blair, distilled much of the thought of the Scottish Enlightenment into his *Essays on Taste*. His essays refer repeatedly to Beattie, rely heavily on Adam Smith's *Theory of the Moral Sentiments*, "the most eloquent work on the subject of MORALS, that Modern Europe has produced" (2: 191), are dedicated to Dugald Stewart, and derive their authority from the fact that "The opinion I have now stated . . . has been maintained in this country by several writers of eminence, by Lord Shaftesbury, Dr Hutcheson, Dr Akenside, and Dr Spence, but which nowhere has so firmly and so philosophically been maintained, as by Dr Reid" (2: 416–17). These acknowledgements read like a roll call of the Common Sense school of philosophers and apparently give equal weight to Reid and Smith. In fact, however, Alison's thought owes much more to Smith than to Reid and may very well explain Stowe's sentimentalism, especially in light of her sister's greater utilitarianism. Thus, it is worthwhile to examine in some depth both Alison's precepts and how they relate to Stowe's practice in *Uncle Tom's Cabin*.

VI

> Sleeping or waking, dreaming or talking, the thoughts which swarm through our heads are almost constantly, almost continuously, accompanied by a like swarm of reminders of incidents and episodes of our past. A man can never know what a large traffic this commerce of association carries on in his mind.
> — Mark Twain, Autobiographical Dictation, January 6, 1907 (Kiskis 194)

In his *Essays on Taste* Alison seeks to explain the nature of what eighteenth-century philosophers called the emotions of taste, that is, the emotions of beauty and sublimity; to examine in particular the sources of these emotions; and to explain the purpose these emotions serve in our lives. Secondarily, he offers a practical aesthetic. His analysis follows the fundamental assumptions of the Common Sense philosophers: first, that human beings have a limited number of senses which when stimulated by the external world give rise to certain subjective inner states such as emotion or memory; second, that human beings can objectify their reactions to the external world by comparing them with the reactions of others, that is to say, human beings can rest assured of the accuracy of their empirical knowledge if it is gained through the senses common to most human beings; and third, that human beings have a moral sense in addition to their physical senses.

Furthermore, Alison subscribed to an associationist model of human psychology. According to this model, human beings react to the world by classifying the unknown in terms of certain characteristics of the known. Thus, as they first come to know themselves and the people in their immediate environments through experience, human characteristics become their associational categories for understanding all further experience. Of primary importance to each child, says Alison, are the emotions, what he calls "expressions of mind," of its mother, so that human traits such as love, hatred, piety, and so forth become the primary categories each person uses to analyze the world. Secondarily, each child learns to associate the physical manifestations of emotions with the emotions themselves; thus the physical signs of feelings can evoke emotional responses in a person who perceives these signs. Naturally, as a person's experience widens, other perceptions of the real world, placed in these associative categories, in turn become new categories of perception. Through widening circles of association, then, human beings know the world. This progression of understanding through association is the basis of the emotions of taste, and, more importantly, of the ability of artists to evoke emotions of taste by mere representations of reality.

In some cases, the physical signs of emotions are constant for all human beings, as in the case of smiles being associated with happiness. In other cases, physical signs of emotion are "accidental," as Alison makes clear in his discussion of the beauty of certain sounds:

> That the Beauty of such sounds arises from the qualities of which they are expressive, and not from any original fitness in them to produce this Emotion, may perhaps be evident from the following considerations. . . . To those who have no such association, or who consider them simply as Sounds, they have no beauty. . . . They who are not accustomed to the Curfew, and who are ignorant of its being the evening bell, and, as such, associated with all those images of tranquillity and peace which render that season of the day so charming, feel nothing more from its sound, than from the sound of a bell at any other hour of the day. (1: 214–15)

Thus Alison accounts for differences in taste by suggesting that association, especially in youth, gives to things their ability to evoke emotion. Different events in the lives of each person lead to different associative categories of beauty.

Stowe accepted this idea, as we can see in her depiction of Rachel Halliday's squeaky rocking chair in *Uncle Tom's Cabin*:

> It had a turn for quacking and squeaking, — that chair had, — either from having taken cold in early life, or from some asthmatic affection, or perhaps from nervous derangement; but, as she gently swung backward and forward, the chair kept up a kind of subdued "creechy crawchy," that would have been intolerable in any other chair. But old Simeon Halliday often declared it was as good as any music to him, and the children all avowed that they wouldn't miss of hearing mother's chair for anything in the world. For why? for twenty years or more, nothing but loving words, and gentle moralities, and motherly loving kindness, had come from that chair. (140)

The Hallidays appreciate the sound not for itself but because "accidentally" it is associated with pleasant human qualities of mind, namely "motherly loving kindness." To Stowe there are no more important qualities of mind, and in her reading of Alison she would have found support for this opinion.

But not all of the Scottish philosophers agreed. Blair, like Reid and Kames, follows Locke in believing that association merely leads to error. From this premise he concludes that true taste relies on an innate common sense of taste. In the absence of any unnatural categories of associative taste, he argues, people have direct sensory awareness of absolute, eternal beauties. Alison, without leaving the basic model of Common Sense, turns to Locke's concept of complex ideas to reinforce his belief in the relativity of beauty. He suggests that the emotions of taste are not the simple consequences of a single human sense that enables human beings to recognize absolute beauty inherent in material objects, in poetry, or in sounds. On the contrary, the emotions of beauty and sublimity are compounded of "some Simple Emotion, or the exercise of some moral affection, and, 2dly, the consequent Excitement of a peculiar Exercise of the Imagination" (1: xxiii). In other words, any of the senses, including the moral sense, coupled with the associative faculty of memory, can produce emotions, either pleasurable or not. When these emotions in turn stir a chain of emotional reflection, yet another emotion arises out of the combined efforts of imagination and memory on the one hand and sensory perception on the other.

Thus we see in the Common Sense school itself divergent tendencies, some of which, as Henry Nash Smith suggests, do reinforce a manneristic, aristocratic aesthetic very much at odds with the realities of the American scene, but the other of which provides an aesthetic relativism that does not require rigid proprieties. This is not to say that Alison felt that the commonplace was the best material for aesthetic contemplation. He did feel that certain narrow trades contract the affections of the mass of humanity, and further that the mundane repetition of daily activites dampens the vitality of the affections even in the refined. Furthermore, he says that no emotions weaken so readily as those of the moral sense, "Which it is the melancholy tendency of the vulgar pursuits of life to diminish, if not altogether destroy" (2: 438).[21] Thus, for art to evoke the emotions of beauty, it must strip away all semblance of the quotidian to get at the emotional center of any experiences, even commonplace ones. By modern definitions, the artistic proprieties such a definition encourages are anti-realistic, but by nineteenth-century standards, these proprieties reinvested reality with its most important components. Such a conflicted theoretical conjunction of propriety and realism explains some of the anomalies in Stowe's use of vernacular and high styles, but the stylistic inconsistency throughout her novel apparently did not bother Stowe as long as the emotional effects she sought in any episode were consistent. On the other hand, the potential discrepencies between the proprieties of emotion and the actualities of circumstance played a significant role in Samuel Clemens's vexed efforts to define his own aesthetic.

A related difficulty for Clemens that over the course of her career also came to disturb Stowe lay in the puzzling connection forged by Common Sense aesthetics between realism and idealism through mental association. According to Alison's definition of taste, the power of association is the most important source of the pleasure people take in art. An associative train of emotional reflections is stirred in an audience by art accurately and properly displaying moving qualities of the human mind, such as what Alison calls the "masculine" qualities of "Spirit, Thought, and Resolution" and the "feminine" qualities of "Humility, Timidity, Sensibility and Kindness" (2: 278). To display these qualities effectively, an artist must evoke emotion by stripping away ambiguity:

> When the circumstances of the scenery are all such as accord with the peculiar emotion which the scene is fitted to inspire; when the hand of the artist disappears, and the embellishments of his fancy press themselves upon our belief, as the voluntary profusion of Nature, we immediately pronounce that the composition is perfect; we acknowledge that he has attained the end of his art; and, in yielding ourselves up to the emotion which his composition demands, we afford him the most convincing mark of our applause. In the power which . . . art thus possesses . . . of withdrawing from its imitations whatever is inconsistent with their expression, and of adding whatever may contribute to strengthen, or to extend their effect, consists the great superiority which it possesses over the originals from which they are copied. (1: 123–24)

In thus espousing an art that hides art, Alison is not far from Sir Philip Sidney or Ben Jonson in his aesthetic; the artist must remain true to nature's materials, only arranging them for a pure effect.

The most significant part of Alison's aesthetic has less to do with how to make an effect, though, than with the basis of the effect, specifically, the viewer's associations of art with "expressions of mind":

> Every one, perhaps, has formed to himself some general conception of the Beauty of the Human Countenance, under the influence of Innocence, Gaity, Hope, Joy, Rapture, — or under the dominion of Sensibility, Melancholy, Grief, or Terror, &c. If he attends to the nature of this operation of fancy, he will find that the principle which governs this ideal composition is that of unity of expression; that he admits into this sketch no feature or colour which does

not correspond with the character which interests him; and that he is at last only satisfied when he has formed the conception of one uniform and harmonious whole. (2: 288–89)

Primarily, then, Alison tells the artist not to copy the essences of external reality but rather to copy the essences of human subjectivity. Nature to Alison merely symbolizes these internal states, and, therefore, an artist tries in copying nature merely to copy the symbolic representations of human characteristics. Consequently, art must not merely strip away quotidian encrustations that hide from a viewer the salient emotional characteristics of a piece of art, but it must also strip away any conflicting symbolic elements in its representation of nature. Thus, while Alison professes a mimetic aesthetic, it is a purified mimesis, closer in fact to what we would now term allegory than to what we would now term realism.

At least one contemporary critic, Jane Tompkins, has drawn the conclusion that Stowe wrote allegory, more specifically, typological allegory consonant with her Calvinist upbringing. Certainly this is to some extent true, as Eva and Tom work as anti-types of Christ in *Uncle Tom's Cabin*.[22] But given Stowe's rejection of Calvinist orthodoxy, she could see what is difficult for us to see, that sentimental aesthetics, in spite of their tendency toward abstraction, promote realism rather than allegory.

In all allegory, including Puritan typology, truth lies outside of nature in God, in the Bible, or in some realm of the ideal. Allegorical categories of representation, then, are supernatural, and any treatment of the supernatural in natural terms is designed to appeal to human beings through their limited capacities. Sentimental realism, on the other hand, takes its categories from the human mind, from the senses and experiences common to all human beings. That there were common categories impressed enlightenment moralists as a sign that God had created nature, but the source of the categories as far as human beings are concerned was definitely natural, not supernatural. Looked at in this way, *Uncle Tom's Cabin* appears to rely more on character type or stereotype than on Biblical type and anti-type.[23]

Early in her career, Stowe followed Alison's aesthetic, as in her depiction of Rachel Halliday in *Uncle Tom's Cabin*:

[Rachel Halliday's] face was round and rosy, with a healthful downy softness, suggestive of a ripe peach. Her hair, partially silvered by age, was parted smoothly back from a high placid forehead on which time had written no inscription, except peace on earth, good will to men, and beneath shone a large pair of clear, honest, loving brown eyes; you only needed to look straight into them, to feel that you saw to the bottom of a heart as good and true as ever throbbed in woman's bosom. (139–40)

Indeed, rather than merely follow Alison's aesthetic, Stowe wished to promote it. For readers who lack the willingness or the knowledge to interpret Rachel Halliday's meaning according to Common Sense aesthetic principles, Stowe explains that Rachel's "face and form made 'mother' seem the most natural word in the world." While the word "natural" implies that Rachel is a product of nature, she most obviously is a perfect type, without confusion or ambiguity. On the other hand, while the name "Rachel" and the fact that Biblical lines are inscribed in this woman's face tease the reader into trying to find a Biblical type for her, Rachel Halliday bears no resemblance to the Biblical Rachel, excepting, perhaps, that she obviously loves her children.

In any event, Stowe's contemporaries accepted her aesthetic as a realistic one. Had *Uncle Tom's Cabin* been seen as merely an allegory, the Southern reaction to the book would not have been so vigorous in its claims that Stowe got her facts wrong, nor would Southern authors have responded with other pieces of sentimental "realism," such as William Gilmore Simms's *Woodcraft* or Mary Eastman's *Aunt Phillis's Cabin*, to refute Stowe's "misinterpretation" with the "reality." Certainly Stowe's northern audience accepted her book as realistic. Consider, for instance, the Rev. E. P. Parker's 1868 assessment of *Uncle Tom's Cabin*[24]:

> It was a perfectly natural, thoroughly honest, truly religious story, with nothing unwholesome in its marvellous fascinations, but contrariwise, fairly throbbing in every part with a genuine Christian feeling. No wonder that ministers, and deacons, and quiet Quakers too, and all the godly folk who had always been accustomed to frown with holy horror upon novels, did unbend themselves to read, and diligently circulate the words of this woman. . . . Great statesmen like Mr. Seward and Mr. Sumner had argued the question of slavery. Able divines had given the testimony of the Scriptures upon it. Eloquent platform orators, and vigorous writers had discussed all its aspects and relations. And still a mist of romance, and an atmosphere of sanctity, or at least of privilege, enveloped and concealed its real features. Mrs. Stowe treated the subject, not as a question of law, or of logic, or of political economy, or of biblical interpretation, but as a simple question of humanity; not as an "abstract theory of social relations, but as a concrete reality of human life." She does not tell, but shows us what it is. She does not analyze, or demonstrate, or describe, but, by a skilful manner of indirection, takes us over the plantation, into the fields, — through the whole Southern country in fact, — and shows us

not only the worst but the best phases of the slavery system, and allows us to see it as it really is. And all the while the power of her own intense sympathy for the oppressed millions whose cause she pleads, is felt throbbing in every line of the narrative. (316–18)

As a clergyman, Parker, if anyone, would have been sensitive to the presence of typological allegory in Stowe's work, yet he stresses its realism as its most important characteristic. His conception of realism appears quite clearly in his insistence that logic and reasoning cannot yield truth as well as can direct perception. Parker prefers intuitive understanding to rational understanding; he accepts the power of the mind to perceive truth directly through sympathy.

Obviously, by claiming that sentimental characterization is not allegorical, I do not mean to imply that it is not didactic. On the contrary, both allegory and sentimental realism serve the purpose of moral uplift. However, while typological allegory has its source immediately in God, suggesting that God must inspire a person's improvement, sentimental realism places the source of uplift in human nature, suggesting that human beings have their own power to grow toward God.

Alison postulates this potential for spiritual growth as the very purpose of the emotions of taste altogether. Because his aesthetic allows for individual variations in taste on the basis of associations and for the possibility of beauty in the practical as well as in the fine arts, Alison concludes that the emotions of taste were designed by God to spur human progress: "The sensibility of imagination thus follows the progress of genius and of usefulness; and . . . a new motive is thus afforded to its improvement, and a new reward provided for the attainment of excellence" (2: 433). Furthermore, because his aesthetic emphasizes that the most powerful emotional associations come from the expressions of human characteristics, he suggests that the emotions of taste are yet an even more powerful goad to our moral improvement. And while vice tends to destroy taste, since "the habits of vice tend to obliterate all the genuine Beauty of Nature to the vicious" (2: 271), beauty can call even the vicious to virtue:

> In ages of civilization, this union of devotional sentiment with sensibility to the beauties of natural scenery, forms one of the most characteristic marks of human improvement, and may be traced in every art which professes to give delight to the imagination. . . . Even the thoughtless and the dissipated yield unconsciously to this beneficent instinct; and in the pursuit of pleasure, return, without knowing it, to the first and the noblest sentiments of their nature. (2: 444–45)

When, at the end of *Uncle Tom's Cabin*, Stowe encourages all of her readers to "feel right" as an important first step in abolishing slavery, she worked not only within the parameters of the "woman's sphere" of influence, but also within the framework of Alison's ideal of progress. If benevolent feelings spur beneficent action, then art in service of progress should devote itself to eliciting benevolent feelings.

In any event, according to Alison, the ability to feel, especially through the moral senses, leads human beings to virtue, and in so doing, seduces them into believing in God: "Perhaps it is chiefy for this fine issue, that the heart of man is thus finely touched, that devotion may spring from delight: that the imagination, in the midst of its highest enjoyment may be led to terminate in the only object in which it finally can repose" (2: 441–43).[25] This is the moral aesthetic that drives *Uncle Tom's Cabin*. By being sentimental, that is, by engaging her readers' human affections in her purified representations of life, Stowe attempts to train her readers beyond the human, toward the divine.[26]

VII

Intellectually we are really no great things; . . . we seldom really know the thing we think we know; . . . our best-built certainties are but sandhouses and subject to damage from any wind of doubt that blows.
— Mark Twain, "The Great Dark" (125)

The Grotto of the Dog claimed my chief attention, because I had heard and read so much about it. Everybody has written about the Grotto del Cane and its poisonous vapors, from Pliny down to Smith, and every tourist has held a dog over its floor by the legs to test the capabilities of the place. The dog dies in a minute and a half — a chicken instantly. . . . I wanted to see this grotto. I resolved to take a dog and hold him myself; suffocate him a little, and time him; suffocate him some more and then finish him. We reached the grotto at about three in the afternoon, and proceeded at once to make the experiments.
— Mark Twain, letter to the *Alta California*, October 6, 1867 (*TIA* 93)

Of the 464 specifications contained in your Public Prayers for the week, and not previously noted in this report, we grant 2, and deny the rest. To wit: Granted, (1) "that the clouds may continue to perform their office; (2) and the sun his." It was the divine purpose anyhow; it will gratify you to know that you have not disturbed it.
— Mark Twain, "Letter to the Earth" (120)

Perhaps the idea that God seduces people to heaven through the emotions attracted Stowe more than any other aspect of sentimentalism, certainly more than its sanguine acceptance of empiricism as compatible with Christian piety. Insofar as she was committed to the reality and importance of the world, Stowe did grudgingly accept the "rationalism" of the "masculine sphere," even to the point of applying it in limited ways to the "feminine sphere." Following her sister's lead, Stowe felt that practical action requires the order and efficiency that only reason can give. Hence both sisters devoted much of their professional life to rationalizing domestic economy into a "science." In *Uncle Tom's Cabin*, Stowe even attaches moral valences to efficient housekeeping, comparing and judging people by their respective skills:

> Dinah . . . was a native and essential cook, as much as Aunt Chloe, — cooking being an indigenous talent of the African race; but Chloe was a trained and methodical one, who moved in an orderly domestic harness, while Dinah was a self-taught genius, and, like geniuses in general, was positive, opinionated and erratic, to the last degree. Like a certain class of modern philosophers, Dinah perfectly scorned logic and reason in every shape, and always took refuge in intuitive certainty.

Stowe at this point reveals her willingness to stand between the extremes of Common Sense philosophy, accepting both natural and cultivated abilities, finding advantages in Chloe's mixture of intuitive and reasoned understanding over Dinah's pure intuitionism.

But rationality to Stowe was dangerous, substantially because it left her in perpetual doubt about ethics, politics, and most of all religion (Lynn 107–9; Sklar 239). After all, it was the highly rational, systematic nature of Calvinistic theological hairsplitting and introspection that first disturbed her faith. After years of orthodox brooding on the state of her soul, she complained in two separate letters to her good friend Georgiana May that she intended "to give up the pernicious habit of meditation" (Fields, *Stowe* 70) because

> In America feelings vehement and absorbing . . . become still more deep, morbid, and impassioned by the constant habits of self-government which the rigid forms of our society demand. They are repressed, and they burn inward till they burn the very soul, leaving only dust and ashes. (Fields, *Stowe* 82)

By the time she wrote *Uncle Tom's Cabin* Stowe had so turned against reasoned belief in God that she even attacked the kind of scholarly biblical exegesis on which her husband's livelihood depended:

> As for Tom's Bible, though it had no annotations and helps in margin from learned commentators, still it had been embellished with certain way-marks and guide-boards of Tom's own invention, and which helped him more than the most learned expositions could have done. . . . He would designate, by bold strong marks and dashes . . . the passages which more particularly gratified his ear or affected his heart. (150)

She advocated an intuitive rather than a rational approach to religion and to morality because she found that the "habit of doubting" (*Uncle Tom's Cabin* 308) required by rationality destroyed her own faith.

Reason's inability to resolve doubt, Stowe implies, prevents moral action. In *Uncle Tom's Cabin*, at any rate, dispassionate argument resolves nothing and trivializes important matters, as when Alfred and Augustine St. Clare, unable rationally to solve the problem of slavery, decide that they might as well drop the subject: "Well, [said Alfred St. Clare,] there's no use in talking, Augustine. I believe we've been round and round this old track five hundred time, more or less. What do you say to a game of backgammon?" (275). Stowe implies that reason without feeling finds no more point in resolving momentous questions than in playing an idle game; worse, when reason can resolve nothing, it merely ignores problems.

As an alternative to this kind of intellectual paralysis, Stowe adopted the radical intuitionism inherent but usually dormant in Common Sense philosophies, developing it into a pietistic alternative to America's increasing skepticism, a skepticism she blamed substantially on the frigid rationality of orthodox puritanism. Nor was she alone in her attempt to save religion in an increasingly secular, increasingly utilitarian society; many readers reacted to *Uncle Tom's Cabin* less for its antislavery rhetoric than for its pietistic evangelism.

Although Stowe blamed mainly Calvinism for destroying faith, she was not blind to the fact that the utilitarian side of moral philosophy led easily to scientific materialism, and, conversely, that science encouraged utilitarianism. After *Uncle Tom's Cabin*, when Stowe grew more explicit in her condemnation of the practical effects of Calvinism, she articulated in her historical novel *The Minister's Wooing* an affection for the moral seriousness of orthodox religion at the same time she expressed increasing anxiety about the direction scientific inquiry was taking. Since Stowe's pietism required a personal God with whom human beings could interact through prayer, she was especially concerned that the God depicted by the light of nature alone, the God whom scientists credited with creating the universe according to fixed natural laws, was too impersonal to care about human beings, or at least too far removed from particular events to intervene in human affairs.

She embodied her anxieties in the novel's villain, Aaron Burr, a man who, having rejected the possibility of a personal God, "assumed pleasure to be the great object of human existence" (817). In pursuit of his two greatest pleasures — exercising power and indulging his curiosity — he experiments constantly with human souls: "Burr was practised in every art of gallantry, — he had made womankind a study, — he never saw a beautful face and form without a sort of restless desire to experiment upon it and try his power over the interior inhabitant" (658). As a good utilitarian materialist, Burr not only wishes to maximize his pleasures, he wishes to minimize pains. "To live as far as possible without a disagreeable sensation was an object which Burr proposed to himself as the summum bonum" (817; note the congruence with Locke's terminology), yet his "experiments" with women's feelings constantly subject him to emotional distress through his own natural sympathies. He responds not by submitting to his natural feelings but by suppressing them according to his "perfect logic of life" (817). That is, he allows reason to mediate between his experience of life and his motivations to action.

In one case in particular, Burr suppresses his emotions by "drawing himself some maps of new territories [and] set[ting] himself vigorously to some columns of arithmetical calculations on the margin; and thus he worked for an hour or two, till his mind was as dry and his pulse as calm as a machine" (779). Whether or not Stowe had in mind Locke's vision of systematic morality based on the model of mathematics, Shaftesbury's moral algebra, or even her sister's mechanistic model of the human will, she clearly felt that a purely scientific approach to human behavior always runs the risk of combining pure selfishness with cold rationalism. The result according to Stowe is pure evil.

Yet she did not want to reject science unequivocally. Stowe herself felt the pull of the natural sciences as a way of understanding the world. In her description of her childhood in "Early Remembrances," she praised her Aunt Esther as a devotee of natural philosophy (392) and attributes much of the inspirational power of her first school master in Litchfield to his being "widely informed, an enthusiast in botany, mineralogy and the natural sciences generally" (397). In defending her faith, then, Stowe tried to co-opt the opposition in the fashion typical of her common sense philosophical tradition at the same time that she moved the grounds of her faith closer to the idealistic extreme of that tradition.

In *The Minister's Wooing*, for example, she tries to etherialize the scientific impulse as a way of transcending its materialism:

> No real artist or philosopher ever lived who has not at some hours risen to the height of utter self-abnegation for the glory of the invisible. There have been painters who would have been crucified to demonstrate the action of a muscle, chemists who would gladly have melted themselves and all humanity in their crucible, if so a new discovery might arise out of its fumes. (541)

In her effort to coopt science, she doesn't ignore its destructive potential, its willingness "to melt all humanity." However, in conflating art and science, she implicitly justifies that danger as arising from a devout impulse.

She further tries to domesticate science by suggesting that the empirical impulse, which she attributes to the masculine side of human nature, discovers a more practical religion than does systematic Calvinism with its emphasis on rationality over experience. In explaining the conversion of the story's hero, James Marvyn, to Christianity, Stowe has James say that Calvinist systematic religion "never impressed me much in any way. I could not make any connection between it and the men I had to manage and the things I had to do in my daily life" (838).

Yet on reading of Jacob's pact with God to secure his fortune, James decides:

> Now there was something that looked to me like a tangible foundation to begin upon. Now if I understand Dr. Hopkins, I believe he would have called that all selfishness. At first sight it does look a little so; but then I thought of it in this way; 'Here he [Jacob] was all alone. God was entirely invisible to him; and how could he feel certain that He really existed, unless he could come into some kind of connection with Him? The point that he wanted to be sure of, more than merely to know that there was a God who made the world; — he wanted to know whether He cared anything about men, and would do anything to help them. And so, in fact, it was saying, 'If there is a God who interests Himself at all in me, and will be my Friend and Protector, I will obey Him, so far as I can find out his will.' I thought to myself, 'This is the great experiment, and I will try it.' (839)

According to Stowe, when once a person tries to pray for help, whether selfishly or not, God's responses will experimentally "prove" His existence and utility. So as long as science remains experiential and avoids systematic, logical, abstract thought, it serves much of Stowe's evangelical purpose.

The question of greatest importance to Stowe here, however, is not so much whether God exists as whether he interferes in human affairs. And on this point, natural philosophy as most of her contemporaries understood it offered her little hope. In fact, Stowe at one point equates the intractable rigidity of natural law with Calvinist fatalism. Referring to her fictionalized Hopkins, she says that "the sublime fatalism of his faith made him as dead to all human considerations as if he had been a portion of the immutable laws of Nature herself" (672). Stowe seems to have perceived—even on the eve of the Civil War—the fatalistic implications of a naturalism that would not blossom in American literature for another quarter century, though its seeds lay far back on the rationalist side of the Common Sense tradition and though it did shortly after the Civil War quite markedly influence moral philosophy in the hands of such thinkers as Herbert Spencer, William Graham Sumner, and John Fiske.

Stowe responds both by calling on the authority of faith alone and by using the language of natural science itself not only to defend her faith, but to call for a scientific investigation of it:

> Our fathers believed in special answers to prayer. They were not stumbled by the objection about the inflexibility of the laws of Nature; because they had the idea, that, when the Creator of the world promised to answer human prayers, He probably understood the laws of Nature as well as they did. At any rate, the laws of Nature were His affair, and not theirs. . . . Is it not possible that He who made the world may have established laws for prayer as invariable as those for the sowing of seed and raising of grain? Is it not as legitimate a subject of inquiry, when petitions are not answered, which of these laws has been neglected? (855)

At first glance it seems strange that Stowe, whose books so assiduously attack the Calvinist world-view for promoting skepticism, would appeal occasionally to its habits of faith to suppress her culture's tendency to doubt the personal importance of religion. But clearly she refers here not to the Calvinistic theological system but to its fundamental idealism, its belief in God and heaven.

She blamed Calvinism not for this belief, but for the inability to teach people how to reconcile this world with heaven:

> There is a ladder to heaven, whose base God has placed in human affections, tender instincts, symbolic feelings, sacraments of love, through which the soul rises higher and higher, refining as she goes, till she outgrows the human, and changes as she rises, into the image of the divine. At the very top of this ladder, at the threshold of paradise, blazes dazzling and crystalline that celestial grade where the soul knows self no more, having learned, through a long experience of devotion, how blest it is to lose herself in that eternal Love and Beauty of

which all earthly fairness and grandeur are but the dim type, the distant
shadow. This highest step, this saintly elevation, . . . to raise the soul to which
the Eternal Father organized every relation of human existence and strung
every cord of human love, for which this world is one long discipline, for
which the soul's human education is constantly varied, . . . to which all its
multiplied powers tend with upward hands of dumb and ignorant aspira-
tion, — this Ultima Thule of virtue had been seized upon by our sage [Hop-
kins] as the all of religion. He knocked out every round of the ladder but the
highest, and then, pointing to its hopeless splendor, said to the world, "Go up
thither and be saved!" (579–80)

Stowe reverts to Calvinist typology at the same time that she echoes
Platonic idealism,[27] but she never renounces the utility of this world for
teaching people how to attain heaven and for fulfilling the divine plan. She
even chastises people for wanting to renounce this world:

Through the sudden crush of a great affliction, [the heroine] was in that state
of self-abnegation to which the mystics brought themselves by fastings and
self-imposed penances, — a state not purely healthy, nor realizing the divine
ideal of a perfect human being made to exist in the relations of human life.
(753)

Still, in *The Minister's Wooing*, Stowe insists that emotion is the impetus
toward salvation, only rarely gesturing toward a balanced evaluation of the
importance of reason as she did in *Uncle Tom's Cabin*. By 1859, then, Stowe
had pushed Alison's Common Sense aesthetic to the very limits of dualism,
leaving a disproportionately small emphasis on the reality of this world and
virtually no room for rational discourse.

VIII

It was a comfort in those succeeding days to sit up and contemplate the
majestic panorama of mountains and valleys spread out below us and
eat ham and hard boiled eggs while our spiritual natures reveled
alternately in rainbows, thunderstorms, and peerless sunsets. Nothing
helps scenery like ham and eggs.
— Mark Twain, *Roughing It* (139)

When Samuel Clemens began to write professionally during the mid-1860s,
Common Sense dualism had already reached this schism. By 1871, when he
moved to Hartford and began writing as both a humorist and a moralist,

his writings would have reflected the tension between the material and ideal halves of moral philosophy. Then, too, the deepening rift in moral philosophy left an unoccupied artistic middle ground. With sentimentalists veering toward idealism from their earlier stance as realists, they left a large opening in *belles lettres* for another kind of realism, one predicated more on ostensibly objective standards than on emotional ones.

Critics conventionally see Mark Twain's development as a writer as a move toward this kind of empirical realism, but they tend to see it as a radical move away from a uniform cultural idealism. My analysis suggests that Clemens's realism may just as well have begun as a conservative attempt to rebuild the Common Sense consensus. If so, this might explain some of the contradictions of his early years as a writer in that any effort to rebuild the consensus would have partaken of the fundamental contradictions of the school in the first place.

In the years before 1870, however, Clemens rarely wrote with such a serious agenda. Nonetheless, in his humorous writings of the 1860s, Common Sense philosophy influenced his work. Even his least morally serious writings of the 1860s were shaped by the conventions spawned by moral philosophy, and these conventions in turn shaped the way he approached all moral issues over the course of his career. How the Common Sense treatment of humor informed Clemens's thinking will be the subject of the next chapter.

3. A "Sensation Parson": or The Moral Philosophy of Newspaper Humor

I

On October 19, 1865, Samuel Clemens wrote to his brother that he had abandoned his first two career choices, preacher and river-boat pilot, because he lacked the "necessary stock in trade [for the first] — i.e., religion," and that the war had ruined the second. Instead he found he had a "call to literature, of a low order — i.e., humorous." His purpose in life now was "To excite the laughter of God's creatures" (Kaplan 14). But it was strange that he would discuss such a profession as a "calling"; to the orthodox Calvinist mind that used such terminology, "humor" was not a calling at all and secular literature generally was suspect. Clemens had been brought up by a Presbyterian mother whose prudish opposition to entertainment of any kind often amused a young Clemens who had seen enough of the world to have broken many of the bonds of his early training, but his letter nonetheless reveals his anxiety about making a profession of fun.[1]

That he could see humor as a profession at all attests not only to the possibility of making money at it, but also to the rise of Common Sense justifications of humor that had gained prominence in the culture at large, even if they had not swayed his mother's orthodoxy.[2] Common Sense philosophers listed humor as one of humankind's innate senses and assumed, therefore, that it had positive values. To Hutcheson, for example, these were primarily two. For one, humor served as a source of pleasure that relieved people of unhealthy seriousness. "Everyone is conscious that a state of laughter is an easy and agreeable state, that the recurring or suggestion of ludicrous images tends to dispel fretfulness, anxiety, or sorrow" ("Reflections," 35). Besides being innately valuable for causing happiness, humor has practical value in balancing the mind. "The application of ridicule is the readiest way to bring down our high imaginations to a conformity to the real moment or importance of the affair. Ridicule gives our minds as it were a bend to the contrary side, so that upon reflection they may be more capable of settling in a just conformity to nature" (36–37). Hutcheson's second value of humor centers on the chance to correct small faults through gentle derision. "If smaller faults, such as are not inconsistent with a character in the main amiable, be set in a ridiculous light, the guilty are apt to be made sensible of their folly, more than by a bare grave admonition" (37).

As these ideas came into American moral philosophy, the value of humor as a relief gained prominence over its value as a means for improving character. As Catherine Beecher's very popular *A Treatise on Domestic Economy* (1841) puts it: "All medical men unite in declaring that nothing is more beneficial to health than hearty laughter, and surely our benevolent Creator would not have provided risibles, and made it a source of health and enjoyment to use them, and then have made it a sin so to do" (261).[3] As is typical of her thinking in her battle against Calvinist orthodoxy, Beecher defends pleasure in a rather restricted way. While arguing that humor has value, she limits its use:

> Jokes, laughter, and sports, when used in such a degree as tends only to promote health, social feelings, and happiness, are neither vain, foolish, nor "not convenient." It is the excess of these things, and not the moderate use of them that Scripture forbids. The prevailing temper of the mind, should be cheerful, yet serious; but there are times, when relaxation and laughter are proper for all. (262)

Such restrictions may have generated part of the anxiety Clemens felt in accepting his new profession; his impulse, even in joking, was to preach. In his *Autobiography* years later, he declared:

> I have always preached. That is the reason that I have lasted thirty years. If the humor came of its own accord and uninvited I have allowed it a place in my sermon, but I was not writing the sermon for the sake of the humor. I should have written the sermon just the same, whether any humor applied for admission or not. (Neider 298)

By the end of his career when he stated this, he had grown comfortable with a broad definition of the humorist's role as moralist, but through much of his career, it rankled him that the freedoms granted him as a humorist also prevented him from being taken seriously: "Now isn't it infamous that a professed humorist can never attempt anything fine, but people will at once imagine there is a joke about it somewhere, and laugh accordingly" (*ET&S* 2:383).

Nonetheless, and in spite of his recollection that he always preached, at the beginning of his career he felt bound by the proprieties of humor to excite the laughter, not the moral senses, of God's creatures. And if it bothered him that he could do nothing "fine," he also felt obliged to give his audiences what they paid for. When defending his humorous lectures to his friend Mary Mason Fairbanks, he explained that he had an implicit contract to fulfill: "What the societies ask of me is to relieve the heaviness of their didactic courses — & in accepting the contract I am just the same as giving my word that I will do as they ask" (*MTMF* 46).

II

As a humorist, Clemens accepted the prevailing definitions of humor as the pleasure arising from the perception of incongruities. Again, according to Hutcheson:

> That then which seems generally the cause of laughter is the bringing together of images which have contrary additional ideas, as well as some resemblance in the principal idea: this contrast between ideas of grandeur, dignity, sanctity, perfection, and ideas of meanness, baseness, profanity, seems to be the very spirit of burlesque; and the greater part of our raillery and jest is founded upon it. (32)

In other words, when ideas are taken out of their usual associative contexts, they appear ridiculous. By this mechanism, as Hutcheson makes clear, humor varies tremendously over time, place, and among people depending on their individual associations. Thus, for humor to work for large audiences, it must be based on broadly accepted conventions with which most people have predictable, expected associations.

The definition of humor as the perception of incongruity was the dominant one through the mid-nineteenth century, serving as the basis of Romantic as well as Sentimental notions of humor. As Kant put it, "Laughter is an affection arising from the sudden transformation of a strained expectation into nothing" (Morreall 47). The strained expectation is what Clemens tried to create throughout his humorous writings, setting up one conventional voice in opposition to another and, in thus violating his audiences' expectations, making them see incongruities.

This is not to say that Clemens read Hutcheson or, less likely, Kant. He learned his art from practitioners, not from theorists. But the ideas of these theorists were extremely widespread and informed the work of most of Clemens's preceptors. Throughout his career, he defined the source of humor as the revelation of incongruity, and as he learned his trade under the aegis of people like Charles Farrar Browne, he often revealed incongruities by exaggerating the differences between conventional types and thus exploiting his audiences' associations.

At the beginning of his career, he often did this without satirical intention, as for instance in his June 6, 1867 letter to the San Francisco *Alta California*, in which he imagines his narrator, Mark Twain, mistaking a cheap New York saloon for a highbrow men's club where the nation's "savants were in the habit of meeting to commune upon abstruse matters of science and philosophy — men like Agassiz and Ericsson and people of that stamp" (*MTTB* 270). The humor that comes of this implausible juxtaposition of expectation and reality has no satiric or irreverent bite; it does not attack the savants so much as mock Mark Twain's own bumbling inability to understand what goes on around him.

But burlesque can easily create an irony that looks both ways, reducing everything in its view to absurdity. Consider a mild case in point, Mark Twain's complaint in his March 15, 1867 letter to the *Alta* about a form of greeting common throughout the U.S.:

> Don't you observe, they [old friends] all ask that same old question: "How do you like San Francisco? — How do you like New York? — How do you like St. Louis?" It is almighty aggravating. Cannot people think of something else besides that? It wouldn't make any difference if only one or two people asked the question; but to be bored with it twenty times a day is insufferable. It has set me to speculating about the other world. A man who has lived a long life . . . will probably meet as many as twenty or thirty thousand people there he was acquainted with on earth; they say we shall preserve our natural instincts — now, think of being bored all through Paradise or perdition with that same wretched old question of "how you like it." Why, it wouldn't make any difference which locality you landed in — you would get so harried and badgered that you would wish you had gone to the other place. (*MTTB* 129)

Here Clemens manipulates a convention of Christian teaching, namely that worldly events should inspire meditation on "the other world," in order to show in an extended conceit how "almighty boring" he finds the question of "how you like it." Interestingly, the conventional outlook he chooses as one half of his juxtaposition of "grandeur" and "deformity" is shaped by Butler's ideas that heaven and earth are analogous, ideas that, as I mentioned earlier, were at the heart of the Common Sense tradition as it influenced American moral philosophy. There is nothing blatantly irreverent in Clemens's juxtaposition of an annoying earthly mannerism with its likelihood in heaven. But over the next few years, he pushed this idea to its ironic extreme in "Captain Wakeman's Travels in Heaven," an intentionally satirical attack on the very concept of heaven, an attack he began to work out shortly after he wrote this "innocuous" letter. This *Alta* letter contains the earliest use of Butler's philosophy in Clemens's oeuvre; it is more than coincidental that the next time he referred to Butler's ideas he deliberately attacked them. The point is that Clemens's technique of juxtaposing conventional expectations tended to lead him to larger criticisms than he first intended.

This happened to him repeatedly over the course of his career, ever more traumatically as he intellectually and psychologically increased his commitment to any of the various "truths" he promulgated. He seems usually to have begun his satirical moralizing with an unself-conscious confidence in his own standards of judgment, only to find that his ironic vision, shortly after it reduced its original targets to absurdity, always turned back upon and consumed his own certainties. While such a vision did over time undercut all the conventional pieties he addressed in his writing, it also ultimately undercut his own "realism" as well.

Hutcheson was aware of some of the unsettling potentials of humor; in fact, he first addressed the topic to "defend" humor against Hobbes's explication of the source of laughter in a realization of superiority.[4] Hutcheson, always trying to find socially redeeming value in anything human, tried to dismiss the aggression often inherent in humor, partly by defining humor as the perception of incongruity, and partly by explaining that people of refinement will never allow humor to be used to attack anything worthy of reverence:

> This engine of ridicule, no doubt, may be abused, and have a bad effect upon a weak mind; but with men of any reflection, there is little fear that it will ever be pernicious. An attempt of ridicule before such men, upon a subject every way great, is sure to return upon the author of it. (39)

By this precept, readers of humor would laugh not at the target of irreverence, but at the perpetrator of it.

Humorists used this idea that the cultivated can turn humor to positive account in order to sanction their irreverence. They often built a genteel frame around their "base" characters in order to guide their readers' responses. But as American "deadpan" humor developed, humorists dropped the genteel or elevated frame in favor of a persona who would serve as a socially acceptable butt of laughter. Clemens had already begun to use this technique in his early humor when he met Charles Farrar Browne, who used the persona "Artemus Ward" in his humorous sketches and lectures. Browne convinced Clemens of the value of this technique, as perhaps can be seen in Clemens's many drafts of the jumping frog story, written at Browne's request for a book Browne was having published in New York. Clemens's first draft uses the old-style frame to distance the reader from the "low" characters (*ET&S* 2:262–78). Eventually, he settled on using his character Mark Twain to serve as the target of laughter. Thus, Hutcheson's description of how a "man of reflection" responds to humor sanctions much of Clemens's humor, with the character Mark Twain serving as the ultimate butt of many jokes. Even when Mark Twain ridicules subjects "every way great," and whatever the manifold real sources of pleasure may have been, Mark Twain served as the legitimate target of laughter.[5]

Since Hutcheson acknowledges that ridicule can be harmful to weak minds, he establishes rules of propriety by which humor can be used without hurting anyone:

> First, either never attempt ridicule upon what is every way great, whether it be any great being, character, or sentiments; or, if our wit must sometimes run into allusions, on low occasions, to the expressions of great sentiments, let it not be in weak company, who have not a just discernment of true grandeur. And, secondly, concerning objects of a mixed nature, partly great, and partly mean, let us never turn the meanness into ridicule without acknowledging what is truly great, and paying a just veneration to it. (39)

By following these rules of propriety, Hutcheson suggests, humorists can use their art to support truth and morality without sacrificing the value of humor as a source of recreation and moral reformation. Correlatively, by the double standard encouraged by the social ideology of the sexual spheres, humorists could only make fun of "great sentiments" on "low occasions" in the company of men, the audience assumed to be best able to take unbridled humor in its proper spirit without incurring moral harm.

III

These aspects of humor as sanctioned by moral philosophy help to explain the contradictory attitudes toward sentimental ideology in Clemens's early humor. By the contemporary understanding of the source of humor as the revelation of incongruities, moral philosophy, both as an intellectual discipline and as social ideology, would provide a constant source of conventional ideas with the associated qualities of "grandeur, dignity [or] sanctity" that a humorist needed as foils for "meanness, baseness [or] profanity."

In the 1860s, Clemens found these foils more readily in the sentimental social ideology supported by Common Sense moral philosophy than in the theology and epistemology that he ultimately chose for much of his subject matter. The relative shallowness of this early humor, of course, is conventional. Humorists such as Browne found their subjects more in social relations than in the philosophies behind them. Clemens followed the patterns of his predecessors in exploiting the humorous value of sentimental social conventions. For instance, many conventional ideas about the purity and sensitivity of women and children served him as suitable foils for comic visions of mean characters.

Clemens's June 1865 sketch for the Virginia City *Territorial Enterprise*, "Just 'One More Unfortunate,'" is a case in point. As Branch and Hirst put it in their introduction to the tale, the title "alludes to a popular poem by Thomas Hood, 'The Bridge of Sighs,' the first line of which . . . had become a cliché for 'wronged innocent'" (*ET&S* 2:236) In this title Clemens elicits expectations about femininity; he then adds to these expectations by describing the subject of his sketch as "petite and diffident, and only sixteen years and one month old. To judge by her looks, one would say she was as sinless as a child"—so sinless that the policemen who hear the tale of her seduction "pitied her and said feelingly . . . she was an ignorant, erring child and had not done wrong wilfully and knowingly." The sketch then describes her in crude terms that make it clear she really is "competent to take charge of a University of Vice." In contrast to slang descriptions of her living arrangements, the sketch employs a false high style in an apostrophe to the prostitute as typical of her gender: "O, woman, thy name is humbug!" (*ET&S* 2:236–38). The readers' conventional associations of women with purity allow Clemens to develop the incongruity that made this sketch funny to its original audience.

Here I will have to beg indulgence for my way of describing the roots of Clemens's humor. If I seem to take jokes too seriously, it is only because to explain how he consciously tried to establish his jokes, I have to explain the "straight" meanings in order to reveal the incongruities that he tried to exploit.

That he was self-consciously trying to play conventional associations off against one another shows in his December 28, 1866 letter to the *Alta*, in which he claims to repeat Captain Wakeman's story of the first time he saw a whaling ship at sea, trying oil out of blubber in the middle of the night. Wakeman assumed he saw a ship afire, stopped his ship, dispatched a boat to help the survivors, and waited to retrieve the wounded. His passengers all assembled "on deck anxious for the boat to come back with the awful news," but the boat didn't return for hours. Nine o'clock passed, ten, then:

> Eleven — no boat; and one by one [the passengers] sidled off to roost — give it up, you see — all gone but me and one solitary motherly old soul — me marching slow up and down the deck and she gazing out across the water at the burning ship. We were just so until half-past 11, and then we heard the sound of oars. We closed up to the railing and stood by for them. Pretty soon the boat ranged up alongside — I tell you I felt awful — something made me hanker to look down into that boat, and yet something held me back. The officer of the boat reported: 'The ship ain't burning, sir; (I felt relieved then;) he says he's in big luck — is full of oil, and ready for home, and so they're cooking doughnuts in the fat and having a grand blow-out, illumination and jollification. But he's uncommon thankful for the good intentions you've shown, and hopes you'll accept this lot of A 1 sea-turkles.' The old woman leaned over the rail and shaded her eyes from the lantern with her hand, and she see them varmints flopping their flippers about in the boat and she says: 'For the land's sake! I've sot here, and sot here, and sot here all this blessed night cal'latin' you'd fetch a boat-load of sorrowful roasted corpses, and now it ain't nothing but a lot of nasty cussed mud-turkles — it's a dern thieving shame, that's my opinion of it!' (*MTTB* 37–38)

The humor, as Clemens deliberately develops it, lies in the reader's expectations of womanly solicitude being violated by the old woman's selfish and morbid disappointment at not seeing the sensation she had counted on. He exaggerates the contrast between expectation and reality by postulating Wakeman as a low character observing a moment of sublime danger in the company of a "motherly old soul." The expected danger stands in incongruous contrast to the reality of relaxation and "jollification," and the audience's likely response of relief is turned to laughter when the sailor's colloquial description of the ship's pleasure is upstaged by the apparently dignified woman's transformation into a paragon of meanness.

The degree to which Clemens exploited the inherent incongruity in the story can be seen in the changes he made between the version in his journal and the published version. In the original, Wakeman refers to his fellow watcher as "an old woman"; Clemens elevates her status with the diction in calling her an "old soul," and he specifies her gender at the same time he calls out a whole range of sentimental associations with the adjective "motherly." The reader then expects feminine solicitude far superior to Wakeman's offer to render the ostensibly stricken ship "all the help I can."

Here, another significant change from Clemens's notes to the published draft heightens the contrast between the expected and actual denouements. In the original notes, Wakeman demonstrates no greater sensibility than does the old woman. He, too, rushes to the returning boat to hear the news and see the worst. In the revision, however, Clemens fills Wakeman with conflicting feelings of curiosity and dread, all stemming from powerful sympathy. When he hears that his fears are groundless, he generously experiences the relief that any right feeling person should. Given that Wakeman is a "low" character to begin with, by contrast, the old woman's response seems even meaner and more morbidly selfish than it did in the original. Clemens then changes "cal'lating to see" (N&J1 250) to "Cal'lating you'd fetch" and "it's too dern bad" to "it's a dern thieving shame" in order to suggest that this woman even blames Wakeman's sailors for depriving her of her anticipated thrill. Altogether Clemens's changes heighten the contrast between expectations of "grandeur, dignity [and] sanctity" with "baseness" and "profanity."

In this passage, the source of incongruity is the age-old contrast between high characters and low, making fun of people on the basis of class characteristics. Even at this early stage of his career, though, Clemens went beyond the usual sources of humor in the ideology of social relations to the more abstruse ideas of moral philosophy. In fact, given the particularly inconsistent nature of sentimental moral philosophy and the wide scope of its intellectual battles, it served Clemens as an ideal source of inconsistencies that his quick wit turned to humorous account. His sketch "Those Blasted Children," published in the New York *Sunday Mercury* in early 1864, for instance, relies on the conflicting views of human nature offered by Calvinists and Sentimentalists.

In this sketch, Clemens characterizes Mark Twain as a drunken reprobate who, though trying to write sentimental literature, actually perceives the world through Calvinist lenses. The title itself implies Twain's perspective, with the euphemistic "blasted" standing in for "damned." Twain's first reference to the children reinforces this impression:

> Here come those young savages again — those noisy and inevitable children. God be with them! — or they with him, rather if it be not asking too much.

They are another time-piece of mine. It is two o'clock now; they are invested with their regular lunch, and have come up here to settle it. I will sooth my troubled spirit with a short season of blasphemy, after which I will expose their infamous proceedings with a relentless pen. They have driven me from labor many and many a time; but behold! the hour of retribution is at hand. (*ET&S* 1:352)

No noble savages in Mark Twain's view of the world — these savages are only good if dead. And taking the stance of judge, Mark Twain promises to expose their evil by telling the truth with his "relentless pen." That he needs to "expose" them implies that the reality of childhood has been obscured by some other image, and, of course, that image is the sentimental image Mark Twain sarcastically evokes and mocks in the closing lines of the sketch:

O infancy! thou art beautiful, thou art charming, thou art lovely to contemplate! But thoughts like these recall sad memories of the past, of the halcyon days of my childhood, when I was a sweet, prattling innocent, the pet of a dear home-circle, and the pride of the village. Enough, enough! I must weep, or this bursting heart will break. (356)

The bulk of the sketch tries to show that children generally motivate themselves by less than charitable impulses. Mark Twain merely "reports" the dialogue of children at play, in which they fight over toys and food they refuse to share and over the relative social positions and ethnic backgrounds of their parents, among other things. The only things the children do in harmonious concert is make war on other people, namely Mark Twain and a "foreign nurse," both of whom can defend themselves, and on a "Chinaman," who cannot:

"Hi, boys! Here comes a Chinaman!" (God pity any Chinaman who chances to come in the way of the boys hereabout, for the eye of the law regardeth him not, and the youth of California in their generation are down upon him.) "Now, boys! grab his clothes basket — take him by the tail!" (There they go, now, like a pack of young demons.) (353)

Mark Twain's ostensibly realistic description of children at play shows human behavior to be at root narrow-minded, vindictive, and aggressive.

Mark Twain's children here do not talk in the elegant style conventional in sentimental literature; instead their speech is riddled with solecisms and slang: "'Flora Low, you quit pulling that doll's legs out, it's mine.' . . . 'Sandy Baker, I know what makes your pa's hair kink so; it's 'cause he's a mulatter; I heard my ma say so.' 'It's a lie!'" (353). Again Clemens is using the age-old humorous convention of contrasting low style reality with high-style expectation in order to make fun of characters. In so doing, however, he casts doubt on the innocence of the children themselves. In accordance with sentimental aesthetics, slang was discouraged not merely because vulgarity had negative social implications, but also because it ostensibly caused immorality by vitiating taste. Poor grammar held the same status as blasphemy because, in the sentimental world-view, anything that tended to weaken one's taste tended to weaken one's moral sense. Through a conflation of cause and effect, then, sentimentalists condemned slang as sinful. Clemens plays with this convention — whether he endorsed it fully or not — by having the children speak slang throughout. He implies that they are therefore "kids" — offspring of the goats who will be consigned to hell at the day of judgment — rather than naturally innocent lambs of God.

These young demons appear to have innate impulses to mischief, though admittedly they do parrot much of their information and their spite from their elders. But in suggesting that children can learn evil from their parents, Clemens is again establishing a contrast with the sentimental vision of childhood innocence. By convention, children were supposed to be able to redeem hard-hearted adults from their vicious ways.[6] Instead, here the children learn evil from their parents, and the parents never grow out of it. And the fact that Mark Twain responds in kind merely suggests that all humankind is of a piece: innately and totally depraved.

Since the sketch requires an understanding of the moral opposition of Calvinism and Sentimentalism, the tensions Clemens creates here could easily be construed as satirically attacking sentimentalism. This is an unwarranted assumption; he as readily judged Calvinists by sentimental standards as vice versa, as in this character sketch of one of the *Quaker City* "Puritans":

> Another passenger — a solemn, unsmiling, sanctimonious old iceberg that looked like he was waiting for a vacancy in the Trinity, as Henry Clapp said of Rev. Dr. Osgood — walked in the other day and stood around for some time, and finally said he had forgotten, when he took passage, to inquire if the excursion would come to a halt on Sundays. Captain Duncan replied that he hardly expected to anchor the ship in the middle of the Atlantic, but that on shore everybody would be free — no restrictions — free to travel on Sunday or not, just as they saw fit; and he had no doubt that some would do one and some the other. The questioner did not groan audibly, but I think he did inwardly. Then he said it would be well for people to calculate their chances before doing wrong; that he had always got into trouble when he travelled on the Sabbath, and that he should do so no more when he could avoid it; that he

lately travelled with a man in Illinois who would not lay by on Sunday because he could not afford the time, but he himself laid by and still beat the sinner and got to the end of the journey first. Now I respected that man's repugnance to violating the Sabbath until he betrayed that he would violate it in a minute if he were not afraid the lightning would strike him, or something else would happen to him, and then I lost my reverence for him. I thought I perceived that he was not good and holy, but only sagacious, and so I turned the key on my valise and moved it out of his reach. I shall have to keep an eye on that fellow. (*MTTB* 276–77)

Here Mark Twain voices a common sentimental complaint about the utilitarian bias in much of the motivation of Calvinists. They do not do right out of respect for right or even for the joy of doing right, but because they fear retribution. Their moral behavior is compelled, and they see human beings as unable to find salvation through works of their own choosing. Clemens cashes in on the humorous value of this when he envisions a man waiting for an opening in the Trinity — in other words a man playing for the highest of stakes in his afterlife — being willing to steal Mr. Mark Twain's valise if he could get away with it. Again, Clemens takes a serious debate in moral philosophy, here about the value of Calvinist piety, and exploits it as a source of humor. One can find no consistency on large philosophical positions between these sketches. Although his interest in these subjects perhaps foreshadows a greater seriousness in his philosophical ruminations, at this point, he follows the proprieties of humor in exploiting incongruity where he finds it.

This is not to say, however, that some of his readers did not take him seriously at times. Ada Clare of the San Francisco *Golden Era*, for example, complained that in "Those Blasted Children" "Mark Twain had misunderstood 'God's little people' " (*ET&S* 1:349). Clare's reaction to Clemens's wit was not unusual; people often bridled at his attempts to ridicule "great . . . character and sentiments" and at the aggression implicit in much of his early humor. The aggression was, in fact, not merely implicit; sometimes it served as the overt and primary source of humor in a sketch, as in the October 1865 Virginia City *Territorial Enterprise* piece, "Steamer Departures":

I feel savage this morning. And as usual, when one wants to growl, it is almost impossible to find things to growl about with any degree of satisfaction. I cannot find anything in the steamer departures to get mad at. Only, I wonder who "J. Schmeltzer" is? — and what does he have such an atrocious name for? (*ET&S* 2:322)

By Hutcheson's proprieties of humor, this is a perfectly acceptable attack inasmuch as the ridicule reflects back on the aggressor.

But Clemens, like most newspaper humorists, did not always contain the socially disruptive nature of his humor by turning it on himself. Often, in good American newspaper tradition, he deliberately attacked fellow journalists on other newspapers in order to generate something to write about and to generate readership. His 1865 to 1866 battle with "Fitz Smyth," that is, Albert S. Evans of the San Francisco *Alta*, is a case in point; their battle of insults gave Clemens material for seven articles over a two month span. Such battles, while convenient for writers and enjoyable for a broad public audience, could, however, be dangerous. While the facts are fuzzy, it seems very likely that Clemens had to leave Nevada because his adversary in a newspaper battle challenged him to a duel.[7] It is small wonder that "genteel" folks were skeptical of the ultimate moral value of humor when it seemed so readily able to encourage "base" passions.

IV

It is important to note here that newspapers were the primary outlet for Clemens's humor before 1869. Insofar as newspapers were businesses that profited by entertaining their audiences, the medium was perfect for his humor. At the same time, it taught him to expand the range of his writing beyond the humorous sketch. According to the psychology of sensations, contrast is a source of pleasure, and by sympathy, one human being could vicariously delight in the experiences of another. As a journalist, one of Clemens's purposes, then, was to be his readers' agent; he was to experience novel sensations for the benefit of his readers.

His travel letters, like so many newspaper travel letters of the nineteenth century, filled this purpose, as Clemens even reminded his readers on occasion. For instance, in one of his dispatches to the *Alta* from New York City, he explains that he could not fill his promise to go "with a detective policeman through all the underground dens of vice and rascality in the Five Points last night" because the officer had been temporarily reassigned:

> We had to put off the expedition until next Saturday night. So, as human nature delights in contrasts, and I have considerable human nature in me, I thought I would go through one of the chief among the fountain-heads of civilization in this great city . . . and compare to-day's experiences with next Saturday's, and see which I like best. (*MTTB* 202)

In an effort to provide thrilling interest to his readers, then, he sought to describe things that were not only interesting in themselves but were also interesting by contrast. From contrast to incongruity was a short step that he took often, but not so often as to dull the value of his humor altogether. He learned, here, a technique of composition that served him throughout his career in his writing and in his lectures, namely, that each of his works should be a "narrative plank, with square holes in it, six inches apart, all the length of it & then in my mental shop I ought to have plugs (half marked 'serious' and the other marked 'humorous') to select from and jam into these holes according to the temper of the audience" (in Henry Nash Smith, *Mark Twain* 35).

As a journalist, then, his purpose was not just to provide laughs, but to provide "thrilling interest" (*Territorial Enterprise*, March 7, 1868) to his readers. In the process, he learned most of the conventional literary techniques for evoking emotion, not, of course, with the genteel purpose of guiding people to feel right, but with the sole purpose of creating emotion. Consider, for instance, the following piece of political reporting. In a letter to the *Territorial Enterprise* about Congress's efforts to impeach Johnson, Mark Twain reports the following facts:

> The scene within was spirited — it was unusual, too. The great galleries presented a sea of eager, animated faces; above these more were massed in the many doorways; below, in the strong light, a few members walked nervously up and down, outside the rows of seats; . . . in every countenance strong feeling was depicted. . . . No committee yet. Something must be done. Motion to adjourn, "in honor of Washington." Amendment — to read Washington's Farewell Address. Both were voted down. . . . Before the roll call was finished, Boutwell came in [sensation]; afterwards, at intervals, Bingham [sensation], Paine [sensation], several other committee men, and finally Thad. Stevens himself [Super-extraordinary sensation!] (*Territorial Enterprise*, March 13, 1868)

The high importance of the occasion would seem to call for this elaborate style, heavily loaded with alliterative cues to reinforce the dramatic phrasing, which is already marked by elaborate punctuation of small phrases. The drama, though, is not the drama of action, but of a remarkable stasis. Note the overuse of the verb "be," the passive verbs "is depicted," "were voted down," and "was finished," and the sentence fragment that uses "motion" without a subject instead of a full sentence predicated with the verb "move." The scene Clemens creates has no real motion but the purposeless movement of nameless Congressmen nervously pacing, getting nowhere.

When the sketch climaxes with the mere entrance of a few Congressmen, Clemens gives his readers emotional cues, namely "sensation" and "super-extraordinary sensation!" Altogether, he gives us a tableau, over which we are to gush and palpitate on cue, and the style itself, so self-consciously literary, so thoroughly punctuated for oral declamation, makes it seem an effort to convey feeling rather than news.

The effort to find sensation of any kind for the sake of sensation itself of course militated against any moral consistency on Clemens's part. He developed items of emotional interest on an ad hoc basis, evoking high sentiments as readily as low; endorsing sentiments in one sketch that he burlesques in another. As Franklin Rogers points out in the first chapter of *Mark Twain's Burlesque Patterns*, burlesque in Clemens's early works does not always imply criticism, and given the exigencies of journalism, it is easy to see why. But even though newspapers did not have philosophically consistent moral purposes, they often did have consistent practical ones. They served not only to entertain, but also to advocate political agendas and to promote economic schemes of various kinds. What moral consistency one can find in Clemens's early journalism comes from his acceptance of these practical programs of most newspapers.

In particular, Clemens often endorses the economic interests of his audiences, usually promoting capitalistic ideas of progress where possible. For instance, his letters from Hawaii to the Sacramento *Union* report on the sugar and whaling industries and editorialize repeatedly about the economic benefits the West Coast and the United States would reap if the nation were to strengthen its ties with the Hawaiian Islands. As he bluntly puts it in his March 1866 letter from Honolulu, "It is a matter of the utmost importance to the United States that her trade with these islands should be carefully fostered and augmented. Because — it pays. There can be no better reason than that" (*MTLH* 20).

Correlatively, he attacks "barbarism" where he finds it because he sees non-Western mores as an impediment to "progress." In this spirit, in his letters from the *Quaker City* expedition, he repeatedly attacks "Mohammedans" of all nationalities and especially the Syrians. Similarly, in his letters from Hawaii, he usually praises the missionaries for bringing free-market values to a once feudalistic land:

> The missionaries have clothed [the Hawaiians], educated them, broken up the tyrannous authority of their chiefs, and given them freedom and the right to enjoy whatever the labor of their hands and brains produces, with equal laws for all and punishment for all alike who transgress them. The contrast is so

strong — the wonderful benefit conferred upon this people by the missionaries is so prominent, so palpable, and so unquestionable, that the frankest compliment I can pay them, and the best, is simply to point to the condition of the Sandwich Islanders of Captain Cook's time, and their condition today. Their work speaks for itself. (*MTLH* 54–55)

The contrast here between Clemens's high praise and his usual disgust with the narrow-mindedness, complacency and self-righteousness of missionaries shows how much he reflected the economic agenda of his employers.

Besides promoting specific schemes, such as a steamship line between Hawaii and San Francisco (*MTLH* 18–24), and the general ideas of progress that facilitated such schemes, Clemens also wrote sketches to build the image of businessmen and trade generally. For example, his November 1864 sketch in the *Californian*, "Daniel in the Lion's Den — and Out Again All Right," ironically defends stock traders as, in the words of Branch and Hirst in their introduction to the sketch, "men of the world essential to an economy based on mineral wealth — expert operators of an intricate social mechanism as intriguing to Clemens as a complex amalgamator or a typesetter" (*ET&S* 2:100).

In the context of sentimentalist attacks on capitalism, Twain's sketches often took a decidedly anti-sentimental stand. In his 1868 burlesque of sentimental Christian tracts, "Mamie Grant, Child Missionary," for instance, Clemens attacks concern for the other world as being inappropriate, irresponsible, and ultimately childish. When Mamie, visiting her aunt and uncle, answers every caller with an exhortation to reform, she drives the callers away. As each caller has a business connection vital to her uncle's financial well-being, she in a single day's effort manages to bankrupt him completely.

Mamie, however, is oblivious to how unschooled in the ways of the world she is. Aware that Sunday School moralists following the sentimental psychology of associations always try to speak to people in terms that have emotional resonance for them, Mamie tries to speak a worldly idiom, as when she tells her uncle's debtor to "lay up treasures" in heaven and to "examine into [his] prospects in the hereafter." If he does, she says, he will find that his "account with sin grows apace" and that he should "Cash in & open the books anew" (*N&J1* 503). To this point, Mamie's metaphors are apt and appear calculated to reach the understanding of commercial man. Were her understanding of the world greater, she would continue in this vein, trying to show the worldly consequences of an obsessive concern for the merely worldly. This, of course, is what Mamie's hero, T. S. Arthur, professed to do in his most famous tract, *Ten Nights in a Bar-room and What I Saw There* (1854). Arthur suggests that Simon Slade, once an "honest miller," took the first step on the path toward worldly as well as spiritual corruption when he abandoned productive labor for the fatter profits of pandering to men's desire for recreational drinking. Arthur saw alcohol as only a small part of the greater problem: greed.[8]

But Mamie, not really understanding the sentimental argument, abandons her appropriate assault in favor of a more spectacular tract, one titled "The Blasphemous Sailor Awfully Rebuked." In paraphrasing the story of God punishing a sailor for blasphemy, Mamie describes, among other impossibilities,

> the dog-watch whipp[ing] clean out of the bolt-ropes quicker than the light-ning's flash! Imagine, Oh, imagine that wicked sailor's position! I cannot do it, because I do not know what those dreadful nautical terms mean, for I am not educated & deeply learned in the matters of practical every-day life like the gifted theological students, who have learned all about practical life from the writings of other theological students who went before them. (*N&JI* 503–4)

Throughout her rendition of the story, Mamie demonstrates a powerful interest in the lurid details for their sensationalistic effect, even though she is unable to garner any meaning from them. Clemens heavy-handedly implies that all sentimental moralists share Mamie's childish attachment to sensation for sensation's sake while lacking any real, practical knowledge by which they can properly judge the world's ways.

Sentimentalists, such as Stowe or Arthur, criticized the pursuit of wealth precisely because it seemed to sacrifice principle to worldly concerns. And in the sentimental world view, ideal principles did act in the world so that deviation from principle would yield worldly destruction. To this Clemens responds, saying that such a simplistic vision of cause and effect is the vision of children and that those who wish to eat in this world will pay more attention to their bread and butter than to the condition of other people's souls. The reader sides quickly with Mamie's "unregenerated Aunt" who responds to Mamie's otherworldly "No, Auntie, I cannot, I dare not eat batter-cakes while your precious soul is in peril," with a healthy "Oh, stuff! eat your breakfast, child, and don't bother" (*N&JI* 500).

But as much as he attacked conventional pieties in an effort to show the practical value of mundane business, Clemens also used those pieties in order to elevate the stature of practical endeavors. Typically, he indulged in the technological sublime, showing that human attention to practical affairs is the highest of human aims, and that in exercising the intellect, human beings aspire to divinity. Take, for example, this passage on the science of navigation:

> "They that go down to the sea in ships see the wonders of the great deep" — but this modern navigation out-wonders any wonder the scriptural writers dreampt of. To see a man stand in the night, when everything looks alike — far out in the midst of a boundless sea — and measure from one star to another and tell to a dot right where the ship is — to tell the very spot the little insignificant speck occupies on the vast expanse of land and sea twenty-five thousand miles in circumference! Verily, with his imperial intellect and his deep-searching wisdom, man is almost a God! (*MTTB* 77–78)

Here Clemens evokes the grandeur of Biblical associations and of nature in order to elicit what Alison would call the emotion of sublimity. He then associates this feeling with practical science in order to create an emotionally compelling justification of the practical, masculine sphere in a culture that increasingly defined morality in idealistic terms. Of course Alison, occupying the middle ground of Common Sense discourse, argued emphatically that God gave human beings their "imperial" intellects precisely so they could aspire to divinity, but by the time Clemens wrote, many sentimental moralists had rejected this middle ground. By asserting it, Clemens hopes to reestablish the moral value of practical endeavor.

So even though his use of sentimental discourse is contradictory between many of his writings, his journalistic efforts to support business explain some of those contradictions. His support for the political agendas of newspapers explains a few more. He did not, at least after his Nevada days, write much about partisan politics; in fact, his Washington correspondence is strangely devoid of partisan opinions.[9] But in a wider political vein, Clemens always encouraged patriotism. His travel letters generally try both to exploit and to build regional and national pride.

A Western audience valued this particularly, for Westerners felt keenly their isolation from the rest of the country. As Clemens lamented in his June 5, 1867 letter from New York to the *Alta California*:

> An educated and highly-cultivated American lady, who speaks French and Italian, and has travelled in Europe and studied the country so faithfully that she knows it as well as another woman would know her flower-garden, said to me yesterday that she had some dear friends in San Francisco and other parts of Idaho, and these Indian rumors gave her unspeakable uneasiness; she believed that for seven nights she had hardly slept at all, with imagining the horrors which are liable at any moment to fall upon those friends; and she said she had

friends in Santa Fe and Los Angeles, but she did not feel so worried about them because she believed the Indians did not infest the Cariboo country as much as they did the Farrallone Mountains and other localities further West. I tried to comfort her all I could. I told her I honestly believed that her friends in San Francisco and other parts of Idaho were just as safe there as they would be in Jerusalem or any other part of China.

Here she interrupted me, and told me with a well-bred effort to keep her countenance, that Jerusalem was not in China. I apologized, and said it was a slip of the tongue — but what I had meant to express was that her friends would be just as safe in Santa Fe and other parts of Cariboo as they would be in Damascus, or any other locality in France.

And she interrupted me again, and this time she did laugh a little bit, and told me modestly and in a way that could not hurt anybody's feelings, that Damascus was not in France.

I excused my stupidity again, and said that what I was trying to get at was, that her people might be even in the perilous gorges of the Farrallone Mountains and districts further west and still fare as well as if they were in Hongkong or any other place in Italy.

And then she did not laugh, but looked serious and said, "Are you so preposterously ignorant as all this amounts to, or are you trying to quiz me?" And I said, "Don't you go to Europe any more till you know a little something about your own country." I won. (*MTTB* 264–65)

Here he anticipates what part of his problem will be in writing travel letters that are designed to promote patriotism. The "educated and highly cultivated" tended to look east for their culture, and the cultural standards they found in literature all tended to reinforce the primacy of Europe over America. After all, Americans learned their aesthetic theory from Kames, Blair, and Alison, all of whom, as Europeans educated in the classics, naturally drew their examples of beauty, of the picturesque, and of the sublime from European examples and traditions. The American readers who accepted their aesthetic theories relied on their examples as the standards by which all beauty should be judged.[10] In writing patriotic travel literature, Clemens had to confront this tendency in the "well-bred" to denigrate their own culture in favor of Europe's. Not surprisingly, this dilemma is yet another source of Clemens's contradictory uses of "genteel" conventions.

On the one hand, he found in the psychology of associations a legitimate way to substitute American scenes for European without sacrificing the conventional terminology by which the "well-educated" described beauty. According to associationist aesthetics, described in the last chapter, if human beings define beauty by attaching their innate conceptions to the particular scenes and events of their own lives, then no absolute standards of beauty exist outside of the human mind. By this psychology, Clemens has Mark Twain gush about natural beauty according to all of the proprieties while simply substituting New World for Old World scenes as his associative standards.

In his European letters, for instance, Lake Tahoe serves him as his ultimate gauge of natural beauty, first in his descriptions of Lake Como and then more extensively in his depiction of the Sea of Galilee:

> The celebrated Sea of Galilee is not so large a sea as Lake Tahoe by a good deal—it is just about two-thirds as large. And when you speak of beauty, this sea is no more to be compared to Tahoe than a meridian of longitude is to a rainbow. The dim waters of this puddle cannot suggest the limpid brilliancy of Tahoe; those low, shaven, yellow hillocks of rocks and sand, so devoid of perspective, cannot suggest the grand peaks that compass Tahoe like a wall, and whose ribbed and chasmed fronts are clad with stately pines that seem to grow small and smaller as they climb, till one might fancy them reduced to weeds and shrubs far upward, where they join the everlasting snows. . . .
>
> In the early morning one watches the silent battle of dawn and darkness upon the waters of Tahoe with a placid interest; but when the shadows sulk away and one by one the hidden beauties of the shore unfold themselves, in the full splendor of noon, when the still surface is belted like a rainbow with broad bars of blue and green and white, half the distance from the circumference to centre; when, in lazy summer afternoons, one lies in a boat, far out to where the dead blue of the deep water begins, and smokes the pipe of peace and idly winks at the distant patches of snow from under his cap brim; when the boat drifts shoreward to the white water, and one lolls over the gunwale and gazes by the hour down through the crystal depths and notes the colors of the pebbles and averages the spots upon the school of trout a hundred feet below; when at night he sees moon and stars, mountain ridges feathered with pines, jutting white capes, bald promontories, grand sweeps of rugged scenery topped with bald, glimmering peaks, all magnificently pictured in the polished mirror of the lake, in richest, softest detail, the tranquil interest that was born with the morning deepens and deepens, by sure degrees, till it culminates at last in resistless fascination. (*TIA* 225–26)

In only three ways, here, does Clemens try to Americanize his standard of beauty. For one, he explicitly names it and locates it in the American West. For a second, in contemplating the landscape, his persona, Mark Twain, smokes a Native American "pipe of peace." And third, while Twain does not clearly state his pretext for visiting the lake, he implies that it is a lazy man's escape from work rather than a cultured man's search for scenes suitable to contemplate, and that the natural beauties, rather than being the objects of a leisured mind's trained gaze, actually are so enchanting as to conquer the indolence of an American rough.

Beyond these points, though, by using standard aesthetic diction that includes such trite terms as "limpid brilliancy" and "crystal depths"; by framing all views with spatial "perspectives"—note the peaks that "compass" the lake, distances defined by the lake's "Circumference," "colors" "belted" so they cannot escape perfect order and the reader's understanding, and especially the "rugged" "promontories" tamed by the "polished mirror of the lake"—; by evoking Biblical associations through the repeated comparison to the "rainbow" with its promises of beauty in peace and order, and the sanctifying of glaciers by the reference to their "everlasting" and thus vaguely divine permanence; by alluding in the first paragraph to the viewer's, or reader's, aesthetic control over the landscape through the "fancy" that "seem[s]" to reduce the sublimity of the scenery to picturesque proportions; and finally by fabricating the entire second paragraph out of a single elaborate and self-consciously controlled periodic sentence, Clemens evokes almost the entire range of literary conventions by which literate nineteenth-century readers understood, judged and mastered beauty. He uses this range of techniques here to replace the old examples of associative beauty with his preferred American ones in order to convince his readers to take pride in their own land. His highly literary treatment of the lake shows his willingness and ability to take seriously American scenes in "highly-cultivated," that is to say, European, terms.

But Clemens's literary artistry itself undercuts the ultimate value of American scenes as potential standards of beauty. The conventionality of his description, by making the scene familiar to a literate audience, actually de-emphasizes the particularity of the American landscape. And the fact that his sketch may be the only way most of his readers know of Tahoe makes Tahoe just one more in a series of purely literary standards, only accessible through a series of ideal types. Unless his experience is shared by his readers, his effort to replace European literary models becomes yet another exercise in Kamesian aesthetics, ultimately undercutting the value of American experience. Further, by following European aesthetic theory, Clemens merely adds American scenes to the list of conventional models of beauty; he does not argue that America is actually better.

Often, then, Clemens turned to an anti-literary aesthetic in order to attack the European models that, according to Kames, had transcendental value or that, according to Alison's associationism, were at least the associative standards of the literate classes. This is the source of the philistinism for which Mark Twain's Holy Land letters, eventually collected into *Innocents Abroad*, are so well known. But it is not an unprincipled philistinism; Clemens had good philosophical justification in the utilitarian side of moral philosophy for preferring the hard data of experience over any vague associations based on the hearsay of a tradition.[11]

So while his alternative to conventional aesthetics consists partly in attacks on literate pretenses to superiority, it also consists partly in his journalistic reports of "practical" matters — facts of commerce, industry, technology, geography, demography — stripped of conventional reflections. For instance, he describes in curiously neutral tones a new railroad coming to the gates of the ancient city of Ephesus:

> A railway here in Asia — in the dreamy realm of the Orient — in the fabled land of the Arabian Nights — is a funny thing to think of. And yet they have got one already, and are building another. The present one is well built and well conducted, by an English Company, but is not doing an immense amount of business. The first year it carried a good many passengers, but its freight list only comprised 800 pounds of figs! (*TIA* 172)

The beginning of his discussion leads one to expect either a denunciation of the modern intrusion into the poetic garden, or perhaps a humorous inversion by which he praises modern technology, but neither occurs.[12] Instead, we get a dry recitation of the facts and the mild observation that the existence of such a line — doing poor business as yet though well run — is "funny," or, as he puts it later in the passage, "curious." "Curious," but not an abomination. Clemens does not attack this railroad according to the proprieties of European aesthetic theory because, as he has Mark Twain say in an earlier passage describing Italy's turnpikes and railroads: "These things win me more than Italy's hundred galleries of priceless art treasures, because I can understand the one and am not competent to appreciate the other" (*TIA* 66). He knew that much of his American audience was in similar circumstances, so he simply bowed to the integrity of sticking with what one knows over the pretense of book learning.

As Clemens's series of letters from the Holy Land progresses, this idea that personal experience serves as a better, perhaps more natural, standard of judgment than does book-learning becomes the dominant theme. And naturally, as a humorist, he advances this theme through the comic juxtaposition of literary expectations and perceived reality. Thus, under the aegis of his political agenda, he often moves his humor into the realm of satire, positing the superiority of one of the juxtaposed positions over the other.

For instance, in his nineteenth *Alta* letter, dated "Constantinople, August, 1867," Clemens has Mark Twain recite the legends that literary tradition associates with the celebrated dogs of Constantinople before describing the reality that he sees. One cannot help but draw the conclusion that Mark Twain's sources were wrong, though he concludes no more than the modest: "I do not say they do not howl at night, nor that they do not attack people who have not a red fez on their heads. I only say that it would be mean for me to accuse them of these unseemly things who have not seen them do them with my own eyes or heard them with my own ears" (*TIA* 125). His next letter, a New York *Tribune* letter dated "Constantinople, Aug. 31, 1867," recites Twain's dreams of the "wonders of the Turkish Bath." But the picture of bliss he describes "just as I got it from incendiary books of travel" is no more like the reality than "the Five Points are like the Garden of Eden." When he actually experiences the bath he finds

> The cadaverous, half-nude varlets that served in the establishment had nothing of poetry in their appearance, nothing of romance, nothing of Oriental splendor. They shed no entrancing odors — just the contrary. Their hungry eyes and their lank forms continually suggested one glaring, unsentimental fact — they wanted a "square meal." (*TIA* 129)

This time he explicitly attacks guidebooks for deliberately misleading him: "When I think how I have been swindled by books of Oriental travel, I want a tourist for breakfast" (*TIA* 128).

Here, in asserting the mendacity of literary representations of the world, Clemens satirically rejects poetry, romance, and sentiment as lies. The implicit syllogism he postulates, then, is that since lies are immoral, all literary representations of the cultural value of the East are also immoral. By this implicit reasoning, Clemens tried to make room for America as the source of its own standards of beauty. But while such satirical reasoning may have cleared some room for American beauties, Clemens did not give up his use of romantic, poetic, sentimental rhetoric when he described American scenes.

Clearly, Clemens's attitude that one should accept reality over ideality did not hold consistently throughout his early journalism; much of his early work suggests to the contrary that such a vision was not, as Henry Nash Smith suggests, his fundamental way of looking at the world at all. In pursuing another of his journalistic tasks, the discovery of political corruption, he was more likely to use sentimental standards of morality than utilitarian ones. This shows most clearly in his correspondence from Washington, D.C., where he saw first hand the pernicious consequences of obsessive concern for one's personal estate at the expense of one's sense of responsibility to the community.

In his third Washington letter to the *Territorial Enterprise* (January 11, 1868), for example, Mark Twain asks his readers whether California's new Senator's democratic ideals are "of the poetical stripe" or "of the practical stripe that looks to the most goods to the greatest number." His play on Bentham's famous dictum suggests that the spoils system in politics secures a very narrow definition of the greatest good, leaving no room for morality. Implicitly, he prefers the "poetical stripe."

More explicitly, in his ninth Washington letter to the *Enterprise* (March 7, 1868), Mark Twain endorses Sunday School morality as being superior to worldly, self-interested Washington standards:

> Right here in this heart and home and fountain-head of law — in this great factory where are forged those rules that create good order and compel virtue and honesty in the other communities of the land, rascality achieves its highest perfection. Here rewards are conferred for conniving at dishonesty, but never for exposing it. . . . I meet a man in the Avenue, sometimes, . . . [who] was a clerk of a high grade in one of the Departments; but he was a stranger and had no rules of action for his guidance except some effete maxims of integrity picked up in Sunday school — that snare to the feet of the unsophisticated! — and some unpractical moral wisdom instilled into him by his mother, who meant well, poor soul, but whose teachings were morally bound to train up her boy for the poor-house.

Assuming that by "morally bound" he means by the natural morality of cause and effect, one sees that the ideas here are the same as in "Mamie Grant." The judgment of them is, however, completely changed by the opening condemnation of Washington hypocrisy.

As in "Mamie Grant," purely moral actions have horrible consequences:

> Well, nobody told this stranger how he ought to conduct himself, and so he went on following up those old maxims of his, and acting so strangely in consequence, that the other clerks began to whisper and nod, and exchange glances of commiseration — for they thought that his mind was not right.

Eventually, after trying to expose corruption where he finds it, he is fired from his job and can't find employment again. His practical failure would be, in sketches such as "Mamie Grant" or in the burlesque Sunday school stories "The Christmas Fireside" (1865) and "The Story of the Good Little

Boy Who Did Not Prosper" (1870), a condemnation of Sunday school morality. Here it condemns the standards of Washington for putting practical concerns above all moral ones.

The greatest moral concern that practical thinking neglects, according to this letter, is honesty. Still ironically speaking from the point of view of worldly Washington in order to reveal the immorality of the political world, he says at the end of the tale:

> Everybody shuns [the clerk] because everybody knows he is afflicted with a loathsome leprosy—the strange foreign leprosy of honesty—and they are afraid they might catch it. There isn't any danger, maybe, but then they don't like to take any chances.

By invoking the whole range of sentimental pieties about motherly influence, childhood purity, and the power of a moral education to inculcate unswerving honesty, Clemens clearly contradicts his frequent condemnations of sentimentality. But again, the contradiction is based on *ad hoc* needs. Both as a humorous and as a satirical journalist, he needed to establish contrasts between conventional voices; the voices he chose at any moment to endorse depended on the particular needs of the occasion of his writing.

One other aspect of journalism goes far to explaining Clemens's apparently inconsistent attitude toward sentimentality in the 1860s. He assumed that he wrote for a predominantly masculine audience—in his New York City correspondence for the Alta, for example, he explicitly addresses his readers as men at least twice—and such an audience appreciated, to use Hutcheson's words again, "allusions" against the "great sentiments" of domesticity on "low occasions." As a humorist, Clemens wrote for occasions that were by definition low, and he often attacked the "great sentiments" of a man's own house with his own wife, and his own mother, "and his wife's mother, and her various friends and relatives, and all the other little comforts that go to make married life a blessing and create what is known as 'Sweet Home,' and which is so deservedly popular—I mean among people who have not tried it (*ET&S* 2:165). Such moldy chestnuts as mother-in-law jokes were, and unfortunately still are, conventional among many men. Although the psychological purposes of such jokes may now be debated among psychologists and anthropologists, of importance to understanding Clemens's use of such aggressive humor is that it would not then have been taken as a serious challenge to the social order. At the same time, it would have been considered harmful to women. Only given the audience of men were such jests considered funny, and only in these circumstances did Clemens scorn domestic ideology.

But when Clemens felt that his audience was, as they said in the nineteenth century, "promiscuous" (*MTTB* 136), meaning of both genders mixed together, he did not impugn the ideals of sentimental domesticity. His letters of March, 1867 to the St. Louis *Democrat* show how quickly he changed his tone when certain that his audience contained women.[13] The first of these letters, a crude satire against women's suffrage, suggests that women worthy of the name lack both the experience and the interest to make a difference in politics. On the contrary, once in office "there would be no more peace on earth" because they would show no interest in practical governance but would instead "go straight after each other's private moral character" (March 12, 1867). Further, they would be so busy running for office, that they would fail to run their homes, leaving poor, abused husbands like Mark Twain with "the one solitary thing I have shirked up to the present time [falling] on me[,] and my family would go to destruction; for I am not qualified for a wet nurse."

When, however, his first satire evoked a powerful response from a female reader, Clemens says that he will "for once drop foolishness, and speak with the gravity the occasion demands." He claims that while it would be just for women to vote, it would not be expedient:

> An educated American woman would . . . vote with fifty times the judgment and independence exercised by stupid, illiterate newcomers from foreign lands, . . . the ignorant foreign women would vote with the ignorant foreign men — the bad women would vote with the bad men . . . [and] a very large proportion of our best and wisest women would still cling to the holy ground of the home circle, and refuse to either vote or hold office — . . . and, behold, mediocrity and dishonesty would be appointed to conduct the affairs of government more surely than ever before. (March 14, 1867)

Rather than end with this argument for expediency, he invokes the social ideology of the sexual spheres to remove the argument to a moral plane:

> That must be a benefit beyond the power of figures to estimate, which can make us consent to take the High Priestess we reverence at the sacred fireside and send her forth to electioneer for votes among a mangy mob who are unworthy to touch the hem of her garment. . . . There is something revolting in the thought. It would shock me inexpressibly for an angel to come down from above and ask me to take a drink with him (though I should doubtless consent); but it would shock me still more to see one of our blessed earthly angels peddling election tickets among a mob of shabby scoundrels she never saw before.

One hopes that the one joke is a sign that the whole saccharine speech is yet another burlesque, but the tone throughout is more that of a sermon than of a satire, leaving the conclusion that Clemens meant his audience to accept his comments as a serious treatise on female suffrage.

However, no sooner does Clemens return his attention to his usual California newspaper audience than the mocking tone returns; he treats the question of voting rights not with the "gravity the occasion demands," but with the levity his role as humorist among men warrants. In his March 25, 1867 letter to the *Alta*, he describes his debate in the pages of the *Democrat* as the battle of real men against the "henpecked husbands, or bully-ragged old bachelors [who] had been driven into a support of" the Missouri petition for women's suffrage that was the occasion for Mark Twain's first *Democrat* satire. In mock fear he claims he did not maintain his side in the battle:

> I attacked the monster in the public prints, and raised a small female storm, but it occurred to me that it might get uncommon warm for one poor devil against all the crinoline in the camp, and so I antied up and passed out, as the Sabbath School children say. (*MTTB* 134)

One cannot conclude that the attacks on sentimental ideology more truthfully state Clemens's opinions about the supposedly angelic nature of womanhood than do his comments supporting it. The best explanation for his apparent vacillation is once again that his role as newspaper humorist opened him to the possibility of mocking domesticity even though his sense of propriety encouraged him to endorse it.

V

In spite of what I have said about the medium, the circumstances, and the genre of Clemens's writing determining his uses of sentimental moral philosophy and social ideology, some trends in his thinking can be discerned in his journalism, most especially in his use of domestic ideology. Clearly, he accepted the general idea of the sexual spheres. He believed that the masculine sphere, the sphere of the business he did so much to promote, should be "utterly unpoetical and essentially practical" (*MTLH* 138). The feminine sphere, on the other hand, should, he felt, be the sphere of angels, of idealism, of beauty and of poetry, and should therefore be withdrawn from the sordid concerns of managing the world.

Clemens was not unusual in making such distinctions. The culture's moralists distrusted the moral consequences of responding to worldly exigencies; they believed in an alternative to the world's tendency to corruption in feminine withdrawal from the responsibilities of public life. From a position of retirement, women were supposed to exercise a benign moral influence on men. Ostensibly, weakness would call out the natural tendency of men to protect others; hence, the idea of feminine influence required women to be weak. But they could only act as agents of civilization by serving as models of purity at the same time they allowed themselves to suffer at the hands of masculine corruption. Their suffering alone could shame men into controlling themselves. Clemens's *Alta* letter of May 26, 1867 shows him sharing this model of feminine influence:

> They do not treat women with as much deference in New York as we of the provinces think they ought. This is painfully apparent in the street-cars. Authority winks at the overloading of the cars . . . instead of compelling the companies to double the number of their cars, and permits them, also, to cruelly over-work their horses . . . The result of this over-crowding is to set the people back a long stride toward semi-civilization. What I mean by that dreadful assertion is, that the over-crowding of the cars has impelled men to adopt the rule of hanging on to a seat when they get it, though twenty beautiful women came in and stood in their midst. That is going back toward original barbarism, I take it. (*MTTB* 226)

By describing this failure of masculine authority to regulate worldly greed, Clemens drives home a little moral about the failure of men to work toward progress, his yardstick for measuring civilization apparently being the status and treatment of women. In using this yardstick, he puts women on the same level as the horses, creatures that should be well cared for under masculine authority.

But of course, he believes women have greater power than animals to encourage the advancement of men; women by virtue of their "angelic" sympathies are able to guide the baser and weaker sympathies of men through domestic attachments, especially those of paternity, as one can see in Mark Twain's discussion of the Czar's daughter's "influence":

> Taking the kind expression that is in the Emperor's face and the gentleness that is in his young daughter's into consideration, I wondered if it would not tax the Czar's firmness to the utmost to condemn a supplicating wretch to misery in the wastes of Siberia if she pleaded for him. Every time their eyes met, I saw more and more what a tremendous power that weak, diffident school-girl could wield if she chose to do it. Many and many a time she might rule the

Autocrat of Russia, whose lightest word is law to 70,000,000 of human beings!
(*TIA* 154)

He sees in the girl's gentleness the source of her power, but only insofar as it presumes on her father's love for her. In his fantasy of her pleading for mercy, Clemens imagines her gentleness — that is, her feminine compassion for all human beings — pitted against the Czar's firmness — that is, his masculine resolve to do what is expedient — with the bridge between the two his kindness toward his daughter. Thus his ability to be an agent of civilization depends as much on her sympathy toward his subjects as it does on his power.

Given that weakness itself supposedly gave women their influence over men, the culture drew the conclusion that children generally and girls in particular would have the greatest influence over masculine sympathies. Clemens generally shared this judgment of girls, but at first he refused to include boys in the domestic sphere, as this description of a home for blind children shows:

> In another part of the house a dozen or so of blind young ladies were knitting all manner of elaborately-figured tidies, and such things. . . . The knitters were talking with all their mights, and seemed perfectly jolly and contented — at least the majority of them did. But it didn't cheer me up a particle. It was the saddest place I ever got into. I don't mind blind boys — they ought all to be blind, for that matter — and deaf and dumb, and lame and halt and paralyzed, and shaken up by earthquakes and struck by lightning — just to make them behave themselves, you know — but I felt so sorry for those girls. (*MTTB* 217)

American culture generally did not make such a marked distinction between the sentimental value of boys and girls, though it did prefer girls as the ideal "civilizing agents." In coming to accept a sentimental vision of girls, Clemens took the first step to committing himself to a consistent moral vision. In the context of his strong reservations about the practical value of sentimentality, this first step led Clemens ultimately into serious questions about the nature of boys, questions that found expression in both *Tom Sawyer* and *Huck Finn*. Clemens had to find what he called a "sound heart" in a boy before he could even conceive of Huck Finn, and then he had to explain how any such heart could fall under the sway of a "deformed conscience."

Clemens's journalism, although necessarily situational, includes the beginning of his serious moral use of domestic ideology in his writing. After 1867, his attacks on home, hearth, and womanhood grow rare while his straight use of ideas of womanly influence grow more frequent. This shift coincides with his search for a wife, whom he found in the miniature portrait of Olivia Langdon carried by her brother, Clemens's fellow passenger on the *Quaker City*, Charles Langdon. As Dixon Wecter puts it in *The Love Letters of Mark Twain*, Clemens was "in love with love" (2). He was so intent on consummating this love affair with an idea that he wooed and won Olivia's hand in spite of all objections to his "low" career and turbulent past.

And these objections were not trivial; Olivia was born to nouveau-riche parents who were trying to climb socially, and a "low" humorist did not fit their idea of a suitable match for their daughter. Their anxiety about Clemens's calling as a humorist surely added to his own. Furthermore, he was concerned that he could not support a family on a newspaper correspondent's earnings. In a letter to Mrs. Fairbanks in which he jokingly tells her he cannot marry even though she thinks he should, he tells her "I can't turn an inkstand into Aladdin's lamp" (*MTMF* 7–8). In these ways, Clemens's growing seriousness about domesticity helped lead him away from his "call."

Not that he did not have impetus enough already. He often wrote disparagingly of journalism, complaining frequently of newspaper sensationalism even while he cashed in on "bloody details" (*MTTB* 232) himself.[14] He disliked the power of the press and its cold-blooded manipulation of public passions to suit a publisher's interests. He lost himself a berth on the San Francisco *Call* because it was unwilling to publish one of Clemens's reports on the persecution of the Chinese by the Irish for fear of losing its sizable Irish readership. Ever the preacher, Clemens scorned these cold-blooded "newspaper reptile[s]" (*MTTB* 214).

It is small wonder, then, that by the early 1870s Clemens abandoned his career as a newspaper humorist and turned to a life as a writer of "higher" literature. As a literary man, though, Clemens found that the tensions between the proprieties of humor and those of literature were greater than those he had experienced as a journalist, partly because his new audience explicitly included women and children, and partly because he was now, by the Common Sense literary theory that required "high" literature to serve moral ends, going to be a moralist. New standards of propriety and ethical consistency would be required of him, even as he was to continue to write humorously about a culture that had a very confusingly contradictory set of moral ideas. How he responded to the heightened ambiguities of his new calling is the subject of the next chapter.

4. Becoming a "Littery Man"

I

> Under his nom de plume of Mark Twain, Mr. Clements is well known to the very large world of newspaper-readers; and this book ought to secure him something better than the uncertain standing of a popular favorite.
>
> —William Dean Howells, unsigned review of *The Innocents Abroad*, *The Atlantic Monthly*, December, 1869, quoted in *MTHL* 5

In his appreciative review of *The Innocents Abroad*, William Dean Howells welcomed Clemens the journalist into a new profession, that of literary artist. Although Howells did criticize Clemens's humor for being "not delicate," he nonetheless found it to have "a base of excellent sense and good feeling" and a large "amount of pure human nature," precisely those qualities that Common Sense aestheticians said art needed to promote good taste, good sense, and good morals. In welcoming Clemens into what Clemens eventually called "our guild," Howells implied much of what Clemens would have to do to earn an enduring fame, that is, to promote the Common Sense compromise that he had earlier exploited in his humor.

Not that Clemens didn't already know what his new profession would require. When revising his newspaper correspondence into *The Innocents Abroad*, he anxiously altered the features that made it so successful as journalism but that would, he felt, destroy his fledgling reputation as an artist. Leon Dickinson correctly points out that, besides adding bridges between letters and removing repetition in order to shape the material into a book, Clemens removed much slang and many "irreverent" passages in order to accommodate the demands of his new audience. Indeed, in writing to Mary Mason Fairbanks about revising the *Alta* letters for *Innocents*, he stated that he did not "like any of those letters that have reached me from California so far. I may think better of those you weeded of slang, though. There will not be any slang in this book except it should occur in a mild form in dialogues" (*MTMF* 21). And when he learned that the *Alta* planned to collect his unrevised letters into a book, he was worried that "if the *Alta*'s book were to come out with those wretched, slangy letters unrevised, I should be utterly ruined" (*MTMF* 24).[1]

The requirements as Clemens then saw them were primarily two. For one, he had to purify his diction in order to avoid the charge that his language would vitiate taste. As indicated in the previous chapter, he already knew about this moral commonplace as it arose out of Common Sense aesthetics. That he accepted it at this stage of his career shows in one of his courtship letters to Olivia Langdon, in which he tells her not to read *Gulliver's Travels, Don Quixote*, or Shakespeare's plays because "portions . . . are very coarse & indelicate" and are not "proper . . . for virgins to read until some hand has culled them of their grossness. No gross speech is ever harmless. 'A man cannot handle pitch & escape defilement,' saith the proverb" (*LLMT* 76). In writing of "coarseness," "indelicacy," and "gross speech," he quite clearly means any language discussing sex. At the same time, however, when he says that "no gross speech is ever harmless" he does not speak euphemistically. He accepts the moralist's "slippery slope" argument that coming into contact with immoral ideas will debase a person's thoughts. When morality was judged more by intention than by action, "impure thought" (*LLMT* 76) was the ultimate moral danger.

In revising his travel letters for book publication, Clemens deleted much sexual innuendo, for instance the long passage in the *Alta* letter dated "Odessa, Russia, August 22d," 1867, in which he describes the Russian practice of nude bathing:

> I was never so outraged in my life. At least a hundred times, in the seven hours I stayed there, I would just have got up and gone away from there disgusted, if I had had any place to go to. . . . Incensed as I was, I was compelled to look, most of the time, during this barbarous exhibition, because it forced them to make a show of modesty, at least. (*TIA* 140)

The mock outrage to justify obvious prurience made a funny newspaper joke for a masculine audience, but, by his widely shared double standard, Clemens would not publish such a piece in a book that would be consumed by a mixed-gender audience. Rather than risk the conventional purity of any American girls — or the outrage of his audience — he struck the passage from *The Innocents Abroad*. By the same general standard of moral purity, Clemens also expunged references to drinking, gambling, and swearing. And finally, he "weeded out" substantial amounts of slang, though he did not purge it all. That he felt "mild" forms could remain without damaging anyone's moral purity suggests that Clemens did not wholly accept the aesthetic criticism of slang.

The second important feature of his letters he addressed was the question of "irreverence." According to sentimental psychology as it developed through Hutcheson, the sense of reverence was one of the key senses to encouraging moral growth. It seemed often at odds with the sense of humor, which was given a valued place in sentimental psychology because it supposedly relieved life's debilitating tensions. But since humor was consigned to a distinctly lower position in the moral hierarchy of senses in sentimental moral psychology, the task of any humorist who wished also to win respectability in literary circles was to find a humor, usually described as "dainty" or "subtle,"[2] that would not cultivate irreverence while it relieved seriousness.

Following these standards, Clemens dumped many of his most scurrilous and delightful barbs. For instance he stopped calling the Bible a "guide-book" (*TIA* 180) and stopped blaming God for the existence of idiotic people (*TIA* 160–61); he blamed biblical commentators rather than the Bible itself for contradictions he found in Christianity (*TIA* 164–65); he dropped some of his most outrageous attacks on "The Old Masters," as when he compared frescoes by the Old Masters to camel dung piled against the walls of Syrian huts (*TIA* 232–33); and he dropped many attacks on the purity or delicacy of women of the Middle East, as when he described a Syrian woman who collected camel dung while entertaining her suitor (*TIA* 245–46).[3] Thus he took into account the reverence in which religion, high art, and women were held.

In spite of his effort to modify both the vulgarity and irreverence of his original letters, he still failed to suit the taste of many reviewers. As Henry Nash Smith notes, Bret Harte's review of *The Innocents Abroad* complained of its "lawlessness and audacity" and the "lack of 'moral or aesthetic limitation' in its humor" (quoted in *Mark Twain* 25) And as Walter Blair notes:

> Literary critics . . . stressed the author's limitations. He was first publicized as "The Wild Humorist of the Pacific Slope." When *Innocents Abroad* appeared, although some reviewers said that he ranked a cut above other jokesmiths, many disagreed; according to the New York *Tribune* he showed "an offensive irreverence" toward things "which other men hold sacred." The note recurred for years. On April 6, 1871, *The Nation* noted that he "was sometimes vulgar and low . . . not refined." In September, 1872, *The Southern Magazine* maintained that the huge sale of *Innocents Abroad* had led to the decision "that the person of refined and polished sensibility will not permit the perusal of this

vicious school of publications." . . . Some [critics] felt that his doom was to be a low comedian forever. The Chicago *Tribune*, on February 27, 1871, said that he "has no aspirations or abilities in any other direction." (25)

It is easy to over-emphasize this criticism, though, and to conclude that Clemens from the beginning was at odds with the literary community while being in touch with the masses. In truth, his revisions did succeed in winning the approval of significant portions of the literary elite. Among those who early accepted him as a literary artist, of course, was Howells, who, though admitting that Clemens's book was often irreverent, found more than enough good points to weight the moral scale in Clemens's favor:

> It is out of the bounty and abundance of his own nature that [the author] is as amusing in the execution as in the conception of his work. And it is always good-humored humor, too, that he lavishes on this reader, and even in its impudence it is charming; we do not remember where it is indulged at the cost of the weak or helpless side, or where it is insolent, with all its sauciness and irreverence. (*MTHL* 5)

In finding the "good-natured" intention of Clemens's humor, Howells finds its conventional moral value.

After *The Innocents Abroad* proved a smashing success, the literati of Hartford, too, decided that they could accept a bit of irreverence; the owners of the Hartford *Courant*, who had snubbed Clemens's advances to buy a share in the paper in June of 1869, actively solicited his investment in the paper's owning partnership and encouraged him to move to Hartford's fashionable intellectual community, Nook Farm (*LLMT* 101, 123–24, 131). Granted, they were inviting him into journalism, but this time as an owner of a very successful highbrow newspaper, not as a lowly comic writer.

One can see the pleasure he took in being recognized for his literary success in his December 27, 1869 letter to his fiancée:

> To-day we came upon a democrat wagon in Hartford with a cargo in it composed of Mrs. Hooker & Alice [one of Livy's good friends] . . . Mrs. Warner & another lady. — They all assailed me violently on the *Courant* matter & said it had ceased to be a private desire that we take an ownership in that paper, & had become a public demand. — Mrs. H. said Warner & Hawley would do anything to get me in there (this in presence of Mrs. W. who did not deny it by any means) & Mrs. H. said she had been writing to Mr. Langdon to make us sell out in Buffalo & come here. (It afforded me a malicious satisfac-

tion to hear all this & contrast it with the insultingly contemptuous indif-
ference with which the very same matter was treated last June (by every one of
them.) (*LLMT* 131–32)

In the letter, this information follows his remark that *The Innocents Abroad*
is selling better than anything "since *Uncle Tom's Cabin*." He realizes that his
success as a writer of books has earned him his entry into Hartford's best
circles. The gloating note shows how much he appreciates the good opinion of this community and at least suggests the anxiety he felt about being
worthy of such a community.[4]

Though Clemens did not immediately accept these solicitations, within two years he did move to Nook Farm, not, however, as a newspaper
publisher, but as a professional writer of books. As such, he worked assiduously not only at developing his craft, but at demonstrating refinement in
taste and at developing erudition appropriate to his position. As Annie
Fields said, "It is curious and interesting to watch this growing man of
forty—to see how he studies and how high his aims are" (Walter Blair 29).[5]
Clemens tried very hard to learn the ropes, to create an image of himself
that was consistent with conventional standards of taste and status.

II

To this point I am agreeing with the conventional opinion that Samuel
Clemens's "reformation" from frontier bohemian to respectable family man
and from journalist to man of letters had a profound impact on his writing
by pushing it toward conventionality. But this narrow reading of the impact
of Clemens's move to Hartford misses a much larger point; his "reformation" also pushed him toward taking stands on all of the central issues raised
by nineteenth-century moral philosophy. During his first decade as a literary man, when trying to accept the dominant culture's intellectual as well as
social underpinnings, Clemens had to confront seriously the inconsistencies in moral philosophy. Hitherto he had merely exploited them for comic
effect; now they threatened to undermine his sense of belonging in genteel
culture.

He first confronted the problems inherent in promoting the Common
Sense agenda in his effort to transform his travel letters into *The Innocents
Abroad*. Take, for instance, his treatment of "associations" as an appropriate

way to promote patriotism. In writing for an Eastern audience, he could not assume that his readers shared his knowledge of the West; in fact, as I demonstrated in the last chapter, he assumed Easterners' ignorance. On this assumption, he expands substantially on the original letter when he first refers to Lake Tahoe in *Innocents*, and, in his next reference, he explains in a footnote:

> I measure all lakes by Tahoe, partly because I am far more familiar with it than with any other, and partly because I have such a high admiration for it and such a world of pleasant recollections of it, that it is very nearly impossible for me to speak of lakes and not mention it. (507)

Significantly, he does not here say that Tahoe fits any abstract conception of what a lake should be; he instead insists on his pleasant associations with the lake, assuming that his audience will accept the value of emotional experience as a legitimate source of aesthetic appreciation. In making this assumption, he argues for it, encouraging Americans to take pride in their own experiences of their own country rather than to undervalue America because it fails to measure up to the idealized European standards their books have given them.

But Clemens's literary artistry itself, as I noted in the last chapter, perversely fails to promote the ultimate value of American scenes as standards of beauty. To repeat, in describing American places in conventional terms, he robs American scenes of their particularity. The book, written for an Eastern audience, is even more likely to be the only way his readers know of Tahoe than was a newspaper sketch for a California audience; consequently, the problem of his writing actually undercutting the value of American experience is even greater for the book than it was for the newspaper sketches. Worse, in turning to an anti-literary aesthetic to solve this problem, he undermines the value of his own book. This is the epistemological problem of *The Innocents Abroad*: it is a travel book that attacks travel books, a report of reality that says one cannot know reality by report, an authority that calls into question its own truth.

His second book, again a collection of travel sketches published by subscription, addresses this problem at large in a way he once used locally in some of his travel letters; he blames errors of understanding primarily on the perceiver's expectations rather than on the report. As he did *Innocents*, Clemens prefaces *Roughing It* with an assertion that he reports facts based on personal experience. But to prevent him from undercutting his own authority again, he establishes a retrospective point of view that enables him to comment on both expectation and reality from the point of view of personal experience.

The opening chapter sets the stage by creating the narrator as a character who seems lost in a daze of fantasy:

> My brother had just been appointed Secretary of Nevada Territory . . . I was young and ignorant, and I envied my brother. I coveted his distinction and his financial splendor, but particularly and especially the long, strange journey he was going to make, and the curious new world he was going to explore. He was going to travel! I had never been away from home, and the word "travel" had a seductive charm for me. Pretty soon he would be hundreds and hundreds of miles away on the great plains and deserts, and among the mountains of the Far West, and would see buffaloes and Indians, and prairie-dogs, and antelopes, and have all kinds of adventures, and maybe get hanged or scalped, and have ever such a fine time, and write home and tell us all about it, and be a hero. And he would see the gold-mines and the silver-mines, and maybe go about of an afternoon when his work was done, and pick up two or three pailfuls of shining slugs and nuggets of gold and silver on the hillside. And by and by he would become very rich, and return home by sea, and be able to talk as calmly about San Francisco and the ocean and "the isthmus" as if it was nothing of any consequence to have seen those marvels face to face. (1–2)

When the narrator is invited to go along, he quickly agrees, proposing

> to stay in Nevada three months — I had no thought of staying longer than that. I meant to see all I could that was new and strange, and then hurry home to business. . . . I dreamed all night about Indians, deserts, and silver bars, and in due time, next day, we took shipping at the St. Louis wharf on board a steamboat bound up the Missouri River. (2–3)

Ironically, this character, whose authoritative "personal experiences" the reader is supposed to trust, is mostly a fabrication. By the time he left for Nevada to escape the Civil War, Clemens, a journeyman compositor, had already traveled over much of the Old Northwest, to Pennsylvania, and to New York before "learning the river" to become a Mississippi steamboat pilot. He was hardly the romantic homebody. But his romantic character, Mark Twain, serves Clemens's authorial needs by embodying imagination unbridled by reality. This boy babbles inconsistencies with disarming faith. The paratactic sentence structure Clemens uses echoes the chaotic working of his character's untested mind, one that tumbles imaginings together unbroken by reflection, that mixes real plans with dreams, that acts impulsively in accord with fantasy. Only such a mind could conceive of one day as "due time" to prepare for a trek across a partially settled continent. His expectation to see "all I could that was new and strange" in three months fits the kind of frenetic imagining and impulsive haste suitable to such "poor innocents" (5).

By the second page Clemens establishes the retrospective counterpoint to such fantastic expectations. "I little thought that I would not see the end of that three-month pleasure excursion for six or seven uncommonly long years!" Here the voice of experience gently points out the absurdity of the expectation by relating the facts that the excursion took much longer than the greenhorn could have imagined, and that there was little "pleasure" in those years that felt "uncommonly long" when actually lived. These two voices in contrast provide the rhythm of much of the book—the voice of experience contradicts with facts the misconceptions of romantic fancy. Incidentally, this becomes the source of the incongruity that constitutes much of the book's humor.

Throughout the book, then, Clemens mainly blames Mark Twain's misconceptions on his own desires rather than on his poor sources of information. By blaming faulty expectations on individual character and ignorance, rather than on report or even on a characteristic mode of seeing through the tropes of literary description, he promotes a certain kind of realism without undercutting the authority of his own report of reality. In so doing, he restores to himself many of the tropes of conventional literary aesthetics while diminishing their tendency to undercut themselves or to veer toward the extreme of literary idealism.

Thus his fictionalized autobiography, based on personal experience to be sure, tried not to make a photographic "record" (*Roughing It*, preface) of fact but rather to uncover a moral truth to nature. He seems to justify his fiction the way Common Sense philosophers justified novels as moral preceptors that uncover essential truths about human beings regardless of the accidental characteristics of actual people. At the same time, his primary message, that too much idealism prevents a person from seeing the truth, supports the Common Sense compromise between idealism and materialism.

III

Clemens struggled with the contradictions inherent in realistic fiction because he valued truth very highly. As he put it in his notebook in 1878, "The one evidence of high civilization must surely be to not lie" (*N&J2* 176), and he did not seriously question this fundamental moral precept until much later in his life. Nonetheless, he did not find truth easily nor stably defined, especially when it came to writing pure fiction that purported to be realistic, that is to say, when he turned from sketches to novels. He started *Tom Sawyer* soon after he finished *Roughing It*, but abandoned the novel shortly thereafter, perhaps in part because of the moral and epistemological difficulties he found in the genre. His first full effort at writing a novel turned out to be a collaborative effort with his neighbor and then good friend, Charles Dudley Warner.

Since Clemens always had a penchant for collaborative literary endeavors, one should not overemphasize the significance of his choice of Warner for a co-author of his first novel, but I suspect he relied on Warner's college education for support in confronting the new medium he wished to master. In any case, he certainly did seem anxious about writing a novel, in part because it was yet another new start for him, and he "was scared. When a man starts out in a new role, the public always says he is a fool & won't succeed" (April 22, 1873 to Whitelaw Reid; quoted in French 12). In Warner he found a writer who was sure of himself as a writer and as a critic of novels. In the fifth installment of his "Back-log Studies," a fictionalized dialogue with one of his old college companions, with a local parson (probably Clemens's good friend Joseph Twichell), and with Clemens, Warner without hesitation condemns the "great body of novels" for treating their subjects "without any settled ethics, with little discrimination of eternal right and wrong, and with very little sense of responsibility for what is set forth. [They] are as chaotic as the untrained minds that produce them" (48).[6]

While the two men agreed about the "demoralizing" nature of novels, Warner did not seem to share Clemens's doubts about his ability to find "eternal truth," because he had, he felt, subjected himself to "study, training, [and] mental discipline" ("Back-log" V, 48). His epistemological certitude, and his belief that his audience shared that certitude, shows repeatedly in *The Gilded Age*. Consider, for instance, that in questioning "Whether medicine is a science, or only an empirical method of getting a living out of the ignorant race" (194), Warner shows his awareness of Locke's distinction between a priori systematic knowledge and knowledge based on simple experience. Our use of the term "science" began in the nineteenth century as "natural philosophers" tried to suggest that their knowledge had advanced to certainty from the imprecision of empirical probabilities. In playing with the older meaning, Warner subtly suggests that medicine is often a fraud based less on any science of the human body than on experience of human gullibility.

Similarly, he uses his understanding and assumes his audience's understanding of Common Sense epistemology in order to characterize Harry Brierly's opportunism. When Brierly meets Ruth Bolton, whom he finds very attractive, he tries to impress her by encouraging her ambition to become a doctor:

> "Medicine is particularly women's province."
> "Why so?" asked Ruth, rather amused.
> "Well, the treatment of disease is a good deal a matter of sympathy. A woman's intuition is better than a man's. Nobody knows anything, really, you know, and a woman can guess a good deal nearer than a man." (283)

Brierly parrots, here, the radical intuitionist challenge to Locke's empiricism. As Hume, and to some extent Smith, put it, we in fact know nothing for certain, but can operate in the world by following our sympathetic intuitions with other people. Warner does not accept this, as his little deflating "you know" shows, and at the same time he shows Brierly's hypocrisy in citing as knowledge a skepticism that if consistent could not be so assertive. Ruth, whom the novel shows ultimately to have a woman's intuition (although she usually suppresses it in her effort to don a mantle of "pure intellect"), sees right through Brierly's flattery and accuses him of scoffing at her ambitions. Warner's subtle satire here not only requires some knowledge of epistemology, but requires agreement with the Common Sense compromise that our knowledge comes in part from reason and experience and in part from intuition, and that we can know this to be true. Clemens had been struggling with epistemological problems in his writing; he probably found security in college-educated Warner's absolute faith in the fundamental moral soundness of Common Sense epistemology.

IV

While Clemens may have relied on Warner's certainties about the epistemological questions of fiction, he needed no help to decide on the rest of the moral agenda the two tried to promote in their novel. They agreed enough in the abstract on moral questions to apply the same solutions in almost every practical case, following the Common Sense (and, of course, Classical) agenda to promote "that just mean in life which is so rarely attained" (197). The novel consistently tries to find mediating positions between possible extremes in order to encourage the moral development of its readers. This shows substantially in the novel's attack on the content and use of much literature in America. Warner's and Clemens's excuse for writing the novel in the first place was that they had been complaining about the moral tendencies of modern novels, and their wives challenged them to do better.[7] One of their ways of doing better is to describe not only what to read but how to read and to show the consequences of reading correctly and incorrectly.

Laura Hawkins's fall from feminine "purity" into the roles of Washington lobbyist (persuasive by virtue of her "charms"), of murderer of the man who first seduced her, and finally of a public lecturer, stems substantially from her misuse of literature. Clemens first shows Laura under a social cloud on account of the mysterious circumstances of her birth. When one of her suitors is chased off by the rumors, Clemens has her turn bitter in disappointment, not merely because the man fails to support her, but because she has false expectations raised by her favorite romances:

> "The coward! Are all books lies? I thought he would fly to the front, and be brave and noble, and stand up for me against all the world, and defy my enemies, and wither these gossips with his scorn! Poor crawling thing, let him go. I do begin to despise this world!" (107)

To Warner fell the task of developing this germ into Laura's seduction at the hands of a Confederate colonel. He has her withdraw from the society that shuns her because "she had will, and pride and courage and ambition," but unfortunately her isolation throws her deep into the world of romance that so warped her expectations in the first place:

> There was another world opened to her — a world of books. But it was not the best world of that sort, for the small libraries she had access to in Hawkeye were decidedly miscellaneous, and largely made up of romances and fictions which fed her imagination with the most exaggerated notions of life, and showed her men and women in a very false sort of heroism. From these stories she learned what a woman of keen intellect and some culture joined to beauty and fascination of manner might expect to accomplish in society as she read of it; and along with these ideas she imbibed other very crude ones in regard to the emancipation of woman.
>
> There were also other books — histories, biographies of distinguished people, travels in far lands, poems, especially those of Byron, Scott and Shelley and Moore, which she eagerly absorbed, and appropriated therefrom what was to her liking. (172–73)

Warner complains mostly about the trashy romances she reads that give her an "immoral" philosophy of life. He also, however, has her read what he considered excellent literature.[8] The problem, as he develops it, is that "she was left to be very much her own guide at the age when romance comes to the aid of passion, and when the awakening powers of her vigorous mind had little object on which to discipline themselves" (169), so she does not know how to read the "masterpieces," only "appropriat[ing] therefrom what was to her liking." Consequently, she is, as Clemens sardonically puts it later in the book, "not a person of exaggerated refinement" (312).

Nor is Laura a woman of exaggerated moral character. Early in her career as her own avenger against men, she turns Harry Brierly into one of her targets. Warner's description of her manipulation of Brierly relies on a significant trope of American fiction, that of the experimenter with other people's souls.[9]

> [A girlish] woman would have attracted Harry at any time, but only a woman with a cool brain and exquisite art could have made him lose his head in this way; for Harry thought himself a man of the world. The young fellow never dreamed that he was merely being experimented on. (181)

That she lacks appropriate human, and in this case especially "feminine," compassion shows the reader how immoral Laura has become. Warner goes on to explain that romance rather than science is to blame for this moral lack, turning the standard use of this trope around:

> He was to her a man of another society and another culture, different from that she had any knowledge of except in books, and she was not unwilling to try on him the fascinations of her mind and person.
>
> For Laura had her dreams. She detested the narrow limits in which her lot was cast, she hated poverty. Much of her reading had been of modern works of fiction, written by her own sex, which had revealed to her something of her own powers and given her indeed, an exaggerated notion of the influence, the wealth, the position a woman may attain who has beauty and talent and ambition and a little culture, and is not too scrupulous in the use of them. She wanted to be rich, she wanted luxury, she wanted men at her feet, her slaves, and she had not—thanks to some of the novels she had read—the nicest discrimination between notoriety and reputation; perhaps she did not know how fatal notoriety usually is to the bloom of womanhood. (181–82)

So Laura's moral decay comes about substantially because she tries to live in an ideal world presented by books; she trains herself in them according to her own romantic inclinations, by what Clemens calls "one's little modicum of romance secreted away in one's composition" (104). The authors do not condemn "dreams" out of hand; they do suggest that it is dangerous to dream in isolation, to lose track of the reality that Common Sense philosophers found in social action and social continuity.

In discussing morality in the domestic sphere, Warner shows the positive alternative to Laura's moral collapse in Ruth Bolton's intellectual and social awakening in the home of her friend, Alice Montague:

> If Ruth did not find so much luxury in the house as in her own home, there were evidences of culture, of intellectual activity and of a zest in the affairs of all the world, which greatly impressed her. Every room had its book-cases or book-shelves, and was more or less a library; upon every table was liable to be a litter of new books, fresh periodicals and daily newspapers. . . . The life of the world flowed freely into this hospitable house, and there was always so much talk there of the news of the day, of the new books and of authors, of Boston radicalism and New York civilization, and the virtue of Congress, that small gossip stood a very poor chance. All this was in many ways so new to Ruth that she seemed to have passed into another world, in which she experienced a freedom and mental exhilaration unknown to her before. Under this influence she entered upon her studies with keen enjoyment, finding a time for all the relaxation she needed, in the charming social life at the Montague house. (197–98)

In the first place, Ruth's experience in medical school had already shown her that she needed a liberal education in order really to "know anything."[10] She stays at the Montague household in order to attend the nearby seminary that "offered almost collegiate advantages of education" (195). So she begins her real training in the life of the mind after having gained a desire for it from experience. She then turns to reading, but only uses it as food for the discussions that all the members of the household engage in. And she balances her reading between daily journalism, literary magazines, and books. Only, suggests Warner, in this social context of academic authority, of communal activity, and of wide-ranging interest does one find healthy "zest," "freedom," and "keen enjoyment." Ruth only "seemed to have passed into another world" by the contrast to the narrow range of her medical studies and of her earlier domestic life in an intellectually dead house. Now she finds herself involved "in the affairs of all the world" rather than in her own dreams or in the idealized world of romance. One attains the "just mean" (197) in life, says Warner, by coupling practical experience with abstract learning in the catalytic presence of community interest.

Both authors present this kind of social and intellectual life as the apex of moral culture, not just for the happiness it brings individuals, but for its social consequences. Clemens's discourse on the three types of Washington aristocracy, namely the Antiques, the Parvenus, and the Middle Ground, suggests the public consequences of certain kinds of domestic behavior. He accuses the Antiques of being virtually dead, stuck in the rigid formalities of an idealized caste system; he scorches the Parvenus for their narrowness and pretense based exclusively on money and the shows of culture that money can buy, and praises the Middle Ground for turning its culture and education to the best account not only of their own families but of the country at large:

> These gentlemen and their households were unostentatious people; they were educated and refined; they troubled themselves but little about the two other orders of nobility, but moved serenely in their wide orbit, confident in their own strength and well aware of the potency of their influence. They had no troublesome appearances to keep up, no rivalries which they cared to distress themselves about, no jealousies to fret over. (311–12)[11]

The rest of the novel shows precious few of these people in action, suggesting the conclusion that their "wide orbit" was more a question of their broad interests than of the size of their community. In any event, much of the book tries to show the difficulties of cultivating this kind of public personality through a combination of education and experience, through domestic attachments and public responsibilities.

Like Harriet Beecher Stowe, Warner and Clemens here suggest that home and hearth provide the best moral impetus for worldly success by providing both an ideal for which to strive (and by which to strive) and practical balance against idealistic excess in the exigencies of earning a living. According to Stowe, the apex of these ideals was self-sacrifice for others. Clemens applies this standard equally to his male and female characters. For instance, before Laura degenerates into a villain, when caring for her adoptive father in his final illness, Clemens shows Laura's willingness to break her health as a sign of her intuitively high moral character:

> From this time forth, three-hour watches were instituted, and day and night the watchers kept their vigils. By degrees Laura and her mother began to show wear, but neither of them would yield a minute of their tasks to Clay. — He ventured once to let the midnight hour pass without calling Laura, but he ventured no more; there was that about her rebuke when he tried to explain, that taught him that to let her sleep when she might be ministering to her father's needs, was to rob her of moments that were priceless in her eyes; he perceived that she regarded it as a privilege to watch, not a burden. (96)

Clay could understand such stoicism insofar as he lived his own life by the same standards:

> When Clay bade his home good-bye and set out to return to the field of his labors, he was conscious that henceforth he was to have his father's family on his hands as pensioners; but he did not allow himself to chafe at the thought, for he reasoned that his father had dealt by him with a free hand and a loving one all his life, and now that hard fortune had broken his spirit it ought to be a pleasure, not a pain, to work for him. (74)

Interestingly, Clay has first to rely on his reason to convince him not to chafe and to do as he ought, whereas Laura simply feels her responsibility as a joy. By sentimental convention, women were supposed to have quicker feelings and were more willing to sacrifice themselves. Clay does live up to his reasoned commitment, though, and when watching Laura at her father's deathbed, comes to feel the nobility of such self-sacrifice.

Clemens and Warner both frequently echo sentiments about the power of familial relations to inspire both practical and moral action, often putting these thoughts in the mouths of their characters, often leaving them in the narrative voice. The widespread appearance of these comments, often without any irony, often ironically criticizing characters for not living up to these standards, suggests that they were not, as Bryant French believes, burlesquing every element of the domestic novel. Far from it, in fact, they used the ethical and aesthetic standards novels professed to follow to show the shortcomings not of the genre itself but of the current examples of it. They did, after all, rise to the challenge of writing a better novel, not of writing a better kind of fiction.

Again as did Stowe, Warner and Clemens suggest that the home should serve as a counterweight to the often visionary schemes of the business world. When Colonel Sellers, for example, finds one of his many schemes falling through, he has to "bolster up his wife's spirits" by telling her of the fortunes they will have by the next year, but since she is the one who has actually to cook the meals that Sellers can't seem to provide, he has a difficult time of it:

> "Just stop and fancy a moment — . . . Bless your heart, you dear women live right in the present all the time — but a man, why a man lives — "
> "In the future, Beriah? But don't we live in the future most too much, Beriah? We do somehow seem to manage to live on next year's crop of corn and potatoes as a general thing while this year is still dragging along, but sometimes it's not a robust diet." (245)

Polly Sellers's insistence on practical day-to-day living is supposed to be the incentive Sellers needs to provide something. Sellers misses the point, though, because he cannot discriminate between real work and idle "speculation." "I know you are the very best little woman that ever lived . . . And I know that I would be a dog not to work for you and think for you and scheme for you with all my might" (245–46). Sellers, then, stands as a lesson in how not to respond to domestic responsibilities.

According to *The Gilded Age*, when the home works properly as a balance to masculine speculation, it does so because housekeeping cultivates pragmatic attention to detail. When Clay Hawkins, for instance, earns enough money to pay off the family debts, only Mrs. Hawkins has the practical ability to use the money wisely (74). Clay himself, the only other practical Hawkins, learned his pragmatic attention to work from his natural mother in the ten years of his life before the Hawkins family adopted him: "My mother — my other mother that's gone away — she always told me to work along and not be much expecting to get rich, and then I wouldn't be disappointed if I didn't get rich" (55–56). To a ten-year-old, this is merely theoretical knowledge, but since women as both mothers and wives are supposed to be the ideals for which men strive, their very practicality serves as an ideal source for masculine practicality in business.

As Stowe projected this image in *Uncle Tom's Cabin*, the reins of domestic management should be extended to include business so that feminine pragmatism and morality come to run the world. Neither Warner nor Clemens interpreted sentimental morality in this way. On the contrary, in spite of their repeated complaints about the absurd idealism of masculine speculation, they see women as able only to provide the impetus for men to abandon pure idealism for a pragmatic balance between speculation and hard work. Besides having Laura stand as an example of a woman unable to earn her own fortune, Warner and Clemens also have the moral heroine, Ruth Bolton, fail in her attempts to support her family. She, with "feminine" clarity of insight, sees that her father's speculations may ruin the family's fortunes, and studies medicine in part to be able to support the family when her father's business fails. But when events come to pass as she anticipates, she does not have the stamina. So Warner sends in a finally successful Philip Sterling to marry Ruth and to bail out the Bolton family.

A substantial part of the novel is intended to show the way a young gentleman should grow out of the romanticism of youth into practical and moral adulthood. Here, both Clemens and Warner emphasize the "gentle" part of man. Clemens's comment on the Middle Ground, quoted above, suggests that real gentlemen are bred to civic responsibilities. But both authors worry that gentility too often leads to a kind of romanticism and a consequent withdrawal from practical responsibilities. Clemens puts it most directly when describing the Hawkins's general attitudes toward work and particularly toward women working. They all come to rely on their undeveloped lands as their fortune, because they

> were born and educated dependents. They had never been taught to do anything for themselves, and it did not seem to occur to them to make an attempt now. The girls would not have been permitted to work for a living under any circumstances whatever. It was a Southern family, and of good blood; and for any person except Laura, . . . to have suggested such an idea would have brought upon the suggester the suspicion of being a lunatic. (74)

The authors find nothing wrong with keeping women from working outside the home, but for gentlemen to be born and bred dependents is to give them a false sense of gentility. As Warner complains, "There are many young men . . . in American society . . . who have really been educated for nothing and have let themselves drift, in the hope that they will find somehow, and by some sudden turn of good luck, the golden road to fortune" (455–56).

Philip Sterling, hero of that plot in the novel designed to show the middle way for a gentleman to find fortune and happiness, first appears to the reader as a new Yale graduate who lives in New York City while waiting for his future to call him. He seeks, of course, fame, fortune and happiness. He is already in love with Ruth Bolton, and he dreams of winning her love, but he has no inkling how to realize his imaginings:

> Philip Sterling used to say that if he should seriously set himself to ten years to any one of the dozen projects that were in his brain, he felt that he could be a rich man. He wanted to be rich, he had a sincere desire for a fortune, but for some unaccountable reason he hesitated about addressing himself to the narrow work of getting it. . . . Especially at night in the crowded theatre . . . the world seemed full of opportunities to Philip, and his heart exulted with a conscious ability to take any of its prizes he chose to pluck. Perhaps it was the swimming ease of the acting on stage, where virtue had its reward in three easy acts. (114–15)

Warner seems to be building on Clemens's earlier observation that "One never ceases to make a hero of one's self" (104); at any rate Sterling makes a hero of himself, imagining himself a great writer, a new Horace Greeley, a new Dr. Livingstone. But rather than apply himself so as to reach any of these goals, the most he does is a little scribbling. In an unfortunate hour, he had two or three papers accepted by first-class magazines, at three dollars the printed page, and behold, his vocation was open to him. He would make his mark in literature. Life has no moment so sweet as that in which a young man believes himself called into the immortal ranks of the masters of literature. It is such a noble ambition that it is a pity it has usually such a shallow foundation. (117–18)

On the basis of this slim success, and without, as Warner's sarcasm makes clear, enough ability to do the job, Sterling decides to take up newspaper work:

With his talent he thought he should have little difficulty in getting an editorial position upon a metropolitan newspaper; not that he knew anything about newspaper work, or had the least idea of journalism; he knew he was not fitted for the technicalities of the subordinate departments, but he could write leaders with perfect ease, he was sure. The drudgery of the newspaper office was too distasteful, and besides it would be beneath the dignity of a graduate and a successful magazine writer. He wanted to begin at the top of the ladder. (118)

Suffering from speculative and romantic delusions about his own abilities and about the ease of attaining his desires, Philip simply refuses to work. As the two authors say about almost every character in the book, he "appears to be a little bit visionary, . . . the worst thing in the world for a business man" (276).

When he fails to land any such job at the top of the ladder, Philip snaps up a chance to go to Missouri to help his friend Henry Brierly speculate on a new railroad. Henry, even more of a dreamer than Philip, dismisses the one practical question Philip raises:

"But in what capacity would I go?"
"Well, I'm going as an engineer. You can go as one."
"I don't know an engine from a coal cart."
"Field engineer, civil engineer. You can begin by carrying a rod, and putting down the figures. It's easy enough. I'll show you about that. We'll get Trautwine and some of those books." (120)

Philip assumes that Henry acts as the Lord's agent in giving him his "call," ostensibly to railroad speculation, though time proves that all Brierly does is give Philip the tools by which he can finally apply himself seriously to a profession; discouraged with the wait-and-see life of land speculation in the West, he turns his attention to the engineering books and learns the theory of a new profession (215–16). He gets the chance to practice some of his theory, too, giving him the capacity finally to earn his fortune.

Philip's Western life teaches him the value of experience in more ways than one. He no longer waits for a "call" to extricate himself from doubts about his life's course; he learns that one must "find out by . . . experience what [one's] heart really want[s]" (195). Having learned what he wants, he sets himself about getting it "with an energy and concentration he was capable of" (216). He does this because he has learned, again by experience, though tempered by the morality he learned "at his mother's knee," that speculation is all too often a combination of laziness and fraud. Now, in his search for a fortune, he turns to hard work.

Philip couples his willingness to labor for his fortune with a belief in using his education and understanding to guide his work. When he is hired by the Bolton family to prospect a new piece of property in the wilds of the Appalachians, his study of his profession gives him confidence and faith:

> The landlord at Ilium endeavored to persuade Philip to hire the services of a witch-hazel professor of that region, who could walk over the land with his wand and tell him infallibly whether it contained coal, and exactly where the strata ran. But Philip preferred to trust to his own study of the country, and his knowledge of the geological formation. He spent a month in traveling over the land and making calculations; and made up his mind that a fine vein of coal ran through the mountain about a mile from the railroad, and that the place to run in a tunnel was half way towards its summit. . . . It was true that there were no outcroppings of coal at the place, and the people at Ilium said he "mought as well dig for plug terbaccer there," but Philip had great faith in the uniformity of nature's operations in ages past, and he had no doubt that he should strike at this spot the rich vein that had made the fortune of the Golden Briar Company. (272–73)

Here he uses his powers of reason and observation, coupled with his cultivated understanding of nature's laws, to determine his course of action.

Philip finds, to his chagrin, that his faith was a bit too sanguine at first, because it was based solely on his theoretical knowledge of his profession. He learns the profession fully with experience:

> There is no difficulty in digging a hole in the ground, if you have money enough to pay for the digging, but those who try this sort of work are always surprised at the large amount of money necessary to make a small hole. The earth is never willing to yield one product, hidden in her bosom, without an equivalent for it. And when a person asks of her coal, she is quite apt to require gold in exchange. (440)

Here he experiences a "natural law" of compensation and of work. This knowledge gives him the heart to push on long past the point where others' capital makes digging the hole easy. Philip finally has to dig the hole with his own hands before he strikes the coal that makes his fortune.

So while Philip does speculate in mining, he succeeds where others fail because he balances his aspirations with theoretical knowledge, and augments his theory with practical experience, and makes all these possible through diligent application of all his powers to the task of earning his fortune. He has luck, it is true, so it would appear that virtue in this novel, as in so many sentimental stories, has its reward, but it takes two full volumes rather than three easy acts, and virtue deserves its reward because virtue earns its reward.

Clemens wrote the parts of the novel that serve as the cautionary counterpoint to Philip's hard-earned maturity, with Washington Hawkins serving as Philip's opposite. Hawkins is characterized as an "evidently . . . pretty fair theoretical book-keeper, and experience would soon harden theory into practice" (92). But raised by his father to count on riches from the ultimate sale of "the Tennessee land," Washington never can settle down into work. He leaves his job time and again under the spell of Colonel Sellers's visionary mind, goes to Washington, D.C., to lobby for the sale of his family's land, watches helplessly as the speculative bubble bursts, and finally returns to the West and his fiancée as a thoroughly chastened and prematurely old man. Of all the pure dreamers in the book, only Sellers never loses heart, though he never makes a dime.

Of course, both Washington Hawkins and Colonel Sellers, caught up so in their own private dreams, can never see the corruption of those around them. Naive dreamers themselves, they are blind to the possibility of any other motives that people might have. Even the more practical and eminently moral Mr. Bolton cannot tell if the smooth-talking speculators he frequently deals with are "sharpers, or fools." But Clemens and Warner profess to know that at least many of them are sharpers who use the public's sentimentality to manipulate affairs to their own profit. For instance, Clemens has two of his confidence men explain how they work the public for money and votes respectively:

> Perhaps the biggest thing we've done in the advertising line was to get an officer of the U.S. government, of perfectly Himalayan official altitude, to write up our little internal improvement for a religious paper of enormous circulation — I tell you that makes our bonds go handsomely among the pious poor. Your religious paper is by far the best vehicle for a thing of this kind, because they'll "lead" your article and put it in the midst of the reading matter; and if it's got a few Scripture quotations in it, and some temperance platitudes and a bit of gush here and there about Sunday Schools, and a sentimental

snuffle now and then about "God's precious ones, the honest hard-handed poor," it works the nation like a charm, my dear sir, and never a man suspects that it is an advertisement. (256–57)

Or consider this diatribe that Clemens put in the mouth of Senator Dilsworthy:

> Give us newspaper persecution enough, and we are safe. Vigorous persecution will alone carry a bill sometimes, dear. . . . It changes the tide of public opinion. The great public is weak-minded; the great public is sentimental; the great public always turns around and weeps for an odious murderer, and prays for him, and carries flowers to his prison and besieges the governor with appeals to his clemency, as soon as the papers begin to howl for that man's blood. – In a word, the great putty-headed public loves to "gush," and there is no such darling opportunity to gush as a case of persecution affords. (392–93)

In both of these cases, Clemens rejoins his frequent attack on sentimentality, because its emotionalism is inappropriate to public policy. It is, says Clemens, appropriate to the domestic sphere as the copious tears and platitudes about home and hearth make clear throughout the book. But while sentimentality can be the source of morality—what the con men call "sentimental squeamishness" against participating in public frauds—for it to have value in influencing public policy, it must be more than "mere matters of temperament"; it must be backed up by "habits and principles" (366).

Thus when the sovereign people turn their attention to public behavior, they have responsibilities to balance emotions with reason and moral precepts with policy, and to sacrifice individual needs to the good of the nation:

> Philip's conscience told him that it was his plain duty to carry the matter into the courts, even with the certainty of defeat. He confessed that neither he nor any citizen had a right to consult his own feelings or conscience in a case where a law of the land had been violated before his own eyes. He confessed that every citizen's first duty in such a case is to put aside his own business and devote his time and his best efforts to seeing that the infraction is promptly punished; and he knew that no country can be well governed unless its citizens as a body keep religiously before their minds that they are the guardians of the law, and that the law officers are only the machinery for its execution, nothing more. (268–69)

Philip believes he should subordinate his selfish feelings to a higher sense of "duty" on which he can act only if he keeps it clearly before his "mind." In their conception of the Common Sense balance between reason and feelings, Warner and Clemens disagree with Stowe about the relative value of emotion as the proper guide to moral public behavior.

Between selfishness on one hand and sentimental naïveté on the other, the nation, according to Warner and Clemens, is going to the dogs. Their solution to the problems of the public sphere is the same as their solution to the problems of the private: restore a balance between idealism and pragmatism, between natural ability and education, between precept and practice, between reason and feeling, between self-indulgence and selflessness. In other words, they try to promote what by then had become a conservative middle ground between the growingly divergent extremes of moral philosophy.

V

In trying to promote an ideal of life rather than just trying to exploit ideas for the sake of humor, Clemens demonstrates a serious acceptance of Common Sense moral philosophy. Neither his new medium of literature nor his belonging to the Hartford community caused him to take seriously this moral agenda; he chose both because he already accepted the basic Common Sense justification of literature. But in the intellectual life of the Hartford community, a life as varied and vigorous in its social uses of literature and learning as the ideal Warner and Clemens expressed in their novel, Clemens found an impetus to deepen his understanding of moral philosophy in a serious study.

Part of this impetus came from his membership in Hartford's Monday Evening Club, a Franklinesque "junto" of prominent Hartford men who met from seven to fourteen times yearly to read and discuss original essays. On the authority of Kenneth Andrews's 1950 study, *Nook Farm: Mark Twain's Hartford Circle*, the impact of this Club on Clemens's thinking has been generally dismissed.[12] According to Andrews:

> One area in which the Nook Farm Neighborhood opened into the larger community was the organized intellectual life, of which the literary men were the acknowledged leaders. The zest with which cultural development was pursued reflects again the congeniality of the society and the multiple sources of its satisfactions. In comparison with these social benefits, the intellectual advancement attained was in itself negligible. (102)

The implied premise, that fun and serious "intellectual advancement" are incompatible, is, I hope, invalid; in Clemens's case, anyway, it seems more likely that he would pursue intellectual questions with zest if he had a pleasant social forum in which to examine them.

In any event, it seems absurd to dismiss the group as intellectually insignificant if one looks at the titles of the papers delivered.[13] Indeed the titles of some papers, such as "Moose and Caribou Hunting" (January 10, 1876), do suggest that the group treated trivial topics on occasion, but most of the papers deal with questions of political, moral, or philosophical importance. Consider, for instance, "Immortality" (April 4, 1876), "Is Restriction of Suffrage in this Country Desirable?" (January 29, 1877), "The Province of Legislation in Enforcing Moral Duties" (October 27, 1873), "John Stuart Mill" (December 15, 1873), "Sphere of Influence of the Pulpit" (January 29, 1874), "Reverence" (November 15, 1875), "Calvinism" (December 17, 1877), "Agnosticism" (March 14, 1871), "The Proper Limits of Common School Education and its Defects in Hartford" (February 11, 1878), and "Conscience" (March 20, 1876).

These topics are not light, and considering that the group's membership included Horace Bushnell and his theological followers Nathaniel Burton, E. P. Parker, and Joseph Twichell, all Congregational ministers; several faculty members and the president of Hartford's Trinity College; James Hammond Trumbull, listed in the club's roster as "Historian, Philologist, bibliographer; First Librarian, Watkinson Library of Reference," who also collaborated with Clemens and Warner on *The Gilded Age* by supplying Chapter mottoes[14]; the owners and editors of the Hartford *Courant*, including Warner; and five fellows of the Yale Corporation, it seems likely that these subjects were treated authoritatively even if not exhaustively. If nothing else, Clemens must have learned from Club members what to read in his approach to almost any subject of intellectual importance to him. It comes as no surprise that Clemens read some of the fundamental texts of moral philosophy during his years in Hartford.

The last of the titles I noted above helps demonstrate yet another way in which the Club aided Clemens's intellectual development. William Hamersley's March 20, 1876 essay titled "Conscience" was delivered just three meetings after Clemens presented his "The Facts Concerning the Recent Carnival of Crime in Connecticut," his first extended examination of conscience. In letters to Howells, Clemens called the piece an "exasperating metaphysical extravaganza" (*MTHL* 123) that would "bring out considerable discussion among the gentlemen of the Club" (*MTHL* 119).[15] If Hamersley's title is a valid indicator, then the discussion spilled over into other meetings, allowing Clemens to take into account considered responses to his ideas.[16] Such response suggests, too, that the members took their thinking as well as their socializing seriously.

At least Clemens took the Club meetings seriously. Even Andrews admits that Clemens used the Club as a forum for trying out new ideas, none more important to the development of his moral philosophy than his ideas about what motivates human behavior. By January 1876, when he wrote "The Facts Concerning the Recent Carnival of Crime in Connecticut," he had already read for the first time W. E. H. Lecky's *History of European Morals from Charlemagne to the Present* (1869).[17] Few books had such impact on Clemens's thinking and writing as Lecky's, which he first discovered when he was working on *Tom Sawyer*.

In reading Lecky, Clemens found a concise statement of the major controversies of Common Sense ethics. Lecky, seeing the world through the dualistic lenses of the Common Sense tradition, divided all moral thinkers into two camps, what he called the "sentimental" and the "utilitarian." Any ethical system that argued that human beings have some innate sense of right or wrong he lumped with the sentimental; any that argued that morality is merely learned he lumped with the utilitarian. That he would willingly classify the stoic Marcus Aurelius with Adam Smith and David Hume on the one hand or Epicurus, Hobbes, and John Stuart Mill on the other shows how insistent was Common Sense dualism and how its primary mode of categorization was by the definition of conscience. Lecky wrote his history to support the sentimental point of view, but in articulating the counter-arguments he gave Clemens a full explanation of both ways of looking at conscience.

Clemens probably owned and marked a copy of the two-volume *History* as early as 1874 (Gribben, *Library*). His marginal comments indicate that he usually disagreed with Lecky, though he wanted Lecky to be right: "It is so noble and beautiful a book, that I don't want it to have even trivial faults in it" (quoted in Walter Blair 131). We do not, however, know when he marked the volume we now have, so we do not know when he came to disagree with Lecky and how fully he ever did disagree in practice rather than just in conception. As Baetzhold points out, Clemens tended to waffle on many of Lecky's points, trying to conflate the intuitionist desire to educate the sensitivity of the moral sense with the utilitarian belief that morality was wholly trained. At any rate, when writing *Tom Sawyer*, Clemens combined some of the precepts that Lecky argued for with his long-held understanding of the importance of intention in judging moral behavior to show that harum-scarum Tom Sawyer was, in sentimental terms, really a good child.

Essentially, *Tom Sawyer* continued Clemens's arguments with Sunday School literature in which model children always get rewarded and children who step out of the straight and narrow path get seriously punished — punished not in proportion to their "crimes," but because "the child is but a prophecy of the man" (*MTS* 67), and therefore early influences cultivate the moral proclivities that lead to success or failure. In Lecky's terms, such an insistence on outcome over intention shows a confusion of utilitarian ethics with sentimental ethics. The best sentimental moralists, such as Adam Smith, acknowledged that good intentions did not always yield positive results, but insisted that, in the development of moral character, intention was far more significant that consequence.

Clemens used this argument about himself when courting Olivia Langdon. The Langdons were concerned about his reputation as a Western reprobate. Clemens admitted that he drank and swore out West, but insisted that he never did anything unredeemable, and he excused his "wildness" as mere high spirits: "the intent was blameless — & it is the intent, and not the act that should be judged, after all. Even men who take life are judged by this rule only" (*LLMT* 39; see also 25–26 and 36).

The Adventures of Tom Sawyer argues the same for boys, who Clemens once said should be deaf, dumb and lame in order to prevent their viciousness. Having adopted the sentimentalist's view of family and childhood, however, he needed to redeem boys as well as girls, finding in their behavior nothing more harmful than youthful high spirits. As he has Aunt Polly put it when she thinks Tom is dead: "He warn't bad, so to say — only mischeevous. Only just giddy, and harum-scarum, you know. He warn't any more responsible than a colt. He never meant any harm, and he was the best-hearted boy that ever was" (128). The three chapters following this speech culminate in the proof that Tom's heart was good in that he at least intended to tell Polly that, rather than being dead, he was just off pirating. When she finally proves this to be true, she bursts into tears and says "I could forgive the boy, now, if he'd committed a million sins" (152).

Under Lecky's tutelage, Clemens found a way better to forgive the sins of boys than just to assert their fundamental good nature.[18] In explaining the operation of the moral sense as a combination of imagination and memory yielding sympathy, and sympathy yielding good intentions, Lecky gave Clemens a way of understanding the development of morality in childhood play.[19] Tom, like all children, does little in life except exercise his imagination in play—or in an effort to lie his way out of a scrape. His imagination works for the most part without positive moral purpose, as in the beginning of Chapter Twenty, when, rebuffed in his effort to make up with Becky Thatcher, he mopes "into the school yard, wishing she were a boy, and imagining how he would trounce her if she were" (153). As is usually the case, his imaginings are the inconstant effect of his emotions, as for that matter are all of his actions as "his mood always determined his manner" (153).

Shortly thereafter, when Tom sees Becky tear the color plate in the schoolmaster's prized anatomy book, he finds himself baffled at the girl's fear to be whipped in school. After all, his experience of a licking makes him scorn the master's rod; unable to imagine himself in Becky's situation, he finds himself having relatively little sympathy. But he does see that her anxiety is real; he does care for her; and he slowly begins to imagine that such punishment might be different for a girl. When finally Dobbins discovers the torn page, "Tom shot a glance at Becky. He had seen a hunted and helpless rabbit look as she did, with a gun leveled at its head" (155). At this point, Tom couples his imagination with his own experience: he has seen a rabbit about to be shot, and he imagines Becky's circumstances to be parallel. This evokes his sympathy in a very powerful way, forcing him to act to remove her from what he imagines to be for her a deadly danger. He "confesses" to her crime and takes her punishment.

In a conventional Sunday School book, self-sacrifice is of course the highest good, but would be rewarded not punished. It also could not be "evil" in its means, as Tom's lie was, by conventional standards, an evil means to a noble intention. In spite of his public punishment, Tom does get a private reward: "the gratitude, the adoration that shone upon him out of poor Becky's eyes seemed pay enough for a hundred floggings" (156). This gratitude reinforces the value of the spontaneous act, but Clemens makes clear that Tom, as much as he usually loves to "show off," does not act here in order to earn praise; he sacrifices himself out of sympathy. Out of the hodge-podge of childhood emotions and imaginings he develops the essential ingredients of moral behavior. Clemens thus outflanks his Sunday School-book enemies on the sentimental side.

But Clemens did not rest with the sentimentalist's model of conscience. Sentimentalists held that the moral sense pained a person only when he or she either planned to do or did something wrong. When he or she did something right, the moral sense supposedly felt pleasure. As the highest sense, the moral sense supposedly rectified all conflicting desires in the human organism by yielding the most intense feelings. In his writings after *Tom Sawyer*, Clemens acknowledged the intensity of moral feelings, but suggested that they yielded only pain because they inconsistently identified all behavior as wrong behavior. Yet, if moral intuitions of sympathy created the beneficent intentions that led to moral behavior, then why should the proddings of conscience be so painful and inconsistent?

This is essentially the conundrum Clemens raised for the Monday Evening Club in "The Facts Concerning the Recent Carnival of Crime in Connecticut." One answer, which Clemens at this point did not seriously consider, was that the universe itself was not fashioned according to consistent moral principles, so that no innate sensitivity could make human behavior consistently moral. Such ideas would come in the last two decades of his life. At this early point in his career, he turned on the very idea of conscience itself, questioning the two possible models of conscience that Lecky postulated by juxtaposing them with the Calvinist model of conscience in order to cast doubt on all three possibilities.

"The Carnival of Crime" challenges the sentimental model of conscience as a moral sense by suggesting that the conscience is fundamentally at odds with the person it belongs to and is appointed by "higher authority." This challenge is in keeping with the etymology of the word conscience itself, suggesting knowledge of one's self along with God's knowledge of the self. In the older Christian tradition, this knowledge was never for a "natural man" a pleasant knowledge. As Henry James, Sr., put it:

> Conscience is the badge of a fallen nature. It is only after we have eaten of the tree of knowledge of good and evil, that its voice is heard investing us with responsibility. . . . It was never designed as a minister of peace and reconciliation with God, but only as a voice of disunion and menace. It was never designed, according to the apostle, to give a knowledge of righteousness, but only a knowledge of sin, that every mouth might be stopped, and ALL THE WORLD BECOME GUILTY before God. (144–46)

James essentially repeats the Calvinist line about conscience, that it is a vengeful voice that chastises the natural man for his total depravity. Without conscience, man "must surely have forgotten the very name of God" (145).

The conscience as Clemens depicts it resembles the Calvinist model of conscience in important ways. For one thing, when his conscience is first made visible to him, the narrator has an "incomprehensible sense of being legally and legitimately under his authority," and without doubt the conscience is an external being, in fact a spirit "appointed by authority," rather than an internal sense or intuition. For another, this conscience will not grant any pleasure:

> "Is there any way of satisfying that malignant invention which is called a conscience?" . . .
> "Well, none that I propose to tell you my son. Ass! I don't care what act you may turn your hand to, I can straightway whisper a word in your ear and make you think you have committed a dreadful meanness. It is my business — and my joy — to make you repent of everything you do." ("Facts" 316–17)

Surely this conscience is "a voice of disunion and menace," designed to castigate all human behaviors, whether right or wrong.

Calvinists were concerned, however, not with carnivals of crime, but with the sin to which the flesh is naturally heir. Unlike the Calvinist conscience, the one in Clemens's tale is appointed not to remind man of his fallen state, but to "improve" him and to regulate society. Thus, while this tale's conscience acts the part of a Calvinist conscience, its purpose of "improvement" implies an Arminian conception of salvation by degree through gradual change of behavior. In this purpose, this conscience is distinctly anti-Calvinist and much more in line with either a sentimental or a utilitarian definition of human motivation.

But while the conscience's "purpose . . . is to improve the man" and by improving the man to improve society, consciences

> are merely disinterested agents. . . . We obey orders and leave the consequences where they belong. But I am willing to admit this much: we do crowd the orders a trifle when we get a chance, which is most of the time. We enjoy it. We are instructed to remind a man a few times of an error; and I don't mind acknowledging that we try to give pretty good measure. (315)

Here, consciences themselves are motivated by the pleasure principle; hence, while a higher authority may govern their purpose and while that purpose may actually be fulfilled by the actions of consciences — as the list of virtuous people with powerful consciences attests and as the story's conclusion shows the conscienceless narrator indulging in his new business of crime and enjoying it as much as "savage" consciences enjoy harrowing people to suicide — the behavior of consciences themselves is marked by wild moral inconsistency.

The "devilish" egotism of the conscience, according to the narrator, explains this:

> I think I begin to see now why you have always been a trifle inconsistent with me. In your anxiety to get all the juice you can out of a sin, you make a man repent of it in three or four different ways. For instance, you found fault with me for lying to that tramp, and I suffered over that. But it was only yesterday that I told a tramp the square truth, to wit, that, it being regarded as bad citizenship to encourage vagrancy, I would give him nothing. What did you do then? Why you made me say to myself, "Ah, it would have been so much kinder and more blameless to ease him off with a little white lie, and send him away feeling that if he could not have bread, the gentle treatment was at least something to be grateful for!" Well, I suffered all day about that. Three days before I had fed a tramp, and fed him freely, supposing it a virtuous act. Straight off you said, "Oh, false citizen, to have fed a tramp!" and I suffered as usual. I gave a tramp work; you objected to it . . . Next I refused a tramp work; you objected to that. Next I proposed to kill a tramp; you kept me awake all night, oozing remorse at every pore. Sure I was going to be right this time, I sent the next tramp away with my benediction; and I wish you may live as long as I do, if you didn't make me smart all night again because I didn't kill him. (316)[20]

Neither the Calvinist nor the sentimentalist version of conscience could account for such absurd inconsistencies as this; this conscience resembles the ego in its purely selfish pursuit of pleasure even in fulfilling its assigned function.

In fact, the parallels between the narrator after he kills his conscience and the conscience itself are striking. The conscience describes himself as the narrator's "most pitiless enemy" (312), showing that, while consciences may force people to have pity for one another, these spirits themselves have none, and implying that all consciences are humankind's collective worst enemy. When the narrator frees himself of his conscience, he, too, loses all compassion for human beings, expressing willingness to kill his Aunt Mary, the person he "loved and honored most in all the world" (302), as readily as people against whom he held grudges. The narrator becomes an enemy to his own kind.

Most important, the conscience repeatedly describes his malignant work as a joy. The biggest conscience in the region so loves his work that "he never sleeps. . . . Night and day you can find him pegging away at Smith, panting with his labor, sleeves rolled up, countenance all alive with enjoyment" (321). The narrator, when free of his conscience at tale's end, similarly develops a profession of deviltry and takes tremendous pleasure from it:

Since that day my life is all bliss. Bliss, unalloyed bliss. . . . I settled all my old outstanding scores, and began the world anew. I killed thirty-eight persons during the first two weeks—all of them on account of ancient grudges. I burned a dwelling that interrupted my view. I swindled a widow and some orphans out of their last cow, which is a very good one, though' not a thoroughbred, I believe. I have also committed scores of crimes, of various kinds, and have enjoyed my work exceedingly, whereas it would formerly have broken my heart and turned my hair gray, I have no doubt. (325)

Early in the story, the narrator says that "only a conscience could find pleasure in heaping agony upon a spirit like that" (321), but by story's end the narrator is just as "devilish." One of the implicit answers to Clemens's conundrum, then, is that the conscience reflects all of a human being's "malignant" (316) traits in order to balance them in action.

In killing his conscience, the narrator suddenly transforms his life, much as a conversion experience is said to transform the life of the regenerate. The language here echoes the language of conversion, with the narrator declaring that he "began the world anew" and found himself living a life of "unalloyed bliss." But this is of course a reverse conversion, a conversion from part saint/part sinner to pure sinner. By killing off God's agent of castigation, the natural man frees himself of divine influence and falls into the pure bliss of ego gratification, even tormenting or killing other human beings for the pleasure of making a business of it.[21]

Thus does the story attack utilitarian ideas of morality by suggesting that unbridled ego yields purely evil selfishness; it also seems to attack the Calvinist idea of conscience by conflating it with utilitarian selfishness. If the story did only this, it would endorse the sentimental conception of conscience that so many of Clemens's Hartford neighbors accepted. But he conflates the sentimental conscience with the Calvinist as readily as he identifies Calvinism with selfishness. For one, as I mentioned earlier, this tale does show conscience serving the purpose of public morality. More importantly, the way Clemens shows the conscience as being trained into effectiveness echoes sentimental ideas of developing the moral sense.

The narrator's conscience reveals that it is born with the man, suggesting that it is part of the spiritual equipment of the person, even though a child's conscience is underdeveloped, "thirteen inches high, and rather sluggish, when he was two years old—as nearly all of us are at that age" (321). Consciences can grow either direction from this nascent state, depending both on how well the conscience plays its cards and on how willing the ego is either to acquiesce or to rebel against its proddings:

> Some of us grow one way and some the other. You had a large conscience once; if you've a small conscience now I reckon there are reasons for it. However, both of us are to blame, you and I. You see, you used to be conscientious about a great many things; morbidly so, I may say. . . . Well, I took a great interest in my work, and I so enjoyed the anguish which certain pet sins of yours afflicted you with that I kept pelting at you until I rather overdid the matter. You began to rebel. Of course I began to lose ground, then, and shrivel a little — diminish in stature, get moldy, and grow deformed. The more I weakened, the more stubbornly you fastened on to those particular sins, till at last the places on my person that represent those vices became as callous as shark-skin. (318–19)

The conscience describes other consciences ranging from a microscopic one to a particularly beautiful one so large it needs to live outdoors. Significantly, the narrator's conscience has grown callous, that is, he has lost his sensitivity to the moral character of certain kinds of behavior. In his fanciful way, then, Clemens describes the growth or demise of conscientious behavior as a function of cultivating moral sensitivity, much as sentimental moralists would.

But at the same time that this passage relies on a sentimental definition of conscience, it also challenges the validity of this definition. That the conscience says certain of the narrator's pet sins "afflicted him with anguish" suggests that the feeling of remorse is innate to the human being, while it is the conscience's function simply to bring the remorse to mind. Clemens here hints that there might be a difference between the conscience and the moral sense, though sentimental moralists usually defined them as the same thing.[22] But Clemens found this conception at odds with the operation of conscience as he felt it. In fact, insofar as he accepted the idea that conscience is external to the man, he found no reason that the human being could not have both a conscience and a moral sense. Nevertheless, when the narrator kills his conscience, he kills his sympathy, too. Clemens thus asks whether conscience and the moral sense are indeed the same thing, or whether the conscience is only a necessary external spiritual force needed to activate the moral sense.

Here Clemens's characteristic mode of thinking by juxtaposing conflicting voices and ideas calls into doubt the validity and value of all three definitions of conscience. In his letter to Howells in which he describes the piece, he makes clear the irony of the title by italicizing the word "facts"; the only fact the piece makes clear is that the educated in Hartford, as well as

throughout the country, were confused about what motivated moral behavior. His Hartford peers apparently could not solve this conundrum to
his satisfaction, because he turned repeatedly to the problem of human motivation throughout his career, especially in *Adventures of Huckleberry Finn*,
which he began writing within a few months of presenting his "Facts."

VI

Clemens's voracious reading did nothing to help him solve this or any other
conundrum of moral philosophy. While he seems over the 1870s to have actively tried to ground his thinking in the fundamental texts of moral philosophy, his reading, by its very eclectic nature, began to increase his doubts.
In many cases, the very incompatibility of different bits of knowledge he
gleaned from his reading did more than cast doubt on the Common Sense
compromise; it destroyed it, especially when he applied what he learned of
the "certainties" of science to the vague hypotheses of metaphysics.

Actually, science had long threatened Clemens's attempt to climb to
artistic, cultural and intellectual respectability. In his courtship letters, for
instance, his interest in science foreshadows the intellectual difficulty of his
efforts to convert himself to conventional Christianity. He no doubt took
his efforts at conversion seriously; the body of his letters to Olivia leaves
little doubt. Sentiments such as "We shall never be separated on earth, Livy;
& let us pray that we may not in Heaven" (*LLMT* 109), written in
September of 1869, show that he at least tried to accept conventional
definitions of the afterlife. But just four months later, he wrote a long letter
about an astronomy book he had been reading, and in this letter he
interjects virtually no small talk, no endearments, and none of the Christian
platitudes in which he often couched his endearments.

The tone of the letter, on the contrary, shows Clemens's rapt fascination with science as a different and perhaps better way to explain the origins
of the earth than those given by Christian metaphysics.

> I have been reading some new arguments to prove that the world is very old &
> that the six days of creation were six immensely long periods. For instance,
> according to Genesis, the stars were made when the world was, yet this writer
> mentions the significant fact that there are stars within reach of our telescopes
> whose light requires 50,000 years to traverse the wastes of space & come to our
> earth. And so, if we made a tour through space ourselves, might we not, in
> some remote era of the future, meet & greet the first lagging rays of stars that

started on their weary visit to us a million years ago? — rays that are outcast &
homeless, now, their parent stars crumbled to nothingness & swept from the
firmament five hundred thousand years after these journeying rays departed —
stars whose peoples lived their little lives, & laughed & wept, hoped & feared,
sinned and perished, bewildering ages since these vagrant twinklings went
wandering through the solemn solitudes of space? (133)

And so on for almost twice again as much, concluding one paragraph by
quoting scripture, "Verily, What is Man, that he should be considered of
God" (134).

The tone of this piece is quite at odds with the usual tone of his letters;
he found himself swept up in the subject, even to the point not only of
writing by hand so many pages on a distinctly unromantic subject, but also
of violating the tenor of his entire correspondence with Olivia. His enthusiasm has its own conventionality, of course, as he uses the vast panorama of
nature as a way of appreciating the greatness of God's works. But enlightenment theologians, as much as they used the book of nature to reject
interpreting the Bible literally, evoked the moral sublime in order to exalt
humankind as the apex of this fabulous creation, not as totally "insignificant" (133). Thus, while the language never explicitly suggests doubts
about the existence of God as a creator of the universe, it does cast doubt on
the entire fabric of American Christianity.

But generally through the 1870s, Clemens tried to hold the Common
Sense compromise together both by gently satirizing scientific certitude
and by rebutting the idea that science destroys idealism. In "Old Times on
the Mississippi," for instance, he mocks scientific efforts to extrapolate a
small amount of data gathered over a few years into grand theories about
origins and destinies. In describing how the Mississippi's channel decreases
in length every time one of its meandering loops gets cut off at the base, he
writes:

> Now, if I wanted to be one of those ponderous scientific people, and "let on"
> to prove what had occurred in the remote past by what had occurred in a given
> time in the recent past, or what will occur in the far future by what has
> occurred in late years, what an opportunity is here! Geology never had such a
> chance, nor such exact data to argue from! Nor "development of species"
> either! Glacial epochs are great things, but they are vague — vague. Please
> observe:
>
> In the space of one hundred and seventy-six years the Lower Mississippi has
> shortened itself . . . an average of a trifle over one mile and a third per year.
> Therefore, any calm person, who is not blind or idiotic, can see that in the Old
> Oolithic Silurian Period, just a million years ago next November, the Lower

Mississippi was upward of one million three hundred thousand miles long, and stuck out over the Gulf of Mexico like a fishing rod. And by the same token any person can see that seven hundred and forty-two years from now the Lower Mississippi will be only a mile and three-quarters long, and Cairo and new Orleans will have joined their streets together, and be plodding comfortably along under a single mayor and a mutual board of aldermen. There is something fascinating about science. One gets such wholesale returns of conjecture out of such a trifling investment of fact. (*LOM* 155–56)

His terms "ponderous" and "conjecture" cast strong doubts on the entire enterprise of science, attacking the persons of scientists as well as their techniques. Particularly, he attacks the analogical mode of thought inherent in extrapolation. To extrapolate from a limited bit of data, one must assume a consistency of states of affairs that transcends time and place. Clemens reduces this faith in analogy to the absurd by applying the analogical method to a case in which the analogy physically cannot hold through time because of the limits of space.[23]

Nonetheless, the remainder of the series of articles tries to show that "the science of piloting" is also an art, and Clemens freely analogizes from his mastery of this art and science to all arts and sciences. He repeats the platitude that science, by revealing the secrets of nature, causes one to lose his awareness of its beauty. But at the same time, he captures a new beauty, a new sublimity, in human mastery of nature. Essentially, he sentimentalizes science in order to reconcile the material and the ideal.[24] But Clemens's fascination for astronomy in particular kept leading him away from the comfortable compromises of Common Sense theology. At about the same time he was reading William Paley's *Natural Theology*, one of the old standby efforts to reconcile materialistic science and spiritual belief, he was also reading Amédée Victor Guillemin's *The Heavens: An Illustrated Handbook of Popular Astronomy* (1878).[25] His comments on Paley's tome are all derisive (Gribben, *Library*); on Guillemin's book, they are all rapt expressions of awe or are working notes to add to his most recent incarnation of "Captain Wakeman's Visit to Heaven."

"Captain Wakeman's Visit to Heaven" was a very important expression of Clemens's moral philosophy, so important that he did not dare publish it when he wrote it for fear of ruining his reputation with the devout. The tale started innocuously enough in 1868 after a conversation with Captain Ned Wakeman. After talking to Wakeman on shipboard during his return to California to secure the rights to his Holy Land travel letters, Clemens first jotted down, he said, a version of one of Wakeman's dreams about visiting heaven.[26] Clemens was fascinated with Wakeman as a character: his speech was colorful, his ignorance profound, and the gaps in his ignorance were all capriciously filled by his own peculiar course of study, mostly of the Bible without any help from professional commentators. Accordingly, his interpretations disproved the liberal Christian belief that the Bible spoke best to individual believers; Clemens found Wakeman's interpretations so peculiar, and so incongruously larded with sailor's profanity, that they undermined Christian belief. Wakeman also was an excellent Captain, a real scientist in his trade and a marvelous leader, making him the kind of exceptional man whom Clemens found interesting throughout his career.[27]

In any event, what started out as merely an outrageous dream became, in 1869, the seed for Clemens's satirical attack on Elizabeth Stuart Phelps's *The Gates Ajar*. The blasphemous but pious Wakeman struck Clemens as the perfect foil to Phelps's perfectly correct and pious characters, and the dream seemed a good starting place to reveal the absurdity of Phelps's vision of heaven. Clemens redrafted the piece three times before 1878, but apparently destroyed these early drafts. After extensive discussions with Howells about the piece, he wrote virtually all the manuscript we now have between 1878 and 1880.[28]

Phelps's book, a major best-seller in 1868, tries to describe heaven in accordance with the principles of analogy laid down by Joseph Butler in his *Analogy of Religion*. The heroine of Phelps's story, having lost her brother in the Civil War, is inconsolable because, according to the Calvinistic tenets of her religion, she has no chance of seeing her brother again. Her aunt and niece arrive just in time to catechize her about the real way of God as can be discerned by the organization of His earthly domains. Life on earth is merely a transitional period in which we learn the ways of God through the signs of nature, with, of course, a little help from the Bible. Nature teaches that heaven will be essentially like earth, only with no pain or suffering, both of which are designed to make us willing to exchange earthly connections for heavenly love. The main point of the story is that human beings will be rejoined in heaven, never to part again.[29]

Clemens, in his skepticism about heaven generally, took Phelps's main point as one of the primary targets of his satire. Echoing Phelps's reliance on dialogue between an older person who knows heaven and a younger one who has yet to learn the ways of the afterworld, Clemens introduces Wakeman to "an old bald-headed angel by the name of Sandy McWilliams" (*Report* 43), who stands in for the author.[30] McWilliams explains to Wakeman that in heaven people grow and change as they do on earth. As

Wakeman points out, while this makes "heaven pretty comfortable in one way, . . . [it] play[s] mischief with it in another."

> "Imagine a sweet young mother seeing her little baby die, twenty years ago, & keeping her heart from breaking by saying a million times, through her tears, 'I shall see my darling again in heaven' — & imagine that mother soaring into this place now, crazy with hunger to get that child in her arms again — & suppose — "
>
> "Sh! — hold still," says Sandy, "I've see it a hundred times. I had an instance last week. Mildred Rushmore — neighbor of ours below — lost a baby sixteen months old, a couple of years before I died. It was her first — she was about 15 years old — & it seemed as if she would go stark mad with the grief of it. . . . All the comfort she could get was out of those very words, 'I shall see my child in heaven — I shall see her in heaven & there we'll be parted no more forever.' — & then she would break down & wail & cry again.
>
> "Well last week, Mildred died & arrived here; I was passing by that house yonder when I heard the whir of wings, & down she lit by me and fell flat. I lifted her up & brushed her off. . . .
>
> "She was all aglow, her eyes were dancing. 'My child!' she says, 'take me to my child! O, take me to my baby, take me to my darling!'
>
> "Just that minute, out of that house steps a woman of about 30, with 5 children following behind her.
>
> " 'This is your baby,' says I, — your daughter, I mean — she is Mrs. McLaughlin, now, & these are her children.'
>
> "The poor old thing stopped stock still, her eyes stared glassy as a corpse's, & her wings drooped till they trailed the ground; never did I see anybody so stricken. She moaned out —
>
> " 'This is my sweet lost baby? — O, there is some dreadful mistake, some cruel mistake! — Take me back to the grave — O, please, I cannot bear to live.' "[31]

The ability to grow and change, perfectly analogous to life on earth, makes the possibility of rejoining in heaven a dubious consolation.

Worse, it suggests the possibility of pain in heaven. By analogy to life on earth, of course, pain would have to exist in heaven. Another of Wakeman's interlocutors, again speaking for the author, explains why:

> There's plenty of pain here — but it don't kill. There's plenty of suffering here, but it don't last. You see, happiness ain't a thing in itself — it's only a contrast with something that ain't pleasant. . . . As soon as the novelty is over and the force of the contrast dulled, it ain't happiness any longer, and you have to get something fresh. (*Report* 42)

In both of these cases, Clemens challenges Phelps's conclusions about heaven by using her methodology. He simply presses the analogy between heaven and earth much further than she in order to imply the invalidity of some of her conclusions.

Primarily, he accuses her of having a narrow mind, of failing to assemble enough evidence to draw proper analogies between heaven and earth. When describing how Mrs. Rushmore gets over her disappointment at not being rejoined to her baby, who incidentally has developed a consuming interest in astronomy and therefore has nothing to talk about with her ignorant mother, McWilliams explains that she

> has got acquainted with a lot of simple-minded, harmless, ignorant Jersey people, — regular gossips — and they get together every day & pull other people's reputations to pieces, & slander the elect in general, wholesale & retail, & have a noble good time. Much she will be bothered about her lost child a month from now. (*Report* xvi)

Wakeman is shocked that they "deal in that kind of gossip in heaven," but McWilliams explains that heaven wouldn't be heaven without it, implying that slander is one of the chief joys on earth. Clemens does not say whether drinking, gambling, theft, murder, adultery, and other sources of human pleasure will also exist in heaven, but in pushing the analogy on the point of slander, he suggests that heaven will have vice as well as virtue. More important, he says that different kinds of people take pleasure in different kinds of things. "The trouble on earth is, that they leave out the *some people* class — they try to fix up a heaven for only one kind of people. It won't work. There's all kinds here — & God cares for all kinds" (*Report* xvi). Insofar as the world shows tremendous variety and contrast, by analogy so should heaven. Consequently, Clemens's parody of Phelps's tale includes in heaven people of all nationalities, and people from all eras, and room enough to accommodate them, all in a scale model of the earth, many times larger than the original. Pushing these analogues to the extreme, Clemens begins to make the entire exercise in analogy appear absurd.

Clemens does in principle accept the epistemological value of analogy; he accepts the idea that nature's laws are consistent throughout the universe so that what we know of earth may have value to teach us about the universe. For instance, he agrees with Guillemin's analogical supposition that, if the earth has life, then so must all other planets. Nonetheless, his reading of Guillemin's astronomy undermined his willingness to accept analogy as a practical way of finding truth because human beings cannot trust their perceptions of the universe to give them a real account of their place in it. As Wakeman discovers while whizzing through the voids of the heavens on his way to Heaven, "The stars ain't so close together as they look to be" (*Report* 23). Judging by his marginalia in Guillemin's book, the vastness of the cosmos is what impressed Clemens the most. Given the inability of the unscientific mind to see and understand this immensity, his examination of it in Wakeman's travels suggests the average person's inability to analogize accurately.

But if our insufficient knowledge alone were not an adequate reason to mistrust our ability to extrapolate from our own experience to an understanding of the afterlife, our hubris would be. Much as he did in his letter to Olivia in 1869, Clemens concludes that the immensity of space really shows our cosmic insignificance. When Wakeman, after racing with a comet, gets lost in the void so that he arrives at the wrong gate to heaven, the bureaucrat at the gate tries to find Wakeman's proper place, to be identified by planetary system and then by planet. Wakeman doesn't know the cosmic name for the earth, so he can do no better than describe our solar system. So the bureaucrat

> got a balloon and sailed up and up and up, in front of a map that was as big as Rhode Island. He went on till he was out of sight, and by and by he came down and got something to eat and went up again. To cut a long story short, he kept on doing this for a day or two, and finally came down and said he thought he had found that solar system, but it might be fly-specks. So he got a microscope and went back. It turned out better than he feared. He had rousted out our system, sure enough. He got me to describe our planet and its distance from the sun, and then he says to his chief—
> "Oh, I know the one he means, now, sir. It is on the map. It is called the Wart."
> Says I to myself, "Young man, it wouldn't be wholesome for you to go down there and call it the Wart." (*Report* 27)

In spite of his humbling experience, Wakeman still obviously shares human pride in the earth, pride that is willing to fight against the superior wisdom of heaven to assert its importance. But to Clemens, the vastness of the universe reveals as mere stupidity the pride that makes human beings believe that all the heavens are merely reflections of our own states of affairs, and that the creator of all the heavens would care so greatly about one small planet "in one of the thinly worlded corners of the universe" (*Report* 27). Like Robert Browning's "Caliban on Setebos," Clemens's story attacks the very principle of analogical thinking that is the methodological centerpiece of natural theology by suggesting that human beings lack the capacity to understand their place in the divine plan. But while Browning attacked "reasoned" religion that is based on analogy in order to support the need for subjective faith, Clemens's attack cut the other way. Rather than suggest that human beings should retreat into the subjectivity that he felt prevented them from seeing reason's truths, he found the failures of natural theology to be sufficient grounds to turn to scientific "objectivity" to find truth in the material world. In other words, in rejecting the Common Sense analogy between the material and the spiritual worlds, he opened himself intellectually to the materialistic monism that was beginning to be promoted by Herbert Spencer, John Fiske, and William Sumner.

VII

Clemens's growing disillusionment with the intellectual footings of Common Sense dualism was reinforced by his growing frustration with the concomitant social ideology, especially as it governed his career as a literary man. He had been from the first concerned that literature was too idealistic, and that literary men, in order to support their ideas by living them, could not make a living. As a gentleman's occupation, writing literature did not traditionally have to make money, but in the late nineteenth-century economy, publishing had long since become big business, and writing itself was becoming professionalized. Without strong copyright laws, this development was difficult, and Clemens's life-long battle against literary pirates and publishers attests to his concern to make his writing a valuable property.

By the end of the 1870s, his battle against piracy had been so unsuccessful that he began to lose faith in the value of literature as a profession. He began to turn to many other business enterprises, including the development of a self-pasting scrapbook he invented and, more importantly, to writing popular plays. As he put it in a letter to his British agent, Moncure Conway, on December 13, 1876, "We find our copywright [sic] law here to be nearly worthless, & if I can make a living out of plays, I shall never write another book" (quoted in N&J2 2). He did not profess to want to write high drama, only plays that sold well, as can be seen from his September, 1876 suggestion to Howells that Howells turn a scene from one of his stories into a scene for the stage. Clemens complains that the piece as written would be too highbrow to be successful, so he suggests the inclusion of a comic character to make the piece more broadly appealing:

> Of course the thing is perfect, in the magazine, without the train-boy; but I was thinking of the stage & the groundlings. If the dainty touches went over

their heads, the train-boy, & other possible interruptions would fetch them every time. Would it mar the flow of the thing too much to insert that devil? I thought it over a couple of hours & concluded it wouldn't, & that he ought to be in for the sake of the groundlings. (*MTHL* 152)

Clemens gave this advice from experience. His dramatic representation of *The Gilded Age*, which he acknowledged lacked most of the moral seriousness of the book, serving instead as a loose framework on which to hang the character of Colonel Sellers, proved enormously profitable. As he noted in a postscript to his October 11, 1876 letter to Howells: "Check for 1,616.16 has just arrived — my clear profit on Raymond's first week in Philadelphia. Write a drama, Howells" (*MTHL* 159). Subsequently, he seriously devoted himself to writing several dramas, once in collaboration with Bret Harte and frequently with Howells, whose financial success as an author was as much smaller than Clemens's as his critical reputation as a serious writer was larger.

As concerned as he was with the conditions of publishing that made it so difficult for writers to make money on literature when they wanted to, Clemens was at least as concerned with the tradition that writers should be gentlemen concerned only with the social and intellectual, rather than the cash, value of their writing:

No doubt you & I both underrate the <value> worth of the work far enough; but that you are warrior enough to stand up & charge anything above a week's board is gaudy manliness in a literary person. Our guild are so egotistically mock-modest about their own merits. — We make a wretched bargain — caressing our darling humility the while — & then when we come to think how much more we could have got, we go behind the house & curse. — By George I admire you. I suppose "consuling" is not without its uses — it breeds common sense in parties who would otherwise develop only the uncommon. (*MTHL* 20)

Clemens wanted literature to occupy a "common sense" middle ground, one in which practical values — such as making a living — corresponded with the social and intellectual values of literature as seen by moral philosophers. When the practical values did not naturally follow, he grew ever more willing to reject the whole package.

Not that Clemens was ever satisfied that he really fit into the moral and intellectual upper crust at all. His niche in the literary world caused him great anxiety, primarily because his role as a humorous writer put him a notch or two lower in the hierarchy of literature than he wanted to be. Howells sensed this anxiety when reading Clemens's first installment of

"Old Times on the Mississippi" for publication in the *Atlantic Monthly*. He told Clemens not to worry about the audience, but to "yarn it off as if into my sympathetic ear." Clemens replied:

> It isn't the *Atlantic* audience that distresses me; for it is the only audience that I sit down before in perfect serenity (for the simple reason that it don't require a "humorist" to paint himself stripèd & stand on his head every fifteen minutes.) (December 8, 1874; *MTHL* 49)

He protests too much; the *Atlantic*'s audience obviously did bother him because he had to live down his reputation as a "mere" humorist. He felt that his reputation made it impossible for people to take him seriously. For instance, when Howells in August of 1876 asked Clemens publicly to support Hayes's candidacy for the presidency, Clemens said he was flattered to be asked, but intended to be very careful in fulfilling the request, because "When a humorist ventures upon the grave concerns of life he must do his job better than another man or he works harm to his cause" (*MTHL* 146).

He had found this to be true of his literary reputation, too. While he had found a fairly successful way to make serious money out of literature, he had in the process compromised his ability to sell his literature as serious. To add to the damage done to his reputation by being a humorist, he published his books by subscription, a distinctly "low class" way of selling books. As Howells put it in *My Mark Twain*, "No book of literary quality was made to go by subscription except Mr. Clemens's books" (quoted in French 7). Although Clemens defended his use of subscription publication to Howells, Aldrich, and Warner in the early 1870s, saying that "Anything but subscription publication is printing for private circulation" (quoted in Howells, *Literary Friends and Acquaintances* 312), he nonetheless knew that publishing by subscription lowered his caste even as it raised his income.

At least he believed that he was considered a low-caste writer. When he proposed to Howells that the *Atlantic* solicit novelettes based on a skeleton plot of Clemens's contrivance, Howells was unable to find anyone to contribute. Clemens blamed the failure on his reputation:

> I see where the trouble lies. The various authors dislike trotting in procession behind me. I vaguely thought of that in the beginning, but did not give it its just importance. We must have a new deal. The Blindfold Novelettes must be suggested anonymously. . . . Now I would suggest that Aldrich devise the skeleton-plan, for it needs an ingenious head to contrive a plot which shall be prettily complicated & yet well fitted for lucid & interesting development in

the brief compass of 10 *Atlantic* pages. My plot was awkward & overloaded with tough requirements.
Warner will fill up the skeleton — for one. No doubt Harte will; will ask him. Won't Mr Holmes? Won't Henry James? Won't Mr. Lowell, & some more of the big literary fish? (*MTHL* 160)

Since both he and Howells thought the idea a grand one, Clemens could not accept that other authors did not want to collaborate, period. So he assumed that, if nobody knew that he had suggested the idea in the first place, and if everyone knew that Aldrich contrived the plot, then the upper crust of America's literati would play along. And perhaps he was right. When, years later, Howells put together a collaborative novel, he managed to get a great school of literary big fish to write it when Clemens had no part in it.

Clemens had other reasons to question his acceptance in the sphere of literary greats. For one, when he and Warner wrote *The Gilded Age*, at least one critic accused him of defrauding the public with one of his notorious literary hoaxes (French 17–18). And when he tried to interject a little humor into the 1877 Whittier birthday dinner, commentators throughout the country excoriated Clemens for not appropriately revering such an exalted literary figure.[32] This social and professional fiasco occurred just before the Clemens family left for an extended tour of Europe. Of course, people in their circle were expected to tour Europe frequently in order to soak up culture and to buy artifacts, and the Clemens family had been to Europe before on these grounds. But this time, they traveled substantially because life in Europe was cheaper than in America, and the Clemens family needed to reduce expenses since Samuel's book sales and Livy's coal fortune had both been hurt by the long economic depression that followed the financial panic of 1873. His inability to live up to the financial and cultural standards to which he aspired perhaps contributed to his willingness to challenge the conceptual underpinnings of this entire social system. The substance of that challenge is the subject of the next chapter.

5. "Training is Everything"

I

The evening of January 19, 1877 saw Samuel Clemens, Nathaniel Burton, E. P. Parker, and Charles and Susan Warner dining at the home of their good friend Joseph Hopkins Twichell. Twichell had invited his friends over to help him entertain Joseph Cook, whose Boston Monday Lectures had, since 1875, created quite a stir in the world of New England letters (Twichell, *Diaries*). In Cook, Clemens met one of America's last outspoken defenders of Common Sense dualism. Cook's Monday Lectures were designed primarily to rebuild support for a theological world view that was increasingly threatened by social and intellectual forces alike. He accordingly broke his very popular and widely printed lectures in two parts: the "preludes" always treating some contemporary social problem, and the "lectures" themselves "present[ing] the results of the freshest German, English, and American scholarship on the more important and difficult topics concerning the relation of Religion and Science" (Cook, *Conscience* v).

These topics were difficult to Cook and his contemporaries because the dualistic attempt to bridge the gap between science and scripture had been under pressure from the discoveries of geologists and astronomers for some time, and after the 1859 publication of Darwin's *The Origin of Species*, the comfortable belief that science revealed an eternal, static creation appeared significantly less defensible than it had. Many thinkers responded by abandoning dualism altogether in favor either of idealism or of materialism.[1] Cook did neither. Not quailing before Darwin's evidence, he accepted evolutionary principles while attacking Spencer's monistic interpretation of Darwin, opposing "the materialistic, and not the theistic, theory of evolution" (v) in order to insist on the congruence of science and religion. At the same time, he belittled the idealists for not accepting the provable truths of empirical research. He tried to "proceed according to the principles of inductive science" (17) in order to demonstrate the limitations of the utilitarian idea, as articulated by "the Mills and the Spencers on the one hand," that conscience is wholly learned, and the idealists' notion, as articulated by "the Kants and Rothes on the other" (30), that the moral sense is purely intuitive.

His argument proceeds by the usual Common Sense tautologies before concluding with a rhetorical flourish:

> Our cheeks may well grow white and the blood of the ages leap with a new inspiration, when, standing between Christianity and science, we find the thunders of the one and the whispers of the other uttering the same truth. It is a familiar doctrine to Christianity, that our bodies are the temple of Somewhat and Some One not ourselves. That Some One Christianity does, though physical science does not, know by an Incommunicable Name. There are connections between religion and science here of the most overawing moment. (32)

Thus does Cook argue that both the material and the spiritual are combined in the lives of human beings, and that the physical evidence of the senses supports such a dualistic belief in the equal and separate realities of both body and spirit.

But although Cook's discussions of social problems were very influential, leading to the development of the "Social Gospel" (Ahlstrom, *History* 791), his theology blanched few cheeks with new inspiration. Even Twichell, a college acquaintance of Cook and fellow Congregationalist minister, found Cook's reasoning weak (Twichell, *Diaries*, January 19, 1877). Especially given the growing monistic challenge to Common Sense dualism articulated by Herbert Spencer and his American popularizers, John Fiske and William Graham Sumner, most writers and thinkers who wished to support Christianity veered toward idealism.

Warner, for instance, in his April 1883 *Atlantic* essay "Modern Fiction," wrote:

> Art requires an idealization of nature. . . . When we praise our recent fiction for its photographic fidelity to nature we condemn it, for we deny to it the art that would give it value. We forget that the creation of the novel should be . . . a synthetic process, and impart to human actions that ideal quality which we demand in painting. (464)

The comparison to painting here refers to the artistic medium that sentimental realists held as their model. One of the primary sentimental genres, the sketch, metaphorically invokes the visual arts in its very name, and many sentimental writers referred to their works as kinds of painting. Stowe, for instance, often referred to her works as "portraits."

But Warner's complaint is not merely formal. He goes on to make clear that his attack has less to do with "modern" fiction itself than with the "petty," "commonplace," and "vulgar" state of thought that the literature reflects: "Literature is never in any age an isolated product. It is closely related to the development or retrogression of the time in all departments of life" (466). Warner was in part lamenting the increasing polarization of intellectual life into idealistic and materialistic camps.

What Warner saw as a retrograde absence of ideality "in all departments of life" was precisely what Herbert Spencer saw as progress. He intended the ethical part of his "synthetic philosophy" to fill the "vacuum" left by the loss of the "supposed sacred origin" of traditional "moral injunctions" with a more attractive "moral rule" stripped of and "undistorted by superstition and asceticism" (iv–v). The "ultimate purpose" of his entire philosophical system was "that of finding for the principles of right and wrong, in conduct at large, a scientific basis" (iii).

This purpose, as Locke had envisioned it much earlier, was to relieve the church of moral authority by placing it in the hands of morally aware individuals. But by the mid-nineteenth century when Spencer wrote, "scientific" no longer meant undebatable knowledge based on a priori truths, but systematic knowledge based on empirical observation of the material world. And although he acknowledged that some higher power may drive evolution, he saw no reason to believe in any intrinsic connection between this power and human beings. His materialism eliminated the human soul, and he therefore judged morality not on the basis of good for "character" but on the basis of good for the body, of which the mind is but a part. "Here might be urged," he says after enumerating the absurd privations incurred by people who assume that human beings have souls that need to be cared for at the expense of the body, "the necessity for preluding the study of moral science by the study of biological science" (109). The materialism on which Spencer predicated his system was the bogey that drove so many nineteenth-century Americans into the idealistic side of their philosophical tradition.

Contingent on his belief that mind and body are the same, Spencer judged the moral quality of all actions on the basis of utility rather than intention. That moral acts could ever be in conflict he explained by enumerating three ends—those of the self, of the family, and of society—that occasionally disagree in the short term. Of course, since he takes evolution as his first principle, all of these ends ultimately refer to the self; in fact, he sees survival of the fittest as a moral imperative. Thus, any social ends, such as those of family or society, ultimately arise from personal needs. Familial impulses, he claims, arise from sexual instincts, and the nuclear family is the natural result of sexual desires. Social needs arise from the survival value of working in concert, so that human beings contract to live in larger communities.

Taking the survival value of following personal pleasure and of avoiding pain as the corollary to his belief that evolution guides progress, Spencer strenuously argues against the moral value of self-sacrifice. Excepting this point, though, his moral system generally promotes the behavior advocated by religious moralists. His belief that intellectual pleasures were greater than physical and that long-term benefits were generally of higher importance than immediate ones basically supported the Common Sense hierarchy of values as articulated by Hutcheson. His theory about the origin and value of the family supported the conventional ideology of the sexual spheres. His belief in the value of competitive individualism supported free-market capitalism. Altogether, Spencer provided a full, systematic apology for America's dominant social ideology without the embarrassing encumbrance of guilt and loving one's neighbor to get in the way of economic competition and familial pleasures.

Not surprisingly, the great American vogue of Spencer's philosophy arose from its power to justify American business practices. In historical hindsight, the philosophy promulgated by Spencer has been named social Darwinism, but in its own day, as the quotation from Joseph Cook shows, it was called "materialistic" and "utilitarian." Not surprisingly, when Clemens had grown doubtful of his ability to fill his role as provider by living the life of a literary man, and as he simultaneously began to see himself as a man of business, he opened himself intellectually to utilitarian moral philosophy, much of it from his reading of Spencer, whom he wished to publish in America, and much from his acquaintances William Graham Sumner and John Fiske.

But to those literary and intellectual men who were less inclined to equate the masculine sphere with American free-market business, Spencer's philosophy was an abomination because, in part, it redefined morality to exclude altruism. Spencer rejected the sentimentalist's belief in a gregarious impulse and in sympathy. He redefined the moral sense and sympathy, both commonly held to be empirically proven aspects of the human psyche, as the accumulated experience of the survival value of cooperation. Since his brand of evolution was Lamarckian rather than Darwinian, he believed that learned experiences could be inherited; thus, the pleasures arising from successful cooperation were passed down from generation to generation as senses of sympathy and altruism. Human beings may have found survival value in social behavior, but they were not, according to Spencer, social animals.

Among Spencer's fellow advocates of the theory of evolution, this was a point of contention. In particular, America's two most important popularizers of Spencer's philosophy disagreed on this point. As promoted by William Graham Sumner, Spencerian philosophy took on a decidedly somber cast.[2] Sumner emphasized the selfish components of Spencer's work, especially advocating free-market economics and the survival value of hard work in a competitive environment. He argued against governmental or social efforts to ameliorate most social conditions because he felt that social engineering was in defiance of natural laws of evolution that we could not hope to control. As Richard Hofstadter puts it, Sumner

> tried to convince men that confidence in their ability to will and plan their destinies was unwarranted by history or biology or any of the facts of experience — that the best they could do was to bow to natural forces. Like some latter-day Calvin, he came to preach the predestination of the social order and the salvation of the economically elect through the survival of the fittest. (66–67)

Sumner, perhaps the most pessimistic of the important American popularizers of evolutionary theory, rejected almost all of the altruistic, emotional values of the sentimental tradition as impediments to evolution. Consequently, he attacked government and most philanthropic organizations for their interference with the laws of economic nature. Regarding government, for instance, he says, "There are two chief things with which government has to deal. They are the property of men and the honor of women. These it has to defend against crime" (101). While he defines the social purpose of government as purely defensive, it is worth noting that he tacitly endorses the traditional sexual spheres in his belief that women need defending. Traditional familial gentleness did not seem to Sumner a violation of natural laws of competition, though he did not stress this in his reading of evolution.[3]

John Fiske, another important American popularizer of Darwin and Spencer and a friend of Clemens, on the other hand, did.[4] Fiske in general did not share Sumner's pessimistic interpretation of evolutionary theory. He, on the contrary, found the theory of evolution consonant with a belief in the kindlier human feelings. He devoted much of his own work, *The*

Meaning of Infancy (1883), for example, to developing a theory of the evolution of altruism and sympathy (Hofstadter 94). In part, his optimism was a consequence of his continued belief in God and spirit, modifying traditional Christian ideas of the divine relation to time by suggesting that God acts "'through time' rather than 'from all time'" (Ahlstrom, *History* 770). He found Spencer's material utopia a new statement of millenialism and he considered it easy to infuse Spencer's idea of progress with the motive power of divine providence. Thus, Fiske was one of the rare supporters of evolution who, though he believed in the rigidity of natural laws acting through time, nonetheless tried to maintain at least a modified dualism.

In this position, Fiske remained closer to Darwin than did either Spencer or Sumner. Darwin himself did not publicly surrender his belief in God, and, unhappy that his theories were used by Spencer and others to promote pure materialism, he wrote *The Descent of Man* (1872) to argue, in part, that God inspired evolution to bring life to the point where it transcends amoral competition. Altruism is the moral telos of evolution according to Darwin. To make this point, he argues that the social impulse is not based in contractual self-interest but is rather an instinct that gives human beings tremendous pleasure. Although it may be at odds with purely selfish survival instincts at times, it is a higher impulse that we are duty-bound to follow.

II

Spencer's ideas had a profound impact on Clemens's moral philosophy. Yet through the accidents of time, we do not have any of his marked copies of Spencer's works, nor do we have his copies of the influential articles in *Popular Science* (to which Clemens subscribed) that Sumner and Fiske wrote to promote Spencerian philosophy. It is easiest, then, to see Clemens's reaction to the ethical implications of utilitarian materialism by noting his responses to Lecky and to Darwin's *The Descent of Man*. In both of these cases, we have Clemens's marginalia to give us an accurate picture of his thinking, especially on the question of altruism. As Blair and Baetzhold both indicate, Clemens disagreed with Lecky's sentimentalism, holding instead that the utilitarians were right in declaring selfishness to be the root of all human behavior.

Clemens's marks in *The Descent of Man* reinforce that conclusion.[5] In arguing that instincts of sympathy are the same as altruism, Darwin actually explains impulses toward moral behavior as the product of material evolution by the survival of the fittest. Insofar as this is true, his distinctions between altruism and selfishness are semantic. He distinguishes the two primarily on the basis of consciousness, describing instincts as behaviors stemming "from the mere force of inheritance, without the stimulus of either pleasure or pain," whereas truly selfish behavior requires a conscious calculation of benefits and costs (76–78). "Hence," he concludes, "the common assumption that men must be impelled to every action by experiencing some pleasure or pain may be erroneous."

But Clemens noted that if sympathy is an instinct, it is not therefore any less selfish. Its power still comes from a regard for self. In the margin on page 78 he wrote, "selfishness again / — not charity / not gene / rosity / (save to- / ward our- / selves.)"[†] Although he saw this instinctive human connection as essentially selfish, Clemens, unlike Spencer, nonetheless accepted it as a fundamental human characteristic. In the passages in which Darwin describes other animals as social in order to build proof that social instincts are the roots of sympathetic morality, Clemens's comments, such as "Sheep eat with their heads all turned the same way on the hillside — cows, mostly, too" (71),[†] attest to his interest in and agreement with Darwin's argument that animals are instinctively gregarious. Although he found this gregariousness to be morally selfish at root, he rejected Spencer's social contract theory of human society in favor of the sentimental idea that social impulses are natural human attributes.

So in his "discussion with Lecky" that Blair argues informs *Huckleberry Finn* and Baetzhold suggests was at the center of Clemens's moral vision throughout his career, Clemens was joining the central philosophical debates of his day. In utilitarian, scientific naturalism he found, at least temporarily, answers to the moral conundrums of Common Sense dualism. He consequently attacked that dualism, especially on the grounds of its definition of realism. While Warner was defending Common Sense "realism" for its ability to abstract from common life the ideals that make life morally worthwhile, Clemens attacked it for being unnecessary at best, dishonest at worst. He concurred with Howells, who had long since replaced Warner as Clemens's literary mentor and confidant, that "the ideal perfection of some things in life persuades me more and more never to meddle with the ideal in fiction: it is impossible to compete with the facts" (*MTHL* 385).

On the contrary, the "photographic" realism against which Warner protested became the standard by which Clemens and Howells professed to judge literature. In his January 21, 1879 letter to Howells about *The Lady of Aroostook*, Clemens wrote, "It is all such truth—truth to life; everywhere your pen falls it leaves a photograph" (245).[6] Photographs, he implies, tell the truth, whereas the painting that Warner and his sentimental predecessors held up as the model art that literature should imitate cannot reach the same level of truth. Obviously, Clemens had not changed his fundamental moral principle, that honesty determines morality, and the principle of honesty attracted him to naturalism. He came to see sentimental realism, with its effort to abstract essential reality from mundane facts, as an exercise in lying. Much of his writing from the late 1870s to the early 1890s serves to promote precisely that point.

This purpose shows first in *A Tramp Abroad* (1879), written during the Clemens family's attempt to economize by living in Europe at the end of the 1870s. One of the central motifs of this travelogue is a parody of the grand tour as an exercise in refining one's higher sensibilities, and one of the primary targets of his satire is that model art according to sentimental aesthetics, painting.

The first chapter lists as one of the narrator's primary purposes the study of painting (1:1), and the audience reads satiric art lessons throughout the book. In satirizing the idealism of the painter's craft, Clemens once again establishes an opposition between his naive self and his educated self, but not surprisingly, since his definition of realism now is at odds with cultivated idealism, he ironically uses his ignorance as the standard by which he judges the moral legitimacy of art:

> What a red rag is to a bull, Turner's "Slave Ship" was to me, before I studied art. Mr Ruskin is educated in art up to a point where that picture throws him into as mad an ecstasy of pleasure as it used to throw me into one of rage, last year, when I was ignorant. His cultivation enables him—and me, now—to see water in that glaring yellow mud, and natural effects in those lurid explosions of mixed smoke and flame, and crimson sunset glories; it reconciles him—and me now—to the floating of iron cable-chains and other unfloatable things; it reconciles us to fishes swimming around on top of the mud—I mean the water. The most of the picture is a manifest impossibility—that is to say, a lie; and only rigid cultivation can enable a man to find truth in a lie. (1:219)

In calling physical impossibilities "lies," Clemens denies that there could be a higher moral truth represented in art. In other words, he denies the fundamental precept of sentimental art, that inconsistencies between actual fact and ideal fact must be stripped from art if it is to have the emotional power that it needs to serve its moral ends. Here Clemens says art can serve no moral ends if it is not completely and immediately true to physical reality alone.[7]

By sentimental standards, the key to "truth" in art is self-awareness of the moral attributes of human character. By Clemens's naturalistic standards, truth in art depends on careful observation not of internal qualities of mind, but of specific experiences, that is, of particular events rather than eternal characteristics. In his June 22, 1882 letter to Howells on Chapters XXIII–XXVI of *A Modern Instance*, Clemens reveals these standards in his praise of Howells's writing:

> That's the best drunk scene—because the truest—that I ever read. There are touches in it which I never saw any writer take note of before. And they are set before the reader with amazing accuracy. How very drunk, & how recently drunk & how altogether admirably drunk you must have been to enable you to contrive that masterpiece! (*MTHL* 408)

The teasing note in accusing Howells of having been drunk notwithstanding, Clemens makes clear that realistic writing must come from experience.

In some ways this idea strikes at the very heart of the moral effectiveness of sentimental literature in that it denies the capacity of people to experience one another's truths through the power of sympathetic imagination. Repeatedly in *Tramp Abroad* Clemens mocks the idea that one can experience life sympathetically. For instance, when viewing some famous Swiss ladders by which the locals ascend a precipice, Mark Twain orders his agent, Harris,

> to make the ascent, so I could put the thrill and horror of it in my book, and he accomplished the feat successfully, through a subagent, for three francs, which I paid. It makes me shudder yet when I think of what I felt when I was clinging there between heaven and earth in the person of that proxy. At times the world swam around me, and I could hardly keep from letting go, so dizzying was the appalling danger. . . . When the people of the hotel found that I had been climbing those crazy Ladders, it made me an object of considerable attention. (2:76)

The absurdity of his horror at watching someone climb for the person who was supposed to climb for him suggests that he is concocting the feelings out of whole cloth. Of course, he makes clear that the feelings are merely a literary exercise designed to load his book with thrills and excitement. Since his readers can do no more than experience the event vicariously, there is no reason, he suggests, to do more than necessary to give his readers a thrill.[8]

But he obviously strays far from truth in doing so. The deceitful nature of sensational literature becomes explicitly clear in Mark Twain's ascent of Mont Blanc by telescope. He credits himself with the capacity to experience from afar everything the climbers he watches experience in fact. But when he tries to adopt the climbers' perspective in describing the view from the top, all he can do is imagine. The geographic inaccuracies and impossibilities he describes reveal the absurdity of his claim to be able in sympathetic imagination to share fully other people's actual experiences.

That people try, Clemens suggests, comes from their own selfish desires. Mark Twain's effort to have Harris climb the ladders, for instance, is intended to give him thrilling material for his book. Similarly, his chagrin at witnessing a child *almost* fall off a cliff is grounded in his own selfishness. He complains that Harris is

> glad the girl was saved because it spared him any anguish, but Harris cared not a straw for my feelings, or my loss of such a literary plum, snatched from my very mouth at the instant it was ready to drop into it. His selfishness was sufficient to place his own gratification in being spared suffering clear before all concern for me, his friend. Apparently, he did not once reflect upon the valuable details which would have fallen like a windfall to me: fishing the child out — witnessing the surprise of the family and the stir the thing would have made among the peasants — then a Swiss funeral — then the roadside monument, to be paid for by us and have our names mentioned in it. And we should have gone into Baedeker and been immortal. I was silent. I was too much hurt to complain. (2:85)

Here, too, his literary interests override real compassion. In suggesting that such "details" — which he manages to put into his book through imagination anyway — are of greater value to him because of greater value to his readers than real human life, he implies that sentimental compassion is in fact selfish revelry in feeling for its own sake. The pleasure comes in vicariously experiencing feelings — danger and grief in this case — safely, without the real concern that would make them unpleasant. That Harris could feel real sympathy shows that Clemens does not reject the possibility of real feeling, though as his marginalia in Darwin suggest it is still selfish rather than altruistic feeling. So even though real feeling is possible, suggests Clemens, feelings trained according to a literary model are in fact perniciously selfish.

This concept is central to *Adventures of Huckleberry Finn*. The literary response to human feeling according to sentimental aesthetic and moral theory requires writers first to purify situations in order to evoke pure, ideal emotions. Truth, as Clemens defined it in the early 1880s, must be sacrificed by such purification, leading people who try to act on such sentimental idealities to act inappropriately in most circumstances. And worse, as I mentioned in the introduction, Clemens thought that the pleasure of vicarious emotion leads people to be reckless of consequences.

I have already described how Clemens uses the scene from Chapter 5, when the new judge tries to reform pap, as an example of this reckless indulgence in intentions at the expense of consequence. Part of the reason, suggests Clemens, that an idealistic over-emphasis on intention is morally reprehensible is that it keeps people from seeing the truth. In this case, it blinds the judge to the truth that, as Clemens put it a few years later in *Pudd'nhead Wilson*, "habit is . . . not to be flung out the window by any man." Habit is a more powerful aspect of human character than sympathy, and in trying to fling another man's habit out the window, the new judge indulges his own sensation habit, but consequently allows Huck to be put in great physical danger under the influence of a drunken, violent brute.

Clemens is especially interested in driving home the point that sentimental reformism, even when it takes appropriate action to help people, is fundamentally selfish. Using Huck's innocent repetition of ideals he has learned by rote but has little stake in to best make the point, Clemens has Huck congratulate himself in sentimental terms for trying to rescue the murderers he stranded on the wreck of the *Walter Scott*:

> I couldn't rest easy till I could see the ferry-boat start. But take it all around, I was feeling ruther comfortable on accounts of taking all this trouble for that gang, for not many would a done it. I wished the widow knowed about it. I judged she would be proud of me for helping these rapscallions, because rapscallions and dead-beats is the kind the widow and good people takes the most interest in. (91)

As he finds out a moment later, his efforts were futile, but it bothers him little because his true interest was in the feeling of pride he got out of conforming to a convention of the social gospel.[9] He helps the worst kind of people in order to prove the validity of his intentions as well as to magnify the admirability of the effort. Insofar as he is concerned about other people's reactions at all, he is concerned about his fellow "do-gooders'" praise, not the gratitude of those he helped. This incident, then, demonstrates the problem of following morality as dictated by sentimental moral philosophy; true sympathy finds itself drowned in theatrical expression of good intentions and in the feeling of bliss attendant on such intentions.

In describing *Huck Finn* as part of Clemens's discussion with Lecky, Baetzhold argues that "the final triumph of Huck's 'sound heart' over his 'ill-trained conscience' dramatizes the fact that Clemens had not yet entirely lost faith in the existence of innate moral perceptions" (97).[10] As my earlier discussion should make clear, I agree. No doubt Clemens did not have a fully consistent moral system that eliminated altruism as his standard of morality in spite of his apparent agreement with the utilitarian school. His unself-conscious confusion shows, too, in a letter to Howells about copyright in which he says he has decided that international copyright would be bad because it would deprive the American public of cheap, pirated editions of literature that would improve the characters and minds of those who read it. Thus, he has come to favor piracy:

> Morally, this is all wrong — governmentally it is all right; for it is the *duty* of governments — & families — to be selfish, & look out simply for their own. . . . [E]ven if the treaty *will* kill Canadian piracy, & thus save me an average of $5,000 a year, I'm down on it anyway. (*MTHL* 34–36)

He seems to miss the point that if it is a duty, then it is moral, so obviously he simultaneously judges morality here by the sentimental standards of altruism and by the Spencerian standard of self-interest. Furthermore, he relinquishes his duty selfishly to promote his family's financial interests in altruistically promoting his country's best interests. So, as Baetzhold says, Clemens clearly was not completely consistent in his new-found utilitarianism.

Nonetheless, by expanding the moral "discussion" to include Darwin and Spencer as well as Lecky, Clemens's vision of Huck's moral motivations is more consistently utilitarian than it would appear if we were to abide by Lecky's rather rigid and narrow definitions. As I noted above, the idea that human beings are born with sympathies for one another was not exclusively the intellectual property of old-style sentimentalists. According to Darwin and Spencer, social sympathies do exist, either as the product of natural selection according to Darwin or as the product of inherited training according to Spencer.[11] In both cases, the motive power of sympathy was, as Clemens interpreted it, selfish.

Particularly, Clemens seems to have been influenced by Darwin's account of the origin of morality in social instincts common to all social animals. When he has Judith Loftus ask Huck "if fifteen cows is browsing on a hillside, how many of them eats with their heads pointed the same direction?" and Huck answers, "The whole fifteen, mum" (74) he repeats a bit of knowledge he used to support Darwin's thesis.[12] Social animals have, Clemens agreed, a powerful instinctive drive to be together. In this, he continued to accept the sentimentalists' belief in a gregarious instinct, a belief Darwin did his best to promote in order to show a biological basis for altruism. Clemens, in interpreting this instinct as essentially selfish, explains much of the motivation of moral behavior as a selfish attempt to belong to society.

This shows clearly in Huck's reaction to isolation. Innumerable critics say that Huck is running away from society to preserve his natural innocence. Uncomfortable with "sivilization" and with pap's brutality, he flees humanity to return to the innocence of his inborn nature. But importantly, Huck gets used to the "sivilization":

> At first I hated the school, but by and by I got so I could stand it. Whenever I got uncommon tired I played hookey, and the hiding I got next day done me good and cheered me up. So the longer I went to school the easier it got to be. I was getting sort of used to the widow's ways, too, and they weren't so raspy on me. . . . I liked the old ways best, but I was getting so I liked the new ones, too, a little bit. (18)

He learns remarkably easily to accept the new ways, and he only leaves these because pap abducts him. Then, although Huck at first fears his father, he gets used to living in the woods in a very short time. As long as he is with people, he finds a way to be content.

In fact, when he lives with the Grangerfords, he becomes more than content, even though he has to live by very orderly ways. He even has to go to church regularly to hear sermons "all about brotherly love, and such-like tiresomeness" (147), but he stands it easily given how much he likes the place. That he acclimates quickly shows in that he "read considerable," apparently on his own, in " 'Pilgrim's Progress,' about a man that left his family it didn't say why" (137). Huck cannot imagine leaving a family without good reason, and the abstract reasons of Puritan piety are completely alien to Huck's natural affinity for human beings. As Clemens put it in the early 1880s, "To become a right Christian, one must *hate* his brother, his sister, his wife, etc. The laws of God and nature being stronger than those of men, this one must always remain a dead-letter" (*WIM* 58). The "interesting but tough" statements of Calvinism certainly never overcome the laws of Huck's nature.

Isolation, on the other hand, Huck always equates with death. In Chapter One, for instance, he says, "I felt so lonesome I most wished I was dead . . . I did wish I had some company . . . the house was all as still as death" (4–5). In Chapter Six, he lists lonesomeness as one of the main reasons he wished to escape from his father's cabin: "But by-and-by pap got . . . to going away so much, too, and locking me in . . . It was dreadful lonesome" (30–31). His pleasure in his escape itself is reduced by the fact that he has nobody to share it with: "I did wish Tom Sawyer was there, I knowed he would take an interest in this kind of business, and throw in the fancy touches" (41). In Chapter Eight, his enjoyment of his stay on Jackson's Island decreases as his loneliness increases:

> When it was dark I set by my camp fire smoking, and feeling pretty satisfied; but by-and-by it got sort of lonesome, and so I went and set on the bank and listened to the currents washing along, and counted the stars and drift-logs and rafts that come down, and then went to bed; there ain't no better way to put in time when you are lonesome; you can't stay so, you soon get over it.
> And so for three days and nights. No difference — just the same thing. (48)

Without human companionship, Huck finds he just "mainly . . . wanted to put in the time" (48). Although critics often note Huck's defenses against society, relatively few note the centrality of his defensive efforts against the ennui of isolation.[13]

In Chapter Twenty-four, Huck hears explicitly what his feelings already told him, that loneliness can be fatal:

> You see, he [Peter Wilks] was pretty old, and George's g'yirls was too young to be much company for him except Mary Jane the red-headed one; and so he was kinder lonesome after George and his wife died, and didn't seem to care much to live. (206)

The gregarious impulse, suggests Clemens, is central to life, and Huck's life is no exception. Society promises life in community as the alternative to the death of isolation. The gregarious impulse leads people to community, but it is conscience that mediates between the individual and society.

Even though, says Clemens, conscience is necessary to social interaction, the social codes contained in conscience impede the human community they should encourage. Huck's "innocence" serves to drive this point home. His innocence is not that of Rousseau's "noble savage" completely untainted by society's conventions. He cannot escape society's codes insofar as he can speak or think at all. Huck remains innocent only because, while he knows the various social codes and while his conscience has internalized most of what it needs for him to be completely socialized, he has not committed himself to society. He prefers a passive approach to society that allows him to maintain a conscientious isolation even when surrounded by other human beings.[14] He guides his behavior by the principle of avoiding trouble, as for example when he accommodates the king and duke on the raft:

> The duke done it [shook the king's hand], and Jim and me was pretty glad to see it. It took away all the uncomfortableness, and we felt mighty good over it, because it would a been a miserable business to have any unfriendliness on the raft; for what you want, above all things, on a raft, is for everybody to be satisfied, and feel right and kind towards the others.
>
> It didn't take me long to make up my mind that these liars warn't no kings nor dukes, at all, but just low-down humbugs and frauds. But I never said nothing, never let on; kept it to myself; it's the best way; then you don't have no quarrels, and don't get into no trouble. . . . If I never learnt nothing else out of pap, I learnt that the best way to get along with his kind of people is to let them have their own way. (165)

When such an innocent decides to commit himself to society, his motives for joining are likely to show clearly, and the consequences of his choice will show all the more plainly.

As the problem of Jim's freedom brought on Huck's first but finally unresolved contest with conscience, so it precipitates Huck's famous decision to "go to hell." In the latter case, Huck's contest with his conscience begins when he *feels* his commitment to Jim:

> After all this long journey, and after all we'd done for them scoundrels, here was it all come to nothing, everything all busted up and ruined, because they could have the heart to serve Jim such a trick as that, and make him a slave again all his life, and amongst strangers, too, for forty dirty dollars. (268)

Huck's "we" stresses his sense of community with Jim, his emphasis on "heart" shows that he senses the emotional nature of human community, and his belief that the worst part of slavery for Jim now would be to be "amongst strangers" shows the depth of Huck's social feelings. As he commits himself to society, his conscience, the ostensible mediator between these raw feelings and satisfying human interaction, interferes with Huck's feelings for Jim and threatens to turn the love of equals into the cold property relationship between master and chattel.

Significantly, Huck's conscience attacks him in terms he learned from the biblical literalist, Miss Watson:

That's just the way: a person does a low-down thing, and then he don't want to take no consequences of it. Thinks as long as he can hide it, it ain't no disgrace. That was my fix exactly. The more I studied about this, the more my conscience went to grinding me, and the more wicked and low-down and ornery I got to feeling. And at last, when it hit me all of a sudden that here was the plain hand of Providence slapping me in the face and letting me know my wickedness was being watched all the time from up there in heaven, whilst I was stealing a poor old woman's nigger that hadn't ever done me no harm, and now was showing me there's One that's always on the lookout, and ain't agoing to allow such miserable doings to go only just so fur and no further, I most dropped in my tracks, I was so scared. (268–69)

Huck's conscience, working in the Calvinist vein, absolutely denies his relationship with Jim. This model of conscience, with all that it implies for society as a whole, denies the importance of the relationship between person and person in favor of a subservient relationship between each individual and a Providence which, if it "got [a person] there warn't no help for him any more" (14).

Even though Huck's conscience starts him along the way to a Calvinist conversion, he finds the terms of society as expressed by Miss Watson's model inappropriate to his feelings about Jim. As soon as he begins to feel once again, his resolution crumbles; his conscience attacks him again, this time in the terms of the Widow Douglas's Arminian social gospel: "I must help other people, and do everything I could for other people, and look out for them all the time, and never think about myself" (13). When following Miss Watson's model, Huck thinks of nothing but himself and his future, but as he thinks further, his social nature asserts itself in Widow Douglas's terms:

I . . . laid the paper down and sat there thinking — thinking how good it was all this happened so, and how near I came to being lost and going to hell. And went on thinking. And got to thinking over our trip down the river; and I see Jim before me, all the time, in the day, and in the night-time, sometimes moonlight, sometimes storms, and we a floating along, talking and singing, and laughing. But somehow I couldn't seem to strike no places to harden me against him, but only the other kind. (269–70)

His actual experience of human connection then overrides his trained belief in one kind of morality. While the experience itself creates feelings of connection, he still needs the Widow Douglas's terminology to act on these feelings. He eventually embraces the Widow Douglas's ethos because it better fits his real feelings for Jim than does Miss Watson's. Still, he forgets that he once noticed that "there was two Providences, and a poor chap would stand considerable show with the widow's" (14), so he fails to shake Miss Watson's terminology. Therefore, he considers his adoption of the Widow's morality a decision to "go to hell."

Having made the decision to join society, even though he is confused by the terms of his membership, he feels the dangerous power of isolation with a new intensity:

> When I got [to Phelps's] plantation it was all still and Sunday-like, and hot and sunshiny—the hands was gone to the fields; and there was them kind of faint dronings of bugs and flies in the air that makes it seem so lonesome and like everybody's dead and gone; and if a breeze fans along and quivers the leaves, it makes you feel mournful, because you feel like it's spirits whispering—spirits that's been dead ever so many years—and you always think they're talking about *you*. As a general thing it makes a body wish *he* was dead, too, and done with it all. . . . I went around and clumb over the back stile by the ash-hopper, and started for the kitchen. When I got a little ways, I heard the dim hum of a spinning-wheel wailing along up and sinking along down again; and then I knowed for certain I wished I was dead—for that *is* the lonesomest sound in the whole world. (276–77)

Huck here continues to think according to the Calvinist paradigm. After he realizes his "sin" he feels dead before "trusting to Providence" to save him by "put[ting] the right words in my mouth when the time come" (277). Once again, though, Huck's innocence highlights the socially relative nature of Providence. Not only does he have the Widow Douglas's and Miss Watson's providences in his repertoire, he also has the king's, one that puts the right words in one's mouth at the right time: "They couldn't hit no project that suited exactly; so . . . the king he allowed he would drop over to t'other village, without any plan, but just trust in Providence to lead him the profitable way—meaning the devil, I reckon" (204). So Huck is confused about which model of morality he should follow in his efforts to confirm and act on his love for Jim. In trusting in whatever providence he finds appropriate, he finds himself "born again" (282) as Tom Sawyer. From here on, he commits himself to Tom Sawyer's fraternal caricature of genteel, sentimental morality. The so-called evasion chapters all depend on Tom's insistence on following the conventional scripts of romances, scripts that depend on a sentimental model of the aesthetic pleasure of danger removed from all potential consequences and responsibilities. Tom thinks he can patch things up for Jim by simply paying him for his time and giving him a grand "torchlight procession" (360). Tom has no idea of the power and importance of Jim's love for his family, no concern for the real, physical dangers of the escape he plans, no conception of possible consequences or real feelings. Huck, even though his commitment to Jim forced him to accept one of the models of society to which he had been exposed, finds Tom's plan worthless simply because it ignores realities: "The first time I catched Tom, private, I asked him what was his idea, time of the evasion? — what it was he'd planned to do if the evasion worked all right and he managed to set a nigger free that was already free before?" (360). Tom then lists his theatrical plan for adventures and a hero's welcome, but Huck rejects it all with an understated, "But I reckoned it was about as well the way it was" (360).

Huck only embraces the models of society as codified in his conscience because he needs a way to act on his feelings for Jim. Having embraced what looks like a workable model, he discovers that social codes impede precisely that which they should promote. Clemens, in giving Huck a conscience that cannot decide what actions are morally right and what actions are morally wrong, denies the absolute authority and accuracy of conscience implied in all of the nineteenth-century models of conscience. As he put it more succinctly and explicitly but less compellingly in his 1885 "The Character of Man":

> There are certain sweet-smelling sugar-coated lies current in the world which all politic men have apparently tacitly conspired together to support and perpetuate. One of these is . . . that conscience, man's moral medicine chest, is not only created by the Creator, but is put into man ready charged with the right and only true and authentic corrective of conduct — and the duplicate chest, with the self-same correctives, unchanged, unmodified, distributed to all nations and all epochs. (*WIM* 61)

On the contrary, he believed it to be produced by training. As he wrote in the early eighties in a piece published posthumously, "I believe that the world's moral laws are the outcome of the world's experience" (*WIM* 57). In saying that the world's experience, not the individual's experience, provides moral law, he implies that the individual must learn his morality from others.

Clearly, *Adventures of Huckleberry Finn* suggests this, too. Since each competing voice in Huck's conscience can be traced not only to a common social model of conscience but also to a specific individual who taught Huck the moral terms appropriate to each of these models, Twain implies that conscience is in fact relative to society rather than inherent in human beings and is trainable not absolute.

In describing conscience in these terms, Clemens judges it harshly because it is fallible. Huck cannot feel his attachment to other human beings without his conscience "stirring him up," and he cannot act until he chooses the morality implied by one of the confused and confusing models of conscience he has internalized. But in spite of his need to act through conscience in order to find community, Huck cannot actually find within his conscience a social code that doesn't betray the very social feelings it is supposed to facilitate. Thus Clemens describes conscience as the enemy of humankind, a chimera that promises absolute morality and social connection but delivers a painful fraud.

Clemens was unusual in that he both accepted the utilitarian model of conscience as true and condemned it so roundly. Even Sumner, whose writings may very well have encouraged Clemens's pessimism, found a kind of harsh justice in following the law of "the survival of the fittest." Clemens, retaining a sense of the value of altruism, found the selfishness that his utilitarian monism uncovered to be purely abominable. Even more peculiar, although most philosophers of the Common Sense tradition saw the gregarious instinct as a sign of humanity's fundamental morality, Clemens saw the human desire for society itself as morally suspect. In continuing to believe in the absolute morality of strict honesty—honesty he had come to define in naturalistic terms—he found any impulse that would lead people to veer from pure truth to be immoral.

By this standard, he judged the social instinct itself as one of humanity's fundamental immoralities. In "The Character of Man," for example, he said:

> We are discreet sheep; we wait to see how the drove is going and then go with the drove. We have two opinions: one private, which we are afraid to express; and another one—the one we use—which we force ourselves to wear to please Mrs. Grundy, until habit makes us comfortable in it, and the custom of defending it presently makes us love it, adore it, and forget how pitifully we came by it. (*WIM* 62)

In his following list of examples, he points out that, invariably, a person's public opinion is a lie that he espouses for its utility. It may advance his career, maintain his job, or just keep him in the good graces of his community, but in all cases, he does it for his own benefit. "The mainspring of man's nature is . . . selfishness" (*WIM* 64).

III

Clemens's evaluation of humanity's selfish gregariousness partly explains his obsession with slavery, as manifested in *A Connecticut Yankee in King Arthur's Court* (1889). As Clemens understood democracy, each elector must have complete independence of mind. But when human beings have overwhelming needs to earn the respect of others, they have no choice but to be enslaved to the opinions of others. Clemens shows this clearly in the case of the commoners, no doubt, but also in the case of Hank Morgan's hand-picked and trained boys and in the case of Hank himself.

In the case of the commoners, the fear of personal destruction of course provides a strong and, in a strictly utilitarian way, a legitimate motive to going along with the crowd. When, in Chapter Thirty, Clemens has Hank isolate the charcoal-burner from his neighbors, Hank prompts the burner into an admission that he serves his master's interests out of perceived necessity:

> I helped to hang my neighbors for that it were peril to my own life to show lack of zeal in the master's cause; the others helped for none other reason. All rejoice to-day that he is dead, but all do go about seemingly sorrowing, and shedding the hypocrite's tear, for in that lies safety. (299)

Although he finds these words "The only ones that have ever tasted good in my mouth," he could not find the courage to say them until Hank said the equivalent first. The implication is that he needs to follow other people's cues whether he is speaking his true mind or not. It becomes doubtful, then, whether he can have a mind of his own in any circumstances.

Hank says explicitly that no man in a feudal society can have his own mind. "You see, in a country where they have ranks and castes, a man isn't ever a man, he is only part of a man; he can't ever get his full growth" (322). The book makes amply clear that Clemens defines manhood by independence of mind; where "men were men," they "held their heads up, and had a man's pride, and spirit and independence" (67). So in a land where men are only partly men, the conclusion is that they cannot have independence of mind.

While Hank concludes conversely that democratic men who have independence of mind are possible, Clemens ironically has Hank build a man factory to turn those who had the raw materials to make men into *"Men."* But of course, the fact that he needs a factory to turn these folk into independent minds shows how little independence they really have. Clem-

ens shows Hank to be a dreamer on this point. When the Church imposes
its interdict, he assumes that his men will have breathed freedom long
enough to have overcome the power of their feudal environment. Clarence,
with the wisdom of his fundamental skepticism, explains that "our schools,
our colleges, or vast workshops" are filled with people who cannot overcome their fear of their "superiors'" judgments. "Since [the Interdict], they
merely put on a bold outside—at heart they are quaking. Make up your
mind to it—when the armies come, the mask will fall" (418). And Clarence, Morgan finds, is right. Morgan had expected that, by declaring a
republic, he could call the latent manhood out of all Britons.

> Ah, what a donkey I was! Toward the end of the week, I began to get this large
> and disenchanting fact through my head: that the mass of the nation had
> swung their caps and shouted for the Republic for about one day, and there an
> end! The Church, the nobles and the gentry then turned one grand all-
> disapproving frown upon them and shriveled them into sheep! From that
> moment the sheep had begun to gather to the fold—that is to say, the camps—
> and offer their valueless lives and their valuable wool to the "righteous cause."
> Why, even the very men who had lately been slaves were in the "righteous
> cause," and glorifying it, praying for it, sentimentally slobbering over it, just
> like all the other commoners. (427)

Here Hank finally learns that it is not just fear that makes the commoners
support feudalism; it is the sentiment of sociability. They, like all human
beings, want to earn the approval of those whose opinions they value. With
a collective frown, the higher orders subdue the lower not through physical
power, but through the power of this social sentiment.

Hank's faithful fifty-two do not accept the legitimacy of the nobility as
their source of approval. But they, too, want to feel that they belong to a
large group. They see not only the nobility coming to fight them, but also
the commoners, the people that Morgan had taught them to consider the
legitimate nation itself. In these circumstances, they, too, find themselves
wanting to give up the battle against hierarchy in order to feel themselves a
part of a larger community. As their spokesman puts it:

> We have tried to forget what we are—English boys! We have tried to put
> reason before sentiment, duty before love: our minds approve, but our hearts
> reproach us. . . . *all England is marching against us!* O, sir, consider!—reflect!—
> these are our people, they are bone of our bone, flesh of our flesh, we love
> them—do not ask us to destroy our nation! (429)

Hank is only ready for this expression of sentiment because he has finally learned that all people follow crowds, not from reason, but from an irrational desire to belong to the mass.

He is not immune to this impulse himself. He admits from early in the book that he wishes to "be the centre of all the nation's wonder and reverence" (45). Although he does not accept the superiority of any class of human beings and therefore does not see official approval of his behavior as the source of his worth, he nonetheless needs an audience in order to be happy with himself. Of course, part of him wants an audience like the one he has been used to, so much of his purpose at "reforming" Arthur's Britain is to build himself a society that he can call home. His longing for community in his efforts to build a republic shows in his unwillingness to offend anyone while he brings about a complete revolution of political, social, and economic life. On his adventure with Sandy, for instance, he slips into reveries "about how to banish oppression from this land and restore to all its people their stolen rights and manhood without disobliging anybody" (121). When he realizes that he cannot change the course of society so easily, he is very disappointed:

> I rather wished I had gone some other road. This was not the sort of experience for a statesman to encounter who was planning out a peaceful revolution in his mind. For it could not help bringing up the ungetaroundable fact that, all gentle cant and philosophizing to the contrary notwithstanding, no people in this world ever did achieve their freedom by goody-goody talk and moral suasion: it being immutable law that all revolutions that will succeed, must *begin* in blood. (182–83)

But Morgan so wants to have his peace and his republic, too, that he grasps at straws to support his "dream" (300) whenever he can.

He is also obsessed with the idea of rising in society by his own merit, refusing the meretricious honor of nobility in favor of a title, "the Boss," spontaneously bestowed by the nation at large.[15] Nothing delights him more than to be the center of attention. Even when he is masquerading as a commoner in order to learn about common life in the republic he wants to install, Hank cannot abide to remain common; he must always win the adulation of those around him: "I never care to do a thing in a quiet way; it's got to be theatrical, or I don't take any interest in it" (309).[16] So he throws a grand party for the burghers of a small town, alternately humiliating his "peers" and then jollying them up so that he can bask in their reverence and companionship. However, when he thinks he demonstrates his superior intellect on a point of political economy but nonetheless fails to win their agreement, he grows furious:

> Well, I was smarting under a sense of defeat. Undeserved defeat, but what of that? That didn't soften the smart any. And to think of the circumstances! The first statesman of the age, the capablest man, the best informed man in the entire world, the loftiest uncrowned head that had moved through the clouds of any political firmament for centuries, sitting here apparently defeated in argument by an ignorant country blacksmith! And I could see that those others were sorry for me! — which made me blush till I could smell my whiskers scorching. Put yourself in my place; feel as mean as I did, as ashamed as I felt — wouldn't *you* have struck below the belt, to get even? Yes, you would; it is simply human nature. (328)

He remains intellectually sure of his ideas, but he holds his ideas mainly to prove to himself his own worth. When others do not agree with him, it challenges his own high self-estimate, making him blush in humiliation. Clemens thus shows Hank Morgan himself, the symbol of democratic man, the man who holds himself up as the universal judge of manhood, to so lack independent judgment as to be "ashamed" at the *appearance* of being wrong.

The difference between "The Boss" and the Britons, Clemens suggests, lies in nurture not nature. Because all human beings want to belong, they learn how to behave by copying their elders, as do the children who hang their mate: "It was some more human nature; the admiring little folk imitating their elders; they were playing mob, and had achieved a success which promised to be a good deal more serious than they had bargained for" (303). So by copying their elders, children learn behavior, that is to say, they learn to be themselves. In this, Clemens had adopted the Spencerian view of the overriding importance of learning in the composition of human character.

In fact, Clemens had by this time come to see human beings as nothing but the product of training. As he has Hank Morgan say of Morgan le Fay:

> Oh, it was no use to waste sense on her. Training — training is everything; training is all there is *to* a person. We speak of nature; it is folly; there is no such thing as nature; what we call by that misleading name is merely heredity and training. We have no thoughts of our own, no opinions of our own: they are transmitted to us, trained into us. All that is original in us, and therefore fairly creditable or discreditable to us, can be covered up and hidden by the point of a cambric needle, all the rest being atoms contributed by, and inherited from, a

procession of ancestors that stretches back a billion years to the Adam-clam or grasshopper or monkey from whom our race has been so tediously and ostentatiously and unprofitably developed. And as for me, all that I think about in this plodding sad pilgrimage, this pathetic drift between the eternities, is to look out and humbly live a pure and high and blameless life, and save that one microscopic atom in me that is truly *me*: the rest may land in Sheol and welcome, for all I care. (162)

This passage is crucial to understanding the development of Clemens's moral philosophy in several ways.

First of all, it marks a substantial clarification of Clemens's attitudes toward the power and value of education in forming human individuality. Early in his career, he seems to have held a fairly conservative belief in the constitution of the human character as composed more of innate than acquired characteristics. This opinion shows no better than in his attack on the great American exponent of education, Benjamin Franklin. Beginning the sketch "The Late Benjamin Franklin" (1870) with a mock attack on Franklin's motives in writing his autobiography and his maxims, and in his scientific investigations, Clemens turns serious at the end in denouncing those who force their children to follow in Franklin's footsteps:

> I merely desired to do away with somewhat of the prevalent calamitous idea among heads of families that Franklin *acquired* his great genius by working for nothing, studying by moonlight, and getting up in the night instead of waiting till morning like a Christian; and that this program, rigidly inflicted will make a Franklin of every father's fool. It is time these gentlemen were finding out that these execrable eccentricities of instinct and conduct are only the *evidences* of genius, not the *creators* of it. (*SN&O* 278)

Of course, the ultimate target of this attack is Franklin himself, whose belief in the power of "Habitude" to create personality inspired so much of his liberal utilitarianism as an alternative to the religion of his father.[17] Clemens, here, directly denies the power of education to change character, or, as he put it earlier in the sketch, "disposition."

Through a more customary humorous exaggeration, Clemens further suggests that any attempt to change a person's disposition out of the course of nature will have deleterious consequences, from a youth's loss of "natural rest" to the adult Mark Twain's "present state of general debility, indigence, and mental aberration":

> The sorrow that maxim [Early to bed and early to rise, Makes a man healthy and wealthy and wise] has cost me, through my parents experimenting on me

with it, tongue cannot tell. . . . If they had let me take my natural rest where would I have been now? Keeping store, no doubt, and respected by all. (*SN&O* 277)

Not that the early Clemens didn't believe that education could make a difference in one's moral character or abilities. But to some extent, the idea that human beings were nothing but education seemed to him to compromise the idea of intrinsic individuality. His acceptance of some conception of intrinsic individuality was perfectly consonant with prevailing Common Sense ideas of humanity as made both of innate and trainable capacities in service of a distinctive, individual soul.

Over the course of the 1870s, Clemens's conception of this balance shifted, stressing ever more the importance of education until he felt that even genius needed to be developed. Consider this comment he published in the *Atlantic*'s "Contributor's Club":

> Miss Anna Dickinson, I see, again braves her fate with the public on the stage. . . . On her first appearance I found the spectacle of her failure so cruel that it was impossible to look at it steadily. And yet, after I came away, I perceived the justice of what had happened. Here was a lady, with all the good motives in the world, aiming to place herself at the very top in an untried art, over the heads of people who had given years of their lives of hard work to it. If she had succeeded, it would have been an injustice more cruel than her failure was. But it was not in nature, it was not in the justice which orders these things, that she should succeed. Genius itself succeeds only by arduous self-training; and it is not for the beginner in any art to snatch its honors from its devoted student. . . . I count it gain whenever this people, in whatever way, gets a knock down hint to the effect that to do a thing you must learn how; and that to play on the fiddle it is not merely necessary to take a bow and fiddle with it. (unsigned contribution to "The Contributor's Club," *The Atlantic Monthly*, 39 [January, 1877]: 108)

By comparison to the earlier "The Late Benjamin Franklin," this note marks a significant shift in Clemens's thinking toward a view of human psychology more congruent with Locke's and with Locke's utilitarian followers than with Locke's more idealistic followers of the sentimental tradition.

By the 1880s, under the influence of his reading in Spencer, Clemens came to believe that human beings are nothing but the product of learning. Nevertheless, even though the passage I quoted above from *Connecticut Yankee* says that training is everything, it almost immediately contradicts this monistic conclusion. Something remains "original in us," though so small as to be a "microscopic atom." This is all that Hank Morgan, speaking here directly for the author, I believe, finds "fairly creditable or discreditable to us," and that can therefore be held morally to any account or that can be even considered as individual rather than collective. This is the remnant of the idea of soul that Clemens, for all of his monistic attack on sentimental dualism, cannot bear to eliminate from his moral vision. Without it, he sees no purpose to life, no moral value in a mechanical "drift between the eternities." This profound sense of loss that Clemens found monistic materialism to entail is, I believe, one of the forces that drove him back into periodic, serious re-evaluations of the worth of sentimental idealism in his last years as a writer.

The passage about Morgan le Fay's training also raises the question of what Clemens means by "training." On the one hand he says that "Training is all there is *to* a person," but two clauses later he says that human nature is merely "heredity and training." The concept of "heredity" seems to us to be completely at odds with the concept of "training," the one embracing innate physiological characteristics, the other the development of skills or characteristics through cultivation after birth. Clemens's use of "heredity" seems at odds with the utilitarian conception of the mind as tabula rasa. But to Clemens's peers, innate characteristics were those given by God: they were closely allied to the idea of soul. Anything developed through evolution was merely acquired. Further, by Spencer's Lamarckian understanding of evolution, and by Clemens's Spencerian reading of Darwin, learned traits are inheritable. Therefore, all traits one has that evolved through the time before birth as well as those accumulated after birth Clemens attributes to "training."

Thus, Clemens perceives human nature as the result of inherited training, as when he has Morgan explain the King's frequently unjust legal decisions as "the fault of his natural and unalterable sympathies" (239). When the King's conscience goads him into reporting escapees, Morgan notes that the King could see only one side of it: "He was born so, educated so, his veins were full of ancestral blood that was rotten with this sort of unconscious brutality, brought down by inheritance from a long procession of hearts that had each done its share toward poisoning the stream" (292). Each heart grows worse under its own experience, but the accumulated effect is transmissible through inheritance.

By Clemens's Spencerian understanding of evolution, not only were physical traits and moral proclivities inherited, but ideas themselves were part of the innate make-up of each person. This accounts for Clemens's insistence that although we are nothing but training, that training is of such a powerful sort as to be virtually unbreakable, with a rigidity we would now ascribe to physical rather than psychological constitution:

> Inherited ideas are a curious thing, and interesting to observe and examine. I had mine, the king and his people had theirs. In both cases they flowed in ruts worn deep by time and habit, and the man who should have proposed to divert them by reason and argument would have had a long contract on his hands. (65)

Altogether, Clemens seems to have thrown a Sumnerian cast on Spencer's ideas to develop a purely mechanical conception of human beings in which they have virtually no personal identity and have apparently limited capacity to change that identity. But his conception of evolution required him to assume that one can be trained after birth in order to have new traits to pass on to future generations. While being raised in an "atmosphere of superstition" forces most of the products of Morgan's man-factories to revert to their inherited and trained ideas of their place in society, his fifty-two boys were bred in a different environment that apparently destroyed all inherited ideas. Clemens here discovers a confusion in Spencerian philosophy about the relative force of those traits "learned" through inheritance and those soaked up after birth from an "atmosphere."

Although the behavior of the boys in contrast to the older products of the man factory suggests that childhood learning has the greatest impact on personality, the book suggests that "training" is a life-long process. Morgan himself, for all of his heredity and training in Connecticut, finds that a few years' time in feudal Britain begins to change him. He is unable to see the effects on him until he runs across a telephone office that had been installed under his authority; he then sees by contrast how numb he has grown:

> It sounded good! In this atmosphere of telephones and lightning communication with distant regions, I was breathing the breath of life again after long suffocation. I realized, then, what a creepy, dull, inanimate horror this land had been to me all these years, and how I had been in such a stifled condition of mind as to have grown used to it almost beyond the power to notice it. (231–32)

Now that he is noticing again, he sees that his numbness has been at least partly an active process even though he has had no conscious control over it; he has been "breath[ing]" the prejudices of feudal Britain in order to incorporate them into his moral outlook.

When reading a newspaper, for instance, he finds that he is outraged at the very insolence he has been trying to encourage:

It was delicious to see a newspaper again, yet I was conscious of a secret shock when my eye fell upon the first batch of display head-lines. I had lived in a clammy atmosphere of reverence, respect, deference, so long, that they sent a quivery little cold wave through me . . . [T]here was too lightsome a tone of flippancy all through the paper. It was plain I had undergone a considerable change without noticing it. I found myself unpleasantly affected by pert little irreverences which would have seemed but proper and airy graces of speech at an earlier period in my life. (257–58)

So Clemens describes change as something that affects people through the course of their lives as well as something inherited. More important, he shows change as an incremental process that is mostly unconscious and caused by external influences mediated by personal processes necessary to life. As the body breathes air, so does the mind "breathe" ideas. He did not, as many utilitarians did, see the individual having any great capacity to guide change. Human "nature," as he saw it, is a mechanical product of forces, such as "atmospheres," wholly beyond a person's control, and this is partly why he found it so "discreditable." He could not find anywhere in it a moral affinity to the ideas of freedom and independence that make for truly moral behavior.

Finally, the passage about Morgan le Fay's training shows Clemens confronting a fundamental paradox in utilitarian moral philosophy. Ever since Locke wrote that human beings could rationally determine morality, utilitarians had stressed the supremacy of reason to emotion not only in determining morality, but also in shaping the plastic personality according to rationally moral principles. The bifurcation of sentimental domestic philosophy into masculine and feminine spheres suggested further that rationality was a primarily masculine trait, essential to the conduct of practical affairs. Such ideas were widespread in a dilute form as part of the sentimental compromise, and with Spencer's effort to describe all knowledge by a rational and utilitarian system, this set of ideas reached its fullest and most problematic expression.

The problem lay in the utilitarian belief that pleasure and pain motivate all human behavior. If that is so, then reason is merely subsidiary to irrational motivation.[18] Morgan discovers this in realizing that it would be pointless to try to argue le Fay out of her prejudices. In fact he admits that "her intellect was good, she had brains enough," but she is emotionally attached to her training. Reason is not only powerless in the face of "custom" (194), it cannot compete with desire. When thinking of the love he left in Hartford, Morgan "sighed; I couldn't help it. And yet there was no sense in sighing, for she wasn't born yet. But that is the way we are made:

we don't reason, where we feel; we just feel" (94). This feeling comes from a man who professes to be "nearly barren of sentiment" (4), but for someone who is barren of sentiment, Morgan gets excited easily. For example, when Sandy grows agitated as she nears the ogres' castle, Morgan shares her feeling even though he finds no reason to, "for that sort of thing is catching. My heart got to thumping. You can't reason with your heart; it has its own laws, and thumps about things which the intellect scorns" (183).

To Stowe, the heart's independence gives it its superiority to reason. Clemens, on the contrary, sees this irrationality as a fundamental weakness in the utilitarian dream of human perfectibility. After all, it is the irrational desire to appear superior that leads Morgan and the King into slavery and then almost foils Morgan's efforts to save himself and the King: "Well, I had gone and spoiled it again, made another mistake. . . . There were plenty of ways to get rid of that officer by some simple and plausible device, but no, I must pick out a picturesque one; it is the crying defect of my character" (372). Like a grown up Tom Sawyer, this symbol of rationality would rather play games than act rationally, all because he wants to be the center of a good show. Emotion, and usually selfish emotion at that, suggests Clemens, is the organizing principle that gives coherence to trainable human beings. This makes them not only soulless, but also stupid, with no possible source of improvement under their own control. At moments in the story when this bleak vision of humanity dominates, Clemens's nihilism erupts, as, when commenting on human snobbery at the beginning of Chapter Thirty-One, he has Morgan say, "there are times when one would like to hang the whole human race and finish the farce" (302). Thus, Clemens's increasing pessimism stemmed in part from his increasing disillusionment with utilitarianism.

But this bleak view did not exclude all optimism, partly because, as Baetzhold points out, Clemens did not completely relinquish the sentimental conception of morality as articulated by Lecky. Lecky's influence on *Connecticut Yankee* as a source of details about the moral history of feudal Europe was substantial, and even though Clemens was trying to disprove Lecky's ideas by juxtaposing them against those of Spencer, certain aspects of sentimental moral philosophy maintained a hold on Clemens's thinking.

This shows in particular in *Connecticut Yankee* in Clemens's treatment of "moral perceptions." By utilitarian standards, moral perceptions would be nothing more than a compound of trained attitudes and self-interest, both of which are usually in concert but which can occasionally collide. The

King, for example, sees slavery as moral when it serves his self-interest as he sees it through both training and experience. But when sold into slavery, he experiences laws that he had only understood in theory before, and the experience, coupled with new self-interest, changes his moral attitudes: "You see, he knew his own laws just as other people so often know the laws: by words, not by effects. They take a meaning, and get to be very vivid, when you come to apply them to yourself" (346). After experiencing slavery, he comes to understand the injustice of it and decides to abolish it.

But the peculiar thing about the way Clemens presents the King's change of heart is that he speaks of moral perceptions as being independent of training, of being intuitively in touch with eternal rightness. One sees this in his reference to slavery "ossifying what one may call the superior lobe of human feeling" (200), and in his repeated assertions that men are at root "*men*"[19] by virtue of intuitive feelings of rightness:

> Secretly the "poor white" did detest the slave lord, and did feel his own shame. That feeling was not brought to the surface, but the fact that it was there and could have been brought out, under favoring circumstances . . . showed that a man is at bottom a man, after all, even if it doesn't show on the outside. (297)

The idea that there are self-evident truths based on moral perceptions is essential to Clemens's understanding of moral independence. The positive vision of progress that the book often endorses depends on his faltering belief in this principle of sentimental morality. When, on the other hand, Clemens argues that any conception of selfhood, including one of moral independence, is merely the result of training, he slips into his recurrent nihilistic misanthropy. Apparently he was strongly vested in the hope that human beings have some larger morality than pure self-interest, and some access to it more valuable than through "training."

His hope seems to lie in the sentimental idea, prominent in Lecky's *History*, that personal experience coupled with sympathetic imagination brings morality to life.[20] The King himself shows this moral progress at work. When Hank Morgan drills the King in how to travel incognito, the King understands the details but cannot manage the appropriate bearing because no matter how much Morgan

> drilled him as representing, in turn, all sorts of people out of luck and suffering dire privations and misfortunes . . . it was only just words, words, — they meant nothing in the world to him, I might just as well have whistled. Words realize nothing, vivify nothing to you, unless you have suffered in your own person the thing which the words try to describe. (277–79)

But over the course of experiencing life as a commoner and as a slave, the King comes to have compassion for most of his subjects.[21]

Thus, the King himself, the leader of the feudal order, the man who has most to gain from the continuation of that order and all of its superstitions, can change through personal experience of a different, transcendental moral code. Such a vision of selfhood seems substantially at odds with the rest of the book, with its final determination of the immutability of human prejudice in the face of self-interest, superstition, and petrified training. It suggests on the contrary that human beings have, through experience coupled with imagination, the power to transform themselves. This ambivalence would persist through the remainder of Clemens's career, with his mechanical view of personality at odds with a more flexible view of human personality that had its roots in the sentimental tradition.

Significantly, Clemens saw human beings as able to overcome their own training and self-interest when they experience suffering in domestic circumstances. In the "small-pox hut," for instance, the King listens to the lament of a woman whose family has been shattered and left without comfort because it has been persecuted by both state and church. The King is so moved by her circumstances that he sheds a tear of compassion over her plight (286). When she responds by unwittingly attacking the King, he "winced under this accidental home-shot, but kept still." The power of domestic troubles to evoke sympathy is so great as to encourage him to subdue his formidable pride.

In his continued sentimentalization of family life, Clemens is not fully contradicting his Spencerian philosophy. After all, Spencer found the family to be the evolutionary source of sympathy and morality. The peculiar thing is not that *Connecticut Yankee* is pervaded with effusive sentimentality whenever it deals with familial relations, but that to an extreme degree, such sentimentality serves an adult political purpose. For instance, the scene in Chapter Twenty-One in which a slave family is sold apart is reminiscent of sentimental antebellum antislavery literature.[22] In his earlier works, Clemens tended to ridicule sentimental political agitation; he felt that sentiment belonged in the home, not in the political and practical sphere. In blending the domestic and practical spheres in *Connecticut Yankee*, he anticipates his later tendency to use the conventions of sentimentality in writing reformist tracts such as "A Dog's Tale" (1903) and "A Horse's Tale" (1906).[23]

Yet at the end of *Connecticut Yankee* Clemens has Hank renounce the use of sentimentality in political affairs. When Hank's conscience begins to trouble him at the thought of slaughtering England's knights, he proposes to warn them of their danger. Clarence castigates him for his conscientious concern, showing him that the knights not only would disdain his warning but would "dismember" the courier in answer. Hank replies, "How empty is theory in presence of fact! And this was just fact, and nothing else. It was the thing that would have happened, there was no getting around that. I tore up the paper and granted my mistimed sentimentalities a permanent rest" (435). Here is Clemens's typical juxtaposition of "fact," or rather a practical assessment of circumstances (though the "fact" he mentions is really only hypothetical), and sentiment, with the practical Hank Morgan opting for fact. The message should support the value of simple truth over dreaming, but the end of the novel does not carry this idea with conviction. Morgan's "victory" ends up killing his supporters, and he, finally vanquished by Merlin's magic, drifts through the eternities dreaming of a return to the domestic bliss he had discovered with Sandy. Morgan, the self-proclaimed "Champion of hard, unsentimental, common-sense and reason" (384) who describes himself as "practical; yes, and nearly barren of sentiment, I suppose — or poetry, in other words" (4), finds himself unable to defeat the dreamy, imaginative world of chivalric romance. Indeed, in the concluding return to the book's frame, we are reminded that the entire story is likely to be an imaginative extravaganza, a literary delirium tremens of someone who clearly drinks and then dreams too much. Reality and realism may take the final and most devastating blow by book's end.

What Clemens discovered accidentally in *Connecticut Yankee* was the inadequacy of his materialistic monism to explain human morality. What he began as a humorous juxtaposition of feudal reality with nineteenth-century ideals of morality and physical comfort in order to show the absurdity of sentimentalizing the past turned first into a vicious satire of humanity's pretenses to importance, and then to a faint but important lament for the idealism he had lost in his Spencerian thinking. When he considered people as lost in the degradation of slavery, he saw them as having lost all that makes life worth living:

> Their entire being was reduced to a monotonous dead level of patience, resignation, dumb uncomplaining acceptance of whatever might befall them in this life. Their very imagination was dead. When you can say that of a man, he has struck bottom, I reckon; there is no lower deep for him. (182)

The value Clemens puts in imagination places him firmly in the idealist side of the sentimental camp despite his fervent efforts to prove that sentimental conceptions of the human mind and morality are ultimately wrong. In

contrasting his materialistic monism with sentimental idealism, he proved
to himself not so much that utilitarianism accurately described the truth of
this world as that the truth left much to be desired.

IV

The American Claimant, a minor work written in seventy-one days in early
1891 (Baetzhold 166) and published by May 1892 in order to turn a quick
dollar in the face of Clemens's mounting financial difficulties, casts an
interesting light back on the meaning of *Connecticut Yankee* to the development of Clemens's moral philosophy.[24] It, too, is a story built on a contrast
between feudal values and democratic ones, this time by transplanting an
idealistic English aristocrat, who wishes to renounce his unearned title and
wealth, into nineteenth-century America, where he hopes to earn his bread
by his own labor. In both, Clemens develops an essentially utilitarian
conception of morality, but in describing the world that requires selfishness
as the basis for moral behavior, *The American Claimant* discovers the social
relativity of some truths, the first step toward Clemens's serious investigation of moral relativism.

Both books describe the moral workings of political economy in the
same free-market terms. And particularly, both describe legitimate fortunes
as those earned through productive labor: neither inherited wealth nor the
wealth accruing to speculative finance is morally or practically worthwhile.
As Morgan puts it in *Connecticut Yankee*:

> No sound and legitimate business can be established on a basis of speculation.
> A successful whirl in the knight errantry line . . . [is] just a corner in pork, that's
> all, and you can't make anything else out of it. You're rich — yes suddenly
> rich — for about a day, maybe a week: then somebody corners the market on
> you, and down goes your bucket-shop; . . . And moreover, . . . knight-errantry
> is worse than pork; for whatever happens, the pork's left, and so somebody's
> benefited, anyway. (177)

Unless there is a product involved, Clemens implies, risk for profit is not
legitimate. That Clemens speculated in business ventures all the time, and
that at the time he wrote this he was investing heavily in the Paige typesetter, is not really a sign of his own hypocrisy: his investments were all in
inventions rather than financial instruments; he was a venture capitalist, not
a financier. He considered himself part of the productive mechanism of

nineteenth-century progress rather than as making illegitimate profit from financial manipulation.[25]

The value to Clemens of material progress shows equally clearly in *Claimant*. Clemens catechizes his British aristocrat in the value of inventiveness and of practical technology at a meeting of a Mechanics Club. There Berkeley learns that anyone who measures a nation's power or value by the size of its population alone misses the importance of material progress. The mechanic who reads a paper that Berkeley hears encourages us to "take a truer standard: the measure of a man's contributing capacity to his time and his people—the work he can do" (84). By this standard, mechanized America can produce the work of forty billion people for the benefit of its sixty million. Young Berkeley pronounces the moral to this speech:

> How grand that is! . . . What a civilization it is, and what prodigious results these are! and brought about almost wholly by common men; not by Oxford-trained aristocrats, but men who stand shoulder to shoulder in the humble ranks of life and earn the bread that they eat. Again I'm glad I came. I have found a country at last where one may start fair, and, breast to breast with his fellow-man, rise by his own efforts, and be something in the world and be proud of that something. (85)

Productivity, then, is the moral standard by which Clemens feels a man must distinguish himself.

But Berkeley, willing though he may be, cannot earn his living in the face of closed union shops. He then turns apostate on his radicalism, longing instead for his hereditary wealth. Clemens here implies that any impediment to free trade, any artificial barrier to allowing all men free access to work, any institution that would drive a potential democrat back into elitism, is immoral. Because Berkeley is too proud to ask his father to call him back, however, he is forced eventually to find a job too shabby and ridiculous to be worth the notice of unions. He begins to work as a hack-portrait painter in the service of two artists who are so bad that, without Berkeley's help, they sell as many paintings to collectors who value them for their accidentally comic qualities as to patrons who commission them. Berkeley improves the firm's fortunes, and, in spite of his initial disgust with the task, he

> was obliged to confess to himself that there was something about work—even such grotesque and humble work as this—which most pleasantly satisfied something in his nature which had never been satisfied before, and also gave him a strange new dignity in his own private view of himself. (154)[26]

Productive work in service of his customers gives Berkeley satisfaction; in utilitarian terms, it gives the work moral value.

As *Connecticut Yankee* and *The American Claimant* share a common understanding of public morality, they share one conception of human nature — that, in the words of Hank Morgan, "training is everything." In *The American Claimant*, Clemens makes the same point by showing that Berkeley's desire to return to his aristocratic ways is not solely the consequence of his early failure to find productive work but is substantially the result of his discovering his deep-seated training as an aristocrat. Berkeley's radicalism is merely intellectual, not emotional, and, when confronted by the unfamiliar "familiarities" of a relatively caste-free society, he is forced to acknowledge the power of his "training." When introduced to the chambermaid at the boarding house he chooses as his American home, for instance, he reacts badly:

> The young Englishman made the awkward bow common to his nationality and time of life in circumstances of delicacy and difficulty, and these were of that sort; for, being taken by surprise, his natural, lifelong self sprang to the front, and that self, of course, would not know just how to act when introduced to a chambermaid, or to the heiress of a mechanics' boarding house. His other self — the self which recognized the equality of all men — would have managed the thing better if it hadn't been caught off guard and robbed of its chance. (91)

But it never gets the chance, because in order to overcome training, Berkeley discovers, one needs a new group of peers who will applaud new behaviors. Since Berkeley has no money and no job, he quickly earns the scorn of most of the boarders, forcing him back into pride of caste to enable him to hold up his chin in public.[27]

The differences between the two novels have less to do with their evaluations of what constitutes human nature and progress than what the individual must do to be a moral person in the context of this reality. In *Connecticut Yankee*, Clemens's obvious disgust with the shams of caste makes him advocate political revolution. Further, he excoriates all nobles as pirates and brigands. *The American Claimant* at first attacks nobility; for instance, when Berkeley renounces his birthright, he tells his father that their family motto, "*Suum cuique* — to every man his own . . . is become a sarcasm" (4). Later, too, in the Mechanics Club where Berkeley finds himself so impressed by democratic ideas, he hears that no throne exists that has a right to exist, and no symbol of it, flying from any flagstaff, is righteously entitled to wear any device but the skull and crossbones of that kindred industry which differs from royalty only business-wise — merely as retail differs from wholesale. (80)

But the novel's plot proceeds to reject such absolute morality as inappropriate to the real world. Berkeley is shown to be an idealistic fool for renouncing privileges he was born to, not because the privileges are inherently right, but because in an unjust world, every man is entitled to serve his own best interests as best he can.

Berkeley comes to feel this idea in his own case, but as he intellectually believes that he must not hold any dishonest distinction, he feels guilty at his desire once again to take his place in the British aristocracy. But when his roommate Barrow attacks the idea of moral self-sacrifice, Berkeley is emotionally relieved but intellectually confused. Eager to reconcile feeling and thought, he presses Barrow to explain:

"You are inconsistent. You are opposed to aristocracies, yet you'd take an earldom if you could. Am I to understand that you don't blame an earl for being and remaining an earl?"

"I certainly don't." . . .

"Well then, who *would* you blame?"

"The whole nation — any bulk and mass of population anywhere, in any country, that will put up with the infamy, the outrage, the insult of a hereditary aristocracy which *they* can't enter — and on absolutely free and equal terms."

"Come, aren't you beclouding yourself with distinctions that are not differences?"

"Indeed, I am not. I am entirely clear-headed about this thing. If I could extirpate an aristocratic system by declining its honors, then I should be a rascal to accept them. And if enough of the mass would join me to make the extirpation possible, then I should be a rascal to do otherwise than help in the attempt." (129–30)[28]

By purely utilitarian standards, it makes perfect sense not to fight against the impossible.

The key here is that Clemens places the moral burden in the mass of humanity rather than in individuals. As Berkeley paraphrases Barrow's ideas, "You have no blame for the lucky few who naturally decline to vacate the pleasant nest they were born into; you only despise the all-powerful and stupid mass of the nation for allowing the nest to exist" (130). Only an idealist, such as the appropriately named Berkeley, Clemens suggests, would subject himself to the injustices the masses suffer through their own delusions.

So in *The American Claimant*, Clemens inverts his earlier definitions of idealist and realist. Berkeley has here an intellectual access to an absolute, rational morality, what Spencer in his *Data of Ethics* wished to promote by uncovering the natural laws of moral evolution. Clemens does not necessarily reject such a moral vision, but he does suggest that anyone who tries to anticipate a moral end before its time is, by thinking about an abstract morality, actually living an emotional lie. Emotions, on the other hand, are more closely tied to the facts of a culture in its current state of development. Thus, reality as it is useful to human beings is relative to its time rather than transcendental.

Clemens anticipated this idea in *Connecticut Yankee*, but in such a way as to prevent him from pursuing its implications. When discussing Sandy's delusions about the pig princesses, Hank acknowledges

> the power of training! of influence! of education! It can bring a body up to believe anything. I had to put myself in Sandy's place to realize that she was not a lunatic. Yes, and put her in mine, to demonstrate how easy it is to seem a lunatic to a person who has not been taught as you have been taught. (191)

Hank acknowledges the relativity of truth between cultures, but he so roundly condemns the past by the standards of the present as to show which truths are better.

But in *The American Claimant*, Clemens begins to open himself to the possibility that madness may have value, not only by making a person fit into his culture in a practical way, but by giving to life a meaning and purpose that a strictly rational understanding of mechanical "laws of nature" cannot. In this way, the return of Clemens's character Colonel Sellers as a comic hero rather than as a buffoon is quite significant. Sellers continues to live in Washington "all of fifteen years" (12) after the action of *The Gilded Age*, in poverty but with spirits intact.[29] He has managed to keep his family together all these years by making frequent small fortunes that he squanders. When we first see him he is just finishing inventing a toy puzzle that, by book's end, is produced and marketed by an industrious Yankee furniture maker. The puzzle makes the fortunes of all concerned, so Clemens has the madcap tinkerer "make good."

By Clemens's earlier representation, Sellers's inventive imagination was too unbridled and unbalanced ever to be of any value to his family or his associates. Here he still pursues mostly insane dreams based on half-understandings of "scientific" theories. He believes, for instance, that he can rematerialize the dead, and when, by an absurd mix-up, he believes Berkeley is the rematerialized body of a Western bankrobbing cowboy, he cannot at first understand Berkeley's English speech and bearing. But his half-baked understanding of Spencerian ideas of evolution finally gives him his explanation:

> The whole secret is perfectly clear to me now, clear as day. *Every man is made up of heredities,* long descended atoms and particles of his ancestors. This present materialization is incomplete. We have only brought it down to perhaps the beginning of this century. . . . We've materialized this burglar's ancestor! (172)

While such absurdities earned Sellers a role as a personification of the danger of unfounded dreaming in *The Gilded Age,* here he serves as a mixed character, both as a clown for the sake of fun and as an example of the value of an imagination. His wife, who once served by counterpoint to highlight Sellers's failures, now admits his victories:

> As for suddenness and capacity in imagining things, his beat don't exist, I reckon. As like as not it wouldn't have occurred to anybody else to name this poor old rat-trap Rossmore Towers, but it just comes natural to him. Well, no doubt it's a blessed thing to have an imagination that can always make you satisfied, no matter how you are fixed. (40)

Sellers's dreaming saves him from the knowledge of his own failures, raising the question, in utilitarian terms, whether a happy man may be said to fail.

In *Connecticut Yankee,* although Hank acknowledges that when a man's imagination is dead he has reached bottom, he always expects to attach imagination to scientific realities in order to further progress. In *The American Claimant,* Clemens begins to see imagination as a way of defeating unhappiness in a real world where, even though morality and happiness are supposed to be congruent, human beings experience relatively little happiness under the overpowering workings of natural law. Sellers's dreaming may have made him a fool, but, as his daughter says, "It pleases him, and does no one any harm" (209). In other words, if he saw reality, he'd realize his manifold grounds for unhappiness, but his dreaming, his idealism, protects him. Here, then, in germinal form, is Clemens's interest in the power of imagination and creativity not to find natural law but to transcend it.

Significantly, Mrs. Sellers's acknowledgment of Sellers's powers of happiness concludes by positing the Colonel as an opposite of Calvin: "Uncle Dave Hopkins used always to say, 'Turn me into John Calvin, and I want to know which place I'm going to; turn me into Mulberry Sellers, and I don't care'" (40). As Clemens began to see the power of nature as a kind of fate, the doctrines of Calvinism began to have a new hold on his imagination, repeating themselves through many unfinished works of his later years. In this tentative exploration of idealism, of wish fulfillment on Sellers's part, Clemens prefigures one of his alternatives to predetermined fate, the solipsism of "No. 44, The Mysterious Stranger."

As Clemens's nascent interest in both idealism and solipsism arose from his understanding of sentimental philosophy, so his changing conception of the importance of humor arose from his growing appreciation of some of the tenets of sentimental philosophy. Again, the change is best seen in a contrast between *Connecticut Yankee* and *The American Claimant*. *Connecticut Yankee*, for all of its irreverence and play, is essentially a serious book, and the aristocratic frown that frightens the people back into their feudal ways symbolizes the limited range Clemens perceived humor as having in changing human behavior.

In an interesting echo of *Connecticut Yankee*, Barrow in *The American Claimant* says that the British people could end aristocracy in six months by "electing themselves dukes and duchesses to-morrow and calling themselves so" (97). The very absurdity of such an attack would make it effective. "Royalty itself couldn't survive such a process. A handful of frowners against thirty million laughers in a state of eruption: Why, it's Herculaneum against Vesuvius" (97). Here Clemens advocates revolution by laughter, and the revolution lies not in power, but in perception. Before the people can perform such a revolution, they must first see and expose the absurdity of artificial distinctions. In *Connecticut Yankee*, the people succumb to the aristocratic frown, and Hank Morgan's revolution of blood could not change the hearts of the people. In the sentimentalist's sense of humor, the capacity to see absurdities and to exploit them by juxtaposing incompatible ideas, here the oxymoron of universal distinction, Clemens sees a truly revolutionary capacity to change. Thus, in advocating social transformation through change of feeling, Clemens discovers a new kind of moral suasion. Remarkably similar to Stowe's call to "feel right" to end chattel slavery, Clemens asks his readers to laugh right to end their own spiritual slavery.

Clemens turned to the sensibility of humor in part because over the course of composing *Connecticut Yankee* he saw human beings more as feeling than as reasoning creatures. As I showed above, he then turned to a sentimental idea of an innate feeling of manhood in order to carry his hopes of progress. His despair at finding human beings a mere product of external forces led him to doubt the power of such a feeling of manhood, especially since this feeling is in opposition to feelings of fear and to sentiments of reverence and loyalty. In *The American Claimant*, however, Clemens discovered in humor an emotional capacity as powerful as fear, a source of emotions that could liberate feelings of manhood.

But in order to see humor in this way, Clemens first had to remove it from its limited position in the Common Sense hierarchy of sentiments. Always subdued by the traditional assessment of humor as being below the sentiment of reverence, he had long been ashamed of his role as humorist. Now, having rejected the old Common Sense compromise through his utilitarian phase, he began to rethink the proper hierarchy of senses, and the sense of humor came out much closer to the top. One can see this in part in the way Barrow uses humor to rescue the despairing Berkeley. Barrow's intention is no more than the old Common Sense one of restoring flagging mental health by inducing laughter (140). But in seeing the absurd painting that Barrow uses as a health-giving joke, Berkeley finds the possibility for work that eventually gives him a powerful sense of his own manhood. It is tempting to see a parallel in Clemens's own circumstances as a man finally acknowledging the personal value in a profession he had never fully appreciated.

Although one can explain Clemens's new appreciation for humor in psychological terms, it is easier to document the change in political terms. Quite simply, he had come to see reverence as a sentiment that served illegitimate political ends. Reacting to Matthew Arnold's criticism of Americans generally and the American press specifically as lacking the reverence any high culture needed, Clemens praised irreverence as the best protector of freedom:

> Our press is certainly bankrupt in the "thrill of awe" — otherwise reverence; reverence for nickel plate and brummagem. Let us sincerely hope that this fact will remain a fact forever; for to my mind a discriminating irreverence is the creator and protector of human liberty — even as the other thing is the creator, nurse, and steadfast protector of all forms of human slavery, bodily and mental. (81)

Insofar as he saw humor in this important role as protector of human liberty, Clemens had to grant it scope to attack people and ideas he felt were in conflict with that sense of manhood that he had come to value so highly. Such a point of view allowed Clemens to explore the power of humor in such different pieces as "The Man That Corrupted Hadleyburg" (1899) and "The Chronicle of Young Satan" (composed in the middle 1890s, published posthumously in a bowdlerized edition as *The Mysterious Stranger* in 1916 and published in an accurate edition in 1969), in which he declared that the human race needs to learn to use its "humor-perception," which is the source of its "one really effective weapon—laughter" (*MTMS* 166, 165). And in his use of his own humor-perception as a weapon in his later years, he discovered that "against the assault of Laughter nothing can stand," including his own belief in reality itself. So in liberating the sentiment of humor, Clemens helped push himself toward the explorations of solipsism, dream-visions and idealism that marked his last years as a writer.

V

If the Common Sense middle ground had held through the 1880s and beyond, perhaps Clemens would not have seen in his exploration of certain aspects of sentimental emotionalism a view into radical intuitionism and even solipsism. But given that the middle ground had more or less evaporated and that he had discovered inconsistencies in both sentimental and utilitarian descriptions of the world, he was left waffling over the void, alternately advocating purely mechanistic determinism and various versions of highly sentimental idealism. His tendency in the early 1890s to turn to the idealistic side was reinforced by the deterioration and ultimate failure of his business prospects. He had, after all, hoped to end his writing career with *Connecticut Yankee* (Baetzhold 165).

He had invested heavily in the Paige typesetter which, as a publisher and a former typesetter, he knew would be worth a fortune when perfected. Paige assured him that perfection was imminent. Perhaps the prospect of imminent wealth as a venture capitalist accounts for Clemens's willingness to attack Britain in *Connecticut Yankee* even though his British book sales accounted for a substantial portion of his income. At the very moment his needs for cash were growing rapidly in the face of his investments, publication of *Connecticut Yankee* depressed the British sales of all of his books by two-thirds (Baetzhold 164). In need of cash, Clemens quickly produced a number of short pieces—including some newspaper correspondence for the New York *Sun*, "The £1,000,000 Bank-note," and "The Californian's Tale"—and three novels, *The American Claimant* (1892), *Tom Sawyer Abroad* (1893), and *Pudd'nhead Wilson* (1894).

The character Wilson might to some extent be the person Clemens at this time perceived himself to be: a practical inventor with an understanding of human nature that only earns him the scorn of the common folk who are below his level, above the mob but governed by its opinions. Wilson does not prosper until he proves the superiority of the scientific outlook.[30] Clemens's hopes to do the same died with the failure of his investments. He misjudged the practicality of Paige's complicated invention, and when the infinitely simpler Morgenthaler typesetter proved its worth at about the same time the Paige proved unworkable, he was forced to recognize that he had invested heavily in a dream, not a practicality. His investments had pushed him to the brink of insolvency, and the panic of 1893 pushed him over the edge. By 1894, he declared bankruptcy, and, to earn his living, he promised to renounce business, with all of its pretensions toward rational practicality, in favor of literature: "I will live in literature. I will wallow in it, revel in it, I will swim in ink" (Baetzhold 175).

He was returning to the old stand, starting again as a literary man whose profession was to promote the Common Sense cultural compromise that barely existed in the culture any more. Most writers were now idealists; Clemens found in his return to his role as a writer at least strong encouragement to turn to idealism himself. And, as earlier in his career, the practical setback in the role he had assigned himself helped him to rethink his understanding of human nature and human morality. But as he had already attacked the major philosophical systems he had available to draw on and had reduced these systems to their fundamental inconsistencies, he was left floundering in confusion, and only slowly was able to force himself back into his own creativity to try to forge a system out of the pieces he had earlier rejected.

6. "All Human Rules Are More or Less Idiotic"

I

Toward the end of the nineteenth century, the famous British physicist Lord Kelvin said that physicists had learned virtually everything there was to know about the material universe. He acknowledged that a few facts were unknown, but he believed that all the important laws had been discovered, making completion of the science a foregone conclusion in short order (Thomas 146). His certitude arose from his monistic faith in the power of mathematics to describe the universe by a few, simple natural laws. As Lewis Thomas says, Kelvin typifies the "conventional, established scientific leadership" (143) of his day. On the eve of Einstein's publication of the Special Theory of Relativity, Kelvin was speaking for the scientific community at large in saying that complete, objective knowledge was not only attainable, but imminent. And the world that scientists described was a mechanical one.

For all that he found such a view appalling and found intuitively, rather than mathematically, some important shortcomings of the monistic viewpoint that reduced all knowledge to a purely rational system, a large part of Samuel Clemens's imagination remained under the spell of mechanistic monism. His continued work on *What Is Man?*, begun as a Monday Evening Club paper titled "What Is Happiness" in 1883 and culminating in a privately printed edition of the entire dialogue in 1906, arose out of his desire to prove the scientific doctrine that human beings are merely machines that lack even the power to influence their own characters, much less to shape their own destinies.

This piece, which Clemens called his "gospel," not only denies people any personal merit, but excuses them of any blame for their shortcomings. Given that he blamed himself for his financial failure and for the family tragedies that dogged him from the death of his son in 1872 to the death of his daughter Jean in 1909, it seems likely that his "gospel" offered him solace by palliating his sense of guilt. In addition to this strong personal compulsion to believe in naturalistic determinism, however, his belief that life is mechanically determined according to natural laws was in perfect accord with the general trend of scientific thought. The careers of Spencer and Kelvin mark the high water of confidence not only in the existence of an immutable and all-controlling nature, but also in the human capacity objectively to understand that nature.

But, as I pointed out in the last chapter, Clemens's ironic vision exposed some fundamental problems in the claim of objectivity, and he came to believe that, without the ability to see objectively, human beings lack the capacity to see the truth. In *What Is Man?* itself, Clemens has the authoritative Old Man in the dialogue reveal the irony that the human desire to find objective truth is at root subjective and therefore may keep people from finding the very truth they seek.

> I said I have been a Truth Seeker. . . . I am not that now. I told you that there are none but temporary Truth Seekers; that a permanent one is a human impossibility; that as soon as the Seeker finds what he is thoroughly convinced is the Truth, he seeks no further, but gives the rest of his days to hunting for junk to patch it and caulk it and prop it with, and make it weather-proof and keep it from caving in on him. . . . Having found the Truth; perceiving that beyond question Man has but one moving impulse — the contenting of his own spirit — and is merely a Machine and entitled to no personal merit for anything he does, it is not humanly possible for me to seek further. The rest of my days will be spent in patching and painting and puttying and caulking my priceless possession, and in looking the other way when an imploring argument or a damaging fact approaches. (*WIM* 184–85)

In saying that the old man spends much time patching the holes in his argument, Clemens suggests that he does not fully believe in the absolute "truths" of positivistic science that he so aggressively promotes in the dialogue as a whole. He admits, rather, that humanity's standard of truth is conviction, not fact, and that once convinced of a truth, a person will defend it against facts that may damage the conviction. The corollary is that what human beings think is truth is relative to their desires, and that they may have little or no ability to perceive objective reality, presuming that such a reality exists.

This idea, rather than the mechanistic philosophy of the rest of the work, is consonant with the tenor of much of Clemens's work over the last sixteen years of his life. Of course, the idea that personal desire governs a person's behavior was not new to the work of a man who had long since adopted the utilitarian emphasis on pleasure and pain as the motives to human action. The change lies in his growing sense of emotion as controlling understanding as well as behavior. To show how these ideas developed after Clemens's bankruptcy, it may be useful to look at two works that attended his bankruptcy, *Pudd'nhead Wilson and Those Extraordinary Twins* and *Personal Recollections of Joan of Arc*. In *Pudd'nhead Wilson*, we see Clemens more or less unconsciously recapitulating his career and arriving, as he did in the slightly earlier *American Claimant*, at the idea that cultural mores determine the fictions by which we perceive the world. He tries to end the book with a firm statement that science can find the realities behind social fictions, and he tries desperately to use humor to support such findings. In this attempt to use humor as a means of salvation, Clemens's old habits of irony lead him to a bleak solace at best, with nothing more nor less than a nihilistic exposure of all the tensions inherent in the philosophical tradition on which he had drawn for so long. The other work, of different tone entirely, is not merely the story of Joan of Arc, it is "Personal Recollections of," and we should be careful to emphasize the "Personal." Here, Clemens quite thoroughly retreats into sentimental nostalgia, finding bittersweet fantasized memory a pleasant alternative to despair over a harsh present reality.

II

Judging from the extensive criticism of the thematics of race and gender in the novel, one suspects that Clemens intended *Pudd'nhead Wilson and Those Extraordinary Twins* to exercise the political and moral power of the "humor-perception." But to see the book in such narrowly political terms without acknowledging Clemens's material circumstances when he wrote it is to make the ideological basis of that perception very puzzling. To read much current criticism shows how puzzling the book can be, especially when it treats the question of race. While most critics now treat the problem of race in the novel, few agree about how Clemens viewed the relations between black and white in America.[1] While the line that race is a "fiction of law and custom" seems unequivocal in its statement that race makes no biological difference, the plot of the remainder of the book seems to turn on the virtually natural viciousness of Tom Driscoll, né Valet de Chambres, and at least one character in the book, Roxy, attributes that viciousness to the influence of "black blood" on the boy's character. The plot seems to bear that out. Myra Jehlen, in her recent article in *American Literary History*, makes the case that such plot developments show the degree to which Clemens was fully implicated in the racist ideology of his day.

On the other hand, Adrienne Bond, in her much earlier article, reads the plot against itself, suggesting that Twain had a fully ironic purpose throughout. In particular, she suggests that the ending, in which family bonds are first re-established according to sentimental convention and then disrupted through the laws of slavery, challenges all the reigning pieties of American culture, including racial hierarchies. At the same time, the book shows that all such pieties ultimately enslave all human beings. "He shows that those with power will abuse it, that those without power will make whatever moral adjustments are required for survival, that we are all 'sold down the river'" (Bond 71). The implication here is that the very conventionality of the plot of the "tragic octoroon," viewed ironically, serves to undercut the validity of racial distinctions, especially as they were developed in a slave-holding culture.

The moral confusion on this point is monumental, especially given, as Susan Gillman points out, that Clemens built the novel to emphasize the "melodramatic" and "sensational" murder and trial. He did not foreground the issue of race. "So the problem remains: why does *Pudd'nhead Wilson* alternately acknowledge and then deny the racial issues that constitute for most readers whatever power the novel may claim" (Gillman 70). The obvious, though I think substantially wrong, answer is that our current interests completely dictate our responses. This is essentially what Herschel Parker argues in Chapter 5, "Pudd'nhead Wilson: Jack-leg Author, Unreadable Text and Sense-Making Critics," in *Flawed Texts and Verbal Icons*.

As his chapter's subtitle indicates, Parker believes that the text as finally produced is so thoroughly flawed in plot as to be unreadable. What sense we make out of it, therefore, is really the sense we project into it in the first place. This analysis, while forcefully arguing the importance of understanding a text's history before trying to interpret it, seems to be too facile. Granted, if one tries to find in the plot a monolithic intention, one will be disappointed, but the images and characters of the story, even cobbled together as inconsistently as they are, have meaning insofar as they reflect the cultural concerns of the late 1800s. Because so many of these concerns, especially those of race, continue to be important in our own time, the book continues to challenge us.[2] While Bond wrote before Parker's study and Jehlen did not take it into account in her article, it would be wrong to dismiss their readings out of hand. Both clearly respond to ideas that are central to Clemens's and to our culture's ideologies. Insofar as both respond to plot, Parker's challenge is important; insofar as both respond to ideas that are in the text as it was written, his claim is grossly overstated. Both build arguments about the meaning of the piece based on ideas that were clearly prominent in Clemens's day.

Jehlen, for instance, finds in *Pudd'nhead Wilson* confirmation of what we know to be true, that environmental determinism as expressed in social Darwinism supported racist arguments about the supposed nature of the races. Bond reminds us of what we also know to be true, that environmental determinism as expressed by political Progressives could predicate an argument for a radical similarity between all human beings. Change the environment, say such people, and the qualities of people in society change. What both arguments miss is an understanding that Clemens could not sort these oppositions out, and that in *Pudd'nhead Wilson* he did not really try to. Neither critic looks at the other half of the novel, *Those Extraordinary Twins*, to see what Clemens was doing. I think Parker is correct to look at the genesis of the text in its own right in order to see whether Clemens was trying to do anything more than make money, but it is equally important to see that genesis in terms of Clemens's usual patterns of composition. Only then can we see how sense came out of the chaotic circumstances of composition, and what the fragments of meaning add up to.

III

Like *The American Claimant*, *Pudd'nhead Wilson* was written for cash when Clemens needed cash desperately. But his economic constraints did not lead him into a calculating frame of mind in which he coolly judged what would work best to turn a buck. In needing cash desperately, Clemens became desperate. But money making was not his only motive in writing the book. Like his *American Claimant* hero Berkeley, he also needed a good dose of humor to cheer him up. In "A Cure for the Blues," Clemens noted that he often found such doses in his "Library of Literary Hogwash," a collection of writings that he found so bad as to be hilarious.[3] One can imagine him wallowing in such stuff often during the days of his impending bankruptcy. And again like Berkeley, Clemens often turned what cheered him to practical account. For instance, his sarcastic appreciation of Julia Moore's verses served him well when he transmuted them into delightful satire in "Ode to Stephen Dowling Bots, Dec'd," in *Huckleberry Finn*. Such literary monstrosities as Moore's poems or "Love Triumphant" or any of the other texts in his library of literary hogwash served him both as relief and as inspiration.

There is a tremendous tension between these two purposes. Relief requires a certain frivolity, a willingness to work without moral purpose, whereas inspiration for the humorist who saw himself as a moralist meant finding a serious satirical purpose and hitting it hard with all the ironic power he could muster. This was the tension that plagued Clemens after he turned from being a "mere" humorist to a career as a literary man; it was the problem of turning from burlesque to satire, as can be seen by the dark endings of both his major serious novels, *Adventures of Huckleberry Finn* and *Connecticut Yankee*. Consider the case of *Huck* in particular. Much of the bitterness of the story is a consequence of plot, of the implausible story of Huck and Jim seeking freedom by running South. But of equal importance is the fundamental tension between the frivolity of humor and the moral seriousness of satire. The former is contingent on fantasy, on unreality; the latter insists, as does Huck, on seeing what is really there. What begins as simple burlesque, in finding a moral center loses its levity.

Clemens probably knew that when he added the "Notice" to stand before the entire story. In having G.G. command us, on pain of banishment, not to seek a moral in Huck's story, he both indirectly challenges us to find his moral truth in a child's tale and also warns us of the consequences. We, like Huck, begin the story constrained by authority and wishing to rebel. Perhaps Clemens is telling us, in an implied echo of the New Testament, that we shall know the truth and the truth shall set us free. Yet this proposition suggests a disturbing corollary: if the truth liberates us, then perhaps lies imprison us. Maybe, then, since he tricks us into seeking the truth by telling us a lie, we are being conned, and therefore deprived of our freedom, by a lying author.

As soon as Huck speaks he tells us to suspect just that. Huck reminds us that his story began in "a book by the name of 'The Adventures of Tom Sawyer,' . . . That book was made by Mr. Mark Twain, and he told the truth, mainly. There was things which he stretched" (1). Huck seems honest, here, in telling us about the danger of fraud, yet he understates to the point of dishonesty when he says the book is mostly true. As a fiction, it is nothing but a fabrication, a lie.

Had Huck existed, he would probably have discovered this truth. After all, in his *Adventures* he uncovers lie after lie by the simple test of experience. When, for instance, Miss Watson tells him that one gets what he or she prays for, Huck tries it:

Once I got a fish-line, but no hooks. It warn't any good to me without hooks. I tried for the hooks three or four times, but somehow I couldn't make it work. . . . I says to myself, if a body can get anything they pray for, why don't Deacon Winn get back the money he lost on pork? Why can't Miss Watson fat up? No, says I to myself, there ain't nothing in it. (13)

So Huck finds Watson's rendition of the Good Book to be lies, and in the same chapter, he finds Tom's mixed account of *Don Quixote* and *The Arabian Nights* to be lies as well. After rubbing a brass lamp to find no genie, he concludes that "all that stuff was only just one of Tom Sawyer's lies. I reckoned he believed in the A-rabs and the elephants, but as for me I think different. It had all the marks of a Sunday school" (17).

Thus does Clemens begin the story of Huck Finn, the chronic liar, who, having staged his death, invents a new autobiography for every new person he meets. By tale's end, we trust him implicitly, but why? Haven't we let the son of an alcoholic con-man con us? Or haven't we, if we remember the meta-lie of the fictional nature of the story, let Clemens con us into believing in the reality of Huck in the first place? If so, we have played into the hands of the liar's paradox that Clemens invokes at the outset of the story. Everything his book says, everything any book says, is a lie, even if this point, though made by a lying book, is true. To live the truth, we must trust experience rather than report.

The moralist in Clemens would have us read no books if we are to set ourselves free. But as Tom Sawyer can joyously misread the same truth in *Don Quixote*, so the pure delight of Huck's fictions and of the fiction of Huck enable us to misread this book, too. The pleasure of misreading is great. No matter how miserable it makes us to see Tom Sawyer rob Huck and especially Jim of their freedom by making them live life by the book, no matter that Clemens is thereby telling us that fictions are prisons, our experience of the bulk of the journey, even though it takes us South through the heart of Walter Scott's romances into the heart of slavery, is one of liberation, not of entrapment. We may be conned, and Clemens may be warning us about that con, but he makes it so pleasant that we end up wishing that we had followed G.G.'s command to seek no moral in *Adventures of Huckleberry Finn*. Had we followed orders, we would not have been banished from Huck's fictional world.

This tension between pleasure and moral seriousness in *Huck*, then, is Clemens's constant problem as a comic moralist. Each time he gives us a humorous story to teach us a truth, the pleasure of his humor gets in the way of the truth. This is the absolute opposite of what he hoped to find in laughter, namely a way to explode the pernicious myths of society and thereby expose the truth. Worse, he also found that the hoped for relief from life's seriousness, the aspect of his wit that had always stood in the way of his serious intentions, undercut itself as irony wrested control from humor: moral seriousness erodes the pleasure from humor. Insofar as he wrote *Pudd'nhead Wilson* to escape from his difficulties — by making money and by giving himself a laugh — this self-destructive feature of his humor is a great threat, both because a Mark Twain without humor sells no books and because an anxious Samuel Clemens who wants to feel better about his failure needs the escape from seriousness that laughter is supposed to bring.

IV

One way to view *Pudd'nhead Wilson*, then, is to sketch the novel's genesis in terms of this tension between humor and irony, between play and serious moral purpose. As Clemens himself tells us in describing the composition of *Pudd'nhead Wilson*, a

> "jack-leg novelist" begins a book with no clear idea of his story; in fact he has no story. He merely has some people in his mind, and an incident or two, also a locality. He knows these people, he knows the selected locality, and he trusts that he can plunge those people into those incidents with interesting results. . . . And I have noticed another thing: that as the short tale grows into the long tale, the original intention (or motif) is apt to get abolished and find itself superseded by a quite different one. It was so in the case of a magazine sketch which I once started to write — a funny and fantastic sketch about a prince and a pauper: it presently assumed a grave cast of its own accord, and in that new shape spread itself out into a book. Much the same thing happened with "Pudd'nhead Wilson." (119)

Much the same, we might add, happened with *Huckleberry Finn* and *Connecticut Yankee*. Perhaps most interesting is that Twain qualifies his "intention" with the words "or motif," suggesting even further that, rather than planning to write the story, i.e., the plot, that came out, he had nothing more than a pattern of looking at the characters in their locality. He thus suggests that, unlike in *Huck* or in *Yankee*, in *Pudd'nhead Wilson and Those Extraordinary Twins* Clemens did not intend to write serious literature at all. Rather than looking for a moral point, he was trying to stay light to provide the laughter that would sell the book. The entire serious content of the book is accidental. For my purposes, then, it stands less as a manifestation

of Clemens's conscious attempts to develop his philosophy than as a manifestation of the way his patterns of thought create meaning even if none is
intended and destroy meanings that he hoped to hold.

That pattern of thought in *Pudd'nhead Wilson*, as in so many of Clemens's works, was to burlesque some earlier idea or text. In this case, he tells
us, his initial impulse was to build a burlesque on a "freak," or rather on a
picture of a "a youthful Italian 'freak' — or 'freaks' — which was — or were —
on exhibition in our cities — a combination consisting of two heads and
four arms joined to a single body and a single pair of legs" (119). Like his
treasured volumes in his library of literary hogwash, such a "freak" inspired
laughter in Clemens, a laughter that is simultaneously the pleasure of an
escape from conventionality or normality and a reminder of what things
should be, of what reality "really" is.

Herschel Parker would have us believe that the humor of this initial
burlesque of Siamese twins is "save[d] from sadism . . . [because] almost everyone who sees [the Twins] admires them (after the initial shock
passes)" (123). There is truth to this, but a truth that buries much important information about the problem of humor for Clemens. Clearly his
motive in making fun of "freaks," as it was in mocking "bad" literature, is
sadistic. The satiric impulse here is accurately described by the Hobbesian
notion of superiority, namely that, living in a competitive world, we laugh
when we see our inferiors humiliated. The motive to laugh, in Hobbes's
view, is often amplified by our awareness of our own competitive shortcomings. We are most likely to laugh at our inferiors when we are acutely
sensitive to our own inferiorities to yet others.[4] This statement needs little
amplification in today's neo-Hobbesian critical climate. With the renewed
interest in power relations as governing all human interaction, much current criticism of laughter focuses on the veiled aggression inherent in it.

But Parker is right to a degree — when reading about the Twins, one
quickly forgets the sadism because they seem impervious to it. In one place,
Clemens even has them pity the rest of the world for being alone, though in
other places they obviously would prefer to be more clearly two than they
are. Given their self-satisfaction, they almost seem enviable, admirable. The
commonplace of criticism, that the satirist veils an attraction to the object
of satire, seems applicable here. Clemens admires the Twins for their ability
to attract sympathy and to turn sympathy into admiration. We see both
sides of this coin in the dialogue between the two Cooper brothers, who in
their proclivities to sentiment or practicality resemble Angelo and Luigi
respectively:

The stranger had made an impression on the boys, too. They had a word of talk as they were getting to bed. Henry, the gentle, the humane, said:
"I feel ever so sorry for it, don't you, Joe?"
But Joe was a boy of this world, active, enterprising, and had a theatrical side to him: [i.e., he is another Tom Sawyer]:
"Sorry? Why how you talk! It can't stir a step without attracting attention. It's just grand!"
Henry said, reproachfully:
"Instead of pitying it, Joe, you talk as if—"
"Talk as if what? I know one thing mighty certain: if you can fix me so I can eat for two and only have to stub toes for one, I ain't going to fool away no such chance just for sentiment." (127)

The one of these voices speaks the pity, the other the admiration. The voice behind these partially conflicting perceptions admires, if nothing else, the way a "freak" stands out.

If nothing else stays consistent through the book as written and finally revised, the idea that standing out is a supreme human pleasure does. In the final version of *Pudd'nhead Wilson*, Clemens says of Rowena, on showing off the Twins (now separated and only admirable because they are from Italy and have titles), that she recognized "now for the first time the real meaning of that great word Glory, and perceived the stupendous value of it, and understood why men in all ages had been willing to throw away meaner happinesses, treasure, life itself, to get a taste of its sublime and supreme joy" (29). Roxy, too, tastes the pleasure of the limelight when she returns to Dawson's Landing after her steamboating years:

her wonderful travels, and the strange countries she had seen and the adventures she had had, made her a marvel, and a heroine of romance. . . . She was obliged to confess to herself that if there was anything better in this world than steamboating, it was the glory to be got by telling about it. (34)

The desirability of publicity is an old idea in Clemens's works, one which he turns to humorous account again and again. The narrator in "Old Times on the Mississippi," for instance, is motivated in his desire to become a pilot by his desire to be conspicuous. Time and again in the narrative, Mark Twain describes his admiration for the notorious manifesting itself as malignant envy. For instance, when he describes the "worldly" boy who runs from town only to return as a roustabout on a steamboat, the narrator tells us he "loathes" his former friend. And when later his rival cub defrauds him out of a chance to go out in the sounding boat in order to impress a young female passenger, the cub's envy knows no bounds:

> I looked over, and there was the gallant sounding-boat booming away, the unprincipled Tom presiding at the tiller, and my chief sitting by him with the sounding-pole which I had been sent on a fool's errand to fetch. Then that young girl said to me,—
> "Oh, how awful to have to go out in that little boat on such a night! Do you think there is any danger?"
> I would rather have been stabbed. I went off, full of venom, to help in the pilot-house. (*LOM* 102–3)

Of course, the wished-for danger arrives; the sounding boat is crushed under the wheel of the steamboat, and the rival cub is among the missing men. But he has managed to save himself and swims back to the boat, where he is greeted with accolades from all, especially from the young woman. Mark Twain hears with disgust the cries of pity and admiration meted out to his rival, and concludes with the envious remark that what his rival had done

> was nothing. I could have done it easy enough, and I said so; but everybody went on just the same, making a wonderful to-do over that ass, as if he had done something great. That girl couldn't seem to have enough of that pitiful "hero" the rest of the trip; but little I cared; I loathed her, anyway. (*LOM* 105)

Clemens deliberately shows the source of aggression here to be naked envy, the envy of a boy who had expected distinction but is pushed back into the ranks of the crowd, of the "normal." The boy's "hatred" is comic by contrast to his great hopes, by contrast to his failure to become superior by becoming distinctive. Our laughter, in turn, may stem from our sense of superiority to his disappointment, but it may equally be a shared sense of disappointment that we can cathartically express in the cub's unmitigated bile.

A parallel kind of humor seems to be at work in the early stages of *Pudd'nhead Wilson*. Clemens returns again to his old motif of contrasting the conspicuous with the typical, the average, the undistinguished, and in so doing uncovers the envy of the undistinguished for the conspicuous. So while the laughter in *Pudd'nhead Wilson* seems at one level to endorse normalcy at the expense of "freaks," at the same time it envies the notoriety of the freaks, the fact that their conspicuous position earns them sympathy. Note that sympathy, i.e., "feeling together," is supposed to be easiest among those who are similar. Yet the Twins as originally created, with very little in common with the townspeople either in their physical beings or in their backgrounds or manners, become the cynosure of the village in virtually no time. True, when the Twins first appear, their difference shocks the people, but Clemens has the villagers turn warm to the unusual Twins in extremely short order. He here suggests that the power of sympathy is not a selfless compassion based on a recognition of similarity; it is, rather, a selfish greed to experience vicariously the novel and the unusual.

According to the proponents of sentimental humor, such interest in the different, if cultivated properly, is true sympathy. And therein lies the redemptive power of humor: by making difference appear pleasurable and interesting rather than painful and frightening, humor bridges the gaps between people. It thus allows for a large degree of social tolerance, a tolerance necessary in a free society. Thus, sentimental humor was seen as a social bond, as a way of building the tolerance necessary to make a morally sound society out of free individuals. Humor was used with this purpose in mind by many American sentimental humorists, like Irving, who used humor to reconcile Americans with the British; like Harte, who tried to sentimentalize Westerners in the eyes of an Eastern genteel audience; like Stowe, whose *Old-Town Fireside Stories* tries to soften the Calvinist past through an indulgent humor; and like Mary Wilkins Freeman, whose short stories are populated by eccentrics we are supposed to come to tolerate and even admire in our laughter at them. Each of these authors, in following a sentimental model of humor, tried to knit into a compatible whole at least some of the elements of a diverse country.

Clemens simultaneously sees this generous side of laughter and the aggressive side of laughter — he often exposed the aggressive side in his own humor, as in the passages from "Old Times" cited above, but in so doing, he used the generous quality to redeem his audience's vision of himself as a man whose genial humor has overcome his narrow selfishness. What Mark Twain's writing reveals here is a fact that no theorists of humor of the time noted, that the incongruity that causes laughter is not so much within the object of laughter, but in the tension between two attitudes contained within the person who perceives the object. What Clemens still mistakenly called the humor perception, which suggests that it is an essentially objective faculty that merely perceives incongruity in or between objects, is in fact subjective, as he would finally discover in the early 1900s.

In *Pudd'nhead Wilson*, Clemens's play with the motif of burlesque began with both a simultaneous aggression toward and attraction to the Twins and a simultaneous aggression toward and attraction to those who sympathize with the Twins. Regarding the latter, characters such as Rowena the "light-weight heroine" (120) whom he describes as "a silly young miss" (119) are mocked cruelly for their gullibility. In Rowena's case, she falls in love with the Twins before they arrive and, rather than waste the sentiment, persuades herself to follow her imagination even after the shock of meeting them. Here Clemens is exercising his anger at misplaced sentimentalities, the same anger we see at the end of *Tom Sawyer* when he describes women petitioning for the release of murderers and in *Huckleberry Finn* when he has Huck describe the widow as being most interested in deadbeats and rapscallions. Still, Clemens's own attraction for the Twins persists, in spite of his effort to show that anyone who likes them is intellectually "light-weight."

Still working by pattern without having found a conscious intention by which to shape his material, Clemens used the old pattern of turning aggressive envy into humor. As he had in so many of his biographically based stories, such as "Old Times," Clemens created masks for himself and projected parts of his own character as he perceived it into those masks. In *Pudd'nhead Wilson*, he chose, at about the same moment in composition, at least two such masks: those of Tom Driscoll and David Wilson.[5] Both are similar to Clemens in that their minds run to the "ironical." Of Driscoll he says, "He was furtively, and sometimes openly, ironical of speech, and given to gently touching people on the raw, but he did it with a good-natured semiconscious air that carried it off safely, and kept him from getting into trouble" (23). Tom embodies the mean side of irony, its use as a tool to promote one's own power and glory. Wilson's mind, too, runs to irony, but with a different intention: "For some years Wilson had been privately at work on a whimsical almanac for his amusement — a calendar, with a little dab of ostensible philosophy, usually in ironical form, appended to each date" (25). Wilson's irony is private and meditational, a kind of philosophical inquiry that serves to amuse and console him. Of the two ironists Clemens thought himself to be, Tom embodies his own aggressive envy; Wilson embodies Clemens's sense of victimization at the hands of the aggressive, the envious, and the stupid.

In the case of Driscoll, Clemens begins with the conventional source of envy, the love rivalry that he had used often before, as in "Old Times."[6] But the conventional motif of a love rivalry quickly yields to a larger sense of Driscoll's consuming desire to be important, through birth or wealth or wit, even if unwilling to work for such distinction. While this dissipated aristocrat is also conventional — one need only think of Poe's stories to find parallels — the way Clemens presents some of Tom's distinctive behavior suggests some remarkable parallels to his own circumstances and one side of his own self-image.

Toms's demise as it unfolds through the book stems from gambling that loses him not only his fortune but threatens to rupture his family ties. To recover his losses, he lies and deceives, even to the point of inventing masquerades to hide his identity while he steals money. In parallel, Clemens had been rich, partly by connection to his wife, and he gambled away not only his own, but her money as well in his business ventures. In writing fictions he was "lying" to "steal" his fortune back. Clemens's own sense of constantly deceiving the world, of living a fraud, seems to manifest itself to some degree here. Earlier in his career, he had articulated his sense of the "mixed" character of his authorship, the mixture of low humor and high literature, in a letter to Howells in which he said his relief at having given "birth" to a well accepted book was similar to that of a woman who gave birth to a white baby when she was expecting "otherwise."[7] Now, when he is again seeing himself as a fraud, the old metaphor comes back, and in projecting this anxiety about fraudulence into the Tom Driscoll character, the changeling plot strains to be born.

It is important to bear in mind how late the changeling plot was in coming. After all, as Parker astutely points out, Tom Driscoll began his fictional career under Clemens's pen as pure white, as one of the town's aristocrats. His first role, a role never abandoned even though the love rivalry disappears, is to set a counter-point to the Twins. While he was bloated beyond compassion in his spoiled upbringing, he was interesting to Rowena, Clemens implies, for his putative nobility. Rowena dumps him for the Twins because they are more "romantic" in their superior, because European, claim to nobility. Tom, morally but not physically deformed, gets an object lesson in the power of extrinsic claims to importance when he sees his own social inferiority to an externally deformed person. The power of extrinsic claims, such as a physical peculiarity or a stereotype or a snap judgment, ties very powerfully into the idea of fraudulence that eventually leads, in part, to the changeling plot, and it also helps develop a projection of another of Clemens's images of himself, that of David Wilson.

Wilson appears in the original version of the story when the judge introduces him to the Twins, shortly after their arrival in Dawson's Landing. As Parker tells us, "The Twins both take an immediate liking to Pudd'nhead—a rare instance of their agreeing to anything" (123). This displays, one suspects, Clemens's association of the Twins to Wilson in the "natural" commonality that was supposed to be the source of true sympathy. Clemens implies a parallel between the Twins—ostensibly freakish, natural outcasts who have traded notoriety for distinction—and Wilson. In this latter, Clemens created a new kind of outcast, an outcast who looks normal, but whose superior intelligence and wit have made him seem a clown, an idiot, in the eyes of the people:

> Irony was not for those people; their mental vision was not focused for it. They read those playful trifles [Wilson's calendar entries] in the solidest earnest, and decided that if there had ever been any doubt that Dave Wilson was a pudd'n-head — which there hadn't been — this revelation removed that doubt for good and all. (25)

No playful effort at wit, Clemens suggests, will ever get a sympathetic hearing.

While in the 1890s the humorist was no longer a part of the circus side-show, Clemens, with his wide-ranging reading in medieval and Renaissance history and literature, knew that the clowns, the fools, the court jesters were often idiots and were shown much as were "monsters" such as the Siamese twins. The parallel positions of Clemens, Wilson and the Twins suggest Clemens's own sense of being an outsider as a mere humorist. Certainly, such an anxiety made up a significant part of his sense of America's reactions to him as a writer. As I mentioned in Chapter 4, Clemens wanted to become a literary man because he was tired of his "groundling" audience "re-quir[ing] a 'humorist' to paint himself stripèd & stand on his head every fifteen minutes" (*MTHL* 49). This feeling persisted into the 1890s and beyond. In fact, when he published *Joan of Arc* serially, he chose to publish it not under the pseudonym he used for his clown act but anonymously. Certainly Clemens's sense that his intellect had been neither appreciated nor properly recompensed seems projected into the character of David "Pudd'nhead" Wilson. And equally clearly, while Driscoll may embody an image of himself that Clemens had, he used Driscoll to write that image out of himself, whereas one senses an investment in Wilson, not only in the story itself, but also in the close identification of author of the story with the author of Pudd'nhead Wilson's calendar. These meta-commentaries raise Wilson above the level of the story, above the merely commercial deceit that makes the whole project seem sordid. Instead, we are asked to sympathize with a man whose merits deserve a recognition they do not receive. By analogy, we are asked to sympathize with Clemens himself.

V

Thus we see the development of a significant tension between the aggressive anti-sentimentalism of the initial "motif" of burlesque and the developing plea for sympathy directed to the author and to several of his characters. This tension persists through the rest of the story as Clemens developed it and it supports and complicates a parallel tension in the plot. On the one hand, the story works to find Wilson a proper "sympathetic" acceptance of his real gifts in a community. (I will return to this later when discussing the end of the book.) On the other hand, it extended outward, by association, to other marginalized figures, in particular into the world of the slaves who, by virtue of their literal "familiarity" with their white siblings should be accorded sympathetic acceptance in the community. This is the second of the latent impulses that moves the narrative toward the changeling plot, and it is important to note that, while the idea of racial "fraudulence" I brought up earlier suggests the degree to which Clemens was still an unreconstructed Southerner who held race to be an essential component of identity, the sentimental impulse toward developing the changeling plot suggests just the opposite, that Clemens held racial categories themselves to be the frauds that disguise fundamental commonality between the races.

In fact, we can see the seeds of this entire line of plot development in Clemens's initial choice of target to burlesque. If I am right that the entire book began in Clemens's effort to write something amusing, light, and frivolous that would make money, but also that he began it while in a state of gloom and ire that needed to be dissipated, then in choosing Siamese twins he was actually choosing a fairly safe target. After all, most such "freaks" in the nineteenth century were illusions and thus not to be taken seriously. Aggression directed toward them was completely safe, the stuff of fantasy. But what if the moralist in Clemens took over, as it usually did, and found the seriousness that Clemens at first chose to ignore? On the one hand, the very problem of frauds was one that obsessed the realist in Clemens, the serious moralist who held truth to be the corner-stone of civilization. While the story works on the assumption of the reality of the Twins, the theme of fraudulence, as I already pointed out, rises quickly to the fore as Clemens develops the burlesque.

Secondly, as Susan Gillman points out, the burlesque of Siamese twins in *Those Extraordinary Twins* is a continuation of a pair of much earlier burlesques that Clemens wrote in 1869. Gillman talks insightfully about the importance of these pieces to questions of personal identity; more importantly for my purposes, she also notes that journalistic accounts of the Original Siamese Twins were a commonplace of the Civil War years and in the years immediately afterward (59–61). They were so in part to satirize and in part to continue a very powerful rhetorical convention used to describe the body politic in the years before, during and immediately after the Civil War. As George Forgie shows, the rhetoric of sentimentality came into play in the years before the war in part to suggest, through the images of common paternity in the Founding Fathers, an unbreakable bond of brotherhood between the states.[8] As Gillman mentions, the literature about the Siamese Twins also speaks to the question of national identity through the image not merely of brotherhood but of twins joined by an unbreakable ligature. The questions of how fully invested in each other's lives such twins were, to what extent they could differ, and to what extent they could disagree without endangering their common existence, made the Twins a powerful metaphor to speak to this morally serious sentimental political rhetoric. And the degree of serious interest they did elicit suggests that many people took the metaphorical ramifications of their ligature to heart. But the Twins made their living as "freaks," and consequently their power as a metaphor of national brotherhood tended to work more through bathos than pathos. Many commentators, including ones Twain would have been exposed to during the war years while he was in California and Nevada, used the image of the Twins to trivialize the sentimental rhetoric of brotherhood. No doubt such trivialization was likely when the war itself had already made the value of such claims a moot point.

Strangely, Clemens picked up the motif in his own writing after the war was over. In "Personal Habits of the Siamese Twins" (1869), for instance, he reflects on the differences of the Twins in spite of their inviolable connection. He notes that they differ in almost every respect, even to the point that "During the war they . . . both fought gallantly all through the great struggle—Eng on the Union side and Chang on the Confederate. They took each other prisoners at Seven Oaks" (*SN&O* 209). Here, after the war but during Radical Reconstruction when the Republican party was solidifying central governmental power, Clemens, the former Confederate, was making fun of the rhetoric of brotherhood. In doing so, he could tap into both sides of this traditional rhetoric—that is, he could assert the importance of the "union" and the pains differences between brothers had caused and he could use the image of "freaks" to trivialize those very pains.

Stimulated by a mere poster of a new Siamese twin, Clemens cast back into his memory for the old formula, the image of twins completely joined but radically different. Like the Original Siamese Twins who disagree about everything, Angelo and Luigi are as different as night and day. Angelo is a teetotaler; Luigi is a hard drinker. Angelo abstains from tobacco; Luigi smokes. Angelo is religious, Luigi a "freethinker." Luigi supports the code duello, Angelo is against it. Luigi is a Democrat; Angelo votes Whig. In many ways their positions echo a contrast between the ante-bellum South and West on the one hand, and the North on the other. The one important bit of information we do not get is about how the Twins view slavery, but in light of the earlier burlesque, in which Twain imagines one Twin fighting for the North and the other fighting for the South, and given their different party affiliations, one imagines that they disagree on the fundamental issue dividing the states.

The Twins as developed in the original version of *Pudd'nhead Wilson* do differ in one very significant way from their prototypes in the earlier sketch—they are given physical descriptions. They appear as radically different as they think and act, with Angelo being fair and Luigi dark. This contrast in siblings is an old literary convention, with the dark sibling usually representing passion and worldly desires and the light a stronger affiliation with spirituality. But in American sentimental rhetoric, the question of racial admixture was always implicit in this contrast. Consider, for instance, Cooper's *The Last of the Mohicans*, in which Cooper implies that Cora may be a woman with a "cross," in both the religious and racial senses of the term. The differences in skin coloration between Angelo and Luigi, given their associations with North and South, suggest a different racial makeup. Here Twain's image plays with the ideas of filial connection between the races, a central component of the culture's debate over race.

In particular, many anti-slavery activists found the sentimental conception of interracial brotherhood to be a powerful tool in the conceptual fight against slavery. From Stowe's *Uncle Tom's Cabin* to Henry Ward Beecher's slave auctions to countless other pieces of literature, journalism, and oratory, abolitionists used the images of common humanity and common suffering in explicitly sentimental terms to argue for the natural rights of blacks in a culture that refused to grant these rights. The essential arguments of the abolitionists were sentimental, and as the abolitionist movement matured from its anti-union stance under Garrison and became more aggressive in its willingness to use political means under the federal government to eradicate slavery, the sentimental arguments for union and against slavery began to merge.

This history was loaded into the striking image of Siamese twins, and, as Clemens began to explore the sense of being outcast, this image would provide yet another impetus toward exploring the most significant form of ostracism in American life, the ostracism of those born to slave mothers. With Luigi suggesting the complexity of racial mixture in brothers, and with Clemens's shift toward sentimentalism as the tale unfolded, the con-

ventional sentimental representation of racial mixture in the case of the
"tragic mulatta" came conveniently to Clemens's mind. Then, too, the
concerns of the 1890s would encourage such a re-examination of an old
convention. When Clemens had last used the image of Siamese twins, in his
1869 burlesque, the Republican Party was not only reconstituting the
nation's bond, it was doing so in part by enfranchising the freed slaves. By
the time Clemens turned to the subject again, a resurgence of legal segrega-
tion was making a mockery of all of the legal gains that the freed slaves had
made under Reconstruction. The old conventions were once again applicable, as numerous commentators have pointed out.[9] Thus, pushed by manifold influences, but with little consistent intention to address racial issues
explicitly, Clemens invented the entire changeling plot.

VI

Having come to the conventional plot that reveals the inhumanity of racism
and slavery through the conceptions of sentimental moral philosophy, the
book begs for a development of an argument about slavery. In fact, most
commentators in recent years have attempted to find such an argument. But
given the way in which the book developed, it is just as likely that it would
invert the old formula. Instead of assuming sentimental values in order to
condemn racism and slavery, the book uses the tropes of the standard
argument to test the limits of sentimental values themselves. Clemens was
still more interested in his own sense of being ostracized, of having failed as
a businessman and of not being properly appreciated as a humorist. Rather
than emphasize the importance of race, Clemens concentrates on the common experience of ostracism. What he comes to notice here is the strange
interplay between the way those on the margins are perceived and the ways
in which they are categorized. He sees a tremendous gap between the two, a
gap that suggests a hypocrisy worthy of satire but that also complicates
beyond moral resolution the way a person can find happiness in society.

As the narrative develops after the changeling plot unfolds, Clemens
creates some striking parallels between Roxy and Wilson. The primary
parallel involves the way each is marginalized on the basis of a fiction. In
Roxy's case it is the fiction of race, as we can see clearly in Clemens's
description of the racial composition and physical characteristics of both
Roxy and her son. "To all intents and purposes Roxy was as white as
anybody, but the one-sixteenth of her which was black outvoted the other

fifteen parts and made her a negro. She was a slave, and salable as such. Her child was thirty-one parts white, and he, too, was a slave, and by a fiction of law and custom a negro" (8–9). Clemens gives us a clear picture of a reality, but shows that the way people respond to that reality is governed instead by predetermined systems of interpretation that are "fictions," mere fabrications that appear true but in fact are lies.

The fiction that ostracizes Wilson is the fiction of his stupidity. Despite an "intelligent blue eye," a college degree, and postgraduate law studies, his deadpan humor makes him seem slow-witted to an audience that does not have the capacity to interpret irony. "That first day's verdict made him a fool, and he was not able to get it set aside, or even modified" (6). And yet the author gives readers a sense throughout of how completely mistaken the verdict is. So, like Roxy, he is judged and put in "his place" by a fiction.

Intriguingly, Clemens partially suggests that people on the margins of social fictions have the capacity to see truths others miss. Roxy is one of very few characters who sees Wilson's intelligence, as when she "calculat[es] her chances" of getting away with exchanging the babies:

> Dey ain't but one man dat I's afeard of, en dat's dat Pudd'nhead Wilson. Dey calls him a pudd'nhead, en says he's a fool. My lan', dat man ain't no mo' fool den I is! He's de smartes' man in dis town, less'n it's Jedge Driscoll or maybe Pem Howard. Blame dat man, he worries me wid dem ornery glasses o' his'n; I b'lieve he's a witch. (16)

In calling Wilson a witch, Roxy attributes to him the greatest power she knows by her systems of thought. As for Wilson's perceptions of Roxy, he is the only one in the town who is interested enough in the realities behind the social fictions of race to be able to figure out what she did. Their linkage in similar positions becomes tragic because, instead of supporting one another in their status as outsiders, they refuse to acknowledge their link. Indeed, Wilson uses his knowledge of Roxy to climb into a new status at book's end.

There are similar parallels in understanding between all of the "odd" characters, those characters central to the story who in one way or another are differentiated from the mobs, from the numbered men who give Wilson his nickname (6), from the audiences who grant power and popularity to those who try to find "glory." One of these characters, Tom, has the gift of irony by which he can see through fictions or use them to his advantage. At times he changes costumes to change identities; at others he uses his singular insight into Wilson's insecurities and pains to wound Wilson with ironic barbs. In return, Wilson sees through Tom's masquerades and wreaks his revenge by publicly exposing Tom. These two are similar in many ways, but their similarities, rather than binding them in affection, cause nothing but reciprocal pain. Indeed, excepting the friendship of the Twins for Wilson, almost all of the powerful connections based on knowledge of realities behind social fictions are connections of fear, suspicion, hatred, and pain. To cite the other most obvious example, Tom and his mother, when their connection is acknowledged, are complicit but always mutually vengeful. Understanding does not yield sympathy. The closest of connections are perversely lacking in positive emotional value.

Equally importantly, positive emotions do not make for close connections between people, as the town's treatment of Wilson shows. We learn that he comes to be well liked by the townspeople, who in their acceptance, tacitly admit that their judgment does not tally with their complete perceptions. "In time he came to be liked, and well liked, too; but by that time the nickname had got stuck on, and it stayed." The nickname, the fiction of Wilson's stupidity, keeps him "in his place," that is poor, underworked, undervalued, and "lonely" living at the edge of town in more ways than one. Their prejudice cancels the value of the friendly feelings that the townspeople have for him. According to sentimental moralists, sympathy should not work so; positive feelings are supposed to overcome prejudice by allowing people to see their commonalities. Clemens says that prejudices work independently of human connections, and that friendship and oppression can co-exist without modifying one another.

In its depiction of Roxy, the story paints an even worse picture of the supposed powers of sympathy. Like Wilson, Roxy is appreciated by the town. Also like Wilson, this appreciation gets her nothing — no power, no relief from her position as victim of oppressive fictions. While we are never told directly about the townspeople's attitudes toward Roxy, the indirect evidence is of the most powerful kind: the fact that her son is less black than she, only one thirty-second part, tells us that she has sparked the desire of at least one white man of the town. We later learn that Roxy's son's father was one of the town's leaders, the FFV Cecil Burleigh Essex. That Roxy's child is fathered by one of the most important white men in the town highlights her desirability, but she is not able to barter that desirability for freedom or love. No matter how much like a "white" woman Roxy appears, she will not be the object of the sympathy of slaveholders. The associations that led Clemens down this path, then, suggest that there is a radical disjunction between the reality of human commonality and the "fictions of law and custom" that insist on artificial differences.

Yet at the same time, the story as it unfolds by following this associative track challenges the very way sympathy is accorded. In sentimental anti-slavery stories, a mulatta's whiteness makes her a sympathetic character by emphasizing similarities between whites and blacks. Implicit in the argument is that similarity is the source, too, of sexual attraction, and therefore the real sin of slavery is to combine in mulatta slaves both desirability and vulnerability. Yet Twain's book denies this conventional argument. We are told quite explicitly that white men desire Roxy not for her physical "beauty" and thus not out of a sense of similarity, but rather because she is legally and socially taboo, as Pudd'nhead Wilson's calendar tells us: "Adam was but human—this explains it all. He did not want the apple for the apple's sake, he wanted it only because it was forbidden" (6). In the opening description of Roxy and her place in the town in contrast to Wilson and his, Clemens highlights both the similarities in their positions, and also points out the shallowness of any sentimental recognition of it. Outcasts are "popular" because they are outcast, not because the people see any intrinsic worth in differences that they create by their own fictions and customs. Wilson may want some kind of sympathy to mitigate his loneliness, but if sympathy is as corruptible as Clemens makes it out to be, then he has no way to find the real article.

This is all the more true insofar as Clemens is not sure if it is possible to find a point of view outside such morally debilitating fictions. Even the outsiders, such as Roxy and Wilson, participate in and to some degree accept the governing fictions of the society that spurns them. As I noted before, although Roxy can see Wilson more accurately than can most, she attributes his intelligence to witchcraft, to another fictitious system that governs her perceptions. More importantly, even though she is oppressed by the slave system, she accepts, partly by virtue of necessity, partly on account of her own training, and finally through her own self-deception, the powers such a system grants to others, particularly her son:

> By the fiction created by herself, he was become her master; the necessity of recognizing this relation outwardly and of perfecting herself in the forms required to express the recognition, had moved her to such diligence and faithfulness in practicing these forms that this exercise soon concreted itself into habit; it became automatic and unconscious; then a natural result followed; deceptions intended solely for others gradually grew practically into self-deceptions as well; the mock reverence became real reverence, the mock obsequiousness real obsequiousness, the mock homage, real homage. . . . Roxy [became] the dupe of her own deceptions. (19)

While the rest of the book does not consistently follow the ideas of this passage, Clemens here argues that passions themselves, the perceptions that are supposed by sentimental philosophy to be truer than reason, are not only easily fooled by human fictions, but often even motivate self-deceit. Here Clemens shows mother-love, considered in sentimental psychology to be the source of all that is good and generous in culture, leading a woman into massive self-deception that ends up perpetuating a system that should be torn down. Interestingly, the mechanism by which this self-deceit takes place is habit, which Clemens describes as a mechanical process. So, in larger philosophical terms, ethical free choice, the free choice made under the pressure of generous emotion, is undermined by the mechanical processes of unconscious habituation. Sentiment was supposed to set people free of the onus of predestination, but Clemens suggests that sentiment is just one more piece of the machine.

By the end of the story Clemens leads Wilson into the glory that will end his isolation by sacrificing Roxy, whose situation evokes in the reader the passion of sympathy more powerfully than did Wilson's ostracism. But as Roxy surrenders her freedom to her desire for the company of her own child, so Wilson surrenders his morally superior, because morally uninvolved, position as the community's fool for the tainted position of community leader. The sympathy that makes Clemens want to rescue Wilson from obscurity becomes the cause of the corruption that makes Wilson, finally, an unsympathetic character.

Accordingly, in following a train of sentimental connections between people, Clemens also shows that subjective perceptions are the causes of separations between people in the first place. This thought returns him to the anti-sentimental satirical impulse that arose early in the book's composition in attacking sentimentalities for creating false hopes, false feelings, false perceptions. At the same time, the moral outrage the book develops over the town's hypocritical treatment of Roxy depends on sentimental sympathy for her sufferings. Not only is her sexuality outraged according to the sentimental formula, she also has her maternal willingness to sacrifice herself to her son outraged by his putative "whiteness." The entire book, then, tears itself apart over its inconsistent presentation of the appropriateness of sympathy. In that way it resembles *Huckleberry Finn*, but the discontinuity is more obvious because more extreme.

Nowadays we see the irreconcilable tensions stemming from Clemens's ambivalent reactions to sentimentalism most easily when those reactions crystallize around the problem of race, but these tensions preoccupied

Clemens over the whole range of moral concerns, from the specific cases of lying to the meta-ethical principles by which one discerns what is valuable and what is not. For instance, he plays with the meaning of identity in training and heredity, and displays the conflation of the two in Roxy's talk about racial characteristics. He plays with the possibility of voluntarism in the face of the immutable power of training, as in Roxy's changing of the babies. Note that he does not credit her with doing this intentionally; rather she discovers the possibility by accident. But later, when she struggles to remove her son from his difficulties, she exercises creative powers that seem to defy the earlier fatalistic conception of human behavior.

To take another example, in playing with the image of Siamese twins who compete over everything, Clemens juxtaposes the radical communitarian message of extreme versions of sentimentalism with the radical individualism of social Darwinism. According to the latter, the stronger should, morally, survive at the expense of the weaker, but in the case of inextricably linked brothers, the stronger cannot survive without the weaker and so must become responsible for him. The sections describing this conflict, many of which remain in "Those Extraordinary Twins," are quite painful when one sees the suffering in blighted individuality in the connection between strong and weak, and yet such suffering is only meaningful in sentimental terms. If my explanation of the book's genesis is accurate, then Clemens began to move from the sense of the value of individuality as expressed in the Twins' longings for independence, to a sense of the importance of connection in Wilson's desire to belong to the community and in Roxy's more powerful desire not to have her family broken by the power of the slave system. Again, the novel vacillates wildly over the relative values of communal and familial connection on the one hand and individual independence on the other.

Although *Pudd'nhead Wilson and Those Extraordinary Twins* may have unfolded much as did *Huck Finn*, *The Prince and the Pauper*, or *Connecticut Yankee* with a burlesque impulse ultimately turning serious, Clemens did not, the evidence suggests, try, as he did with the other novels, to sort out his serious moral intentions from the comic impulse that started the book. Rather than turn to explicit and consistent satire, he was at this point more concerned with making the book sell quickly and with finding some sort of comic redemption from his own difficulties. Without the desire to craft a moral intention and under the stress of lost conviction in his utilitarianism but without a corresponding faith in the sentimental alternative, Clemens wrote more or less unconsciously. Thus, in these images of inseparable twins and too-separable slaves, in grotesque ideas of familial honor and equally grotesque manifestations of self-aggrandizement, in examples of love and selfishness, in battles between various kinds of truths and lies, Clemens merely revealed his perplexities about the philosophical tradition on which he had drawn and the degree to which he was without a clear moral vision by the 1890s. In fact, it is not even clear that he knew any longer on what he expected to base a moral system. Did he seek happiness according to utilitarian formula? brotherhood according to sentimental? truth or justice according to any moral systems? Not only does *Pudd'nhead Wilson* not offer solutions to the internal contradictions of Clemens's tradition, it does not even reveal that he knows what he hopes to value in fashioning an alternative.

The only thing that is clear is that Wilson as a character stands as Clemens's fictive hope to master the tangle, both intellectually and socially. While Wilson's irony got him into trouble in the first place, it gives him the leisure he needs to develop the science that will explain the "crimes" that have plagued Dawson's Landing. Wilson uses this science finally to incorporate himself into the community, compensating himself for the "crime" of ostracism; but in sticking to his own purposes, he fails to realign the fundamental moral structure of the community. Unlike Huck, who promises to light out for the territories, Wilson chooses to live in his community. But rather than fully succumb to the perfidy of his community, he maintains his independence in his irony. His calendar, throughout his career in Dawson's Landing, compensates him for being on the outside in the consolation of philosophy.

Indeed, Clemens himself found these aphorisms to have a consoling power; he struggled over them in the first place, but continued to make them through the rest of his life. They figure prominently as chapter headings in *Following the Equator*, and he continued to tinker with them in his notebooks well into the twentieth century. He even made their consoling power a subject of one day's autobiographical dictation (see below, chapter seven). Although by the early twentieth century Clemens would come to explain the value of an aphorism as an exercise in catharsis, in the 1890s he saw the aphorism as a validation of ironic superiority. Consider, for instance the aphorism about discovering America: "It was wonderful to find America, but it would have been more wonderful to miss it" (113). The ironist mockingly says that knowledge of the world is really easy to come by if one simply sees it as it is: sail West from Europe and you will see America. But the ironic pleasure of the aphorism is in condemning all of

American culture, suggesting that in "discovering" the world, we merely reveal our own corruption. Here, then, the irony argues both that knowledge of fact, what Clemens had so often praised as the hallmark of intellectual and moral integrity, is superior to ignorance and that knowledge enlarges the scope of human evil. The ironist's superiority, then, undercuts itself by acknowledging its complicity in the crimes it condemns. How, then, is this a very satisfying moral vision?

In one of the aphorisms, in fact, Clemens acknowledges how weak is the pleasure that comes from ironic carping: "It is easy to find fault, if one has that disposition. There was once a man who, not being able to find any other fault with his coal, complained that there were too many prehistoric toads in it" (40). Clemens demonstrates this disposition, and in fact this disposition, this irreverence that he had vaunted so long as a source of power and independence, leads to a very bitter kind of independence, an independence of mind alone, that does not really free its owner from belonging to the world he criticizes.

So the meta-irony of Wilson's "play" with philosophy is that it gives very little pleasure, or at best the crude and ultimately bitter pleasure of a compromised superiority. Strangely, if one moves away from the expectations of satire, one can find that the real fun of this bizarre and fractured book, even in its watered-down condition with the Twins separated, lies in the absurd play with drunkenness, with brotherly squabbles, with lovesickness, with humbug honor, with the windbag Southerners. Humor, as opposed to irony, makes idiots into clowns and makes laughter rather than anger the appropriate response. So here is Clemens, in his bitterness, trying to write a redemptive piece of hogwash by juxtaposing incompatibles to find hilarity. In doing so, he is confronted by seriousness, the stuff of irony, and his effort at redemption turns dark again, leaving him damned by his own drive for moral monism.

VII

At about the same time he was writing *Pudd'nhead Wilson*, Clemens worked on a book of radically different tone, *Personal Recollections of Joan of Arc*. In noting some of the broad outlines of the story, one could imagine this novel at the center of interest in Twain's work. Like *Connecticut Yankee*, it uses history to make sense out of contemporary society; like so many of his works, it both challenges and participates in a Romantic vision of a medieval past; like *Huckleberry Finn*, it raises questions of justice in politics and uses a child-figure as a foil to the hypocrisies of an adult world. But the book does not occupy the center of the Twain canon for the simple reason that its sentimentality seems overt and uncomplicated.

The entire tale is told as the nostalgic reverie of Joan of Arc's childhood playmate and later secretary, Sieur Louis De Conte, and his nostalgia tinges even the book's humor — of which there is much — with a morbid and sticky bittersweetness. In some few places Clemens uses the narrator's rejection of humor to make fun of the narrator himself, but for the most part the narrator's serious bitterness — the bitterness of an old age made gloomy by the martyrdom of Joan — casts what appears to be Clemens's gloom over even the most comic of scenes. For instance, in Chapter XXXVI, Clemens re-works George Washington Harris's "Burn's Bull Ride," both depriving the story of its scandalous and malignant energy, and also turning the bull ride, here of Joan's father, from an accidental ride away from a wedding into a deliberate ride toward a funeral. Gloom pervades even the lightest parts of this book.

It is easy, and probably correct, to speculate about how Clemens turned to sentimental nostalgia to compensate himself for his losses. Current taste finds irony more interesting, but in the intellectual context I have developed here it is important to look at more than one aspect of this book, both to see how thoroughly Clemens was willing to indulge himself in sentimentalism and to see how even at his most earnestly sentimental he cannot quite maintain his hope in the sentimentalist's link to ideality.

What is most conspicuous from the very beginning of this most fully sentimental of Twain novels is the author's fascination both with Joan's putative ability to discern the truth unerringly and with her ability to sustain selfless devotion to community in the face of all the apparent cynicism and hypocrisy human beings can demonstrate. She stands as hero to her time or any time in exactly the opposite way that Wilson stands to his.

Fascination with Joan's veracity and selflessness opens the book in the "Translator's Preface," the part of the book least distanced from the author's own voice:

> She was truthful when lying was the common speech of men; she was honest when honesty was become a lost virtue; she was a keeper of promises when the keeping of a promise was expected of no one; she gave her great mind to great thoughts and great purposes when other great minds wasted themselves upon pretty fancies or upon poor ambitions; she was modest and fine and delicate

when to be loud and coarse might be said to be universal; she was full of pity when a merciless cruelty was the rule; . . . she was a rock of convictions in a time when men believed in nothing and scoffed at all things; she was unfailingly true in an age that was false to the core. . . .

She was perhaps the only entirely unselfish person whose name has a place in profane history. No vestige or suggestion of self-seeking can be found in any word or deed of hers. (vii–viii)

Notice that the catalogue begins with two clauses stating the basic virtue of honesty, followed by a third stating the related virtue of holding fast to one's promise, that is, of being true to one's word. Later in the same sentence, we see again that she was "unfailingly true." Given the degree to which Clemens held honesty to be the essence of civilization—indeed his entire realist credo was, as we have seen, based on this belief—he held Joan of Arc to be the paragon of civilization.

But the odd points in this catalogue are that she is both true and unselfish. By the utilitarianism that Clemens espoused as part of his realist credo, unselfishness was humanly impossible. The turn here marks the degree to which Clemens was dissatisfied with the ethical implications of his creed. Selfishness makes liars of us all. So if we are to progress toward that reality called truth, we need to be able not only, as does Joan, to see external truth unerringly, but also to see internal motivations honestly and to maintain the integrity that our very selfishness inhibits. The difficulty here leads Clemens out of his former realism squarely into the camp of idealism. In fact, the encapsulated point of this entire catalogue is stated near the beginning of the preface with the claim that Joan of Arc was "ideally perfect" (vii). Here is the man who earlier renounced the ideal as artifice and sham, returning with a vengeance to the hope for an ideal. Is this a full renunciation of the realism that Clemens had so long espoused? Or is it just a more emphatic statement of the sentimental ideal in the battle with the cynical irony of *Pudd'nhead Wilson*?

The rest of the book suggests the latter. Imagining the same material in the hands of Charles Dudley Warner, we would see that the point of the ideal perfection of Joan would be to confirm, through her capacity to hear the voices of angels, the existence of God. This is not, however, the way Clemens develops the story. Strangely, while Joan's visions and voices are the center of Joan's story, Clemens seems remarkably uninterested. True, he does have the narrator come upon one of Joan's visions, and this passage stands as substantial confirmation of the divine source of Joan's abnormal understandings. But in another place, the narrator expresses his skepticism:

> I was frequently in terror to find my mind (which *I* could not control) criticising the Voices and saying "They counsel her to speak boldly—a thing which she would do without any suggestion from *them* or anybody else—but when it comes to telling her any useful thing, such as how these conspirators manage to guess their way so skillfully into her affairs, they are always off attending to some other business." I am reverent by nature; and when such thoughts swept through my head they made me cold with fear, and if there was a storm and thunder at the time, I was so ill that I could but with difficulty abide at my post and do my work. (367–68)

Here, in one of the few places in the book in which he indulges a cynical irony, Clemens reveals his doubts about the ability of such naively superstitious men as those of Joan's day to uncover the truth about anything.

But in spite of this one eruption of ironic skepticism and the occasional straightforward statement that Joan's Voices were not merely imaginary, Clemens seems remarkably uninterested in their historical truth or falsehood. What he concentrates on instead is his sense of Joan's intellectual superiority to all other human beings. When Clemens's narrator reports what happens at the repeated trials of Joan by ecclesiastical courts that try to determine the truth and source of her visions, Clemens concentrates not on the verdicts as true or false but rather on Joan's marvelous intellectual capacities in being able to defeat in debate the most learned minds of her day. The courts all represent the limited minds of the typical human being, caught in logic and experience, but unable, because of epistemological problems stemming from the superstitions of culture, to see Truth. Not only does Joan stand alone in each trial, defending herself against the marshalled intellectual power of Western civilization, she stands alone as the one mind with an acuity great enough to see truth directly. Much of the book serves no other point than to express astonishment that any human being could have such powers:

> A sort of awe crept over us, to think how that untaught girl, taken suddenly and unprepared, was yet able to penetrate the cunning devices of a King's trained advisers and defeat them. Marvelling over this, and astonished at it, we fell silent and spoke no more. We had come to know that she was great in courage, fortitude, endurance, patience, conviction, fidelity to all duties—in all things, indeed, that make a good and trusty soldier and perfect him for his post; now we were beginning to feel that maybe there were greatness in her brain that were even greater than these great qualities of the heart. It set us thinking. (106)

Here is the traditional heart/brain split that is so central to sentimentalism, but the peculiar thing in this book is that it works so hard to show that this split is finally false.

What the story slowly reveals is that Joan's great honesty comes not only from her ability to see to the center of any matter intellectually, but to do so by using her great heart, in conjunction with imagination, to see into the minds of other human beings. Her powers of mind include an incisive intuition that is a combination of emotional and objective mental states:

> Our chief knight says a good many wise things and has a thoughtful head on his shoulders. One day, riding along, we were talking about Joan's great talents, and he said, "But, greatest of all her gifts, she has the seeing eye." I said, like an unthinking fool, "The seeing eye? — I shouldn't count that for much — I suppose we all have it." "No," he said; "very few have it." Then he explained, and made his meaning clear. He said the common eye sees only the outside of things, and judges by that, but the seeing eye pierces through and reads the heart and the soul, finding there capacities which the outside didn't indicate or promise, and which the other kind of eye couldn't detect. He said the mightiest military genius must fail and come to nothing if it have not the seeing eye — that is to say, if it cannot read men and select its subordinates with an infallible judgment. It sees as by intuition that this man is good for strategy, that one for dash and dare-devil assault, the other for patient bull-dog persistence, and it appoints each to his right place and wins. (139)

Here Clemens shows that the sentimentalism of *Joan* is as much an episte-mological one as an emotional one, or rather, that the emotionalism of the book arises from its epistemology. Joan's intuitions are, as David Hume would say intuitions from sympathetic imagination must be, the bridge over the limitations of a strict empiricism. While the external senses see only surfaces, which can deceive, sympathetic intuition yields more.

So while this sympathetic intuition reveals itself most clearly as an intellectual power in Joan's trials, where she defends herself against sophistic traps "by force of her best and surest helper, the clear vision and lightning intuitions of her extraordinary mind" (348), her military and social successes flow from the same source. Her charisma transforms the French armies from cowards to conquerors, simply because she can understand the hearts of all of her hearers and so teach them what they need to know to rise to their best dignity.

But while Clemens here argues that sympathy has both the potential in the hands of a superior person to reveal truth and to galvanize people into their best behavior, the book as a whole still does not endorse sympathy as a fully satisfactory consolation for the trials and tribulations of an average person. It is important to consider that the story of Joan of Arc, like the stories of the various outcasts in *Pudd'nhead Wilson and Those Extraordinary Twins*, is the story of a freak, someone so unusual as to be barely human. The fact that Joan is a saint rather than a sinner in no way mitigates this fact. And while her peculiarities may spark faith, they also lead to her death. On the one hand, Clemens at this stage in his career is seeing death as a "release" from bondage, both literally in Joan's case and figuratively for every person. But as much as the story insistently protests that Joan's exceptional life inspires not only awe but faith, the narrator, speaking from old age, speaks nothing but bitterness.

His is the bitterness of David "Pudd'nhead" Wilson and of Samuel Clemens; that is, it is the bitterness of a man with greater understanding than average, but with no more than average ability to transcend the human limitations he can see all too clearly. We see both his superiority and the kind of limitations common to most human beings in his very condescending examination of the peasants in Joan's village and in her family. In such commentary, the mask of the narrative persona shifts, revealing a Clemens much closer intellectually to the one who narrates *Pudd'nhead Wilson*. Although for Joan the associations of childhood—specifically the memories of her mother and of *L'Arbre Fee de Bourlemont*—are morally redeeming, for the rest of her family and friends associations are merely the prison of habit. Habit, the narrator tells us, "is not to be flung out of the window by any man, but is to be coaxed down-stairs one step at a time" (49).

This statement of the power of habit is the aphoristic distillation of a truth that reveals itself in the inability of Joan's family to adjust to its new status after the King, in gratitude to Joan, proclaims her family noble:

> I may as well say now as later, that Papa D'Arc and [Uncle] Laxart were stopping in that little Zebra Inn, and that there they remained. Finer quarters were offered them by the Bailly, also public distinctions and brave entertainment; but they were frightened at these projects, they being only humble and ignorant peasants: so they begged off, and had peace. They could not have enjoyed such things. Poor souls, they did not even know what to do with their hands, and it took all their attention to keep from treading on them. (281)

Living the bulk of their lives at the bottom of the social hierarchy, they, like Tom Driscoll removed from the slave's quarters at the end of *Pudd'nhead*

Wilson, cannot adapt themselves to their new social realities. They are trapped by their pasts.

The narrator himself is in a middle position. Hanging on to a petty nobility, he is the one literate contemporary of Joan from Joan's village. This gives him a social distinction adequate enough to explain his difference from the peasants, but not to explain his difference from the run-of-the-mill nobles he also comes to hold in patronizing contempt. What distinguishes him is a transcendent connection to Joan through shared childhood associations and even through a shared birthdate. He seems to have a special place in Joan's heart, and, considering that Joan can see aptitudes with unerring accuracy, that she makes him her private secretary indicates the degree to which he is closer to her level than are the others.

But closer is not close enough. He is still caught in the world's lies and deceits, and always judges Joan more by human than by divine standards. The one thing he always wishes is to be closer to Joan spiritually, and thus he longs with an intensity that can only yield disillusionment for Joan's eternal sympathy. While she lives, her sympathetic notice is the one great consolation of his life; after she dies, he is left inconsolable. While he has worked for the rehabilitation of Joan's character, and while he has both worked for and seen the success of Joan's great project, the liberation of France, he remains disconsolate and embittered, hoping for release from the disillusionment of old age into the transcendent beauty of death — described as a return to childhood innocence, faith, and morality built on homely associations. Thus, no matter how transcendent the narrator finds Joan, his own attitude is one of wild vacillation between the cynical realism of old age and the enchanted faith of childhood.

Much of Clemens's later writing participates in this same strange tension between strained, contemptuous laughter at the world and sentimental tears over it, between cynical "realism" and strained "idealism." Often the tension exists simultaneously in a single work, as it does in "Chronicle of Young Satan." Philosophically, this tension does make a gradual large shift in his work; in both the "idealistic" or "sentimental" or antirealist works and in the realist works of his last years, Clemens is trying to explore the philosophical implications of subjectivity.

To mention this philosophical component is not to dismiss the personal value of both kinds of work to Clemens. Even in exploring subjectivity and fantasy he was trying to compensate for the pain of his financial, and later, familial circumstances, and both the sentimental and naturalistic stories serve these purposes. On the one hand, in a world determined by external circumstances, Clemens was able to see that it was absurd to blame anyone for failure. On the other, he found in sentimentalism another way to exonerate himself for his failures. After all, although Sumner's naturalism may suggest that human successes and failures are determined by outside influences, it still, in spite of Clemens's reasonable argument to the contrary, attaches moral opprobrium to failure. By naturalistic standards, Clemens may not have been to blame, but he still proved himself morally "unworthy" of survival by his very failure itself.

In sentimental terms, financial failure is not necessarily judged so harshly. Sentimentalists look to intention, not consequence, to judge morality. In so doing, they also purify situations of emotional ambiguity in order to find the moral tone of a person's intentions. These characteristics made sentimental morality a gentler standard by which Clemens could judge his bankruptcy, and so he often turned to the conventions of sentimental literature to replay his business failure in order to find himself innocent of any moral shortcoming.

For instance, in the unpublished, unfinished novel, "Which Was the Dream?" Clemens writes of a famous man, an upstanding, trusting character, General X, whose business-manager, his wife's cousin, swindles him and leaves him unable to pay his creditors. General X's errors are those of a generous spirit who assumes other men's honesty. When he confesses his naïveté, he expects to be given a chance to right the wrongs that he committed through ignorance rather than through intention:

> "I am to blame. I am to blame, I confess it freely. I trusted Sedgewick as no human being ought to be trusted, and I have my reward. He has destroyed me."
> There was no word of response. I was ashamed. I had expected at least a recognition of my remark, the mere courtesy of a comment of some kind or other; I was used to this much deference — and entitled to it. ("Which Was the Dream?" 62)

But the business mind is unsentimental; it cannot do the right thing. General X finds that a sentimental appeal cannot exonerate him in the eyes of his creditors. They reject "womanish sentimentalities" (63) and all explanatory arguments. Only then does X learn the truth of the world:

> But how little I knew the religion of commerce and its god. The argument fell flat; more — it was received with disdain — disdain of the sort evoked when a person intrudes a triviality into a serious discussion. Mr. Simmons brushed it aside as indifferently as if he were squelching the ignorant prattle of a schoolboy —
> "Men will do anything for money." (65)

The businessmen, in showing their lack of respect for the General, in failing to give him the "deference" to which he was "entitled," show their moral affinity with the embezzler. The General, though in a practical bind, appears innocent by contrast. Thus Clemens establishes a sentimental theater of absolutely pure intention in conflict with impure intention in order to exonerate General X of any moral taint and instead to pin the blame on the business mind for its harshness and lack of sympathy.[10]

In spite of this purifying vision of himself as a suffering victim of unfair business dealings, when Clemens did go bankrupt he was, he says in his *Autobiography*, willing to renounce many of his debts. But he did not because his new friend, H. H. Rogers of Standard Oil, advised him against it. As he explains:

> I was morally bound for the debts, though not legally. The panic was on, business houses were falling to ruin everywhere, creditors were taking the assets — when there were any — and letting the rest go. Old business friends of mine said: "Business is business, sentiment is sentiment — and this is business. Turn the assets over to the creditors and compromise on that." . . . Mr. Rogers was certainly a business man — no one doubts that. People will think they know what his attitude would be in the matter. And they will be mistaken. He sided with my wife. He was the only man who had a clear eye for the situation and could see that it differed from other apparently parallel situations. In substance he said this: "Business has its laws and customs and they are justified; but a literary man's reputation is his life; he can afford to be money poor but he cannot afford to be character poor; you must earn the cent per cent and pay it." (Neider 283–84)

Clemens describes Rogers as the only man who sided with his wife in preferring sentiment to business, albeit not for sentiment's sake, but because it made good business sense for a man who was in a sentimental business. Clemens, determined now to drown in ink, learned the practical value of the sentimental tradition to him.

So with substantial personal motivation, and with the models of important American men of letters, like William James, lending the move a certain intellectual legitimacy, Clemens was quite willing to return to the sentimental intellectual tradition. Sentimentalism, imported into the United States in opposition to Calvinistic doctrines of predestination, was an essentially voluntaristic philosophy, and the epistemology attendant on its voluntarism provided Clemens and other important critics of Spencerian fatalism with the ideas they needed to construct a philosophical alternative. Consider William James's use of sentimental moral philosophy as a case in point.[11]

James's career as a philosopher began in the shadow of Spencerian monism, and he found the deterministic conclusions of Spencer's mechanistic philosophy overwhelmingly depressing. He needed to believe in free will, and he felt that such desire itself was an exercise in will (Hofstadter 127–30). But rather than retreat into a romantic idealism that would deny physical reality, James turned to sentimental moral philosophy to ground his critique, not just of Spencerian monism, but of all monisms.

James stressed that all belief, including the desire to believe in rational systems, is ultimately subjective. The paradoxical title of one of his essays, "The Sentiment of Rationality" (1879), shows that he, like Clemens, perceived the desire to know to be at root subjective. More important, he discovered in Spencer's system a willful confusion of objective description of "reality" and subjective prescription of reality. As he put it in "Remarks on Spencer's Definition of Mind as Correspondence" (1878),

> Is it not already clear to the reader's mind that the whole difficulty in making Mr. Spencer's law work lies in the fact that it is not really a constitutive, but a regulative, law of thought which he is erecting, and that he does not frankly say so? Every law of Mind must be either a law of the *cogitatum* or a law of the *cogitandum*. If it be a law in the sense of an analysis of what we *do* think, then it will include error, nonsense, the worthless as well as the worthy, metaphysics, and mythologies as well as scientific truths which mirror the actual environment. But such a law of the *cogitatum* is already well known. It is no other than the association of ideas according to their several modes. (17–18)

He thus turns back into sentimental moral philosophy for a description of mind rather than for a prescription of morals.

In building on the sentimental tradition, James accepts the effort to find objective reality by empirical methods, but he rejects the possibility of pure objectivity by the very principles of mind that the philosophy entails:

> I, for my part, cannot escape the consideration, forced upon me at every turn, that the knower is not simply a mirror floating with no foot-hold anywhere, and passively reflecting an order that he comes upon and finds simply existing. The knower is an actor, and coefficient of the truth on one side, whilst on the other he registers the truth which he helps to create. (23)

James does not deny the existence of external, physical realities, or even the possibility that human beings can explore it. But he does imply that truth is not monistic and rational, as nineteenth-century science proclaimed, nor is it merely dual, as the Common Sense philosophers had held. It is, instead, plural, as multiform as human subjectivity in collision with external reality can make it. Further, insofar as the mind helps create the reality it perceives through associated ideas colored by desires and irrationality, then neither truth nor human fate can be fixed. Fate is instead the plastic result of a myriad of influences, many of them internally generated, all of them in unpredictable flux.[12]

VIII

By the time he wrote *The American Claimant*, Clemens had decided that all ways of looking at the world were ultimately based in irrational desires.[13] In writing *Following the Equator* (1897), he explored more fully some of the implications of such a way of thinking. In particular, he began to question the superiority of any one culture over another. Rather than looking at a culture's physical progress alone, he chose to look at the moral development of certain important "sentiments," and in so doing discovered the essential similarity of European and non-European cultures.

For instance, in his chapters on New Zealand, he praises the native Maoris in part for their relatively high state of technological development, but most particularly for their character traits of determination and independence, especially in their patriotic defense of their homeland against British invasion. He makes this latter point a lesson in cultural similarity by pointing out the absurdity of two British war memorials at Wanganui:

> One is in honor of white men "who fell in defense of law and order against fanaticism and barbarism." Fanaticism. . . . If you carve it at Thermopylae, or where Winkelreid died, or upon Bunker Hill monument, and read it again — "who fell in defense of law and order against fanaticism" — you will perceive what the word means, and how mischosen it is. Patriotism is Patriotism. Calling it fanaticism cannot degrade it; nothing can degrade it. Even though it be a political mistake, and a thousand times a political mistake, that does not affect it; it is honorable — always honorable, always noble — and privileged to hold its head up and look the nations in the face. (1:307)

He refuses to let the prejudices of the British misname the motives of their enemies because he sees a fundamental likeness in the moral qualities of the behavior of both the Maoris and the British.

Similarly, he compares cultures by their capacities for "reverence," the sentiment his critics had used to disparage his wit. Throughout *Following the Equator*, he demonstrates a reverence for all things non-European that is truly remarkable in light of his earlier travel books, freighted as they were with a powerful Western chauvinism. In this last of his travel narratives, he redefines reverence in such a way that he finds all cultures lacking in that valuable moral characteristic. The seventeenth chapter of Volume Two, for instance, is a virtual sermon on true reverence, beginning with the text, from Pudd'nhead Wilson's New Calendar, "True irreverence is irreverence for another man's god" (185).

In the chapter, Clemens describes his audience with a Hindu holy man who had "attained to what among the Hindus is called the 'state of perfection,'" and is therefore considered to be a god. He goes on to describe the religious ideas that lead Hindus to accept this denomination, and describes further how many Hindus renounce the "vanities and comforts of the world" (2:192) in order to further their spiritual quest for "perfection." He notes the similarity to the Christian practice of renouncing the world in a holy quest, but complains that, although his readers might find such a Christian quest worthy of reverence, in the Hindu devotee they see

> merely a crank. . . . The ordinary reverence, the reverence defined and explained by the dictionary, costs nothing. Reverence for one's own sacred things — parents, religion, flag, laws, and respect for one's own beliefs — these are feelings which we cannot even help. They come natural to us; they are involuntary, like breathing. There is no personal merit in breathing. But the reverence which is difficult, and which has personal merit in it, is the respect which you pay, without compulsion, to the political or religious attitude of a man whose beliefs are not yours. You can't revere his gods or his politics, and no one expects you to do that, but you could respect his belief in them if you tried hard enough; and you could respect *him*, too, if you tried hard enough. (2:193)

Here again, Clemens is not judging the truth of any metaphysical ideas, but he is coming to appreciate the "tremendous forces that lie in religion" (2:192), "that stupendous power, Faith" (2:135), that is a part, whether it makes sense or not, of all human beings.

In judging people by the moral quality of reverence, however, Clemens finds all people falling short. As he says in the continuation of his sermon:

> If the man doesn't believe as we do, we say he is a crank, and that settles it. I mean it does Nowadays, because now we can't burn him. We are always canting about people's "irreverence," always charging this offense upon somebody or other, and thereby intimating that we are better than that person and do not commit that offense ourselves. Whenever we do this we are in a lying attitude. (2:193)

As a defense of his life's output as a humorous writer against the attacks of the righteous, this sermon is interesting enough, but the importance of it to Clemens's moral philosophy is that it argues that human beings are locked in the prejudices of their own cultural "attitudes." Later in the chapter he describes Europeans, who were desecrating the holy places of India without a civilized qualm in the world, revealing their fundamental "Barbarism" (195).

Much of the book serves to show Western barbarism at work in its imperial quests throughout the world. For instance, at one point he notes that "all the territorial possessions of all the political establishments in the earth—including America, of course—consist of pilferings from other people's wash" (2:298). By calling imperialism "pilfering," he shows it, through satiric understatement, to be immoral, but he explains the European inability to see this immorality as a consequence of its universality: "A crime persevered in a thousand years ceases to be a crime, and becomes a virtue" (2:299). By showing the universality of such savagery as land-grabbing, Clemens hopes to show the absurdity of European claims to "superiority." As he put it elsewhere in the book: "There are many humorous things in the world; among them the white man's notion that he is less savage than the other savages" (1:192).

Clemens could not reach this conclusion without first seeing through the differences between cultures' *mores* to the essential similarities between their moral *qualities*. Having gained this insight himself, he notes that most European tourists cannot see past their ideas of what constitutes morality to the impulse behind it. Hence, they all perceive non-European *mores* as proof of the superiority of Western moral character. He describes this best when talking of the sentiment of modesty:

> Without doubt modesty is nothing else than a holy feeling; and without doubt the person whose rule of modesty has been transgressed feels the same sort of wound that he would feel if something made holy to him by his religion had suffered a desecration. I say "rule of modesty" because there are about a million rules in the world, and this makes a million standards to be looked out for. Major Sleeman mentions the case of some high-caste veiled ladies who were profoundly scandalized when some English young ladies passed by with faces bare to the world; so scandalized that they spoke out with strong indignation and wondered that people could be so shameless as to expose their persons like that. And yet "the legs of the objectors were naked to mid-thigh." Both parties were clean-minded and irreproachably modest, while abiding by their separate rules, but they couldn't have traded rules for a change without suffering considerable discomfort. (2:155)

His point is that while rules themselves may change from culture to culture, the impulses behind them do not. No culture, then, is in a position to judge the rules of other cultures, because "all human rules are more or less idiotic" (2:155). One can, he says, judge true morality only by the impulse behind the rule.

The moral impulse, Clemens often finds, is idealistic in the extreme and often at odds with any conceivable notion of practicality. He marvels at how such a diversity of rules could have evolved from common human experience as much as he marvels over the idealistic powers of mind that make morality possible. For instance, referring to the Suttee — that is, the Brahmin wife's practice of committing suicide on her husband's funeral pyre — he remarks that the faith that keeps the practice going "compels one's reverence and respect" (2:135). While he can see how it has been "brought to the pitch of effectiveness by the cumulative force of example and long use and custom" (2:135–36), he "cannot understand how the first widows came to take to it. That is a perplexing detail" (2:136). Similarly, he is mystified at the success of a Trappist monastery he describes:

> There it all was. It was not a dream, it was not a lie. And yet with the fact before one's face it was still incredible. It is such a sweeping suppression of human instincts, such an extinction of the man as an individual. La Trappe must have known the human race well. . . . [He] must have known that there were men who would enjoy this kind of misery, but how did he find it out? (2:323)

Here he states his perplexity in the utilitarian terms that had come to dominate his thinking. Finally, however, he sees these terms to be inadequate. Pursuit of pleasure and avoidance of pain makes rational sense, but the ideals that drive self-abnegation, ideals such as "merely the saving of [one's] soul" (2:324) in the Trappist case and of the reunion of souls in the case of the Suttee, defy reason. They are part of what he called the "idiotic" world of human rules.

Idiotic, but somehow necessary. As Colonel Sellers in *The American Claimant* found happiness in escaping into his own insanity, so, Clemens suggests in *Following the Equator*, human beings need to escape from reality into their own arbitrary rules. As he put it at the beginning of Volume Two, Chapter Twenty-Three, "Don't part with your illusions. When they are gone you may still exist but you have ceased to live" (2:246). He here expresses a belief in an objectively discernible reality outside of human idealism, but he has become so disillusioned with it as to reject it as emotionally untenable.

But much of *Equator* nonetheless tries to expose human fraudulence, the hypocritical pretensions based on desire. He does not simply describe the gulf between human rules and natural reality; he judges it. For instance, when trying to discover the real history of the Jameson raid in South Africa, he says he needs to do this because all accounts so far are too biased to be worth anything. So he himself takes on the task of discovering the truth: "By liquefying the evidence of the prejudiced books and of the prejudiced parliamentary witnesses and stirring the whole together and pouring it into my own (prejudiced) molds, I have got at the truth of that puzzling South African situation" (2:332). He admits that he, too, is prejudiced, so that he, too, will actively color the truth; he therefore, in James's words, "registers the truth which he helps to create." After all, as he puts it a bit later in the book, "The very ink with which all history is written is merely fluid prejudice" (2:366). Like James, he believes that, while there may be an objective truth, it is unlikely that human beings will ever find it or that it is relevant to human life. But, unlike James, Clemens contradictorily continued to judge the value of beliefs by how closely they approximate the objective "truth." He seems to have continued to accept Darwin's explanation of human progress from savage to civilized as the growing ability to distinguish between subjectivity and objectivity (Darwin 63–64). In discovering the subjectivity of all knowledge, Clemens, unlike James, decided that all human beings are savages and, consequently, that progress is a myth.

Clemens's judgment of humanity by this standard shows him unable to make the important distinction between natural law as mere description, what James calls a "constitutive" law, and natural law as prescription, what James calls a "regulative" law. This confusion is inherent in the metaphor of "law" itself, with the implied law-giving creator legislating the best of all possible worlds through his omnipotent and omniscient command. Insofar as Clemens accepted this prescriptive connotation of natural law — as, it must be emphasized, almost all of his contemporaries did — his belief in the purely subjective and irrational and therefore law-defying qualities of human culture were very disillusioning at first. He was caught in a metaphor of human creation that his understanding of human subjectivity should have allowed him to reject, but before he could do so, he had to rail at the cosmic stupidity of human beings and then at the cosmic unfairness of a deity that would make human beings so unable to find happiness. Only then would he be able to confront his intellectual despair and find ways to come to terms with it.

7. Dreaming Better Dreams

I

"The Chronicle of Young Satan" may well mark the nadir of Clemens's personal and intellectual despair. Written in three bursts between 1897 and 1900, this long narrative served the purposes of attacking both humanity and God that his intellectual journey through *Following the Equator* elicited.[1] When Clemens began the piece at the end of 1897, he had finished his lecture tour and *Following the Equator*. He had repaid virtually all his debts and had a small surplus which H. H. Rogers invested profitably for him. He had just suffered through the death of his daughter Susy to meningitis and had recently learned that his daughter Jean had epilepsy. He certainly had formidable personal reasons to vent his spleen, and he had the financial luxury to write for himself rather than for his public. As he said in a letter to Howells, "I couldn't get along without work now. I bury myself in it up to the ears. Long hours—8 & 9 on a stretch, sometimes. And all the days, Sundays included. It isn't all for print, by any means" (*MTHL* 670).

But in his notebook, in a passage written for his own eyes, Clemens explained that he wrote not only to relieve his sorrow or for money but also because he had grown contemptuous of humanity and of the universe. He explained that much of what he wrote was not for print because he wanted to protect his family from embarrassment and financial ruin, but he desired, he said, to attack creation in the broadest possible terms:

> It is the strangest thing that the world is not full of books that scoff at the pitiful world, and the useless universe and violent, contemptible human race—books that laugh at the paltry scheme and deride it. . . . Why don't I write such a book? because I have a family. (Tuckey, *Satan* 26)

In "The Chronicle of Young Satan," he does deride the "contemptible human race," listing human foibles ad infinitum, listing humanity's wars and brutalities, showing people unable to have compassion for each other.

Equally important, the satire attacks God for creating such an absurd world. Clemens shows that human beings are more interested in divine notice than in consoling one another, and while they should direct their attentions to one another, they cannot help but reject their own best interests in the presence of a malignantly compelling higher power. The satire condemns all people for being trapped, but equally condemns God for trapping them.

Similarly, in "Letters from the Earth," Clemens blasts both humanity and God. In the letters, Satan, the embodiment of the irreverent impulse, describes his exploration of the earth, God's "experiment in morals." Satan finds the experiment contemptible, noting human frailty after frailty, absurdity after absurdity. His contempt for the creation itself, though, is directed not so much at human beings as at their creator. The lawgiver himself must be held accountable for the perverse consequences of his laws. Here speaks the Clemens who promoted, in *Connecticut Yankee*, the idea that any subject of unjust laws is morally obligated to protest those laws; here speaks the Clemens of *The American Claimant*, who suggested that irreverence for injustice is the only way to promote justice; here speaks the Clemens of "Chronicle of Young Satan," trying to "blow . . . to rags and atoms" (*MTMS* 166) the absurdities of the entire cosmos through the power of laughter. In this progression from protest to laughter, he finally dropped the idea that natural law provides human beings with a workable moral imperative. Instead, he began to see that one can describe the complexities and confusions of human affairs without insisting on a consistent, transcendental morality in concert with natural law.

Many of his works of the 1900s depend on this kind of relativism. The way he reworked "The Chronicle of Young Satan" into "No. 44, The Mysterious Stranger" in some ways mirrors the course of his own intellectual journey from a philosophical pursuit of objective truth to a belief that truth is the concoction of the subjective mind. In the former tale, human suffering at the hands of a malignant, or at least stupidly indifferent, deity assumes the reality of the human condition. By the time he wrote the dream ending to "No. 44" in 1904 (Gibson, Introduction, *MTMS* 11), he had extended his belief in the relativity of truth to the point of pure solipsism:

> Nothing exists; all is a dream. God — man — the world — the sun, the moon, the wilderness of stars: a dream, all a dream, they have no existence. Nothing exists save empty space — and you! . . . And you are not you — you have no body, no blood, no bones, you are but a thought. I myself have no existence, I am but a dream — your dream, creature of your imagination. . . . But I your poor servant have revealed you to yourself and set you free. Dream other dreams, and better. (*MTMS* 404)

Of course, this extreme solipsism served Clemens as compensation for extreme pain in his life, but the ideas that allowed him to voice such a fantasy of release into a better dream could evolve only after he had freed himself from the idea that natural law was the same as moral law, and only after he abandoned his earlier philosophical monism.

Bernard De Voto suggested that in the dream ending to what we now know is the textually corrupt *Mysterious Stranger* Mark Twain found in art not only an end to pain but also an end to his own creative block. However, pure solipsism is a call not to artistic production, but rather to total silence. Without an audience, why write? Why not just dream? But Mark Twain did continue to write and to publish steadily, even going so far as to publish three texts — "Extracts from Capt. Stormfield's Visit to Heaven," parts of his *Autobiography*, and, in a private, small edition, *What is Man?* — that he originally intended only for private use. He clearly wanted an audience, as he found that truth, if relative, was relative not completely to a single individual, but to that individual and his entire set of circumstances, including his audience. Clemens did find salvation in art, but not in the art of philosophical solipsism. Like William James, Clemens rejected the epistemological claims neither of the physical world nor of mental and spiritual states. What he had found in *Following the Equator* and lamented in "Chronicle of Young Satan" was the gap between the two kinds of claims to truth. This gap permitted his irony to undercut the grounds for beliefs he needed to support his writing and therefore threatened to stifle his creativity. But after grieving over the existence of this gap, he found that the gap itself was a fruitful subject for art. He continued to use his writing to try to tell truth, but now he attempted to tell as many truths as he could find, both those relative to circumstance and those that revealed *how* truth was relative to circumstance. Many of his late works play with epistemological questions in bold ways, in particular by using the metaphor of translation to explore the relationship between individual circumstances in time to larger questions of enduring truth. Having explored these themes fancifully, he applied the understanding his explorations generated to his last major work, his *Autobiography*.

II

One probable motive for Clemens's flirtation with pure solipsism was a fantasy of moral purity, a dream of being so untethered to human community that he would be free to be so morally consistent and good that his conscience would cease to castigate him for everything he did. Throughout his career he fussed about the morally debilitating power of public opinion, and, indeed, this suspicion of public opinion had long been one of his psychological grounds for rejecting the claims of sympathy. The sympathy that Clemens envisioned Puddn'head Wilson seeking, for instance, he presented as a mark of corruption, and he often showed the Tom Sawyerish pranks that are cute in a child as a source of vice in an adult. The degree to which Clemens persisted in finding the moral danger of such a human characteristic is made amply clear in "The United States of Lyncherdom" and "Corn-pone Opinions."

But in the face of his loneliness in his last years, Clemens could not really find much satisfaction in moral isolation, partly because no such fantasy really ended the feelings it was supposed to cancel. Persistent desires to be "petted" by public and private audiences moved him away from his earlier individualistic ethic. In fact, most of his late writings deal with the profound hypocrisy of modesty in that it is usually a show to encourage praise. In the *Autobiography*, he admits that he cultivates a shyness in front of young women in order to get them to love him, and, in "Three Thousand Years Among the Microbes," the speaker of the tale admits that he has practiced in front of a mirror how to appear modest so that he is able to secure the greater love of admiring crowds. Whereas in earlier years such behavior would have elicited his scorn, in the works of the 1900s Twain excuses it as natural:

> The baby microbe shows off before company; the microbe lad shows off, with silly antics, before the little bacillus girls; also he plays pirate, soldier, clown — anything to be conspicuous. After that — well after that, his appetite for notice and notoriety remains — remains always — but he lyingly and hypocritically lets on that he has lost it. He hasn't lost it, he has only lost his honesty. Now then, be gentle with me, for that is all I have lost; all that you and I have lost. (*WWD* 459)

He had often in the past, when using Mark Twain as the butt of humor, implicitly indulged egotistical dishonesty, but his irony usually cut short that indulgence. Here, he holds irony in abeyance and sticks to humor.

He does so not because he merely accepts human egotism — the desire to be "petted" — as a normal, albeit unfortunate, human foible. On the contrary, he has come to see egotism as something essential to the human constitution, as the impulse that holds solipsism and doubt in check. If, indeed, our conceptions of ourselves are virtually unconnected to natural fact, if, indeed, truths as we believe them are entirely contingent on our points of view, then we will constantly be in danger of being lost in total doubt, in the pure chaos of imagination, desire, and shifting circumstance. Egotism, if it does nothing more, ties a person to audience, drives a person to find community. Much of the late work, then, plays with the tension between the isolating potentials of philosophical relativism and the countervailing drive to find community and security in the face of doubt.

This tension shows quite clearly in "Three Thousand Years Among the Microbes," the entire structure of which is designed to show how tenuous our hold on reality is. All of the play with time, space, form, language, etc., shows that perceptions of reality are completely contingent on circumstance, that what is true to one circumstance may be absurd to another. The narrator drives this main point home explicitly when, after first finding his report of the truths of his former life laughed at by his new microbe friends, he confronts the apparent absurdity of Christian Science as promoted by his servant:

> She was so earnest about it that I could not doubt, and did not doubt, that she believed what she was saying. To me it was a delusion; an hour or two earlier I would have said so, and risen superior to her, and looked down upon her compassionately from that high altitude, and would have advised her to put the foolish and manifest fraud out of her head and come back to common sense and reasonableness. But not now. No. An hour or two ago and now — those were two quite different dates. Within that brief space I had suffered a sea-change myself. I had seen a certainty of mine dubbed a delusion and laughed at by a couple of able minds — minds trained to searchingly and exhaustively examine the phenomena of Nature, and segregate fact from fancy, truth from illusion, and pronounce final judgment — and these competent minds had puffed my World away without a moment's hesitancy, and without the shadow of a misgiving. They thought they knew it was an illusion. I knew it wasn't.
>
> The list of things which we absolutely know is not a long one, and we have not the luck to add a fresh one to it often, but I recognized that I had added one to mine this day. I knew, now, that it isn't safe to sit in judgment upon another person's illusion when you are not on the inside. (*WWD* 492)

Not only does the narrator see that point of view determines truth but also he sees that he has changed and so his truths have changed from one moment to the next. What is more, he finds the laughter of his comrades to be extremely unsettling to his pride. Given the power of point of view, given that he has changed so much over the course of the story as to forget much of his English and most of his history, given that he can change attitudes so quickly, what, the story asks, is to hold him down as a self? Where is the security of belief? Solipsism in such a world is as frightening as it is liberating, isolating in its freedom, as likely to deliver horrible nightmares as it is to deliver sweet dreams.

Given the constant danger that reality will blow up in our faces, that simple error will blast our certitudes to doubt, that skepticism can chill the most ardent will to live, Clemens came to believe that we need something outside ourselves to lend credence to our hopes. That something, as developed in so many of his late works, is to find a community that will lend confirmation to belief, that will, in comradeship and sympathy rather than in argument, lend credence to "illusion." The story makes this point in its resolution of "arguments" about immortality. The narrator had been quibbling with conventional conceptions of heaven as being too egotistical, too narrow, in including only microbes. He had a grander hope of a community of all life, but could find no clinching argument. Finally, in seeking support for his belief, he came across a fellow believer:

> When the Brother learned that I longed to have our humble friends and helpers, the lower animals, accompany us to the Happy Land and partake of its joys with us, it went to his heart. He was deeply moved, and said it was a most noble and compassionate feeling, and that he shared it with me to the uttermost. That was good and strong and cheering language; and when he added that he not only longed for the translation of the animals but believed it would happen and had no shadow of a doubt that it would happen, my cup of happiness was full! I had never lacked anything but a support like this to clinch my own belief and make it solid and perfect, and now it was solid and perfect. I think there *was* not a happier Microbe than I. (*WWD* 512)

The narrator receives no new arguments — in fact he is not looking for any. What he finds instead is shared belief couched in "strong and cheering language," and especially in a "compassionate feeling." Belief, then, is made solid in sentimental community, in the happiness that comes from sharing a point of view and a construction of reality. So finally, the desire to show off is neither more nor less than the motive that binds one to a shared vision of the world.

But the word "translation" of the lower animals brings up the final plague to Clemens's sense of happiness in a community of believers. If the final absolute metaphysical truth is that all being is equal and will share in the divine dispensation, then why is belief so contingent on point of view that language gets in the way of understanding? Again and again in Twain's later works, he tells stories as elaborate translations from one language, one construction of reality, to another. Metaphorically, translation serves to suggest the profound isolation of individuals within their private circumstances. This is the point of the fragmentary "The Secret History of Eddypus," an account of politically subversive historians at work in a future age. The narrator of "Eddypus" tries to recover historical fact by translating secret documents from the early twentieth century. He is unable to translate accurately both because time distorts language in the natural course of human events and because those who hold political power actively distort language in order to consolidate their power by manipulating what people can perceive as the truth. If one reads for plot alone, one sees Twain describing language isolating one human being from another, much as Orwell describes in *1984*. But unlike Orwell's book, Twain's tale is filled with levity and the ultimate sense that the very effort to bridge the gaps of time and deceit is the essence of communication, of community. Getting the facts of history may be impossible, but getting the true feeling of community in the effort is what matters much more.

"Microbes," too, projects the same basic message, that the effort to make contact is somehow redeeming. Despite the losses of memory the narrator experiences, despite his troubles with English, despite the final translation by Mark Twain, the story conveys its points with great clarity. As in the passage I quoted above, the final happiness in belief comes from a "compassionate feeling that he shared with me to the uttermost." With compassion, suggests Clemens, human beings can construct a set of beliefs that acknowledges some enduring truths, but mostly satisfies the individual believers by making them feel content in their beliefs.

III

Clemens saw his *Autobiography* as his last major literary work, and in some ways he had been, as James Cox (*Fate* 293) suggests, practicing to write it all his life in his various semi-fictionalized travel writings. Hiding behind the Mark Twain persona, Clemens was able to present, as fictions, many embarrassments of his real life. He was obviously very interested in telling autobiography, both because his semi-autobiographical works were so important to his output as a literary comedian whose work verged on journalism and because his realist doctrine was based on the need to ground all plausible fictions in real experiences. But when confronting autobiography directly, without the mediating filter of a persona or a novel, Clemens confronted the inescapable fact that no effort to tell the whole truth and nothing but the truth of one's own life can be successful because each autobiographer distorts his or her self-image to secure self-respect.

Clemens tells several instances to his knowledge of people re-creating their own life histories to their advantages. For instance, in the dictation of February 23, 1906, he tells of Charles Webster appropriating some of Clemens's actions for his own curriculum vitae, and in the dictations of February 23 and of April 6, 1906, of Orion Clemens's incapacity, in spite of his notorious honesty to the point of self-defeating tactlessness, to tell his own story accurately:

> In the other room you will find a bulky manuscript, an autobiography of my brother Orion, who was ten years my senior in age. He wrote that autobiography at my suggestion, twenty years ago, and brought it to me in Hartford, from Keokuk, Iowa. I had urged him to put upon paper all the well remembered incidents of his life, and to not confine himself to those which he was proud of, but to put in also those which he was ashamed of. I said I did not suppose he could do it, because if anybody could do that thing it would have been done long ago. The fact that it has never been done is very good proof that it can't be done. . . . I urged Orion to try to tell the truth, and tell the whole of it. I said he couldn't tell the truth of course.†
>
> Orion wrote his autobiography and sent it to me. But great was my disappointment; and my vexation, too. In it he was constantly making a hero of himself, exactly as I should have done and am doing now, and he was constantly forgetting to put in the episodes which placed him in an unheroic light. I knew several incidents of his life which were distinctly and painfully unheroic, but when I came across them in his autobiography they had changed color. They had turned themselves inside-out, and were things to be intemperately proud of. (Neider 245)

The repetition of the basic idea here from one rendition of the story to the next, in spite of the minor discrepancy in the detail about how he received the manuscript, shows the importance Clemens attaches to Orion's failure to write a fully and intentionally honest autobiography.

Usually, critics account for Sam's disparaging remarks about Orion as manifestations of his latent hostility toward his older brother, and such critics might suggest that the way I selected lines from the February 23 dictation suppresses that personal animus in order to create an image of a more objective aesthetic philosophy of autobiography. I do not deny the malice in the entry, but in fact the most malicious lines in the day's dictation support my point all the more:

> I urged Orion to try to tell the truth, and tell the whole of it. I said he couldn't tell the truth of course — that is, he could not lie successfully about a shameful experience of his, because the truth would sneak out between the lies and he couldn't help it — that an autobiography is always two things: it is an absolute lie and it is an absolute truth. The author of it furnishes the lie, the reader of it furnishes the truth — that is, he gets at the truth by insight. (February 23, 1906)†

Surely it is malicious for Sam to call his brother a liar. But he calls himself, as an autobiographer who will as a matter of course try to make himself the hero of his life's story, a liar, too. More importantly, he exonerates both by offering the solution to the problem of dishonesty, that the sagacious reader will be able to discern the truth in spite of any attempts an author might make to obscure those truths.

This motif about lying and finding ways to give the reader the truth in spite of the author's lies pervades the *Autobiography*. When Clemens began the autobiographical dictations, he determined not to publish them while he was alive in order to encourage himself to tell the whole truth. He says repeatedly that he intends to release none of the work until after his death because he can only be honest if he is not to be embarrassed by his revelations:

> It is not my purpose, in this history, to be more malicious toward any person than I am. I am not alive. I am dead. I wish to keep that fact plainly before the reader. If I were alive I should be writing an autobiography on the usual plan. I should be feeling just as malicious toward Webster as I am feeling this moment — dead as I am — but instead of expressing it freely and honestly, I should be trying to conceal it; trying to swindle the reader, and not succeeding. He would read the malice between the lines, and would not admire me. Nothing worse will happen if I let my malice have frank and free expression. The very reason that I speak from the grave is that I want the satisfaction of sometimes saying everything that is in me instead of bottling the pleasantest of it up for home consumption. (Neider 271)

But of course, he did publish much of the *Autobiography* in installments in the *North American Review* while he was still alive and while he was still dictating more. He was able to do this partly by deleting many references that would embarrass him, and partly because he felt that he had discovered that the story would tell the truth whether he tried to suppress it or not. Partly, he was concerned to avoid the kind of petty (and perhaps legal) embarrassments that come from slandering living persons, but in a larger sense he was willing to try to write a kind of autobiography that was never written before, one that would deliberately tell the truth of a whole personality, not so much in any single anecdote, each of which Clemens knew to be full of distortions, but more in the plan of the *Autobiography* itself, whereby the juxtaposition of many anecdotes, no one of which was completely true, would nonetheless reveal a more complete truth by revealing and revelling in contradictions and inconsistencies from day to day, memory to memory, impulse to impulse.

Nowhere is this more clear than in his recollections of the John Greenleaf Whittier birthday speech, and in his intentions for publishing those recollections in the various editions he expected his *Autobiography* to go through. In the December 1907 installment of dictations published in the *North American Review*, Clemens tells the story of his changing attitudes toward his speech at Whittier's seventieth birthday dinner. In the dictation he describes how his memory of the event was recalled by a letter he received requesting a copy of the speech. On receipt of the letter, he says he reviewed the speech and found it to be without flaw, and without any irreverence. Yet the dictation of January 11, 1906 (which found its way into the *NAR* and has been subsequently republished as "The Story of a Speech") was not his last word on the topic. In his January 23, 1906 dictation, he says that he has again "changed my notion about it — changed it entirely. I find it gross, coarse — well, I needn't go on with particulars."† Then, at the bottom of the page, in holograph, is the notation. "May 25 . . . day before yesterday . . . I gave it a final & vigorous reading — aloud — & dropped straight back to my former admiration of it. MT."†

This waffling back and forth is characteristic of several stories he tells in the *Autobiography*. As he put it in the January 15, 1906 dictation when trying to get the facts of a story right, "I don't mind excursioning around in an autobiography — there is plenty of room. I don't mind it so long as I get things right at last, when they are important."† Naturally, he would want to get the facts right, but the commentary on why he is willing to "excursion" highlights his willingness to reveal his own errors. The changing opinion about the Whittier birthday speech is a sincere effort to include the embarrassments of his life without necessarily turning himself into a hero. Yet in his first version, he makes his current self a hero in contrast to his former self — he says his speech is perfect, and that had he the opportunity now, with his current confidence, he "would take that same old speech, deliver it, word for word, and melt them till they'd run all over that stage. Oh, the fault must have been with me, it is not in the speech at all" (Kiskis 237). Not content with this version of his past and present, he returned to the speech.

This sequence of versions of a story has a larger point, too. Besides trying to not make himself the eternal hero of all of his stories, he is interested
in showing that his own perception of himself is not consistent. In the
January 23 dictation, he makes this inconsistency the real point of the story:

> How do I account for this change of view? I don't know. I can't account for it. I
> am the person concerned. If I could put myself outside myself and examine it
> from the point of view of a person not personally concerned with it, then no
> doubt I could analyze it and explain to my satisfaction the change which has
> taken place. As it is, I am merely moved by instinct. My instinct said, formerly,
> that it was an innocent speech, and funny. The same instinct, sitting cold and
> judicial, as a court of last resort, has reversed that verdict. I expect this latest
> verdict to remain. [then the asterisk leading to the May 25 revision] I don't
> remove the speech from the autobiography, because I think that this change of
> mind about it is interesting, whether the speech is or not, and therefore let it
> stay.†

Here he makes it explicit that the "facts," that is, the actual words of the
speech, are much less the point of the story than the character behind the
speech. He reveals his inability to give the reasons for his own inconsistency, but trusts that if he gives the facts of his own feelings and judgments,
that the reader will be able to understand what the autobiographer himself
cannot.

    While the *North American Review* chapter does not contain the January
23 or May 25 vacillations, the basic theme of a mind that is tortured by
embarrassment comes through quite clearly, though the self-conscious
awareness of that ambivalence is the explicit text of what Clemens still
expected to be a posthumous edition of the *Autobiography*. He is willing to
expose an embarrassment and inconsistency while he is still alive, but he is
not willing to make overt the fact that that ambivalence and inconsistency is
the real point of the story in the first place.

    Instead, at this point in publication, Clemens relies on the reader to see
the truth in spite of his partial distortions. He believes that "he will tell the
truth in spite of himself, for his facts and his fictions will work loyally
together for the protection of the reader; each fact and each fiction will be a
dab of paint, each will fall in its right place, and together they will paint his
portrait; not the portrait he thinks they are painting, but his real portrait,
the inside of him, the soul of him, his character" (January 31, 1904).† Yet
the later dictation, the part held in reserve for posthumous publication,
makes the effort "to get things right at last" slightly different. In the early

edition, he relies on the reader's sympathetic imagination to translate words into thoughts in order to read the real character of the man. The later dictations suggest that there is not a single character, but instead that there is a multiple character that the autobiographer himself cannot read. Thus, we see yet another function the *Autobiography* was to serve Clemens, not only to communicate the truth of his character to others, but also to help him reveal some parts of himself to the other parts. He needs to tell the truth of himself to himself in order to put the painful pieces of his life into an order that will be less painful. He seeks to dream a better dream that will account for all the facts of his experience, both events and emotions.

But given that the autobiographer "Without intending to lie . . . will lie all the time, not bluntly consciously, not dully unconsciously, but half-consciously—consciousness in twilight; a soft and gentle and merciful twilight which makes his general form comely with his virtuous prominences and projections discernible and his ungracious ones in shadow" (January 31, 1904),† Clemens's problem is to show himself his unconscious mind in spite of the semi-conscious distortions, to bring to full light all of the memories of the past. Here he turned back into the sentimental model of mind to find a technique of remembering truths. He turned to the belief that memories are lodged by association and that the key to knowing one's self is to uncover all of the facts, feelings and beliefs that constitute that self by freely associating one idea to another.

IV

The power of association is a constant theme of the *Autobiography*, beginning with some of the earliest of the dictations, the Florence dictations of 1904. In these, Clemens was not fully confident in the power of free association to tell his story, and he seems to have wanted to go at his autobiography chronologically, trusting to dictation to give it a "flow" that most autobiographies lack. But in trying to tell the story of his first book, he uncovered to his conscious mind the power of association to tell the truth. In trying to tell the embarrassing story of plagiarizing the dedication to *Innocents Abroad* from a collection of Oliver Wendell Holmes's poetry, Clemens uses the power of association to recall an experience that demonstrates that power. When confronted with the fact of his plagiarism, a fact he at first denied, he could not account for the fact:

I could not remember ever having seen Dr. Holmes's dedication. I knew the poems, but the dedication was new to me. I did not get hold of the key to that secret until months afterward, then it came in a curious way, and yet it was a natural way; for the natural way provided by nature and the construction of the human mind for the discovery of a forgotten event is to employ another forgotten event for its resurrection. (Kiskis 181)

He then tells the story of how a letter he received later reminded him that the Honolulu Hotel in which he resided while in the Sandwich Islands had few books. Upon being reminded of this, Clemens recalled having read the Holmes book to death, only to forget consciously the dedication. "It lay in some lost dim corner of my memory a year or two, then came forward when I needed a dedication, and was promptly mistaken by me for a child of my own happy fancy."

This story, an effort, one surmises, to reveal the truth of his life by revealing an embarrassing event, leads to the more important recollection of Clemens's apology to Holmes and Holmes's acceptance of it. In a letter, which Clemens has conveniently lost so that his rendition of it blurs happily with his own philosophy:

> Dr. Holmes laughed the kindest and healingest laugh over the whole matter, and at considerable length and in happy phrase assured me that there was no crime in unconscious plagiarism; . . . that all our phrasings are spiritualized shadows cast multitudinously forth from our readings; that no happy phrase of ours is ever quite original with us, there is nothing of our own in it except some slight change born of our temperament, character, environment, teachings and associations; that this slight change differentiates it from another man's manner of saying it, stamps it with our special style, and makes it our own for the time being; all the rest of it being old, mouldy, antique, and smelling of the breath of a thousand generations of them that have passed it over their teeth before!
>
> In the thirty-odd years which have come and gone since then, I have satisfied myself that what Dr. Holmes said was true. (Kiskis 182)

While trying to explain the embarrassment of plagiarism, Clemens uses Holmes's sympathy to guide his reader's response. Further, Holmes's philosophy suggests the commonality and thus grounds for sympathy among all people. Yet this passage is really a rather strange justification for an act of almost perfect plagiarism, because the explanation talks less of identity between people and more of what constitutes individual identity. And the key here is associations, the particular string of events as associated in memory that makes one individual self different from all others.

When Clemens returned to the dictations almost two years later, what had been a mere digression into the philosophy of association became a dominant theme of the dictations. It is in fact extremely difficult to choose passages to quote here because they are interspersed so liberally to explain so much about how human beings behave, but my purpose here is to show not just that Clemens believed in the power of association to shape personality, but that his understanding shaped his technique of constructing autobiography. In a 1907 dictation, after he had grown comfortable with dictating and had convinced himself that a dictated autobiography would make the most successfully honest autobiography ever written, he began his January 6, 1907 dictation with the phrase:

> "That reminds me." In conversation we are always using that phrase, and seldom or never noticing how large a significance it bears. It stands for a curious and interesting fact, to wit: that sleeping or waking, dreaming or talking, the thoughts which swarm through our heads are almost constantly, almost continuously, accompanied by a like swarm of reminders of incidents and episodes of our past. A man can never know what a large traffic this commerce of association carries on in his mind until he sets out to write his autobiography; he then finds that a thought is seldom born to him that does not immediately remind him of some event, large or small, in his past experience. Quite naturally these present remarks remind me of various things, among others this: that sometimes a thought, by the power of association, will bring back to your mind a lost word or a lost name which you have not been able to recover by any other process known to your mental equipment. (Kiskis 194)

Since part of the purpose of the *Autobiography* was to tell the whole truth of himself, and since he felt that a self was constituted of particular memories, and that the mind would try to forget the painful in order to exalt the self, Clemens fittingly tried to use free association as a way to tell the whole truth of himself, both to others and to himself.

And it more or less works. With most any given day's dictation, Clemens allows his skill as a raconteur to distort facts to make a good story. As he put it in one day's dictation:

> By the privileges of our order [i.e., "professional humorist"] we are independent of facts; we care nothing for them, in a really religious way. If, in their integrity they will not work into our scheme with the kind of effect which we wish to produce, we rearrange them to meet the requirements of the occasion. When we are hot with the fires of production we would even distort the facts of the multiplication-table, let alone the facts of Genesis. (August 10, 1906)†

But more than lying for humorous effect, he often distorted facts to make himself look better. As in his account of the Whittier birthday dinner, he compensated for the earlier embarrassment by claiming a skill born of age that would turn the dross of that evening's performance to gold. Or the way he apologizes for plagiarizing from Holmes by having Holmes himself exonerate him. He does not escape the impulse to make himself a hero. But in freely associating from artifacts, or newspaper stories, or Susy's diary, or what have you, he often tells stories that intersect, and, in the intersections, truths that he tries to suppress come out.

Perhaps the best instance of this is in two related stories about his fiftieth birthday. The first of these was part of a few connected entries that arose from Clemens finding an account of the literary community's celebration of his fiftieth birthday. He re-read several published tributes to him before launching into an account of the trauma of turning fifty: "When a man reaches fifty, age seems to suddenly descend upon him like a black cloud. He feels immeasurably old — very much older than he is ever to feel again, I am sure. I doubt if any person ever crosses his fiftieth parallel without experiencing what I have just described."† This reads like the preamble to an admission of despair twenty years in the past, but the examples he uses to illustrate his point he draws from the lives of James Russell Lowell and of one of Clemens's Hartford neighbors, Major-General Franklin. These two serve to displace his own feelings, so by the time he reaches the end of the story, he can make himself out to be supernatural in his reaction to his own aging:

> Lowell regained his cheerfulness and went to his death a cheerful soul at seventy-two. Franklin reached a greater age, I think, but the depressions which his fiftieth year brought him passed quickly and did not return.
> I do not remember that my fiftieth year brought serious depressions to me, if any at all, but if it did they did not last. (October 30, 1906)†

This last remark rings hollow, and apparently Clemens's technique of letting an idea work into his subconsciousness challenged him to see a more accurate version of his emotional history.

In an installment dated by the typist October 31, 1906, and re-dated in Clemens's hand November 8, 1906, Clemens made his topic of the day memory for faces, and actually published much of this in the *North American Review*. But then, without warning the dictation skips back to the question of his fiftieth birthday with the remark:

It was quite natural that I should think I had written myself out when I was only fifty years old, for everybody who has ever written has been smitten with that superstition at about that age. Not even yet have I really written myself out. I have merely stopped writing because dictating is pleasanter work, and because dictating has given me a strong aversion to the pen, and because two hours of talking per day is enough, and because — — But I am only damaging my mind with this digging around in it for pretexts where no pretext is needed, and where the simple truth is for this one time better than any invention, in this small emergency. I shall never finish my five or six unfinished books, for the reason that by forty years of slavery to the pen I have earned my freedom. I detest the pen, and I wouldn't use it again even to sign the death warrant of my dearest enemy. (Kiskis 190)

Again, we see a deflection from the emotional point that Clemens was very distraught at turning fifty, so distraught that he thought his creative powers had failed him. This time he says as much, though he immediately deflects the point by making a fatuous distinction between writing — that is, the physical act of putting pen to page — and dictating. Usually when he talks about dictating his *Autobiography* he refers to the result as literature, and he obviously spent time, pen in hand, revising the typescript of each day's dictation. But almost as if this day's dictations forged a promise he had to keep to save face, he in several instances actually wrote by hand chapters for the *Autobiography*, but wrote the word "Dictated" and the date as a heading to maintain the illusion in the published editions that the entire work was spieled out into the ear of a stenographer. Still, all pretenses and deflections aside, the return to the fiftieth birthday gets much closer to speaking explicitly the truth of Clemens's emotions than does the first installment, and the two together tell a truth that neither alone would tell.

This, then, is one of the main points of Clemens's approach to autobiography, that in following no plan but the plan to follow no plan, he allowed his memories to speak out in spite of himself. The associations that make up the self reveal themselves more fully the more chances he gave them to make themselves known. In using such a recursive and anecdotal technique, Clemens tried to create a multifaceted portrait of himself to show a character that is much more complicated than any simple monism would allow. In the process, he became true for the first time to the source of his humor and to his real mode of composition, which works from the random association of apparently incompatible ideas. No longer did he label inconsistency with the stigma of hypocrisy; no longer did he reject humor for the absolutism of satire.

V

At the same time Clemens turned away from the absolutism of satire, he seemed to reject the radical relativism of the solipsism he briefly explored in "No. 44, The Mysterious Stranger," instead accepting that a truth extrinsic to a single consciousness may be discernible from some points of view in spite of any effort on the part of one consciousness to obscure such truths. Such an effort to be true to a science of mind was, of course, common to the era, and William James was not the only person to argue that a science of mind had to take into account the irrational processes of thought as well as the rational. Others made the same point but to a different purpose, that in understanding the irrational we would simply prove the power of rational objectivism to account for all phenomena. While James was insisting on the dynamic interplay between desire and reality, other psychologists were trying to construct "objective" sciences of mind, the implications of which were ultimately deterministic.

Freud, for instance, tried to use the model of scientific objectivity to find in free association a way of allowing the conscious mind to recover suppressed memories from the unconscious. In so doing he was following an older trend in nineteenth-century psychology for which Clemens had an affinity, as revealed in his reference to Holmes's model of mind. In fact, in Clemens's reference to Holmes's description of the mechanical nature of the association of ideas, one does not see any clear rejection of positivism. Somehow, Holmes claims, he is outside of the problem of subjectivity himself, and does not therefore need to suspect his own determinism as it arises from a positivist point of view. Clemens clearly had a continued attraction to such positivist determinism, but the very structure of the *Autobiography*, which insists on the variability and inconsistency of the human mind, shows his desire to shed such a vision of the mind.

Throughout the *Autobiography*, one can see Clemens trying to sort out both the relative truth and the relative value of extreme subjectivism and extreme objectivism. At times, especially when he refers to his "gospel," *What is Man?*, he echoes his earlier deterministic monism. And often, in re-ferring to the mechanical association of ideas, he retreats into this position:

> From the beginning of time, philosophers of all breeds and shades have been beguiled by the persuasions of man's bulkiest attribute, vanity, into believing that a human being can originate a thought in his own head. I suppose I am the only person who knows he can't. In my own person I have studied him most carefully these many years — indeed for a quarter of a century — and I now

know beyond doubt or question that his mind is quite incapable of inventing a thought, and is strictly limited to receiving suggestions from the outside and manufacturing second-hand thoughts out of them. . . . The reason that I can come to this dictation-industry every morning unprepared with a text, is that I know quite well that somebody's passing remark, or a paragraph in the newspaper, or a letter in the mail, will suggest something which will remind me of something in my life's experiences and will surely furnish me, by this process, one or more texts. (August 11, 1906)†

I do not know what to make of the vanity of this comment and the claim to apparent originality in discovering something that no one else knows. That he admitted earlier his debt to Holmes makes it likely that he is being ironic, yet he is clearly committed at this point to the idea of mind as machine. Clearly, here, he sees his mind as no different from any other, that in the process of association, he lacks freedom; he acts merely as a machine.

By this standard, he explains that people often believe impossibilities because by early training, by associations accumulated before the age of reason, a person is so thoroughly constructed as to deny the capacity of rational thought to re-create the will. In particular, he often remarks how ideas learned in youth recur in old age in spite of a lifelong effort to shed them:

Lewis's last estate reminds me of David Gray's, and is an impressive revelation of the strength and persistency of impressions made upon the human mind in the early years, when its feelings and emotions are fresh, young, and strong, and before it is capable of reasoning. At five years of age David Gray was a strenuous Presbyterian; at thirty-five he had long been a pronounced agnostic — not to put it stronger. He died as strenuous a Presbyterian as he had been when he was five years old and an expert theologian. (August 11, 1906)†

Again, we have Clemens's apparent positivism under which he describes human beings as mere mechanisms, without will, and he tells us we can know this fact through reason.

On the other hand, though, he is fully convinced that any belief is ultimately contingent on desire, and that desire is stronger than reason. He is not sure, then, to what extent his philosophy really is rational, as can be seen in his October 2, 1906 reference to "a philosophy of mine — or a superstition of mine, if you prefer that word" (*MTE* 384). This reference is not simply modesty. As we have seen, he often expresses his understanding of his own behavior by speaking of others, and he often explicitly says he is just like any other human being who has ever lived. So when he refers repeatedly to people who can will themselves into believing what no evidence supports, the implication is that he knows that he, too, behaves in a similar way.

The tone of some of the discussions of people willing themselves to belief shows a kind of awe for the power of irrationality:

> I knew Rev. Thomas K. Beecher intimately for a good many years. He came from Connecticut to Elmira in his early manhood, when he was a theological fledgling, to take charge of a Congregational church there whose chief financial support was Jervis Langdon, my to-be father-in-law, and he continued in that charge until he died, a few years ago, aged seventy-four. He was deeply versed in the sciences, and his pulpit eloquence fell but little short of that of his great brother, Henry Ward. His was a keen intellect, and he was brilliant in conversation, and always interesting — except when his topic was theology. He had no theology of his own, any more than has any other person; he had an abundance of it, but he got it all at second-hand. He would have been afraid to examine his subject with his own fine mind lest doubts should result, and unsettle him. He was a very frank, straightforward man, and he told me once, in the plainest terms, that when he came on from Connecticut to assume the pastorship of that Elmira church he was a strenuous and decided unbeliever. It astonished me. But he followed it with a statement which astonished me more; he said that with his bringing up he was aware that he could never be happy, or at peace, and free from terrors, until he should become a believer, and that he had accepted that pastorate without any pangs of conscience for the reason that he had made up his mind to compel himself to become a believer, let the cost be what it might. It seemed a strange thing to say, but he said it. He also said that within a twelvemonth or two he perfectly succeeded in his extraordinary enterprise, and that thenceforth he was as complete and as thorough a believer as any Christian that had ever lived. (March 1, 1907)†

Clemens clearly sees such willful belief as a violation of reason and thus to be despised; but, equally clearly, one sees his fascination with the strength of will that such belief entails — that in creating a belief Beecher created happiness for himself. Further, the implication of this story conjoined with those parts of the *Autobiography* when he calls his philosophy a superstition, or those places where he calls it his gospel, or those places where he disclaims the power of the human mind to think original thoughts, all lead to the conclusion that Clemens himself believes that his own thoughts are also merely rationalizations designed to suit moods.

At one point he began directly to confront this idea in a philosophical way, beginning the June 2, 1906 dictation: "Effects wrought by moods — — However, let that subject go until another time."† This nasty little joke seems designed to spite future scholars who want his opinions on everything (but then again, perhaps I deserve it, turning such a sprightly and witty work into a somber philosophical disquisition), but while his mood change here deflects him from moods as matters of philosophy, he dropped the subject only temporarily. The importance of mood is a text of many of the autobiographical stories. For instance, the stream of association of April 11, 1906 was leading Clemens to judge human beings as perfidious and incapable of compassion, when he deliberately arrested the flow of thought to find reason to reach a different conclusion: "I will disengage my mind from this dismal subject and see if I can't find a cheerfuler one among this morning's clippings."† Here he exercises his will to change a belief so that a happier mood will follow.

Or again, in the January 9, 1907 dictation, he says:

> There has been an incident — an incident of a common sort — an incident of an exceedingly common sort — an incident of a sort which always troubles me, grieves me, and makes me weary of life and long to lie down in the peaceful grave and be at rest. Such incidents usually move me to try to find relief in the building of a maxim. It is a good way, because if you have luck you can get the venom out of yourself and into the maxim; then comfort and a healed spirit follow.†

He refuses to give us the particular event but chooses instead to make his subject the relief-giving capacity of cathartic expression. Clearly the conclusion he struggles to reach in the maxim sounds like a ringing and universal truth, but Clemens tells us that, on the contrary, it is merely the condensed expression of a moment's bile. "Universal" truth, then, is merely the product of mood.

No doubt he did feel that the universe has laws that a truly rational mind could discern. But he also had doubts about the capacity of any merely human mind to achieve the dispassionate rationality needed to discern such laws. Furthermore, and most significantly, he continued in the line of thinking developed in *Following the Equator* to reject the value to human beings of any such transcendental truths. The only universal truths that interested Clemens were the truths of our emotional nature, that we all share the capacity to feel a range of emotions and desires. If reason could not discern metaphysical truths, then human beings could fall back into emotions as experiential truths unto themselves. Nowhere is this more clear than in his use of anecdotes of his dead daughter Susy to make clear the importance of human point of view in determining values:

To go back a year — Susy aged seven. Several times her mother said to her:

"There, there, Susy, you mustn't cry over little things."

This furnished Susy a text for thought. She had been breaking her heart over what had seemed vast disasters — a broken toy; a picnic cancelled by thunder and lightning and rain; the mouse that was growing tame and friendly in the nursery caught and killed by the cat — and now came this strange revelation. For some unaccountable reason, these were not vast calamities. Why? How is the size of calamities measured? What is the rule? There must be some way to tell the great ones from the small ones; what is the law of these proportions? She examined the problem earnestly and long. She gave it her best thought from time to time, for two or three days — but it baffled her — defeated her. And at last she gave up and went to her mother for help.

"Mamma, what is 'little things'?"

It seemed a simple question — at first. And yet, before the answer could be put into words, unsuspected and unforeseen difficulties began to appear. They increased; they multiplied; they brought about another defeat. The effort to explain came to a standstill. Then Susy tried to help her mother out — with an instance, an example, an illustration. The mother was ready to go down-town, and one of her errands was to buy a long-promised toy-watch for Susy.

"If you forgot the watch, mamma, would that be a little thing?"

She was not concerned about the watch, for she knew it would not be forgotten. What she was hoping for was that the answer would unriddle the riddle, and bring rest and peace to her perplexed little mind.

The hope was disappointed, of course — for the reason that the size of a misfortune is not determinable by an outsider's measurement of it, but only by the measurements applied to it by the person specially affected by it. The king's lost crown is a vast matter to the king, but of no consequence to the child. The lost toy is a great matter to the child, but in the king's eyes it is not a thing to break the heart about. A verdict was reached, but it was based upon the above model, and Susy was granted leave to measure her disasters thereafter with her own tape-line. (Kiskis 29–30)

This entire story is told in the context of Clemens's trying to come to grips with the emotional devastation wrought in him by Susy's death. Throughout the *Autobiography*, Clemens turns to Susy as the innocent voice of human ignorance and human purity. She stands in opposition to the adult point of view as humanity stands in opposition to the capacities of God. God may be able to evaluate human insignificance cosmically, but only human beings can judge the value of their own emotional experience.

Thus, much of the *Autobiography* serves to try to shake Clemens's skepticism, to move him back into a healthy respect for human emotion. Here, in turning to a child's point of view, Clemens argues for the ultimate value of judging human beings by human standards rather than by superhuman ones. Throughout his career, his ironic vision always tended to push him outside of the range of human emotions to seek some transcendental perspective by which he could shrink sufferings to microscopic size and so dismiss them. But his experiences as a satirist had shown that such thinking merely magnifies bitterness. The weak consolation of *Puddn'head Wilson* turns out to be a nightmare of divine satire, a nightmare that Clemens assiduously struggles to reject:

> I must get that stupendous fancy out of my head. At first it was vague, dim, sardonic, wonderful; but night after night, of late, it is growing too definite — quite too clear and definite, and haunting, and persistent. It is the Deity's mouth — His open mouth — laughing at the human race! The horizon is the lower lip; the cavernous vast arch of the sky is the open mouth and throat; the soaring bend of the Milky Way constitutes the upper teeth. It is a mighty laugh, and deeply impressive — even when it is silent; I can endure it then, but when it bursts out in crashing thunders of delight, and the breath gushes forth in a glare of white lightnings, it makes me shudder.
>
> Every night he laughs, and every morning I eagerly search the paper to see what it is He has been laughing at. It is always recorded there in the big headlines; often one doesn't have to read what follows the headlines, the headlines themselves tell the story sufficiently; as a rule, I am not able to see what there is to laugh at; very frequently the occurrences seem to merely undignify the human race and make its acts pitiful and pathetic, rather than matter for ridicule. This morning's paper contains the following instances:
>
> No, 1.
> SPECIAL TRAIN TO SAVE HER DOG'S LIFE.
> Rich, Childless Woman Spent
> Thousands in Vain Efforts
> for Her Pet.
>
> It is matter for pity, not mirth. No matter what the source of a sorrow may be, the sorrow itself is respectworthy. (October 10, 1907)†

Beginning with delight in a huge sardonic laugh, but turning to unendurable nightmare, this dream recapitulates Clemens's career. For much of his career, Clemens sought in his satire the Olympian perspective of this dream, and his irony moved him inexorably in that direction through his career. By 1906, having become convinced that point of view created the feeling and that the feeling of bitterness that such laughter entailed was overwhelming, he finds such a vision horrifying and the coldness of it too painful to bear. God, in this vision, is the source of a heartless irreverence, and human beings must work to shake such heartlessness in order to find a redemptive compassion. While it is all too easy to find human beings acting without dignity, feelings lend a dignity beyond divinity to the most absurd of heartfelt human behavior.

By insisting that human emotion is the measure of the only truths that should matter to human beings, Clemens turns back to the sentimentalist's vision of humor, that real humor, saving humor, comes out of compassion rather than out of disdain:

> [I]t has always been the way of the world to resent gravity in a humorist. It is a little strange that this should be so, for an absolutely essential part of any real humorist's native equipment is a deep seriousness and a rather unusually profound sympathy with the sorrows and sufferings of mankind. (May 22, 1908)†

Gone is the earlier glory in irreverent laughter as a way of revealing human absurdity. Instead, we see a man relishing the dignity of a deep compassion that can heal emotional pain by understanding it rather than by mocking it.

VI

Arising as it does from a more compassionate view of human feelings, Clemens's clear shift from satire to humor parallels another important shift that the *Autobiography* makes vividly clear. While most of his career marked a progressive move from sentimental realism toward naturalism, the *Autobiography* returns repeatedly to the theme that good literature is a manifestation of the heart. Absolutely gone is the insistence on rendering reality with precision. In its stead is an insistence that any person who sticks to powerful emotion without regard to literary "proprieties" will create literature. Again and again in the *Autobiography*, Clemens asserts this point and follows it up with an example of "literature from the heart."

He introduces this motif in June, 1906, when he first explains this interest in untutored literature as a consequence of his knowledge that all human beings are at heart the same, and he therefore wishes to explore the contents of the heart in as direct and natural a way as possible:

> During five years I have had in my possession a sack of old letters to which I attached no value. They were letters from strangers to each other, in the main, Smiths and Joneses and the like, wholly unknown to the world and to me, persons of not the slightest interest to anybody. I was never expecting to become industrious enough to overhaul that sack and examine its contents, but now that I am doing this autobiography the joys and the sorrows of everybody, high and low, rich and poor, famous and obscure, are dear to me. I can take their affairs into my heart as I never could before. In becoming my

own biographer I realize that I have become the biographer of Tom, Dick, and Harry, the voiceless. I recognize that Tom and I are intimates; that be he young or be he old, he has never felt anything that I have not felt; he has never had an emotion that I am a stranger to. (June 18, 1906)†

Here he acknowledges the change in perception that has come over him. No longer are the external signs of particular individuality of any interest to him; the universal compassion he finds for all stems from his belief in the universality not of circumstances or disposition, but of emotion.

Clemens follows this assertion by inserting the texts of letters of three women, one of whom was sequestering herself in a boarding house to conceal from her family and friends her pregnancy out of wedlock, and another of whom was officiously trying to pry into this first woman's affairs, and a third who ran the boarding house in which the pregnant woman took refuge. Clemens speaks of this group of letters as revealing a fundamental human drama that is rich with heartfelt interest even though the skill of presentation is distinctly unliterary. He expresses deep sympathy for the young woman and admiration for her letter:

That young woman's letter exhibits the fact that she has had very little school-ing. It is unlikely that she has had much practice with the pen, yet how moving and convincing are her simple phrases, her unstudied eloquence! Her letter is literature — good literature — and the most practiced pen cannot surpass it, out of the best-trained head. She speaks from the heart, and the heart has no use for the artifices of training or education or dramatic invention when it has a tale to tell.†

Clemens returns to this theme too often in the dictations, even once finding himself conned by a fraudulent group of letters purportedly from an igno-rant woman but actually from a professional humorist. Despite his lifelong horror of being defrauded by sentiment, Clemens is remarkably mild in his reaction to these letters and shortly thereafter even returns to quoting letters as examples of the superiority of literature from the heart to the studied work of professional writers.

In fact, he even revises his own assessment of how he has always written:

Several weeks ago the editor of Harper's Bazaar projected a scheme for a composite story. A family was to tell the story. The father was to begin it, and, in turn, each member of the family was to furnish a chapter of it. There was to be a boy in the family, and I was invited to write his chapter. I was afraid of the scheme because I could not tell beforehand whether the boy would take an interest in it or not. Experience has taught me long ago that if I tell a boy's story, or anybody else's, it is never worth printing; it comes from the head not the heart, and always goes into the waste-basket. To be successful and worth printing, the imagined boy would have to tell his story himself and let me act merely as his amanuensis. I did not tell the "Horse's Tale," the horse told it himself through me. If he hadn't done that it wouldn't have been told at all. When a tale tells itself there is no trouble about it; there are no hesitancies, no delays, no cogitations, no attempts at invention; there is nothing to do but hold the pen and let the story talk through it and say, after its own fashion, what it desires to say. (*MTE* 243; August 29, 1906)

Like the sentimentalists before him, Clemens has taken to defining realistic literature by subjective standards — if it is true to the emotions, then it is true. Thus, a horse could speak through Clemens; a dog could speak through Clemens; a cat could speak through Clemens, and so forth. No wonder that the late output is so anti-realistic. Beyond the problems of translation, Clemens moves to the power of sympathy, and in so doing completely abandons his earlier insistence on physical plausibility as a standard for judging literature. If it could happen in the mind, then it is good enough to make literature.

This side of Twain was always latent, but with his deliberate effort to use literature as a way to create feelings of happiness, to exalt the human capacity to control one's own emotional, if not physical, fate, even his lifelong anxiety about being "taken" subsides. The bulk of the *Autobiography* reads as one long effort to find and sustain happiness. Satire serves as catharsis, sympathy as confirmation of the value of human experience, and throughout, the power of storytelling is redemptive beyond any effort to understand metaphysical truths. What Clemens seems above all to seek is the capacity to make our stories create new and better lives, to re-create the dream of human existence so that it provides comfort rather than pain.

In the first story of amateur literature from the heart, we see Clemens talking once again about the wide gap between human nature and the conventions of society, and, as one expects, Clemens condemns human conventions as being too painful to endure:

I have an uncompromising detestation of that old cat who writes the first letter. I feel disrespectfully toward that machine-made Christian who writes the second one. I think that in her heart she turned the friendless refugee and the baby into the street in the raw March weather; and so I hold her guilty to the hilt for that uncommitted inhuman act, and I am sure she would have committed it if she could have done it without falling under the artificial censure of the community. I call it artificial because I think that perhaps the majority of the community would have secretly approved the act while publicly denouncing it. I think this because it is human nature — wrought upon by established conventions — to privately exult over certain kinds of baseness and ungenerosity while publicly censuring them to keep on the good side of Mrs Grundy.

All my sympathies and my compassion are for the betrayed and abused ignorant and trusting young widow, who was as yet too young to know the human race. . . . When she says her conscience absolves her, I believe that too. I think she means that she was tempted beyond her strength by a man whom she had know familiarly in her early girlhood, and that by some inborn instinct she realized that she did not create her own nature, that she did not create its limitations and that when those limitations were overpassed she was not strictly responsible for the consequences. There are human laws against her conduct, but her conduct transgresses no law of Nature, and the laws of Nature take precedence of all human laws. The purpose of all human laws is one — to defeat the laws of Nature. This is the case among all the nations, both civilized and savage. It is a grotesquerie, but when the human race is not grotesque it is because it is asleep and losing its opportunity. (June 18, 1906)†

This denunciation of human laws in the second of these two paragraphs echoes those in *Following the Equator*: human laws are absurd because they violate the more compelling laws of nature. Yet the first paragraph shows a human law that, in violating natural proclivities, actually serves a compassionate end. Again, one sees a Clemens operating out of a significantly changed perspective. Rather than simply trying to assault the human laws that he calls grotesque, he wishes to salvage the woman's reputation by exhibiting sympathy for her. Sympathy, not protest, becomes salvation. The hope, here, is that sympathy will create a new story, a new human law that will make human experience less painful.

But even if sympathy does not create a better dream, Clemens does not seem willing to return to the solipsism of "No. 44." More importantly, he argues that human laws, no matter how absurd, are infinitely superior to the brutality of natural laws. For instance, he describes a December 1907 meeting with the British author Elinor Glyn. He told her he agreed with the tenor of her book, that sexual taboos were violations of the laws of nature, but that he would not endorse her book publicly because

we were the servants of convention; that we could not subsist, either in a savage or a civilized state, without conventions; that we must accept them and stand by them, even when we disapproved of them; that while the laws of Nature, that is to say the laws of God, plainly made every human being a law unto himself, we must steadfastly refuse to obey those laws, and we must as

steadfastly stand by the conventions which ignore them, since the statutes
furnish us peace, fairly good government and stability, and are therefore better
for us than the laws of God, which would soon plunge us into confusion and
disorder and anarchy if we should adopt them. (Neider 386)

He suggests here that human convention, which ten years earlier he called
"idiotic," is superior to the greater idiocy of natural laws. Thus, to promote their own happiness, human beings need to promote the "laws" of
convention.

This is the more characteristic late Clemens, the one who, like William
James, continued to believe that while there is an external, physical reality,
and that there are natural laws that are independent of human thought,
human beings operate partially independently of those laws because their
minds create a substantial part of the reality they see. In "A Fable," Clemens
uses the metaphorical mirror of knowledge much as James does. The
various animals who all go to the mirror to see a painting that they have
been told about instead see nothing but their own reflections, which in turn
become their images of truth. Each is the kind of believer William James
rejected when he said that "the knower is not simply a mirror floating with
no foot-hold anywhere, and passively reflecting an order that he comes
upon and finds simply existing" (23). With unself-conscious faith in the
objectivity of their own perceptions, each becomes a dogmatic partisan of
prejudice. In refusing to see their own subjectivity, the animals foolishly
fight, making asses of themselves. One moral is that human beings would
live more happily if they recognized their own subjectivity. Only then could
they create and appreciate beauty; only then could they build a happier
world for themselves.

VII

Part of this happier world for Clemens included a retreat into sentimentality
in a way that violates most of what we now perceive as aesthetically best in
his works. But to dismiss the sentimentality out of hand is to dismiss the
intellectual progress that it helped usher in. It was, after all, the terms of
sentimental moral philosophy that enabled Clemens to criticize scientific
monism. In criticizing science, Clemens was beginning to explore some of
the twentieth century's great intellectual concerns, for instance, the relativity of truth, the absurdity of existence, and the human capacity to abstract

meaning from absurdity. His philosophical ruminations, rarely finished to be sure, often anticipate ideas expressed in some of the most important works of this century. For instance, his investigation in "The Secret History of Eddypus" of the power of language to describe human truths and of the importance of controlling history to lend credence to those "truths" preceded Orwell's *1984* by about forty years.

So although we may dislike the sentimental overtones of much of Clemens's later work, it diminishes that work to explain it exclusively in psychological terms. It is not critically useful to pity a dead man because "comedians, in whatever media they work, are supposed to be essentially tragic figures who sublimate their grief in laughter" (Hill xv). By viewing Clemens's work through such a psychological template, Hill partakes of the determinism that Clemens, at least sometimes, tried to shake.

Nor does it help us understand the development of Clemens's later works by dismissing his philosophy altogether with the damningly faint praise that he "was an artist, not a thinker" whose split personality engendered both the creative tension that inspired his best work and the contradictions that crippled so much of the rest. Surely Clemens did contradict himself frequently, as anyone involved in the philosophy of his time must have. But as he came to accept the discrepancy between external reality and human perception, he became increasingly interested in the discrepancy itself. It is no coincidence that, in talking about his technique of writing autobiography, he used the same metaphor to describe his observations of his own reality that he used in "A Fable" to describe the way all people view reality: "This autobiography of mine is a mirror, and I am looking at myself in it all the time" (dictation of April 4, 1906 as quoted in Hill 138).

In his later years, Clemens passed some of his most interesting judgments on the human desire for consistency and tendency toward inconsistency. In conclusion, he finally developed a grudging tolerance of the hypocrisy that used to torment him so:

> We can't help our nature, we didn't make it, it was made for us; and so we are not to blame for possessing it. Let us be kind and compassionate toward ourselves; let us not allow the fact to distress us and grieve us that from mommer's lap to the grave we are all shams and hypocrites and humbugs without exception, seeing that we did not make the fact and are in no way responsible for it. If any teacher tries to persuade you that hypocrisy is not a part of your blood and bone and flesh, and can therefore be trained out of you by determined and watchful and ceaseless and diligent application to the job, do not you heed him; ask him to cure himself first, then call again. If he is an

honorable person and is meaning well, he will give the medicine you have recommended to him an earnest and honest and sincere trial, but he will not call again. ("Microbes," *WWD* 460)

Clemens himself, the teacher who used to rail at human hypocrisy, now tells himself to be compassionate toward himself. The man who once said training is everything now says that we cannot train this trait out of our nature; in this contradiction he proves at least his own inconsistency.

In accepting his own inconsistency, Clemens began to trust imagination and art, and he allowed himself the capacity to hold opposites in tension in creating such fascinating experimental pieces as "Three-thousand Years Among the Microbes." Without such a willingness to reject monistic prescriptions of human morality, without a willingness to accept the rich confusion of the human mind, he could not have given us, in his autobiographical dictations, such an extraordinary glimpse into the complex and contradictory workings of a powerfully creative mind. After all, his description of humanity applies particularly well to himself: "We could be made better, but we wouldn't be interesting, then" ("Microbes," *WWD* 551).

Notes

Chapter One

1. In using the names "Mark Twain" and "Samuel Clemens," I try to follow the recently established convention of referring to the historical person as Samuel Clemens and to the writer's persona as Mark Twain. As difficult as this distinction often is to make, it is complicated here by my efforts to respect the preference others have for the name "Twain." Thus, in quoting or paraphrasing other critics, I use their choices of names even if they do not draw the same distinction between person and persona that I try to.

2. "Phunny Phellow" was a common name for humorists of the Civil War era, and was often applied to Mark Twain. See, for instance, Twain's own notice of this title in his letter to the Virginia City *Territorial Enterprise*, March 7, 1868. For information on the relative popularity of these books see James D. Hart, *The Popular Book in America*.

3. Which John Tuckey proved is a bowdlerized version of the even bleaker "Chronicle of Young Satan." See *Mark Twain and Little Satan*.

4. The military imagery is interesting, too, but since I am not writing a book on Capra, I'll not elaborate.

5. Quoted in *Current Opinion* 65 (July, 1918): 48.

6. In Sattelmeyer and Crowley, eds., *One Hundred Years of Huckleberry Finn*, pp. 386–403.

7. Henry Nash Smith, *Mark Twain: The Development of a Writer*, p. vii and passim.

8. Wallace's remarks appeared in numerous journals; see E. R. Shipp, "A Century Later, Huck's Still Stirring Up Trouble," *New York Times*, February 4, 1985. It seems odd that I should need to point out that the novel has black readers who defend it, but the fact that some published criticism still considers white and black readers as monolithic, completely opposed interest groups, makes it seem necessary. Consider that James Cox, one of the most influential of Twain scholars, implies that black critics as a "group" have denounced the book as racist; see "A Hard Book to Take," p. 387. By arguing that racial groups contain varieties of opinions within them, I am not disagreeing with Cox's conclusion that the complaints of black critics have disrupted white "complacency" about the book. But since the book has always been controversial, I suspect that, rather than causing the controversy about the book's place as an American classic, such attacks have encouraged white readers to articulate their discomfort with the book, especially with the book's ending, in racial terms. In the years since the civil rights movement, many of the most vigorous published attacks on the book's depiction of Jim have come from white critics. For

an excellent recent treatment of this critical history, see Forrest G. Robinson, "The Characterization of Jim in Huckleberry Finn."

9. See, in particular, Ralph Ellison, "Change the Joke and Slip the Yoke," which slightly modifies his extraordinary praise of Huck Finn in "Twentieth-Century Fiction and the Black Mask of Humanity." For a fully developed account devoted to *Huck Finn*, see Harold Beaver, "Run, Nigger, Run: *Adventures of Huckleberry Finn* as a Fugitive Slave Narrative." I do not mean to imply in any way that these are representative or typical responses of black readers. Presuming that there is a typical response, it seems possible that these accounts are atypical insofar as the institutionalization of academic criticism has until recently militated against negative criticism of "canonical" works in many obvious ways, not least of which is that most scholars do not spend time writing about books they loathe.

10. Robinson, "Characterization of Jim," p. 369. Twain himself, in his platform readings of sections of *Huck Finn* in 1895–1896, said that "Huck is the child of neglect & acquainted with cold, hunger, privation, humiliation, & with the unearned aversion of the upper crust of the community." Consequently, he and Jim are "close friends, bosom friends, drawn together by community of misfortune" (*Huck*, Appendix D, p. 806). Thus, Robinson echoes Twain's own interpretation of their bond, but note that Robinson emphasizes the suspicion inherent in the bond whereas Twain emphasizes the heart-felt community of interest.

11. David Brion Davis, "Religious Sources of Antislavery Thought: 'The Man of Feeling' in the Best of Worlds."

12. David Brion Davis, *The Problem of Slavery in the Age of Revolution, 1770–1823*, pp. 42, 45.

13. Gary Wills, *Inventing America*, 1978.

14. Given the importance of definitions of gender to definitions of sentimentality in Twain's times, it is worth noting that he has mainly women crying over the fraudulent heirs: "Everybody, most, leastways women, cried for joy to see them meet at last and have such good times" (211).

15. For examples of these positions, see the collection of essays in the special issue of the *Mark Twain Journal* 22 (1984) about the problem of race in *Huckleberry Finn* (reprinted and expanded as *Satire or Evasion*). In speaking primarily of Jim as described by the term "Uncle Tom," I limit my discussion to the sentimental stereotypes by which Twain characterizes Jim. The literature Robinson draws on in his essay describes Twain's uses of the minstrel-show character in portraying Jim, but to consider the emotional ramifications of this more pernicious set of stereotypes would require too long a digression from my point here. Let it suffice to say that both stereotypes exist simultaneously in the novel, as Ellison tangentially notes in "Twentieth-Century Fiction and the Black Mask of Humanity," and that readers' varying reactions to one or the other of these stereotypes may well be another reason for the varied responses readers have to the book's moral value as a whole.

16. Clemens had, incidentally, read Hume's histories of England and the essay "Of Miracles," as well as Thomas Huxley's *Hume* in the English Men of Letters Series. See Alan Gribben, *Mark Twain's Library*, entries under Hume and Huxley.

17. And yet we must allow ourselves to react to the emotional "coercion" of literature if we are to be able to analyze it. To remain aloof and then to try to explain

what we have not experienced is akin to eating a meal with plugged nostrils and then trying to analyze the smell.

18. See the new author's introduction to *Invisible Man*, p. xix.

19. Equally importantly, the "scientific" utilitarian worldview that vied with sentimentalism for primacy in post-bellum America shared much of the same genealogy.

20. See Susan Gillman's *Dark Twins*, pp. 1–3, for a brief review of some of this literature. Her book as a whole is a formidable addition to it.

21. As a final example of the limitations of Mark Twain criticism based on a rigid rejection of the potential artistic value of literary convention — especially sentimental convention — I turn to Smith's treatment of *A Connecticut Yankee in King Arthur's Court*, which Smith saw as Mark Twain's last significant work in developing the vernacular voice in American literature:

> Simply as a literary idea, the notion of viewing the European past through the eyes of an adult spokesman for the American vernacular tradition was as promising as any Mark Twain had ever hit upon. It was a misfortune that he allowed himself to be diverted from his original plan into the well-worn ruts of Anglophobia and sentimental melodrama. (81)

In attacking Anglophobia because it is merely conventional, Smith implicitly attacks the vernacular tradition. After all, while American Anglophobia was conventional — enough so for politicians to "twist the lion's tale" in election campaigns — it was a distinctly vernacular tradition. The equation "vernacular is good but conventionality is bad" can neither explain what Clemens was doing here nor teach us how to evaluate it.

Perhaps the more interesting thing to note is that sentimentality, rising as it did from British roots and frequently serving the middle classes in their efforts at social climbing, promoted Anglophilia. Hank Morgan, however, is both sentimental and Anglophobic at times. Thus, Clemens combined in one character two conventional outlooks that were substantially incompatible. If Smith is right that juxtaposing differing world-views is a sign of originality and literary promise, what could be more promising than juxtaposing sentimentalism and Anglophobia in a single character? All communication depends on convention; Clemens's peculiar comic genius stems from his ability to meld conventions to highlight their absurdities. He used the same technique in early failures such as the bland "Ye Sentimental Law Student" (1863) as well as in such successes as "Scotty Briggs and the Parson" and *Huck Finn*. If *Connecticut Yankee* fails, it fails for reasons other than that Clemens followed literary conventions.

Chapter Two

1. The most useful introduction to the development of this philosophy as it bears on American letters is in the last section, "The Didactic Enlightenment," of May's *The Enlightenment in America*. See also Crane, Tuveson, Davis, Howard,

Hall, Nye, Martin, Howe, and Ahlstrom as well as the primary sources listed in the bibliography.

2. See Ammons, "Stowe's Dream of the Mother-Savior," and Tompkins, "Sentimental Power." For a general review of the range of feminist opinion about nineteenth-century fiction written by women, see Mary Kelly, "The Sentimentalists: Promise and Betrayal in the Home." Although her title suggests she might, Kelly does not analyze the roots and intellectual presuppositions of sentimentalism. For a review of and addition to feminist criticism specifically of *Uncle Tom's Cabin*, see Gillian Brown, "Getting in the Kitchen with Dinah."

3. Lyman's one effort at "belles lettres," on the contrary, was a heavy-handed allegory. See the introduction to the Belknap edition of *The Autobiography of Lyman Beecher*.

4. Fisher's interest lies essentially in "the primary psychology of sentimental narration itself" (105), emphasizing its anti-realistic effects. His argument serves as an important counterpoint to my emphasis on the historical development of Stowe's ideas and thus on her "realism." See below for my responses to Tompkins's work.

5. Brown only refers to these philosophers once in a 370-page book, showing how little credence he gives to the sentimentalists' justifications.

6. The only a priori truths Locke explicitly mentions are that we exist and those adduced by mathematics and geometry, though he implies that we can build ethics on intuitive truths (Book 4, chap 12, sections 7–11).

7. See especially IV, 12.

8. Of course, his ideas were quite susceptible to theories of evolution, and the genteel reliance on Paley helps to explain genteel resistance to Darwin and Spencer.

9. In this move we see the origins of the modern social sciences (see Schneider, *The Scottish Moralists*).

10. Most scholars of Scottish realism note its anti-speculative bias.

11. Of course, Locke began the game by suggesting that human beings could develop a moral science with almost the precision of mathematics.

12. She wrote this letter to Edward in 1829.

13. This composition could also have come out of Stowe's imagination in the 1860s, as Stowe often in her reminiscences took liberties with what Mark Twain calls "petrified fact." According to Wilson, "In any public display of her personal affairs, Harriet was seldom frank" (113). He does not say whether she limited her tendency to dramatize her life to exaggeration or included complete fabrication. In any case, though, she shows her familiarity with the works of Blair and Alison.

14. Calvinists, especially, persisted in treating children as miniature adults (and born sinners) well into the nineteenth century, in spite of the growing popularity of sentimental definitions of the sanctity and innocence of childhood. For a rather chilling example of the defensive assertiveness of the orthodox as late as the 1830s, see William McLoughlin, "Evangelical Child Rearing in the Age of Jackson: Francis Wayland's Views on When and How to Subdue the Willfulness of Children." Interestingly, Wayland wrote one of America's most influential adaptations of Scottish moral philosophy, adapting it, however, to support orthodoxy and

authority. That Common Sense philosophies could be so adapted leads Howard to conclude that "the light of this philosophy was rather dim" (71). Could it not be equally true that the liberalizing power of this philosophy cast such a strong light that the orthodox needed to shine it through shades of their own devising? As Ahlstrom makes clear, however, such efforts in turn helped undermine orthodoxy as the ultimately liberal basis of sentimentalism shone through (268–69).

15. It is worth noting that Fields assumes that her audience will be familiar with Butler. This is not surprising considering that not only was Butler's book commonplace in American schools, it was even distributed by the American Tract Society as a fundamental text of Christian learning.

16. See *Common Sense*, pp. 20–21, 24–25, 45.

17. See Chapter 9, "Faith or Belief":

> We have shown that a belief in the reality of the existence, both of mind and of matter . . . is one of the implanted principles of mind. Some philosophers have claimed that there is nothing in existence but mind, and that all that is called matter is simply ideas of things in the mind itself, for which there is no corresponding reality. Others have claimed just the opposite: that there is no such existence as an immaterial spirit, but that soul is the brain, or some other very fine organization of matter. In both cases, the assumptions not only have no evidence to sustain them, but are contrary to the common sense or reason of all mankind, and never can be really believed. (165)

See also Sklar, *Catherine Beecher*, pp. 78–80 and 84.

18. Compare William Dean Howells's *A Hazard of New Fortunes* for a critique of this commonplace of nineteenth-century moral philosophy.

19. It seems that Catherine gave Harriet a way to interpret the Book of Job when her Calvinist older brother could not.

20. Of course, Beecher was not alone in developing the ideology of the sexual spheres, though she was one of the most important and influential popularizers of it. For excellent general discussions of the rise of domestic ideology in America, see Cott and Welter.

21. As Stowe certainly thought they did to men who pursued business.

22. Note also the characters in *The Minister's Wooing*, whose names seem to tie them explicitly to their Biblical types.

23. The shift in American letters away from typological allegory may have been at least in part inspired by the demise of Ramistic logic. Alison's use of the term "accidental" characteristic rings of Aristotelian logic, a logic substantially modified in Common Sense philosophy by empiricism (Howell). Wouldn't a combination of Aristotelian categories and empiricism yield characterization by stereotype?

24. E. P. Parker, one of Horace Bushnell's closest theological allies, was a central figure in the literary and cultural circles of Hartford, Connecticut. Hartford was one of America's most important publishing centers in the mid-nineteenth century, serving as one of America's major centers for subscription publishing (which explains in part why Clemens chose to make his home there). See Andrews, *Nook Farm* and French, *Mark Twain and* The Gilded Age. An essay on Parker's

movement from Calvinist orthodoxy to sentimental idealism would read much like this essay on Stowe.

25. Compare Locke, *Essay*, Book II, chapter vii, Paragraph 5:

> Beyond all this, we may find another reason why God hath scattered up and down several degrees of pleasure and pain, in all the things that environ and affect us . . . that we, finding imperfection, dissatisfaction, and want of complete happiness, in all the enjoyments which the creatures can afford us, might be led to seek it in the enjoyment of Him with whom there is fullness of joy, and at whose right hand are pleasures for evermore.

Alison, like Locke before him, indulges in a Neoplatonism at odds with his fundamental realism. Such a Neoplatonic subtext runs uneasily through the works of many Common Sense philosophers, serving as part of a bridge these thinkers built between their essentially materialistic empiricism and their faith in God.

26. The philosophy of sensibility that the Scots developed in many ways radically changed Protestant Britain's view of art to correspond more with that adopted by the Catholic Church during the counter-reformation. Under the influence of these philosophies, Americans, too, adopted a respect for Catholic attitudes toward art and ritual. See Howe, *The Unitarian Conscience*, p. 172. He places the turn to ritual throughout the Protestant world in the nineteenth century, but it of course began in Britain around the turn of the eighteenth. In any event, one can see the influence in Catherine Beecher's repeated praise of Catholic schools and the philanthropic works of nuns. Harriet Stowe, too, refers in her writings, especially in *The Minister's Wooing*, to Catholic ritual and to Catholic mother worship. See also Elizabeth Stuart Phelps, *The Gates Ajar*:

> In our recoil from the materialism of the Romish Church, we have, it seems to me, nearly stranded ourselves on the opposite shore. Just as, in a rebound from the spirit which would put our Saviour on a level with Buddha or Mahomet, we have been in danger of forgetting "to begin as the Bible begins," with his humanity. (75)

27. Stowe refers to Plato's symposium several times in *The Minister's Wooing* in support of her idealism; she does not refer to Plato once in *Uncle Tom's Cabin*.

Chapter Three

1. To get a sense of the extent to which Clemens had rejected his mother's definitions of moral behavior, see his letter to his brother Orion in which he describes a visit his mother made to him in New Orleans:

> Ma was delighted with her trip, but she was disgusted with the girls for allowing me to embrace and kiss them — and she was horrified at the schottische as performed by Miss Castle and myself. She was perfectly willing for me

to dance until 12 o'clock at the imminent peril of my going to sleep on the afterwatch—but then she would top off with a very inconsistent sermon on dancing in general; ending with a terrific broadside aimed at that heresy of heresies, the schottische.(*MTB* 156)

For an excellent brief account of Clemens's anxiety about his "call," see Branch and Hirst, introduction to "A Voice for Setchell" (*ET&S* 2: 169–72).

2. His exposure to such ideas likely came from many sources. For one thing, his father was a deist, giving young Clemens a set of moral alternatives to rigid orthodoxy. For another, the intellectual battles that I described in the last chapter swept the country through the 1830s, 40s, and 50s. In his autobiographical fragment, "Villagers of 1840–43," he describes the era as "an intensely sentimental age" and his descriptions of his mother in the *Autobiography* suggest that she embodied the conflict between sentimental conceptions of motherhood and Calvinist teachings.

3. In defending a comic stage play in a newspaper review, Clemens shows his agreement with this commonplace justification of humor:

I have experienced more real pleasure, and more physical benefit, from laughing naturally and unconfinedly at [Setchell's] funny personations and extempore speeches than I have from all the operas and tragedies I have endured, and all the blue mass pills I have swallowed in six months. (*ET&S* 2: 172)

4. "Superiority theories" of humor are once again common; they were not widely promulgated in the nineteenth century.

5. This may in part explain why Clemens changed Mark Twain's character so frequently. Mark Twain is sometimes refined, sometimes rough, usually a bachelor, but occasionally married—Clemens gave him whatever characteristics he needed to make him the safe butt of humor. See, too, Cox's *Mark Twain: The Fate of Humor*, which uses Freudian psychology to explain the way humor turns back on Twain.

6. See little Eva in *Uncle Tom's Cabin* or the miller's daughter in *Ten Nights in a Bar-room*.

7. See Lynn and Paine, *MTB*, for different accounts, and see *Roughing It*.

8. Donald A. Koch, in his introduction to the Belknap Press edition of Arthur's temperance novel, notes that Arthur was more than just a "cold-water zealot . . . In an ebullient time of causes he spoke out against smoking, gambling, business speculation, materialism, mesmerism, and credit buying." In other words, he saw all aspects of a leisure culture to be pernicious, and saw the love of money as the root of all evil.

9. He did not, for instance, take a stand on Johnson's impeachment until it seemed very clear that his patrons were in favor of it.

10. See, for instance, Francis Parkman's description of the aftermath of a thunderstorm in Wyoming's Laramie Mountains:

All around us was obscurity; but the bright spot above the mountain-tops grew wider and ruddier, until at length the clouds drew apart, and a flood of sunbeams poured down from heaven, streaming along the precipices, and involving them in a thin blue haze, as soft and lovely as that which wraps the Apennines on an evening in spring. (*The Oregon Trail* 234)

11. See above, Chapter 2, about the differences between Locke's and Alison's assessments of the value of association, of metaphor, and of art.

12. See Leo Marx's *The Machine in the Garden* about the importance of these pro- and anti-technology tropes to American culture.

13. These dates are given in *MTTB*, 287.

14. Of course, in order to secure Livy's hand, Clemens had to prove to her parents that he could support her, and he chose to do so by investing in a newspaper, the Buffalo *Express*, with the financial help of his prospective father-in-law, in August of 1869 (*LLMT* 102). Clemens relished being in a position of control, for a change, promising, in a letter to Livy, to

get the reporters accustomed & habituated to doing things my way . . . I simply want to educate them to modify the adjectives, curtail their philosophical reflections & leave out the slang. I have been consulting with the foreman of the news room for two days, & getting him drilled as to how I want the type-setting done . . . I have eliminated all the glaring thunder-&-lightning headings over the telegraphic news & made that department look quiet & respectable. (*LLMT* 103)

But even though he reformed the lurid excesses of the paper, the business did not satisfy him for long. He took a leave of absence from the *Express* just a few months after he began working for it (*LLMT* 112), and he got out of the newspaper business for good by 1871 (*LLMT* 158).

Chapter Four

1. Dickinson follows the old line in Mark Twain criticism that Eastern standards of gentility governed Clemens's editorial policy. In deleting all local references to California and the West, Clemens did undoubtedly cater to the requirements of his Eastern audience. But this single standard does not explain his editorial changes in the articles he wrote for two New York newspapers, the *Tribune* and the *Herald*, for which he wrote "slangy" and "irreverent" letters. That he toned these letters down for *Innocents Abroad* suggests that his changes had to do with the ostensible purposes of books as opposed to newspapers, and that he made these changes self-consciously to fit these new requirements. (See *Travels with the Innocents Abroad* for detailed lists of changes from the original dispatches to *Innocents Abroad*.)

2. See French, *Mark Twain and* The Gilded Age, for reviews of *The Gilded Age* that discuss Warner's usual style of humor.

3. Not surprisingly, but still inconsistently, many modern critics of Clemens state that *The Innocents Abroad* is superior to the original letters or to any of

Clemens's earlier works because it relies less on such scatological humor, at the same time that they berate him for capitulating to the false standards of decorum that prevailed in the literary East.

4. See Smith, *Mark Twain*, pp. 24–25, for the history of Clemens's climb into the world of letters; see Kaplan for the tension this climb caused Clemens; see Blair, *Mark Twain and Huck Finn*, p. 29, for a quick recapitulation; see Brooks, *The Ordeal of Mark Twain*, for the original condemnation of Clemens's "capitulation"; and for a recent, excellent study of this crucial period in Clemens's literary career, see Steinbrink, *Getting to Be Mark Twain*.

5. Annie Fields was a writer and the wife of Boston publisher and one-time editor of the *Atlantic Monthly* James T. Fields.

6. Supposedly such statements from Warner and Clemens about the "absolutely demoralizing manner of treating social questions" in most novels led their wives to challenge them to write a better one.

7. See French, *Mark Twain and* The Gilded Age, on the legitimacy of this story of the novel's genesis.

8. In an 1883 essay titled "Modern Fiction" he praised Scott as one of the world's greatest literary artists.

9. Compare above, Chapter Two, on Stowe's *The Minister's Wooing*, and consider, of course, Hawthorne's morality tales.

10. In Warner's words:

Ruth found before her first term was over at the medical school that there were other things she needed to know quite as much as that which is taught in medical books, and that she could never satisfy her aspirations without more general culture. "Does your doctor know anything — I don't mean about medicine, but about things in general, is he a man of information and good sense?" once asked an old practitioner. "If he doesn't know anything but medicine, the chance is he doesn't know that." (194)

11. The irony of Clemens's attack on the *nouveaux riches* is patent to anyone who knows of his obsession with money generally and with speculative ventures more specifically. But the irony does not mean that Clemens merely mouthed these ideals; he took quite seriously his involvement in his community, believing it to be a source of moral rectitude and cultural refinement. His collaboration with Warner on *The Gilded Age* is only one of many signs of his belief; I discuss his further involvement in the intellectual circles of Hartford below.

12. Baetzhold's *Mark Twain and John Bull* is an exception in that it does take the Club seriously, but it gives little new information about the Club's impact on Clemens, probably because such information is very difficult to find.

13. Andrews, *Nook Farm*, lists a few, but gives an image of frivolity by his choice.

14. James Hammond Trumbull's letter of July 22, 1874 to Clemens shows that Clemens asked Trumbull for advice about literary plots.

15. The piece was received well enough at least by Joseph Twichell for him to comment favorably on it in his diary, January 24, 1876.

16. I have not yet found any other record of Hamersley's essay.

17. See Walter Blair, *Mark Twain and Huck Finn*; Baetzhold, *Mark Twain and John Bull*; and Gribben, *Mark Twain's Library*.

18. The following discussion of *Tom Sawyer* owes much to Baetzhold, *Mark Twain and John Bull*.

19. Lecky here paraphrases Adam Smith.

20. The narrator's similar description of variable remorse when he describes his attendance at a charity sermon is a parody of Benjamin Franklin's account in his *Autobiography* of listening to Whitefield's plea for money. Franklin may very well have been one source of Clemens's knowledge of utilitarianism.

21. As becomes clear in the final paragraph when he declares that he is in the cadaver business.

22. See Joseph Twichell, "The Religious Experiences of Children," *The Religious Herald*, December 19, 1878: "Conscience, or if you please, moral sense." See also Chapter Two, above.

23. For another parody of scientific investigation, see "Some Learned Fables for Good Old Boys and Girls" (1875; *SN&O* 126–48).

24. For a very different view of the epistemological implications of "Old Times on the Mississippi," see Sherwood Cummings, "Mark Twain's Theory of Realism; or the Science of Piloting."

25. Clemens bought the book in Munich in 1878. It is in the Mark Twain Papers now.

26. See editorial introduction to Notebook 7, *N&J1* 241, and see *Report from Paradise*. No record of any such manuscript exists, and he made no extensive notebook entries about this dream.

27. Consider "Cecil Rhodes and the Shark", Sherburn in *Huck*, Wakeman in the letters collected in *MTTB*, Satan in "Chronicle," etc. See Paul Baender, "Mark Twain's Transcendent Figure."

28. Clemens did not publish any of it until 1907 under the title "Extracts from Captain Stormfield's Visit to Heaven." The extracts he published comprise almost exclusively the material he wrote in the late 1870s, even though he wrote another substantial body of manuscript in the first part of the 1900s. He did make some significant changes in the published parts. Tracing the course of composition of this piece is difficult, substantially because manuscripts of few of the drafts Clemens said he wrote remain. In a March 1878 letter to Orion, Samuel Clemens said:

> Nine years ago I mapped out my "Journey in Heaven." . . . After a year or more, I wrote it up. It was not a success. Five years ago, I wrote it again, altering the plan. That MS is at my elbow now. It was a considerable improvement on the first attempt, but still it wouldn't do. — Last year & year before I talked frequently with Howells about the subject, & he kept urging me to do it again. So I thought & thought, at odd moments, & at last I struck what I considered to be the right plan! (*Letters* 1:323)

He apparently drafted the story on the basis of this plan over the next couple of years, mostly during his European trip. I draw this conclusion in part because he used the paper on which the manuscript is written frequently in 1878 and 1879, and in part because his notebook entries and his marginalia in Guillemin's book all post-date this letter to Orion.

The manuscript as it now exists is in three large sections, each numbered separately. The first of these in terms of plot was written last, in the 1900s shortly before publication, though little of it was used in publication. The other two sections were written on three kinds of paper. The first of these in both plot order and in sequence of composition is on Crystal Lake Mills stationery, the second section is mostly on Smith stationery and on some paper I cannot identify. A title page is on Platner paper, suggesting that Clemens added it in the early 1880s, even though Paine dated it 1868. The manuscript Clemens mentions in his letter to Orion does not survive, so it is not possible to discover how much, if any, of the original drafts made it into the drafts we now have. Judging from his extensive use of Guillemin, I suspect he retained very little of the original.

29. Scholars speculate that the book's success depended on this message of consolation to bereaved families of Civil War dead.

Note, too, the similarity to Locke's explanation of imperfection in this world; see above, Chapter Two, note 24.

30. "McWilliams" is one of Clemens's pseudonyms. See the many "McWilliams" stories, "The Experiences of the McWilliamses with the Membranous Croup" (*SN&O* 85–92) for instance.

31. From the previously unpublished manuscript of "Captain Wakeman's Travels in Heaven," section two, pages 11–14, printed here with the kind permission of the American Academy of Arts and Letters in New York City.

32. Clemens himself was crushed by the response. In a letter to Howells he called himself a "great and sublime fool." See Henry Nash Smith, *Mark Twain*, about the importance of this event to Clemens.

Chapter Five

1. See above, Chapter Two.

2. Clemens owned at least one of Sumner's books, *What Social Classes Owe to One Another*, and may very well have known Sumner personally. Sumner, as a prominent, controversial, yet well-liked professor at Yale, had close contact with the Hartford community's many members of the Yale Corporation, including Joseph Twichell. Sumner also participated in the activities of the New Haven Saturday Morning Club, which often exchanged speakers with the Hartford Saturday Morning Club. (Saturday Morning Clubs, which were combination literary societies and debating clubs for girls, were established in many New England cities. They operated much as did the Hartford Monday Evening Club. In Hartford, at least, it acted as a sort of girls' auxiliary, drawing many of its speakers and topics from the adult organization. It also communicated with at least the Boston and New Haven clubs in order to share other topics and speakers.) Sumner gave a lecture titled "Socialism" to the Hartford group on November 20, 1886 (Saturday Morning Club, typed program of lectures for 1886–1887, "Minutes and Records").

3. Consider his involvement in Saturday Morning Clubs for girls.

4. See Gribben, *Library*; *MTHL* 181, note 5; and see *MTS* 112, in which Clemens refers to "John Fiske, whom I knew well and loved." Clemens kept up on Fiske's work as can be seen from his copy, held in the Mark Twain Papers, of Fiske's *A Century of Science and Other Essays* (1900), which Clemens annotated heavily in places.

5. Clemens's copy is in the Mark Twain Papers. It is heavily marked through the first half of the book with definitions of technical terms. The signatures in the first half of the book are damaged, some with pages torn from the stitching, most loose from the binding, suggesting that he read this part a great deal. The last half is virtually unmarked. The main substantive markings are all in the chapters on morality.

The frequency with which Clemens refers to Darwin in *A Tramp Abroad* suggests he was reading Darwin in the late 1870s. See, for instance, volume 2, page 77 and the Chapter on Mount Blanc and the moon. The 1894 piece titled "Mac-Farlane" (*WIM* 76–78) suggests that Clemens knew of Darwin first and primarily through *The Descent of Man*.

6. See also Clemens's March 1, 1883, letter to Howells in which he praises *A Woman's Reason* for its accurate depiction of characters: "I did not know there was an untouched personage in American life, but I had forgotten the auctioneer. You have photographed him accurately" (427).

7. That his new agenda was to attack sentimental realism may explain in part why Clemens had so much trouble writing *A Tramp Abroad*. He needed to make money, so he turned to the genre he had perfected in *Roughing It*. But in *Roughing It* he had found a form that enabled him to use the conventions of sentimental realism that he now held in contempt. In attacking those forms while trying to use them, Clemens put himself back in the bind of *The Innocents Abroad*: he was writing a travel book that undercut the authority of travel books. This time he wished to undercut his own authority as a way of attacking his readers for wanting appearance rather than reality, for wanting sensation rather than experience, for wanting culture without work, for believing in the value of lies over truth.

In advocating the value of his ignorant approach to high culture over his educated understanding of it, he may have revealed to himself the value of Huckleberry Finn as a character who could comment on the moral value of sentimental culture without having to worry about undercutting his own authority. As an outsider, Huckleberry had no authority to undercut. Thus Clemens could move him in and out of American society in ways that would cast light back on the moral pretenses of that society.

8. Ironic considering that when he sent his friend Riley to South Africa, Clemens really believed he could write a book by proxy.

9. Compare Watson Branch, "Hardhearted Huck: 'No Time to be Sentimentering,'" which tries to prove that Huck is not really as unfeeling as this passage makes him out to be.

10. The note to 127.33–34 in the University of California Press edition of *Huckleberry Finn* points out this apparent contradiction, too.

11. See Loren Eiseley on Darwin's break from Lamarckian evolutionary the-

ory and his slow return to it in the face of uncertainties over the age of the earth. By the time he wrote *The Descent of Man*, he had already retreated a bit from his own theory as articulated in the first edition of *The Origin of Species*.

12. Sherwood Cummings mentions that *Huck* uses Darwin's cows, but Cummings and I draw very different conclusions about Clemens's interest in and understanding of Darwin. See *Mark Twain and Science*, 33.

13. Although in Twain criticism "relatively few" still means "many." To cite a few important predecessors on this point, Sculley Bradley's selection of criticism for the 1961 Norton Critical Edition of *Adventures of Huckleberry Finn* includes Eric Solomon's essay about Huck's "Search for Security," in which Solomon argues that Huck's sense of loneliness is central to his motivations in the novel. I agree. But not every critic who has addressed the point does, as Paul Schacht's "The Lonesomeness of Huckleberry Finn" demonstrates. Schacht's article, incidently, refers to other critics who have addressed the question, as does Robinson's "The Silences in *Huckleberry Finn*."

14. Traditional raft/shore arguments do not really explain Huck's retreat from society. The river is not a perfect symbol of uncomplicated safety; it is fraught with danger for Huck and Jim from the beginning—Jim gets bitten by a rattlesnake; thunderstorms and a rise in the river threaten their comfort and safety—and the river never really protects them from human beings—hence Huck's need to lie about the smallpox, hence their need to run the river at night. Yet by running at night, they get hit by a steamboat. The river is hardly a haven regardless of Huck's statement that "there warn't no home like a raft, after all." And while he likes a raft as a home because "other places do seem so cramped up and smothery, but a raft don't. You feel mighty free and easy and comfortable on a raft" (155), he and Jim both quickly find no place so cramped and smothery as their raft when the king and duke invade it.

15. Hank Morgan as a name is probably significant. "Hank" is a nick-name for "Henry," a common name for English kings. "Morgan," German for "morning," is the root of the term "morganatic," meaning elevated to noble status by gift rather than birth and without having the right of succession granted to heirs. Clemens used the word in *Following the Equator*.

16. Like the Tom Sawyer of the "evasion" chapters in *Huckleberry Finn*, Hank Morgan refuses to spring the King until he can do it in a "picturesque," "dramatic" (353) way.

17. See Mitchell Breitweiser, *Cotton Mather and Benjamin Franklin: The Price of Representative Personality*.

18. Benjamin Franklin, for all his ultimate belief in the need for rational control of human behavior, acknowledged this in his autobiography: "So convenient a thing it is to be a reasonable creature, since it enables one to find or make a reason for everything one has a mind to do" (*Autobiography* 32). Clemens's brother had him read the *Autobiography* when he was still a printer's devil. Years later, in a letter to Howells, he described Franklin's and Cellini's autobiographies as the only two worth reading. Clemens was influenced by his reading of Franklin. Early in his career, in "The Late Benjamin Franklin," he genially mocked Franklin's philosophies, but by the middle of the 1880s his private philosophy, expressed in "Three

Statements of the Eighties" (*WIM* 56–59), parrots Franklin's "A Dissertation on Liberty and Necessity, Pleasure and Pain."

19. He frequently uses the term "man" in italics to suggest an ideal state of manhood in contrast to the real state of development of that ideal, for examples on pages 69 and 157, or in contrast to being a human sheep, for example on page 114.

20. See my discussion of *Tom Sawyer* in Chapter 4.

21. Clemens repeats here one of the main themes of *The Prince and the Pauper* (1881).

22. This is not really surprising since he drew many of the details for his descriptions of the slaves' conditions from antebellum antislavery literature. In particular, he relied on Charles Ball's slave narrative, *Slavery in the United States: A Narrative of the Life and Adventures of Charles Ball*, 1837 edition. See Baetzhold; Gribben, *Library*; and the University of California Press edition of *A Connecticut Yankee*.

23. Of course, *The Prince and the Pauper* does use sentiment to teach children democratic politics, but, as a children's book, it stays within the traditional confines of sentimental domesticity.

24. See Budd for the importance of this novel to Clemens's political ideas.

25. That he endorsed Beard's pro-free trade illustrations is further evidence to support the point.

26. Budd argues that Berkeley's apostasy from his radicalism parallels Mark Twain's return to conservatism. I think this passage shows to the contrary that Clemens's complaints about closed union shops arise from his support not of aristocracy and the British system, but of the value of work. The labels conservative and liberal on these issues apply very poorly.

27. See pages 108–10, and consider the entire plot line of Berkeley's development in the boarding house, especially page 121 regarding the pleasure of being respected.

28. Compare the passage in *Connecticut Yankee* about one's duty to change wrong government:

> I was from Connecticut, whose Constitution declares "that all political power is inherent in the people, and all free governments are founded on their authority and instituted for their benefit; and that they have at all times an undeniable and indefeasible right to alter their form of government in such manner as they may think expedient."
>
> Under that gospel, the citizen who thinks he sees that the commonwealth's political clothes are worn out, and yet holds his peace and does not agitate for a new suit, is disloyal; he is a traitor. That he may be the only one who thinks he sees this decay, does not excuse him: it is his duty to agitate anyway, and it is the duty of the others to vote him down if they do not see the matter as he does. (113–14)

29. In Clemens's time, about twenty years passed between the publication of the two books.

30. Though the book to some extent ironizes this endorsement of the scientific point of view. See Chapter Six below.

Chapter Six

1. Partly, I suspect, this is a carryover from the debate about *Huckleberry Finn*, with critics trying to find more evidence about Clemens's attitudes toward race in order to evaluate the more aesthetically satisfying text.

2. See the first section of Gillman's chapter for a powerful and more detailed statement of this point. For a powerful dissenting view, see John H. Schaar, "Some of the Ways of Freedom in *Pudd'nhead Wilson.*"

3. As Clemens put it in his *Autobiography*: "It is perfection, I think, in many things, and perhaps most things, that fascinates us. A splendid literature charms us; but it doesn't charm me any more than its opposite does — "hogwash" literature" (January 15, 1906; *MTA* 1:324). See also Gribben, "'I Kind of Love Small Game': Mark Twain's Library of Literary Hogwash."

4. It is worth noting the similarities to the Freudian idea of wit, that is, a relief from debilitating sublimation in veiled aggression.

5. Parker is not sure which one came first in order of composition or conception. For a parallel but significantly different discussion of the connections between Wilson and Driscoll, see James Cox, *Fate*, pp 232–46.

6. Perhaps most revealingly in "The Loves of Alonzo Fitz Clarence and Rosanna Ethelton," in which the villain bears a striking resemblance to Mark Twain.

7. Specifically, Clemens was thanking Howells for the favorable review of *Roughing It* that Howells had published in the *Atlantic Monthly*. See the June 1872 letter from Clemens to Howells in *MTHL* 10–11.

8. George Forgie, *Patricide in the House Divided.* See chapter 5, "Sentimental Regression From Politics to Domesticity," pp. 159–99, and chapter 6, "The Literature of Fratricide: Civil War as Memory and Prospect," pp. 201–41.

9. See, for instance, Eric Sundquist, "Mark Twain and Homer Plessy."

10. This image of the General stands both for Clemens himself and for General Grant, I believe.

11. Gribben mentions only James's *Principles of Psychology* (1890), which influenced certain passages of "Chronicle of Young Satan," and *Varieties of Religious Experience* (1902) as works by James that Clemens read, but the ideas of these early works from which I quote here undergird James's entire corpus. See also Clemens's June 12, 1906 autobiographical dictation in which he mentions a published letter by James in the context of a discussion of memory.

12. While of course not all scientists saw fate as fixed, many of those most influential to literary history — in particular, Spencer and Sumner — did. See above, Chapter 5. The idea that all physical events are determined by the rigid workings of natural law has until recently been advocated by many highly respected physicists and by other "hard" scientists. The recent development of chaos theories is finally leading most to abandon the long cherished idea that the universe can be described and predicted on the basis of a single natural law.

13. In imagining such a model of mind, Clemens develops a line of thought parallel to James's.

Chapter Seven

1. Dates courtesy of John Tuckey, whose ground-breaking study of "The Mysterious Stranger" manuscripts essentially opened Clemens's late works to serious study after Paine's deceit and De Voto's unfinished work led to simplistic hypothesizing about Clemens losing his artistic abilities and rediscovering them at the end of *The Mysterious Stranger*.

Works Cited and Consulted

Ahlstrom, Sydney. *A Religious History of the American People*. New Haven, CT: Yale University Press, 1972.
——. "The Scottish Philosophers and American Theology." *Church History* 24 (1955): 257–72.
Alison, Archibald. *Essays on the Nature and Principles of Taste*, 2 vols. Rev. ed., 1810. Edinburgh: Archibald Constable and Company, 1825.
Allen, Charles A. "Mark Twain and Conscience." *Literature and Psychology* 7 (1957): 17–21.
Ammons, Elizabeth. "Stowe's Dream of the Mother-Savior: *Uncle Tom's Cabin* and American Women Writers Before the 1920s." In *New Essays on* Uncle Tom's Cabin. Ed. Eric J. Sundquist. Cambridge: Cambridge University Press, 1986. 161–70.
Andrews, Kenneth. *Nook Farm: Mark Twain's Hartford Circle*. Cambridge, MA: Harvard University Press, 1950.
Arthur, Timothy Shay. *Ten Nights in a Bar-Room, and What I Saw There*. 1854. Cambridge, MA: Belknap-Harvard University Press, 1964.
Aspiz, Harold. "Lecky's Influence on Mark Twain." *Science and Society* 26 (1962): 15–25.
Baender, Paul. "Alias Macfarlane: A Revision of Mark Twain Biography." *American Literature* 38 (May, 1966): 187–97.
——. "Mark Twain's Transcendent Figure." Diss., University of California, 1956.
Baetzhold, Howard G. *Mark Twain and John Bull: The British Connection*. Bloomington: Indiana University Press, 1970.
Ball, Charles. *Fifty Years in Chains; or, the Life of an American Slave*. New York: H. Dayton, 1860.
Baym, Nina. *Woman's Fiction: A Guide to Novels by and about Women in America, 1820–1870*. Ithaca, NY: Cornell University Press, 1978.
Beaver, Harold. "Run, Nigger, Run: *Adventures of Huckleberry Finn* as a Fugitive Slave Narrative." *Journal of American Studies* 8 (1974): 339–61.
Beecher, Catherine. *Common Sense Applied to Religion*. New York: Harper & Brothers, 1857.
——. *The Duty of American Women to Their Country*. New York: Harper & Brothers, 1845.
——. *Treatise on Domestic Economy*. 1841. New York: Schocken Books, 1977.
Beecher, Catherine and Harriet Beecher. *Primary Geography for Children, on an Improved Plan*. Cincinnati, OH: Corey & Fairbank, 1833.
Bellamy, Gladys Carmen. *Mark Twain as Literary Artist*. Norman: University of Oklahoma Press, 1950.

Blair, Hugh. *Lectures on Rhetoric and Belles Lettres*, 3 vols. 1783. Edinburgh: Bell & Bradfute, 1813.

Blair, Walter. *Mark Twain and Huck Finn*. Berkeley: University of California Press, 1960.

Bluefarb, Sam. "*Huck Finn*: Escape from Conscience and the Discovery of the Heart." In *The Escape Motif in the American Novel: Mark Twain to Richard Wright*. Columbus: Ohio State University Press, 1972. 12–24.

Blues, Thomas. *Mark Twain and the Community*. Lexington: University Press of Kentucky, 1970.

Boller, Paul F., Jr. "Mark Twain's Credo: A Humorist's Fatalistic View." *Southwest Review* 63 (1978): 150–63.

Bond, Adrienne. "Disorder and the Sentimental Model: A Look at *Pudd'nhead Wilson*." *Southern Literary Journal* 13 (1981): 59–71.

Brack, O. M., Jr. "Mark Twain in Knee Pants: The Expurgation of *Tom Sawyer Abroad*." *Proof* 2 (1972): 145–51.

Branch, Edgar. *The Literary Apprenticeship of Mark Twain*. 1950. New York: Russell & Russell, 1966.

Branch, Watson. "Hardhearted Huck: 'No Time to Be Sentimentering.'" *Studies in American Fiction* 6 (1978): 212–18.

Brashear, Minnie M. *Mark Twain: Son of Missouri*. Chapel Hill: University of North Carolina Press, 1934.

Breitwieser, Mitchell Robert. *Cotton Mather and Benjamin Franklin: The Price of Representative Personality*. Cambridge: Cambridge University Press, 1984.

Brogan, Howard O. "Early Experience and Scientific Determinism in Twain and Hardy." *Mosaic: A Journal for the Comparative Study of Literature and Ideas* 7 (1974): iii, 99–105.

Brooks, Van Wyck. *The Ordeal of Mark Twain*. Revised ed. New York: E. P. Dutton, 1933.

Brown, Gillian. "Getting in the Kitchen With Dinah: Domestic Politics in *Uncle Tom's Cabin*." *AQ* 36 (1984): 503–23.

Brown, Herbert Ross. *The Sentimental Novel in America, 1789–1860*. 1940. New York: Pageant Books, Inc., 1959.

Budd, Louis J. *Mark Twain, Social Philosopher*. Bloomington: Indiana University Press, 1962.

Butler, Bishop Joseph. *The Analogy of Religion, Natural and Revealed, To the Constitution of Nature*, 4th edition. London: John & Paul Knapton, 1750.

Byers, John R. "Miss Emmeline Grangerford's Hymn Book." *AL* 93 (1971): 259–63.

Clark, Marden J. "No Time to Be Sentimentering." *Mark Twain Journal* 21 (1983): 21–23.

Clemens, Samuel. *Adventures of Huckleberry Finn*. 1885. Ed. Walter Blair and Victor Fischer. Berkeley: University of California Press, 1985.

———. *The Adventures of Tom Sawyer*. 1876. Ed. John C. Gerber, Paul Baender, and Terry Firkins. Berkeley: University of California Press, 1980.

———. *The American Claimant*. 1892. New York: P. F. Collier and Son, n.d.

———. The Autobiography of Mark Twain. Typescript in the Mark Twain Papers,

Bancroft Library, University of California, Berkeley. Also under Bernard De Voto, ed., *Mark Twain in Eruption*, New York: Harper & Bros., 1940; Michael J. Kiskis ed., *Mark Twain's Own Autobiography*, Madison: University of Wisconsin Press, 1990; Charles Neider, ed., *The Autobiography of Mark Twain*, New York: Harper & Row, 1959, and Albert Bigelow Paine, ed., *Mark Twain's Autobiography*, New York: Harper & Bros., 1924.

——. "The Californian's Tale." 1893. *"The $30,000 Bequest" and Other Stories*. New York: P. F. Collier and Son, n.d.

——. "Captain Wakeman's Travels in Heaven." Holograph Manuscript held by the American Academy and Institute of Arts and Letters, New York, New York.

——. "The Christmas Fireside: The Story of the Bad Little Boy That Bore a Charmed Life." 1865. *Early Tales and Sketches*. Berkeley: University of California Press, 1981. 2: 407–10.

——. *A Connecticut Yankee in King Arthur's Court*. 1889. Ed. Bernard L. Stein. Berkeley: University of California Press, 1979.

——. "A Dog's Tale." 1903. *"The $30,000 Bequest" and Other Stories*. New York: P. F. Collier and Son, n.d.

——. *Early Tales and Sketches*. Ed. Edgar Marquess Branch and Robert H. Hirst. Berkeley: University of California Press, 1979.

——. "A Fable." 1909. *The Complete Short Stories of Mark Twain*. Ed. Charles Neider. New York: Bantam, 1958. 600–2.

——. "The Facts Concerning the Recent Carnival of Crime in Connecticut." 1876. *Tom Sawyer Abroad, Tom Sawyer, Detective, and Other Stories*. New York: P. F. Collier and Son, n.d.

——. "Female Suffrage: Views of Mark Twain" and "Female Suffrage: Another Letter from Mark Twain." St. Louis *Democrat*, March/April 1867.

——. "Fenimore Cooper's Literary Offenses." *North American Review* 161 (July, 1895): 1–12.

——. *Following the Equator*, 2 vols. 1897. New York: P. F. Collier and Son, n.d.

——. "A Horse's Tale." *Harper's Magazine*, August and September, 1906.

——. *The Innocents Abroad*. Hartford, CT: American Publishing Co., 1869.

——. *Letters from the Earth*. Ed. Bernard De Voto. New York: Harper & Row, 1962.

——. "Letter to the Earth." *Letters from the Earth*. Ed. Bernard De Voto. New York: Harper & Row, 1962. 115–22.

——. *Life on the Mississippi*. 1883. New York: P. F. Collier and Son, 1917[?].

——. *The Love Letters of Mark Twain*. Ed. Dixon Wecter. New York: Harper & Brothers, 1949.

——. "The Loves of Alonzo Fitz Clarence and Rosanna Ethelton." *Atlantic Monthly* 141 (March, 1878): 320–30.

——. *Mark Twain in Eruption*. Ed. Bernard De Voto. New York: Harper & Brothers, 1940.

——. *Mark Twain's Fables of Man*. Ed. John S. Tuckey. Berkeley: University of California Press, 1972.

——. *Mark Twain's Hannibal, Huck & Tom*. Ed. Walter Blair. Berkeley: University of California Press, 1969.

——. *Mark Twain's Letters*. 2 vols. Ed. Albert Bigelow Paine. New York: Harper & Brothers, 1917.

——. *Mark Twain's Letters from Hawaii*. Ed. A. Grove Day. Honolulu: University Press of Hawaii, 1975.

——. "Mark Twain's Letters from Washington." Nos. 1 to 11. Virginia City, Nevada, *Territorial Enterprise*. January to April, 1868.

——. *Mark Twain's Mysterious Stranger Manuscripts*. Ed. William M. Gibson. Berkeley: University of California Press, 1969.

——. *Mark Twain's Notebooks and Journals, Volume 1 (1855–1873)*. Ed. Frederick Anderson et al. Berkeley: University of California Press, 1975.

——. *Mark Twain's Notebooks and Journals, Volume 2 (1877–1883)*. Ed. Frederick Anderson et al. Berkeley: University of California Press, 1975.

——. *Mark Twain's Notebooks and Journals, Volume 3 (1877–1883)*. Ed. Frederick Anderson et al. Berkeley: University of California Press, 1979.

——. *Mark Twain's Speeches*. New York: Harper & Brothers, 1910.

——. *Mark Twain's Travels with Mr. Brown*. Ed. Franklin Walker and G. Ezra Dane. New York: Alfred A. Knopf, 1940.

——. *Mark Twain's Which Was the Dream?* Ed. John S. Tuckey. Berkeley: University of California Press, 1968.

——. *Mark Twain to Mrs. Fairbanks*. Ed. Dixon Wecter. San Marino, CA: Huntington Library, 1949.

——. "No. 44, The Mysterious Stranger." *Mark Twain's Mysterious Stranger Manuscripts*. Ed. William M. Gibson. Berkeley: University of California Press, 1969.

——. "Old Times on the Mississippi." 1875. Rpt. in *Life on the Mississippi*. 1883. New York: P. F. Collier and Son, 1917[?].

——. *Personal Recollections of Joan of Arc*. New York: Harper & Brothers, 1896.

——. *The Prince and the Pauper*. Boston: Osgood & Company, 1881.

——. *Pudd'nhead Wilson and Those Extraordinary Twins*. 1894. New York: W. W. Norton, 1980.

——. *Report From Paradise*. Ed. Dixon Wecter. New York: Harper & Brothers, 1952.

——. *Roughing It*. 1871. New York: Harper & Row, n.d.

——. *Sketches New and Old*. Hartford: American Publishing Company, 1875.

——. "The Story of the Good Little Boy Who Did Not Prosper." 1870. *Contributions to* The Galaxy: *1868–1871*. Ed. Bruce R. McElderry, Jr. Gainesville, FL: Scholars' Facsimiles & Reprints, 1961. 44–46.

——. "Three Thousand Years Among the Microbes." In *Mark Twain's Which Was The Dream? and Other Symbolic Writings of the Later Years*. Ed. John S. Tuckey. Berkeley: University of California Press, 1968.

——. *A Tramp Abroad*. 1879. New York: P. F. Collier and Son, n.d.

——. *Traveling with the Innocents Abroad*. Ed. D. M. McKeithan. Norman: University of Oklahoma Press, 1958.

——. *What Is Man? and Other Philosophical Writings*. Ed. Paul Baender. Berkeley: University of California Press, 1973.

——. *Mark Twain's Which Was The Dream? and Other Symbolic Writings of the Later Years*. Ed. John S. Tuckey. Berkeley: University of California Press, 1968.

Clemens, Samuel and William Dean Howells. *Mark Twain-Howells Letters*. Ed. Henry Nash Smith and William M. Gibson. Cambridge, MA: Belknap-Harvard University Press, 1960.

Clemens, Samuel and Charles Dudley Warner. *The Gilded Age*. 1873 Hartford, CT: American Publishing Co. 1890.

Coburn, Mark D. " 'Training is Everything:' Communal Opinion and the Individual in *Pudd'nhead Wilson.*" *Modern Language Quarterly* 31 (1970): 209–19.

Cook, Joseph. *Conscience*. Boston: Houghton, Osgood and Co., 1879.

Cooper, James Fenimore. *The Last of the Mohicans*. 1826. New York: Signet, 1962.

Cott, Nancy. *The Bonds of Womanhood: "Woman's Sphere" in New England, 1780–1835*. New Haven, CT: Yale University Press, 1977.

Cox, James. "A Hard Book to Take," in Sattelmeyer and Crowley, eds., *One Hundred Years of* Huckleberry Finn. 386–403.

——. "Humor And America: The Southwestern Bear Hunt, Mrs. Stowe and Mark Twain." *Sewanee Review* 83 (1975): 573–601.

——. *Mark Twain: The Fate of Humor*. Princeton, NJ: Princeton University Press, 1966.

Crane, R. S. "Suggestions Toward a Genealogy of the 'Man of Feeling.'" *ELH* 1 (December, 1934): 205–30.

Cummings, Sherwood. *Mark Twain and Science: The Adventures of a Mind*. Baton Rouge: Louisiana State University Press, 1989.

——. "Mark Twain's Acceptance of Science." *Centennial Review* 6 (1962): 245–61.

——. "Mark Twain's Theory of Realism; or the Science of Piloting." *Studies in American Humor* 2 (1976): 209–21.

——. *"What Is Man?*: The Scientific Sources." In *Essays on Determinism in American Literature*. Ed. Sydney Kraus. Kent, OH: Kent State University Press, 1964.

Darwin, Charles. *The Descent of Man* vol. 1. New York: D. Appleton & Co., 1871. Clemens's personal copy with marginalia, held in Mark Twain Papers, Bancroft Library, University of California at Berkeley.

Davis, David Brion. Chapter 11, "Religious Sources of Anti-Slavery Thought: The 'Man of Feeling' in the Best of Worlds." In *The Problem of Slavery in Western Culture*. Ithaca, NY: Cornell University Press, 1966.

Davis, Philip E. "Mark Twain as Moral Philosopher." *San Jose Studies* 2 (1976): 83–93.

De Voto, Bernard. *Mark Twain at Work*. Cambridge, MA: Harvard University Press, 1942.

——, ed. *Mark Twain in Eruption*. New York: Harper & Brothers, 1940.

——. *Mark Twain's America*. Boston: Little, Brown & Co., 1932.

Dickinson, Leon T. "Mark Twain's Revisions in Writing *The Innocents Abroad.*" *AL* 19 (1947): 139–57.

Ditsky, John M. "Mark Twain and 'The Great Dark:' Religion in *Letters from the Earth.*" *Mark Twain Journal* 17 (1975): 12–19.

Douglas, Ann. *The Feminization of American Culture*. 1977. New York: Avon, 1978.

Doyno, Victor A. *Writing* Huck Finn: *Mark Twain's Creative Process*. Philadelphia: University of Pennsylvania Press, 1991.

Duncan, Jeffrey L. "The Empirical and the Ideal in Mark Twain." *PMLA* 95 (1980): 201–12.

Eastman, Mary H. *Aunt Phillis's Cabin*. 1852. New York: Negro Universities Press, 1968.

Ellison, Ralph. "Change the Joke and Slip the Yoke," *Partisan Review* 25 (1958): 212–22.

———. New author's introduction to *Invisible Man*. New York: Random House, 1982.

———. "Twentieth-Century Fiction and the Black Mask of Humanity." *Confluence: An International Forum* 2, no. 4 (1953): 5–21.

Eiseley, Loren. *Darwin's Century: Evolution and the Men Who Discovered It*. 1958. Garden City, NY: Anchor Books, 1961.

Fields, Annie. *Life and Letters of Harriet Beecher Stowe*. London: Sampson Low, Marston & Company, 1898.

———. *Memories of a Hostess*. Boston: Atlantic Monthly Press, 1922.

Fischer, John Irwin. "How to Tell a Story: Mark Twain's Gloves and the Moral Example of Mr. Lawrence Sterne." *Mark Twain Journal* 21 (1982): 17–21.

———. "Mark Twain, Mount Tabor, and the Triumph of Art." *Southern Review* 14 (1978): 692–705.

Fisher, Philip. *Hard Facts: Setting and Form in the American Novel*. New York: Oxford University Press, 1985.

Fiske, John. *A Century of Science and Other Essays*. Boston: Houghton, Mifflin and Company, Riverside Press, 1900. Mark Twain's annotated copy, held in the Mark Twain Papers, Bancroft Library, University of California, Berkeley.

———. "Charles Darwin." *The Atlantic Monthly* 49 (1882): 835–45.

Fliegelman, Jay. *Prodigals and Pilgrims: The American Revolution Against Patriarchal Authority, 1750–1800*. Cambridge: Cambridge University Press, 1982.

Forgie, George. *Patricide in the House Divided: A Psychological Interpretation of Lincoln and His Age*. New York: W. W. Norton, 1979.

Foster, Charles H. *The Rungless Ladder*. Durham, NC: Duke University Press, 1954.

Franklin, Benjamin. *Autobiography*. 1788. New York: Holt Rinehart & Winston, 1969.

———. "A Dissertation on Liberty and Necessity, Pleasure and Pain." 1725. *The Autobiography and Other Writings*. New York: New American Library, 1961. 321–27.

French, Bryant Morey. *Mark Twain and* The Gilded Age: *The Book That Named an Era*. Dallas, TX: Southern Methodist University Press, 1965.

Fussell, E[dwin] S. "The Structural Problem of *The Mysterious Stranger*." *Studies in Philology* 49 (1952): 95–104.

Gaylin, Willard. "Two Routes to Unselfish Behavior. From Twain to Freud: An Examination of Conscience." *Hastings Center Report* (Institute of Society, Ethics, and the Life Sciences) 6 (1976): 5–8.

Gillman, Susan. *Dark Twins: Imposture and Identity in Mark Twain's America*. Chicago: University of Chicago Press, 1989.

Gillman, Susan and Forrest G. Robinson, eds. *Mark Twain's* Pudd'nhead Wilson: *Race, Conflict, and Culture*. Durham, NC: Duke University Press, 1990.

Girgus, Sam B. "Conscience in Connecticut: Civilization and its Discontents in Twain's Camelot." *New England Quarterly* 51 (1978): 547–60.

Glick, Wendell. "The Epistemological Theme of *The Mysterious Stranger*." In *Themes and Directions in American Literature*. Ed. Ray B. Browne and Donald Pizer. West Lafayette, IN: Purdue University Press, 1969. 130–47.

Gribben, Alan. "'Good Books and a Sleepy Conscience:' Mark Twain's Reading Habits." *American Literary Realism* 9 (1976): 294–306.

——. "'I Detest Novels, Poetry and Theology:' Origin of a Fiction Concerning Mark Twain's Reading." *Tennessee Studies in Literature* 22 (1977): 154–61.

——. "'I Kind of Love Small Game': Mark Twain's Library of Literary Hogwash." *American Literary Realism* 9 (1976): 64–76.

——. *Mark Twain's Library*. Boston: G.K. Hall & Co., 1980.

——. "Mark Twain, Phrenology and the 'Temperments': A Study of Pseudoscientific Influence." *American Quarterly* 24 (1972): 44–68.

——. "Removing Mark Twain's Mask: A Decade of Criticism and Scholarship," Parts I and II. *ESQ* 26 (1980): 100–108 and 149–71.

——. "'Stolen from Books Tho' Credit Given:' Mark Twain's Use of Literary Sources." *Mosaic* 12 (1979): 149–55.

——. "'When Other Amusements Fail:' Mark Twain and the Occult." In *The Haunted Dusk: American Supernatural Fiction*. Ed. Howard Kerr. Athens: University of Georgia Press, 1983. 169–89.

Grove, James. "Mark Twain and the Endangered Family." *AL* 57 (1985): 377–94.

Guillemin, Amédée Victor. *The Heavens: An Illustrated Handbook of Popular Astronomy*. 1878. Clemens's personal copy with marginalia, held in the Mark Twain Papers, Bancroft Library, University of California at Berkeley.

Hall, G. Stanley. "On the History of American College Textbooks and Teaching in Logic, Ethics, Psychology, and Allied Subjects." American Antiquarian Society *Proceedings* n.s. 9 (1895): 137–74.

Harnsberger, Caroline Thomas. *Mark Twain's Views of Religion*. Evanston, IL: Shori Press, 1961.

Harrell, Don W. "A Chaser of Phantoms: Mark Twain and Romanticism." *Midwest Quarterly* 13 (1972): 201–12.

Harris, George Washington. "Old Burns's Bull Ride." *Sut Lovingood*. New York: Dick and Fitzgerald, 1867. 98–107.

Hart, James D. *The Popular Book in America*. New York: Oxford University Press, 1950.

Hays, John Q. "Mark Twain's Rebellion Against God: Origins." *Southwestern American Literature* 3 (1973): 27–38.

Hill, Hamlin. *Mark Twain: God's Fool*. New York: Harper & Row, 1973.

Hobbes, Thomas. From *Leviathan* and from *Human Nature*. Ed. John Morreal. *The Philosophy of Laughter and Humor*. Albany: State University of New York Press, 1987. 19–20.

Hofstadter, Richard. *Social Darwinism in American Thought*. Revised ed. New York: George Brazillier, Inc., 1959.

Howard, Leon. "The Late Eighteenth Century: An Age of Contradiction." In

Transitions in American Literary History. Ed. Harry Hayden Clark. Durham, NC: Duke University Press, 1953.

Howe, Daniel Walker. *The Unitarian Conscience: Harvard Moral Philosophy, 1805–1861*. Cambridge, MA: Harvard University Press, 1970.

Howell, Wilbur Samuel. *Eighteenth-Century British Logic and Rhetoric*. Princeton, NJ: Princeton University Press, 1971.

Howells, William Dean. "My Mark Twain." In *Literary Friends and Acquaintances: A Personal Retrospect of American Authorship*. New York: Harper & Brothers, 1911.

Hutcheson, Francis. From "Reflections Upon Laughter." 1750. In Morreal, ed., *The Philosophy of Laughter and Humor*. 26–40.

———. *A System of Moral Philosophy*, 2 vols. Glasgow: R. and A. Foulis, 1755.

Hume, David. "Of Miracles." *An Inquiry Concerning Human Understanding*. 1758. New York: Liberal Arts Press, 1955. 117–41.

Huxley, Thomas. *David Hume*. English Men of Letters Series. New York: Harper & Brothers, 1879.

James, Henry Sr. *The Nature of Evil*. New York: D. Appleton & Company, 1855.

James, William. *Principles of Psychology*. Authorized ed. 2 vols. New York: Henry Holt & Co., 1890.

———. "Remarks on Spencer's Definition of Mind as Correspondence." 1878. *William James: The Essential Writings*. Ed. Bruce W. Wilshire. Albany, NY: State University of New York Press, 1984. 9–24.

———. "The Sentiment of Rationality." 1879. *William James: The Essential Writings*. Ed. Bruce W. Wilshire. Albany, NY: State University of New York Press, 1984. 25–38.

———. "Spencer's *Data of Ethics*." *The Nation* 29 (1879): 178–79.

———. *The Varieties of Religious Experience: A Study in Human Nature*. London: Longmans, Green, and Co., 1902.

Jehlen, Myra. "The Ties that Bind: Race and Sex in *Pudd'nhead Wilson*." *American Literary History* 2 (1990): 39–55.

Kaplan, Justin. *Mr. Clemens and Mark Twain*. New York: Simon and Schuster, 1966.

Karpowitz, Steven. "Tom Sawyer and Mark Twain: Fictional Women and Real in the Play of Conscience with the Imagination." *Literature and Psychology* 23 (1973): 5–12.

Kelley, Mary. "The Sentimentalists: Promise and Betrayal in the Home." *Signs* 4 (1979): 434–46.

Kenton, Edna. Quoted in *Current Opinion* 65 (July, 1918): 48.

Kiskis, Michael J., ed. *Mark Twain's Own Autobiography*. Madison: University of Wisconsin Press, 1990.

Kolb, Harold H. "Mark Twain, Huck Finn and Jacob Blivens: Gilt-Edged, Tree-Calf Morality in *Huck Finn*." *Virginia Quarterly Review* 55 (1979): 653–69.

Krause, Sydney J. *Mark Twain as Critic*. Baltimore: Johns Hopkins University Press, 1967.

———. "Mark Twain: At Home in the Gilded Age." *Georgia Review* 28 (1974): 105–13.

———. "Olivia Clemens's 'Editing' Reviewed." *AL* 39 (1967): 325–51.

Krauth, Leland. "Mark Twain: The Victorian of Southwest Humor." *AL* 54 (1982): 368–84.

Lathrop, George Parsons. "A Model State Capital." *Harper's New Monthly Magazine* 71 (October 1885): 715–34.

Lecky, W.E.H. *History of European Morals.* 1869. New York: D. Appleton Co., 1874.

Leonard, James S., Thomas A. Tenney, and Thadious M. Davis, eds. *Satire or Evasion? Black Perspectives on* Huckleberry Finn. Durham, NC: Duke University Press, 1992.

Levy, Leo B. "Society and Conscience in *Huckleberry Finn,*" *Nineteenth-Century Fiction* 18 (1964): 389–91.

Lindborg, Henry J. "A Cosmic Tramp: Samuel Clemens' *Three Thousand Years Among the Microbes.*" *AL* 44 (1973): 652–57.

Locke, John. *An Essay Concerning Human Understanding.* 1706. New York: Dutton, 1965.

Lowell, James Russell. "Rousseau and the Sentimentalists." In *The Writings of James Russell Lowell: Volume II, Literary Essays.* Cambridge, MA: Riverside Press, 1892.

Lloyd, James B. "The Nature of Twain's Attack on Sentimentality in *Huck Finn.*" *University of Mississippi Studies in English* 13 (1972): 59–63.

Lynn, Kenneth. *Mark Twain and Southwestern Humor.* Boston: Little, Brown & Co., 1959.

McKay, Janet. " 'Tears and Flapdoodle': Point of View and Style in *Huck Finn.*" *Style* 10 (1976): 41–50.

McLoughlin, William. "Evangelical Child Rearing in the Age of Jackson: Francis Wayland's Views on When and How to Subdue the Willfulness of Children." In *Growing Up in America: Children in Historical Perspective.* Ed. N. Ray Hiner and Joseph M. Hawes. Urbana: University of Illinois Press, 1985. 87–107.

Martin, Terence. *The Instructed Vision: Scottish Common Sense Philosophy and the Origins of American Fiction.* 1961. New York: Kraus Reprint Co., 1969.

Marx, Leo. *The Machine in the Garden: Technology and the Pastoral Ideal in America.* New York: Oxford University Press, 1964.

May, Henry F. "The Didactic Enlightenment." In *The Enlightenment in America.* New York: Oxford University Press, 1976. 307–62.

Monday Evening Club. *The List of the Members of the Monday Evening Club with the Record of Papers Read at Their Meetings. 1869–1954.* Hartford, CT: privately printed, 1954.

Morreall, John, ed. *The Philosophy of Laughter and Humor.* Albany: State University of New York Press, 1987.

Neider, Charles, ed. *The Autobiography of Mark Twain.* 1959. New York: Harper & Row, 1975.

Nye, Russel B. *Society and Culture in America: 1830–1860.* New York: Harper & Row, 1974.

Paine, Albert Bigelow. *Mark Twain: A Biography.* New York: Harper & Brothers, 1912.

———. *Mark Twain's Autobiography*. New York: Harper & Bros, 1924.

Paley, William. *Moral and Political Philosophy* and *Natural Theology* (which were printed together in one volume for wide American distribution by The American Tract Society in about 1803). In *The Works of William Paley, D.D.* London: T. Nelson and Sons, 1860.

Parker, Edwin P. "Harriet Beecher Stowe." In *Eminent Women of the Age*. Hartford: S. M. Betts & Company, 1868.

Parker, Herschel. "Pudd'nhead Wilson: Jack-Leg Author, Unreadable Text and Sense-Making Critics." In *Flawed Texts and Verbal Icons: Literary Authority in American Fiction*. Evanston, IL: Northwestern University Press, 1984. 115–45.

Parkman, Francis Jr. *The Oregon Trail*. 1849. Harmondsworth: Penguin, 1982.

Phelps, Elizabeth Stuart. *The Gates Ajar*. 1868. Ed. Helen Smootin Smith. Cambridge, MA: Belknap-Harvard University Press, 1964.

Rashdall, Hastings. *Is Conscience an Emotion?* Boston: Houghton Mifflin Company, 1914.

Rees, Robert A. "*Captain Stormfield's Visit to Heaven* and *The Gates Ajar*." *English Language Notes* 7 (1970): 197–202.

Rickels, Milton. "Samuel Clemens and the Conscience of Comedy." *Southern Review* n.s. 4 (1968): 558–68.

Robinson, Forrest G. "The Characterization of Jim in *Huckleberry Finn*." *Nineteenth-Century Literature* 43 (1988): 361–91.

———. "The Silences in *Huckleberry Finn*." *Nineteenth-Century Fiction* 37 (1982): 50–74.

Rogers, Franklin R. *Mark Twain's Burlesque Patterns*. Dallas, TX: Southern Methodist University Press, 1960.

Rogers, Rodney O. "Twain, Taine and Lecky." *Modern Language Quarterly*, 34 (1973): 436–47.

Salvaggio, Ruth. "Twain's Later Phase Reconsidered: Duality and the Mind." *American Literary Realism* 12 (1979): 322–29.

Santayana, George. "The Genteel Tradition in American Philosophy" 1911. In *The Genteel Tradition, Nine Essays*. Ed. Douglas L. Wilson. Cambridge, MA: Harvard University Press, 1967.

Sattelmeyer, Robert and J. Donald Crowley, eds., *One Hundred Years of* Huckleberry Finn. Columbia: University of Missouri Press, 1985.

Saturday Morning Club. "Minutes and Records." The Mark Twain Memorial, Hartford, CT.

Schaar, John H. "Some of the Ways of Freedom in *Pudd'nhead Wilson*." In Gillman and Robinson, eds., *Mark Twain's* Pudd'nhead Wilson: *Race, Conflict, and Culture*. 211–27.

Schacht, Paul. "The Lonesomeness of Huckleberry Finn." 1981. In *On Mark Twain: The Best from* American Literature. Ed. Louis J. Budd and Edwin H. Cady. Durham, NC: Duke University Press, 1987.

Schneider, Louis, ed. *The Scottish Moralists on Human Nature and Society*. Chicago: University of Chicago Press, 1967.

Schwartz, Thomas D. "Mark Twain and Robert Ingersoll: The Free-thought Connection." *American Literature* 48 (1976): 182–93.

Sedgwick, Catherine. *A New England Tale*. New York: E. Bliss and E. White, 1822.

Shaftesbury, Anthony Cooper, Third Earl of. *An Inquiry Concerning Virtue or Merit*. In *Characteristicks*. 1711. Gloucester, MA: Peter Smith, 1963.

Shipp, E. R. "A Century Later, Huck's Still Stirring Up Trouble." *New York Times*, 4 February, 1985.

Simms, Kristina. "Mark Twain and the Lady from Decatur." Atlanta *Journal and Constitution*, 12 November, 1972, Magazine Section, 48, 51, 53.

Simms, William Gilmore. *Woodcraft*. 1854. Ed. Charles S. Watson. New Haven, CT: New College and University Press, 1983.

Sklar, Kathryn Kish. *Catherine Beecher: A Study in American Domesticity*. 1973. New York: W. W. Norton & Co., 1976.

Smith, Adam. *The Theory of the Moral Sentiments*. 1759. New Rochelle, NY: Arlington House, 1969.

Smith, Henry Nash. *Mark Twain's Fable of Progress*. New Brunswick, NJ: Rutgers University Press, 1964.

——. *Mark Twain: the Development of a Writer*. Cambridge, MA: Belknap-Harvard University Press, 1962.

——. "The Scribbling Women and the Cosmic Success Story." *Critical Inquiry* 1 (1974): 47–70.

Solomon, Eric. "The Search for Security." 1960. In *Adventures of Huckleberry Finn: An Annotated Text, Backgrounds and Sources, Essays in Criticism*. Ed. Sculley Bradley. New York: W. W. Norton, 1962. 436–43.

Spencer, Herbert. *The Data of Ethics*. New York: Hurst & Company, n.d. (preface dated 1879).

Spengemann, William C. *Mark Twain and the Backwoods Angel*. Kent, OH: Kent State University Press, 1966.

Steinbrink, Jeffrey. *Getting to Be Mark Twain*. Berkeley: University of California Press. 1991.

Stone, Albert E., Jr. *The Innocent Eye: Childhood in Mark Twain's Imagination*. New Haven, CT: Yale University Press, 1961.

——. "Mark Twain's *Joan of Arc*: The Child as Goddess." *AL* 31 (1959) 1–20.

Stowe, Harriet E. Beecher. "Early Remembrances." Ed. Charles Beecher. In *The Autobiography of Lyman Beecher*. 2 vols. 1864. Ed. Barbara Cross. Cambridge, MA: Belknap-Harvard University Press, 1961.

——. *The Minister's Wooing*. 1859. In *Stowe: Three Novels*. New York: Library of America, 1982.

——. *Uncle Tom's Cabin*. 1852. Ed. Kenneth Lynn. Cambridge, MA: Belknap-Harvard University Press, 1962.

Sumner, William G. *What Social Classes Owe to Each Other*. 1883. New York: Arno Press, 1972.

Sundquist, Eric J. "Mark Twain and Homer Plessy." In Gillman and Robinson, eds., *Mark Twain's* Pudd'nhead Wilson: *Race, Conflict, and Culture*.

Tenney, Thomas. *Mark Twain: A Reference Guide*. Boston: G. K. Hall & Co., 1977.

Thomas, Lewis. "Humanities and Science." In *Late Night Thoughts Listening to Mahler's Ninth Symphony*. New York: Bantam Books, 1984.

Tompkins, Jane P. "Sentimental Power: *Uncle Tom's Cabin* and the Politics of

Literary History." In *Sensational Designs*. New York: Oxford University Press, 1985.

Tuckey, John S. *Mark Twain and Little Satan*. West Lafayette, IN: Purdue University Studies, 1963.

——. "Mark Twain's Later Dialogue: The 'Me' and the Machine." *AL* 41 (1970): 532–42.

——. *Mark Twain's Mysterious Stranger and the Critics*. Belmont, CA: Wadsworth Publishing Co., 1968.

Tuveson, Ernest. "The Origins of the 'Moral Sense.'" *Huntington Library Quarterly* 11 (1948): 241–59.

Twichell, Joseph. Personal Diaries. Collection of American Literature, Beinecke Rare Book and Manuscript Library, Yale University, New Haven, CT.

——. "The Religious Experiences of Children." *The Religious Herald*, December 19, 1878.

Waggoner, Hyatt. "Science in the Thought of Mark Twain." *AL* 8 (1937): 357–70.

Warner, Charles Dudley. "Backlog Studies, 1–4." *Scribner's Magazine*, 2 (1871) and 3 (1872).

——. "Modern Fiction." *Atlantic Monthly* 51 (April 1883): 464–74.

Wayland, Francis. *Moral Philosophy*. Second ed. 1837. Cambridge, MA: Belknap-Harvard University Press, 1963.

Wecter, Dixon. *Sam Clemens of Hannibal*. Boston: Houghton Mifflin Co., 1952.

Welland, May. "Mark Twain, the Great Victorian." *Chicago Review* 9 (1955): 101–9.

Welter, Barbara. *Dimity Convictions*. Athens: Ohio University Press, 1976.

Wills, Gary. *Inventing America: Jefferson's Declaration of Independence*. Garden City, NY: 1978.

Wilson, Forrest. *Crusader in Crinoline*. Philadelphia: J. B. Lippincott Company, 1941.

Wilson, James D. "*Huck Finn*: From Abstraction to Humanity." *Southern Review* 10 (1974): 80–94.

——. "'The Monumental Sarcasm of the Ages': Science and Pseudoscience in the Thought of Mark Twain." *South Atlantic Bulletin* 40 (1975): 72–82.

Wood, Gordon S. "Conspiracy and the Paranoid Style: Causality and Deceit in the Eighteenth Century." *William and Mary Quarterly* 39 (1982): 401–41.

Index

This book has been set in Linotron Galliard. Galliard was designed for Mergenthaler in 1978 by Matthew Carter. Galliard retains many of the features of a sixteenth-century typeface cut by Robert Granjon but has some modifications that give it a more contemporary look.

Printed on acid-free paper.